Human Rights as Political Imaginary

José Julián López

Human Rights as Political Imaginary

palgrave
macmillan

José Julián López
University of Ottawa
Ottawa, ON, Canada

ISBN 978-3-030-08952-8 ISBN 978-3-319-74274-8 (eBook)
https://doi.org/10.1007/978-3-319-74274-8

Cover credit: Fatima Jamadar

Printed on acid-free paper

This Palgrave Macmillan imprint is published by Springer Nature
The registered company is Springer International Publishing AG
The registered company address is: Gewerbestrasse 11, 6330 Cham, Switzerland

For Telsing, my imaginary

Acknowledgements

This book has long been in the making, but it would not have been written were it not for the existence of institutions such as the Social Sciences and Humanities Research Council of Canada, which provided funding for the research, and my own academic institution, the School of Sociological and Anthropological Studies at the University of Ottawa. It is an enormous privilege to receive part of the national wealth, generated through taxation, in the form of research funding, and as a salary to teach, research, and participate in communities of knowledges. For this, I wish to express my deepest gratitude.

It is typical in the acknowledgements of academic books to name the readers and interlocutors, both known and anonymous, to thank them for their contributions. Such acknowledgements remind us that academic research is always already a collective effort. I have greatly profited from comments, critiques, and insights from many individuals. They know who they are because I have thanked them in person. I reiterate my profound gratefulness for the collective nature of academic work. However, in the spirit of this book, which draws attention to the conditions of possibility of human rights rather than the idea of human rights, I would like to name, and thank, individuals, who have, in myriad and less obvious ways, contributed to making this book possible. In alphabetical order, they include Telsing Andrews, Leo Alexander, Elan Boaventura, Ela Canela, Cloud, Laura DiMarzo, Carol English, Kellylee Evans, Mark

Ferdinand, Ari Gandsman, Christian Karner, Maurice Lévesque, Angie López, Luna Lucia, Lucero, John McKay, MaAngeles Martin de las Heras, Andrea Matyas, Francoise Moreau-Johnson at the Centre for Academic Leadership, Lisa Mills, Vangelis Nikias, Justin Paulson, Clara Picker, Linda Pietrantonio, Garry Potter, Rebecca Schein, Susan Spronk, the late Michael Stone, Terra Felicity, Anthony Woodiwiss, Nathan Young, and Sabrina Zeghiche. Anyone else who should have appeared but has not as a result of an unfortunate oversight on my part, thanks to you as well.

Finally, thanks to Sharla Plant, at Palgrave Macmillan, for her patience and support.

Contents

1

Introduction

The Human Rights Reflex

We see a picture of a human body, broken; visible signs of unspeakable brutality remain. We know that it is wrong. We know it with our eyes that attempt to avert their gaze; we know it in our minds, powerless to comprehend why; we know it in the phantom sympathetic pain coursing through our own bodies. For those who have souls, they know it with this faculty as well. Some argue that the capacity to understand the pain of others flows from a shared humanity and, in consequence, that the capacity to inflict this kind of pain requires divesting the victim of their humanity, and, in doing so, forsaking one's own.

Today, the automaticity with which we know that what is depicted in the above image is wrong will, most likely, be the product of having been tutored on what is right and wrong by a powerful moral and political worldview, human rights. It is a worldview, invisibly stitched into our ethical and political faculties, that is self-evident to many. It is akin to an involuntary moral reflex. We know immediately and instinctively that this is a violation of a person's fundamental human rights. Human rights are a series of inalienable rights to which each human person is entitled

J. Julián López, *Human Rights as Political Imaginary*,
https://doi.org/10.1007/978-3-319-74274-8_1

for no other reason than their humanity. Freedom from torture, freedom from wrongful imprisonment, freedom of conscience, freedom of speech, and the list goes on. This catalogue of rights is the heritage of all human beings, and lest we forget, it is codified in international law.

We see another picture. This is a little girl, laying back listlessly. Her torso is laced by a protruding ribcage, joints thicker than limbs. Her eyes bulge out in ghastly relief against an emaciated face where the skin is stretched into a death mask. A fly hovers on her forehead. This is wrong too. We know it with every fibre of our moral being. This should not happen. This young girl, any girl, like all human beings, has rights. She has a right to food. She has the right not to be stalked to death by hunger. We live in a world of human rights. Yet, the two images I just have described are not anomalies. We live in a world where human rights are constantly and brutally violated.

My professional entry, as a sociologist, into the universe of human rights was the product of the second image. My moral and political sensibilities, like many of my contemporaries, had been educated by the discourses, the images, and the practices of human rights. A monthly contributor to Amnesty International, the reaction to the image of the shattered tortured body, above, is my own. The image of a young girl deprived of food to the very edge of death is a picture that haunts me. I had seen countless pictures depicting similar situations before, but this one, for reasons that I cannot quite explain, seared itself into my soul. It welded my affective to my professional life. What is this thing called a human right to food? I asked myself. What can it do? Can it be bent to shield humanity from hunger?

As a sociologist, I am trained to understand social phenomena as arising from the interaction of complexly structured, historically situated, and institutionalized social relations that steer people's lives, delimiting what is likely, possible, improbable, and in some cases impossible. My own work, and the work of a wealth of respected scholars, has convinced me that one of the biggest causes of contemporary hunger, and of many other forms of inequality and violence, is capitalism. As I understand it, capitalism is not founded on the mere existence of markets, which predate capitalism, or political liberalism. Capitalism is distinguished from other forms of economic organization by the private ownership and control over the productive capacity of a society, and increasingly of the world. Capitalism is not so much a thing, as it is a complex historically evolving form for organizing economic relations.

Capitalism, willingly or not, inexorably produces inequalities, the effects of which can be devastating if not deadly. To the surprise of many of its critics, it is considerably more resilient and adaptive than had been presumed. At the time of the Occupy protest in Zuccotti Park, New York, I remember seeing a clip where the idiosyncratic Slovenian philosopher Slavoj Žižek announced that while we can readily envision the end of the world, it seemed impossible to imagine the end of capitalism. I reluctantly agreed and still agree that, for the moment, this is an accurate appraisal. But perhaps human rights and, more specifically, the human right to food could be mobilized, not to overthrow but to humanize the face of capitalism. This is certainly what many claim. Given the apparently perennate nature of capitalism for the time being, it is a claim well worth exploring.

Understanding Anew What One Already Understands

This book, however, is not about the human right to food, though I will make occasional reference to my empirical work in this area. This book presents the work that I have undertaken to try to understand exactly what a human right is, initiated while researching the origin and the development of the human right to food. To a lawyer, a philosopher, an activist, or a human rights victim, the idea that one needs to figure out what a human right is might appear odd. Have I not just defined it above as a moral and political reflex, codified as a series of inalienable rights, enshrined in international law? This being the case, if human rights are still violated might it not be because people are not aware of their human rights, or do not know how to assert them? Perhaps what we need to do is foster a deep human rights culture.

The preceding claim was not, to my mind, implausible. Although a long-term advocate of human rights, it was not until I undertook research in this area that I discovered that I, like others, apparently had a human right to food. I just didn't know it. I most certainly did not know how I would go about claiming this very basic right, if circumstances made it necessary. To be honest, I still don't. Perhaps, the reason why the flow of human rights violations has failed to be stemmed is not because of a lack of human rights culture, but because the laws, codifying human rights, are not yet on the books in localities where the violations are taking place, or, if on the books, they are not being implemented, for lack of resources or the absence of political will. Or, maybe, they are just the wrong laws. Consequently, what is needed is more precisely contextualized laws, and so on. At the start of my research on the human right to food, I might have found some of the just mentioned strategies for improving the implementation of the human right to food persuasive. Now I do not. Many of the reasons for this are developed throughout this book.

Sociology has had different publics throughout its existence. In the past, it frequently caught the attention of groups, across the ideological continuum, interested in tackling social problems arising from inequality, discrimination, poverty, and exclusion. In the postwar period, in countries that developed welfare states, sociologists provided models and empirical evidence that fed into the conception, development, and evaluation of a range of social policies. Starting in the 1970s, other forms of knowledge began to displace sociology as a source of understanding for what social relations are and how they might be governed. This is to my mind unfortunate. Not just because I have a professional interest in sociology having a public, but because sociology, I am convinced, provides those individuals who live in society—that is to say, all of us—important insights and knowledge about our lives as social-relational beings. It provides resources for reflecting on how we might make our lives and the lives of those to whom we are unavoidably linked through a variety of social relations, many not of our choosing, more equitable, how we might best mobilize ethical and political energy to this end.

For many, sociology is a bit of gadfly, questioning what everyone already knows, even what sociologists, themselves, already know. The raw materials for sociologists are found in the conceptions, ideas, practices, routines, and occurrences of everyday life. Sociologists are particularly interested in exploring the ideas and practices that people cling to the tightest—the ones that they take to be self-evident, the ones that sociologists themselves take as undeniable. Sociologists, like all persons embedded in social relations, are predisposed to seeing the world in certain ways, through certain categories, judging some modes of action as appropriate and others as not. It could not be otherwise. This is, after all, what makes social life possible, an alignment of ideas and practices, with certain affordances that under certain circumstances modify or even revolutionize the alignment.

Sociological practice, despite its arrays of highly complex qualitative, quantitative, and historical tools of data collection and analysis, is founded on a simple intuition. One that, as it happens, most people nurture at some, or many, points in their lives: namely, that our individual and collective representations of how the social world works, does not quite correspond with reality. This suspicion, in some instances, can manifest in what I like to think of as a proto-sociology, a more basic form of thinking about the lack of correspondence between our representations and the reality of our lived experience, to wit, conspiracy theory.

Conspiracy theory is founded on the distinction of how the social world is supposed to work and how it actually works. For conspiracy theory, the gap between the two is attributed to the alleged inordinate power of a specific group capable of beguiling the masses through mechanisms of mass deception and thought control, and through their direct access to the levers of power. In contradistinction, sociologists try to understand how the way people think about, act, and interact in the world is the product of "public narratives" and their "relational settings", to draw on two expressions introduced by the sociologist Margaret Somers, which I develop at greater length in the next chapter.

Sociologists try to model these narratives and relational settings and then devise research questions that might provide evidence for, or against, the proposed models. The stage of modelling, that is, conceptualizing the social phenomenon of interest—for example, What is a human right?—is a crucial one.[1] It is a cognitive mechanism that serves to interrupt, however imperfectly, the flow of everyday conceptions and practices. Were this not the case, sociologists would merely contribute to providing evidence for what we already know. If successful, however, sociological modeling opens up a space for seeing things otherwise and for empirically putting the explanatory capacity of these modes of seeing things otherwise, these "sociological visualities" (Woodiwiss 2001), to the test. In a way, then, doing sociology is a collective research practice where one attempts *to know anew what one already knows*. Because of the current moral and political self-evidence attached to contemporary human rights, the approach that I take in this book involves the following:

> Where the self-evidence of the social world imposes itself through current affairs and everyday life, a capacity for surprise needs to be maintained [...] In questioning the moral self-evidence by taking it as an object of study rather than an object of judgements and emotions, we drive a wedge into what is generally the subject of consensus. (Fassin 2012, 244)

The purpose of the wedge is neither to be fastidious nor to dismiss the ideas that people hold dear. It is to open up the consensus with an eye to trying to determine its social conditions of possibility and efficacy. In the past there has been consensus on a range of things that today we find surprising. Thinking about how we might live differently, hopefully better, depends on being able to generate a sense of surprise regarding how we now live.

Above, I noted that the raw materials for sociology are taken from the routines and ideas of everyday life. Another category of crucial raw materials, for sociologists, is composed of the theories, models, findings, and explanations developed by other scholars. What in academic parlance is called the literature is, after all, no less a part of the everyday lives of scholars. As I noted above, sociology is a collective research practice. Critically working on and exploring existing explanatory accounts, conceptual tools, and weighing the available evidence is how sociology as a discipline advances, when it does. This book is, in part, intended as an exploration of how sociologists have conceptualized human rights. Although there is much that can be usefully garnered from the work of the scholars that I present here, I have come around to thinking that there are two fundamental limitations in the field of the sociology of human rights, as it exists at the moment. The first is that the field currently takes the form of an academic archipelago, a series of islands of concepts, models, theories, and findings that are relatively isolated from one another. Consequently, one of the goals of the book is to provide a sympathetic, yet critical, overview of the field, to draw out some of the submerged assumptions linking the islands in the archipelago.

The second limitation of the field, as I see it, is that it relies on a thin conception of human rights. A thin conception of human rights, a notion that I spend much of the next chapter unpacking, refers to the practice of conceptualizing human rights as an abstract idea, a moral ideal, or a legal principle. Ideas are important in social life, to be sure. But ideas always come from somewhere; they are carried by all manner of agents, human and non-human. They are connected to particular forms of social organization and are embedded in routine social practices. One needs only think about religious ideas, the manner in which they are depicted visually, inscribed in texts, apprehended through reading practices, disseminated by preachers, and celebrated and reaffirmed in communal practices. Ideas, even powerful ones like religious ones, do not travel on their own steam. They do so through socially enabled public narratives, that is, widely shared and reproducible representations, and through the social pathways enabled by particular social arrangements, that is, social-relational matrices.

Part of the thinness in the conceptions of human rights derives, as I show at greater length throughout the book, from the taken-for-granted status of their backstory, namely, that they arose in the context of an unprecedented consensus in the wake of the postwar period, as crystallized in the Universal Declaration of Human Rights (UDHR) in 1948. It is assumed that it is the moral and political weight of this consensus that has pushed human rights forward. Said differently, it is presumed that human rights have become so central to our contemporary moral and political understanding, and even our individual self-understanding, because they are morally persuasive to the point of being self-evident. Who would deny that the brutality and inequality that human rights activists routinely denounce is wrong? Only compelling moral and legal principles, it is believed, could have secured the consensus that existed then and is still manifest today. Fortunately, in recent years, a new critical historiography has emerged to contest this widely accepted chronicle of the origins and development of human rights. I draw heavily on this historiography in my discussion of the sociology of human rights scholarship, and use it to sketch how we might sociologically thicken our understanding of human rights.

Summary of the Book

Chapter 2 is devoted to drawing attention to the prevalence of thin accounts in the contemporary understanding of human rights. I elaborate on the points introduced in the section above to argue that as sociologists, and as citizens interested in human rights, we cannot be content with a thin conception, not least because if we are, we end up *knowing what we already know* as opposed to *knowing anew what we already know.* I introduce some of the insights arising from the emerging critical human rights historiography. In particular, I highlight the untenability of contemporary accounts of human rights that trace back their origin to the UDHR in 1948. Much of this critical historiography suggests that the 1970s is a better site to excavate the origins of contemporary human rights. In particular, the path-breaking work of the historian Samuel Moyn locates the emergence of human rights, which he defines as a moral anti-politics that seeks to transcend politics, in the context of the exhaustion of the grand postwar political utopias, namely, liberal democratic capitalism, socialism, and post-colonial nationalisms and pan-nationalisms.

This is an insight that I continue to build on throughout the book. I conclude the chapter by briefly sketching my sociological alternative to a thin sociological conception of human rights, the political imaginary model. I propose that human rights are best understood, sociologically, as a mode of representing the world in order to improve it whose origins are in the 1970s rather than the 1940s. This mode of representing the world is patterned by certain social technologies that encourage specific subjectivities, that is, particular ways of being in the world, and pattern social action, that is, specific ways of acting in the world.

To briefly illustrate, let me return to the first image introduced above. For those of us who read it as human rights claim, it depicts the violence as morally unacceptable and requiring remedy and/or redress. The picture itself, documenting the violence, the manner in which it has gotten to me, relies on social technologies, that is to say, patterned ways of collecting and disseminating credible evidence of violations, and organizing a collective form of bearing witness. I am not the only person to have seen the picture or to have reacted as I have. You have probably reacted in the same way, which is why it is important to grasp that a political imaginary patterns, but does not necessarily, determine, social behaviour. The representation—we want a world where this will not happen, or where perpetrators are punished—and the social technologies position us as certain types of beings, subjects, who react to the picture with the conviction that something needs to be done. What we do—letter writing, protesting, lobbying, sending money—is also a product of the social technologies, and organizational forms, for instance, a human rights organization and its campaigns encourage and enable these types of action. It is the complex interaction of these dynamics that the human rights political imaginary tries to conceptually capture.

Chapter 3 returns to the question of the moral and political self-evidence of human rights and explains how we might understand the significance of this certitude. The bulk of the chapter, however, is concerned with examining the work of a number of sociologists—Bryan Turner, Judith Blau and Alberto Moncada, Rhoda Howard-Hassmann, Gideon Sjoberg, Elizabeth A. Gill and Norma Williams, and Michael Burawoy—who have forcefully argued, invoking different rationales, that sociologists should take human rights as their moral compass. Indeed, some have suggested that the discipline should be rethought, in varying ways, in order to enable sociology to participate in the quest for human rights. I develop a respectful, but dissenting reading of their claims. I conclude by arguing that by developing a sociology *for* as opposed to a sociology *of* human rights, we are deprived of the tools to *know anew what we already know*.

Chapter 4 is organized around a discussion of the explanatory work that the concept of practice might do in the sociology of human rights. The concept draws attention to the way in which ideas are embedded in social relations, embodied and embrained by actors located in these social relations, and inthinged in artefacts and organizational forms, which are, also, inseparable from relational and institutionalized settings. After reviewing a number of important sociological contributions, I show that their deployment of the concept of practice does not dislodge the notion that human rights are abstract ideas. Instead, and surprisingly, they reinforce it. Human rights, conceptualized as abstract ideas or legal principles, are opposed to the reality of how they are, or might be, implemented in social life. Following this, I draw on the important work by Fujiko Kurasawa who argues that human rights are best understood as a practice, an ethico-political one. Drawing on a critical reading of his work and that of Kate Nash, I conclude that the human rights political imaginary is usefully conceptualized *as an ethico-political practice where the claims of distant and/or excluded others are brought to the attention of an imaginary ethico-political community, who might, or might not, be triggered into action.*

Chapter 5 addresses another sociological conceptualization of human rights that stands out in the field, namely, that human rights can be understood as an extension or supersession of citizenship rights. I review the arguments of two key contributions—Alison Brysk and Gershon Shafir, and Yasemin Soysal—and identify important weaknesses. I accept their claim that human rights and citizenship rights are related, but not in the way they argue. Their accounts are fundamentally normative. I postpone presenting an alternative social-relational and historical account until Chap. 6.

I then go on to consider another version of the extension or supersession of citizenship by human rights in the form of cosmopolitanism. I discuss a number of proposals that, though normatively compelling, rely on very thin conceptions of human rights. Throughout the chapter, I maintain that the relationship of human and citizenship rights cannot be one of an essential equivalence, which is what is presupposed by the idea that the latter is extended into, or superseded by, the former. I draw on Margaret Somers' wickedly excellent conceptualization of the emergence of citizenship rights and leverage it to highlight the centrality of the figure of the victim in the development of the human rights political imaginary. The latter is, surprisingly but predictably, absent from the conceptualization of human rights reviewed in the chapter. The fact that what is invoked in the human rights political imaginary is the *claim of a distant and/or excluded victimized other* is, to my mind, ethically and politically consequential, and should, of necessity, influence how we think about the relationship between citizenship and human rights. It should also influence our understanding of what human rights might (not) achieve.

In Chap. 6, I explore the entanglement of the human rights political imaginary with law. I develop a critique of law naïveté: the notion that the law has a special capacity to transform social relations, which is surprisingly prevalent in the field of the sociology of human rights. I also question the assumption that human rights have always already been entangled with law. Drawing on sociolegal theory, I sketch out some basic features of law, conceptualized as a social practice, and explore its interaction with the human rights political imaginary, with an eye to unravelling their entanglement. Crucially, I draw on the pioneering sociolegal work undertaken by Yves Dezalay and Bryant Garth, Mikael Rask Madsen, and Anthony Woodiwiss to explore the entanglement of the human rights political imaginary with law in the US, the EU, Chile, Canada, and the UN.

I show how this entanglement turned liberal democratic capitalist societies, virtually overnight, into human rights nations, by linking citizenship to human rights. The particular form in which human rights were juridified, that is, became entangled with law, at the UN, had the effect of making countries, whose social-structural arrangements differed from those of liberal democratic capitalist societies, into human rights laggards. In doing so, it simultaneously deprived them of ability to draw on the human rights political imaginary to mobilize practical means to constrain the exercise and abuse of social power.

In the conclusion, I return to the metaphor of the archipelago and reveal a number of submerged commonalities amongst the different approaches discussed in the book. These include the persistence of thin conceptions of human rights, expressed normatively rather than social relationally, and a surprising law naiveté. I then present a stylized account of the human rights political imaginary developed in the book. Human rights is usefully understood as a political imaginary made up of representations, social technologies, modes of subjectivity and action, and organizational forms. Born of the political minimalism of the anti- or post-political waves of the 1970s, it is embodied, embrained, and inthinged in an embedded ethico-political labour, founded on bearing witness. The ethico-political labour not only involves making visible the claims by, or on behalf of, distant and/or excluded victimized others but also involves the simultaneous construction of the imaginary ethico-political community that receives and potentially acts on those claims.

The juridification of the political imaginary has generally failed to mobilize the power of the law precisely in those places where people are most vulnerable to the types of violations against which human rights are intended to protect. In the final section of the conclusion, I present some insights that can be gleaned from the development of the political imaginary model. I argue that human rights, in their minimalist version, can contribute to the struggle for global justice, but on their own will not radically transform the world.

Much contemporary support for human rights arises from their moral self-evidence and from the conviction that they can change the world significantly for the better. To date, there is little evidence that the latter is the case, as I show in Chap. 6. We can continue to hope that the conviction nurtured by human rights' self-evidence will be rewarded. *We can know what we already now.* Or we can attempt *to know anew what we already know.* The sociological reflection that I develop in the pages that follow is not aimed at discrediting human rights or their advocates. It is an invitation to interrupt the moral automaticity generated by the persuasiveness of contemporary human rights, with the hope of providing new insights into what human rights may and may not achieve. This requires a willingness to engage in a type of thinking that is very different from our everyday thinking. It can be demanding and awkward but also deeply informative. An invitation to sociology is an invitation to think otherwise about ourselves and others, against the background of the social relations that pattern our interaction. This is the invitation that this book extends and that I hope the reader accepts.

Note

1. I don't understand models merely in the formal mathematical sense, though they can certainly be this in some cases. Sociological models are attempts to link together concepts and identify relations that might account for the phenomenon of interest. Also, modelling is not in reality a stage; it is a transversal component that is repeated throughout the research process. An introduction into the many heuristics that sociologists use to interrupt the flow of everyday conceptions is presented in Andrew Abbott's wonderful book, *Methods of Discovery: Heuristics for the Social Sciences* (2004); on the role of metaphors, see López (2003).

Bibliography

Fassin, Didier. 2012. *Humanitarian Reason: A Moral History of the Present.* Berkeley, CA: University of California Press.

López, José Julián. 2003. *Society and Its Metaphors: Language, Social Theory and Social Structure.* London: Continuum Books.

Woodiwiss, Anthony. 2001. *The Visual in Social Theory.* London: The Athlone Press.

2

Human Rights as Political Imaginary

Introduction: Human Rights as a Global Lingua Franca

Human rights appear to have become one of the foundational moral matrices of our time. Its array of elements generates not only a variety of morally based rights claims but also contributes to contemporary conceptions of identity, political community, and legitimacy. For example, the legal scholar Costas Douzinas has drawn on Lacanian psychoanalysis to show how human rights interact with desire to simultaneously stabilize and destabilize a sense of self (Douzinas 2007, 48), while Joseph Slaughter, a literary scholar (2009), has documented the didactic function of human rights law that, like its fictional counterpart the *bildungsroman*, instructs individuals on how to become the citizens that they are already destined to become.[1]

The historian Lynn Hunt has rooted the power of human rights claims in their self-evidence, deeply seeded by the eighteenth-century development of autonomy and empathy as embodied in emotional and cultural forms (Hunt 2007, 29). Thus despite the plodding rate, if not the abject failure, of human rights instruments and associated monitoring and

J. Julián López, *Human Rights as Political Imaginary*,
https://doi.org/10.1007/978-3-319-74274-8_2

enforcement bodies, the vitality of human rights ultimately rests, she argues, on their cultural internalization: that is to say, on the "feelings, convictions and actions of multitudes of individuals, who demand responses that correspond with their inner sense of outrage" (Hunt 2007, 213). Equally, scholars working within the world culture research programme have persuasively drawn attention to the global normative impetus that seemingly compels nation-states to declare their support for human rights, though stopping short of obligating their enforcement, in order to legitimately claim membership in the international community of nation-states (Meyer et al. 1997).

In light of the claims for the deep historical roots of human rights, which I explore in more detail below, it is worth noting that such global normative compulsion is surprisingly recent: "a few decades ago, the concept of human rights was hardly discussed outside a small circle of Western intellectuals. In what amounts to a historical blink of the eye, the idea of human rights has become the lingua franca of international morality" (Normand and Zaidi 2008, 9). The frequently intoned refrain of human rights as a moral lingua franca, at first blush, appears to capture human rights' contemporary pre-eminence in the global moral economy. However, as a sociological heuristic—a mental shortcut—it has its limitations. This is because the idea of a lingua franca grates against what many advocates discern as one of the keys to human rights' contemporary success, its moral thinness or minimalism.

Lingua franca etymologically makes reference to a distinct Frankish tongue made up of a combination of Italian, Greek, Arabic, and Spanish formerly used in Eastern Mediterranean ports. It has subsequently come to denote a language used by speakers who do not share a mother tongue in order to communicate. Today, English plays the role of the contemporary lingua franca of the globalized world (Oxford University Press 2003). Consequently, many believe that human rights are to global morality what English is to world communication: "[human rights] has become the lingua franca of global moral thought, as English has become the lingua franca of the global economy" (Ignatieff 2001, 53). Although a pidgin is also used to communicate in a context where speakers do not share a native tongue, it is distinguished from a lingua franca by two features. One, it is a grammatically simplified version of a language, and, two, it lacks a community of native speakers who speak the language amongst themselves. In other words, compared to a lingua franca, a pidgin is a language that is stripped down to the bare essentials required for communication: a thin rather than a thick language.

As noted above, the global pervasiveness of human rights is frequently attributed to its moral minimalism. To take perhaps one of the best-known examples, which can stand in for many others, Ignatieff argues that "[h]uman rights can command universal assent only as a decidedly 'thin' theory of what is right, a definition of the minimum conditions for any kind of life at all" (Ignatieff 2001, 56). From this perspective, its success is actually imperilled when rendered more thickly as a "secular religion", "creed", or "metaphysics" (Ignatieff 2001, 53).[2] Understood thus, the appellation of pidgin is more appropriate insofar as human rights' ability to circulate globally would seem to depend on its austerity, of not quite constituting a complete moral language. In Ignatieff's words, human rights can be likened to "not much more than the basic intuition that what is pain and humiliation for you is bound to be pain and humiliation for me" (Ignatieff 2001, 95). Were human rights to have the fully developed syntactical and lexicographical components of a genuine moral lingua franca, capable of indexing substantive moral positions, rather ironically it could cease to function as one.[3]

To restrict our sociological understanding of human rights' successful global dissemination and its persuasiveness to a no-frills moral language, however, is to grasp it in terms of synecdoche. That is to say, to take a part—in this case that which is visible—for the whole. Bare normative claims materialized in the language of rights are conceded a social force that obviates the need to explore the complex social processes through which a field of persuasive normativity or social obligation is engendered and maintained. It encourages us to think that the success of human rights relies on its ability to enunciate a series of basic normative demands that any fully developed moral or ethical tradition could accommodate, that any rational and ethical individual would accept, and that any sovereign should be committed to enacting and enforcing as law. It conceptualizes human rights as a minimal normative *passe-partout* capable of unlocking a large number of contemporary moral dilemmas.

Is it not, however, sociology's task to thicken what is socially thinned, to account for why some practices circulate seemingly effortlessly, commanding immediate assent? And to do so, not out of cynicism or condescension, but out of genuine explanatory curiosity? I would argue that it is, and it is what I set out to do in this chapter, and throughout this book. I start by briefly categorizing the thoughtful attempts by philosophers and political theorists to thicken the conception of human rights and show why they ultimately remain wanting. I then draw on Jeffrey Alexander's path-breaking work on the origin of the civil sphere to indicate how human rights might be thickened sociologically.

Following this, I switch gears and explore recent historical scholarship that is both critical of thin historical narratives and offers thicker alternatives. Some of the substantive arguments in this critical historiography will be incorporated into my sociological conceptualization of human rights. However, in addition, the discussion of this historiography also clarifies how the thin/thick distinction might be usefully incorporated into sociological analyses. I then draw on the work of Bob Jessop and his colleagues in the cultural political economy approach and the work of Margaret Somers on public narratives and relational settings to introduce a preliminary outline of the political imaginary model.

Thickening Human Rights Sociologically

There are, of course, different recipes for thickening human rights' moral minimalism. One is through substantive foundational arguments that, conceptually at least, do not undermine claims to universality (Freeman 1994; Habermas 2012; Nickel 1987; Shestack 1998; Wellman 2010). Another is to blend human rights with local or culturally contextualized values, eventuating in substantively different yet in principle morally equivalent sets of rights as in the case of "Asian" (Kausikan 1993; Bell 2000; Mauzy 1997) or "African" values (Cobbah 1987; Donnelly 1984, 400–419; Mutua 2001; Ake 1987). For advocates cognizant of, but not content with, such regional or cultural segmentation, a third option is to further thicken human rights through hermeneutically inspired reflexive multicultural dialogue (De Sousa Santos 2008; Bell 2000).[4]

There is much intellectual and conceptual richness in these methods for making human rights heartier; however, for sociologists, I would argue they should remain ultimately unappetizing. This is not so much due to the substantive arguments themselves, which sociologists would do well not to ignore because they contribute to the social valence of contemporary human rights, but rather to the assumptions that they entail. In the first case, normative argumentation that aims at universality tends to assume the social efficacy of abstracted rationality and, as Jeffrey Alexander writes in a different but nonetheless pertinent context, "avoids the messiness of life, the work that we must do as members of real societies" to deploy or mobilize rational arguments in a socially efficacious manner (Alexander 2006, 14), or to use a term introduced by Fuyuki Kurasawa, discussed in Chap. 4, to perform "ethico-political work" (2007). Said differently, the abstract rationality or coherence of moral systems, though not irrelevant, does not in itself account for the social traction of moral practices.[5] Writing about Habermas, whom I take as an exemplar of the type of abstract moral argumentation in question, Alexander notes, "if we must be moral, according to these philosophical beliefs, we must find a way of staying inside of principle, inside the good, inside of abstraction, and of keeping away, as much as possible, from the concrete messiness, the irrationality of everyday life" (Alexander 2006, 15).

In the second case, that is, contextualizing human rights in local cultures, the attempt to articulate human rights with concrete cultural practices and beliefs provides a richer and more robust understanding of the possible meanings attached to human rights, indicating the manner in which they might be embraced and reproduced in daily life. However, it fails to explain how the unity of human rights is maintained beyond such local diversity namely, what assures the currency of human rights translocally?[6] Summarizing the weakness of both approaches, Alexander writes,

> These are the paradoxes that haunt moral philosophy. Theories of imperative abstraction turn resolutely away from the meanings that define everyday life. Hermeneutic philosophy cultivates meaning but cannot envision its expansion beyond particular communities. (Alexander 2006, 17)[7]

The third approach to thickening human rights, that is, through multicultural dialogue, is advanced by scholars who foreground the distinctiveness of human rights rooted in particular cultural communities, but do not want to forsake the prospect of some form of contingent commensurability amongst the moral commitments of said communities. This is implicit amongst authors who propose to balance the preponderance of Western liberalism in the constitution of human rights, for example, by incorporating Asian (Bell 2000) or African (Cobbah 1987) values.

Boaventura de Sousa Santos is one of the most thoughtful exponents of this strategy (2008). He argues that although all cultures have some conception of human dignity, human dignity is rendered varyingly across cultures. Moreover because all cultures' conceptions of human dignity are incomplete and problematic, and no culture is monolithic, there is space for what he calls "diatopical hermeneutics". This involves teasing out possible "isomorphisms" across cultures though dialogue by critically reflecting on the "overarching rhetorical commonplaces of a given culture", that is, their topoi (De Sousa Santos 2008, 12–15). Under the right conditions, these exchanges could yield a "mestizo-conception of human rights, a conception that instead of resorting to false universalisms organizes itself as a constellation of local and mutually intelligible meanings, networks of empowering references" (De Sousa Santos 2008, 15).[8]

Enticing as this vision undeniably is, it remains a highly abstract one and perhaps necessarily so. What it does not address, however, is the processes and institutional conditions that would underwrite the proposed "hermeneutics". What are the sites where such dialogues are to take place? Who is to participate? How are "the networks of empowering references" to be maintained, mobilized, and rendered socially efficacious? Tellingly, De Sousa Santos' enumeration of the necessary conditions for an "intercultural reconstruction of human rights" (De Sousa Santos 2008, 23–40) is predominantly normative and mimics Habermasian proceduralism, once discourse ethics is replaced by intercultural dialogue.[9]

Consequently, none of the aforementioned accounts provide the necessary ingredients to develop a sociologically thick conception of human rights. In his thought-provoking analysis of the civil sphere, Alexander arrives at a similar conclusion with respect to normative theories of contemporary democracy (Alexander 2006). Consequently, he argues for the need to move beyond

> high theory to discover the imbedded discourse and institutions of every day social life. Rather than an abstract deduction of philosophers, the normative stipulations of civil society turn out to be the language of the street, the television, novels, politics, office and scandal. (2006, 551)

Alexander maintains that the civil sphere is a distinct social sphere relatively autonomous from both state and the market. The product of the institutional differentiation and the cultural complexity of modernity, it is best understood as a "solidary sphere in which a certain kind of universalizing community comes to be culturally defined and to some degree institutionally enforced" (Alexander 2006, 31).[10] It exists as "a moral force, an institutional fact, and a set of interactional practices" (Alexander 2006, 31).

One possible avenue for the development of a sociologically thick conception of human rights, then, is to build on Alexander's work, conceptualizing human rights as a global expansion of the ethos of the universalizing community. Indeed, this would dovetail with some contemporary approaches to human rights. For instance, a number of scholars understand human rights as an extension of the logic of citizenship to the global community or read in human rights the essential cosmopolitan moral script through which to enact global civil society. Illuminating as both of these broad approaches are, they are not without certain shortcomings that I will address in Chap. 5. This said there are a number of aspects of Alexander's analysis that I retain and attempt to develop further in this book.

First is Alexander's persuasive insistence that "culture is not a thing but a dimension, not an object to be studied as a dependent variable, but a thread that runs through, one that can be teased out of, every conceivable social form" (Alexander 2003, 7). It is, of course, indisputable that collective meaning has been a concern of sociology at large and the sociology of culture specifically. Nonetheless, Alexander contends, to a certain extent correctly, that the focus has primarily been on what creates meaning—typically "more material" structures of a "less ephemeral kind" than on understanding culture's role in the co-production of social life (Alexander 2003, 5, 2011; Alexander and Smith 2003; Emirbayer 2004). As a corrective, Alexander and his colleagues have developed what one commentator has called the "Alexander School" of cultural sociology (Emirbayer 2004, 9), more popularly known as the "strong program in cultural sociology" (Alexander and Smith 2003).[11]

Though I share Alexander and his collaborators' commitment to understanding how culture and meaning co-produce social life, I do not exclusively adopt what I view as a key component of the strong programme, namely, "structural hermeneutics" (Alexander and Smith 2003). This is for two reasons. One is that the structural hermeneutics framework is, to my mind, too narrow a conception of cultural analysis, focusing primarily on binary codes, genres, narrative structures, and metanarratives, in effect leaving out important aspects of how meaning is created and circulates in social life.[12] The choice of starkly circumscribing cultural analysis to this limited analytical register is dictated by the attempt to establish the ontological autonomy of culture (Alexander and Smith 2003, 11).[13] However this perceived need to ring-fence the autonomy of culture introduces

> a static quality to Alexander's cultural sociology and a lack of attention to how cultural formations themselves emerge in dynamic relation with other such configurations. Cultural codes always seem to end up unaltered in his empirical work and they are always presented as singular and self-standing. (Emirbayer 2004, 10)

The other reason I do not entirely subscribe to the project of structural hermeneutics is its reliance on a conception of "materiality" that is too strongly opposed to "culture". This limits the strong programme's ability to grasp culture and meaning's hybrid nature (Emirbayer 2004, 11). What I have in mind here are the powerful explanatory frameworks opened up by science studies in which the generation of meaning, but more importantly its transmission through social space and its social efficacy, is understood as an assemblage of human and non-human actants, (Latour 1987), producing a relational and semiotic materialism that promotes ecological analyses that are dynamic and processual

(Sismondo 2011, 74). In other words, the autonomy of culture might be better grasped not by positing a pure realm of culture, but by recognizing, as Somers in an entirely different yet strikingly pertinent context argues, that autonomy is "more often than not contingent upon grids of social relationality" (Somers 1994a, 629).[14]

The second element from Alexander's analysis to be retained is his warning that a mode of sociological engagement with normative social phenomena styled on the disciplinary practices of moral philosophy will, as he says with respect to Habermas, lead us to "losing our sociology" (Alexander 2006, 15), thus obscuring the unique contributions that sociology can make to contemporary normative debates. Indeed, this book is committed to ploughing an explanatory furrow between philosophical normativism and sociological partisan advocacy in the field of human rights. In the latter case, as I contend in the next chapter, it is not sufficient to translate the normative arguments of the human rights community into a sociological idiom with the hope of mobilizing sociologists and broader publics for the realization of human rights.

The autonomy, significance, and social efficacy of human rights' normativity need to be addressed in social rather than in abstract moral terms or through foundational arguments. This requires a commitment to analysing the concrete mechanisms that enable human rights claims to circulate in a meaningful and socially efficacious manner rather than their idealized conditions of possibility. Alexander's work on the social sphere draws attention to its binary semiotic codes, the role of communicative and regulative institutions, and processes of "civil repair" (Alexander 2006). Elsewhere he equally identifies mechanisms such as "symbolic extension" and "emotional identification" (Alexander 2003, 30), as well as the components associated with successful "social performance" of cultural scripts (Alexander 2011).

In contrast, I propose to sketch the social mechanisms underpinning human rights' current normative traction by developing a model of human rights as a political imaginary, constituted by discursive representations, social technologies, modes of individual and collective subjectivity and action, and organizational structures. This notion of imaginary differs from more popular usages, as associated with the works of Laclau and Mouffe (1985, 2), Lacan (1977, 195–99), or Castoriadis (1998,

145)—all which, in differing ways (Castoriadis 1998, 3), understand an imaginary as a discursive or symbolic logic (Neocleous 2003, 1). Equally, though not unrelated to Charles Taylor's conception of a social imaginary (Taylor 2002; Gaonkar 2002), my intention in developing the notion of political imaginary is not to disinter the deep symbolic roots of modernity or previous cultural epochs. A political imaginary, in my usage, is not so much a meta-representation of the world or its deep moral code; it is the coming together of patterned yet dynamic social relationships that act on us, in part because they are meaningful, as we attempt to act on them. From the perspective of actors, it is an active mode of understanding that is both representational and agential.

The third element is Alexander's claim that it behoves us "to understand why morality is so often the claims of the strong, so often falsely universal, and so prone to camouflage and cover-up rather than upholding reciprocity and claims to truth" (Alexander 2006, 16). In other words, it is paramount to understand how the moral claims that sustain contemporary political worldviews such as commitment to solidarity and democratic life are intertwined with power; indeed whatever efficacy they might have is dependent on their entanglement with power (Woodiwiss 2005, 8–11). He adds, however, an important caveat. The technocratic, deterministic, and excessively rationalistic and optimistic accounts of the basis of social solidarity, which characterized nineteenth- and early twentieth-century social thought, must be abandoned. Yet, in so doing, it is crucial not to reduce the social normativity, associated with moral worldviews, to the mere effects of narrowly conceived group interests or the mobilization of "resources" and "capacities" (Alexander 2006, 39, 2011, 87). While group interests, capacity, and resources are indubitably key components of the parallelogram of power, to reduce power to these is "to leave out the independent shaping of power of background symbols and forms, the figures and forms of script, the contingency of *mise-en-scène* and actor interpretation, and the extraordinary significance of audience separation" (Alexander 2011, 88).

A reader unfamiliar with Alexander's work might be tempted to read the preceding quotation's use of "performance" strictly in a metaphorical register. Alexander certainly plumbs performance and dramaturgical theory to analogically generate the analytical elements of cultural performance

(Alexander 2011, 28–33). However, he also claims that seeing politics in terms of social drama is not merely a convenient and fruitful heuristic move: it is necessitated by the simultaneous historical emergence of the theatre and "the public sphere as a compelling social stage" (Alexander 2011, 48–49). It is, he argues, the concatenation of increased social complexity, more critical and reflexive cultural forms and less ascriptive forms of authority that make possible the staging of social dramas where authoritative commands and prescriptions no longer suffice. Actors need to not only perform but also need to perform convincingly (Alexander 2011, 49). In other words, "if power is to be effective, performing power must be a success. To be really powerful means that social actors, no matter what resources and capacities they possess, must make their audiences believe them" (Alexander 2011, 89).[15]

Regardless of whether one concurs or not with Alexander's contention that theatre and social drama are dizygotic cultural twins, his analysis of the intertwined cultural and performative dimension of politics is certainly promising.[16] It is an aspect of contemporary human rights that I also tackle in this book. As I will show in the next chapter, human rights like many persuasive cultural forms are characterized by their self-evidence. When actors successfully define a situation as being within their moral or legal purview, human rights seem to function seamlessly, activating a taken-for-granted moral common sense that no moral actor, collective or individual, could oppose, the involuntary moral reflex of the book's introduction. A successful human rights performance has been staged.[17] In instances of failure, however, human rights advocates tend to attribute the failure to Western liberalism, imperialism, economic globalism, neo-colonialism, or powerful actors' limited and interested deployment of human rights (Blau and Moncada 2005; Bricmont 2006; De Sousa Santos 2008; Douzinas 2007; Kennedy 2005; Mutua 2001; Peck 2011; Sellars 2002; Teeple 2005; Waters 1996; Žižek 2005).

While certainly these and more factors mobilize, refract, and mitigate the potential social efficacy of human rights claims, the underlying logic, in many but not all cases, seems to suggest that absent these obstacles the existing moral consensus would induce socially beneficent results. The consensus is presumed. Alexander's focus on performance and my own on the components of a political imaginary seek to enquire into the social conditions of possibility of such a consensus, its reproducibility, and the social dynamics that underpin it. I certainly do not disagree with a number of authors who persuasively emphasize that a sociological interpretation of human rights must understand them as being political (Armaline et al. 2015; Anleu 1999; Baxi 1998; De Sousa Santos 2008; Hynes et al. 2012; Morris 2013; Waters 1996).

All the same, the sense of "political" cannot be conflated with narrowly conceived interests. It requires taking into consideration the broader register in which politics takes place, exploring the social and cultural forms that seek to grasp the tension between how the world is and how it might be. It must include as Kate Nash argues, understanding human rights as cultural politics, the "more or less organised struggles over symbols that frame what issues, events or processes mean to social actors who are emotionally and intellectually invested in shared understandings of the world" (2009, 1). Likewise, it must contend with the fact that "cultural politics is not only the contestation of symbols. Cultural politics concerns public contests over how society is imagined; how social relations are, could and should be organised" (Nash 2009, 1). I want to show how in the case of human rights, conceiving of them in terms of a political imaginary helps to shed light on how they are socially performed and adds to Nash's conception of cultural politics. However before turning to this task, I first return to the notion of thickening, this time in the context of historical narratives. My aim in doing so is to further fine-tune what the distinction between thin and thick conceptions of human rights might signify in the context of sociological analysis.

Thin Historical Narratives

The counterpart of the thin conception of human rights as a moral pidgin, discussed above, is a thin historical narrative. The historiography on human rights is remarkably recent, emerging in the mid-1990s (Cmiel 2004, 118–19).[18] According to the historian Samuel Moyn, a refreshingly iconoclastic and incisive commentator, this historiography is "the tardy fruit of the fashion of human rights in politics" (Moyn 2014b, 1), predisposing historians to "set out to provide the backstories to the vogue of human rights" (Moyn 2014b, 1–2, 2012, 160).[19] Such backstories identify different historical founts for contemporary human rights—the "Greeks or the Jews, Medieval Christians or early modern philosophers, democratic revolutionaries or abolitionist heroes, American internationalists or antiracists visionaries" (Moyn 2010, 5).[20] Whether one, several, or all of these sources are chosen, the subsequent historical narration of human rights is one of their gradual extension and becoming (Moyn 2010, 2014b). These do not necessarily take the form of whiggish narratives of progress—given the ongoing record of human barbarism an impossible task even for the most motivated of historians. They do, however, cast the trans-historical moral impulse sustaining human rights as an admittedly frequently ineffectual yet ever-present moral beacon. In the words of one of the key historians of the field, "[o]ne may think of the history of human rights as a journey guided by lampposts across ruins left behind by ravaging and insatiable storms" (Ishay 2004, 3).

The thinness of these historical narratives derives from the fact that rather than challenge the ahistorical claims—"grand assertions and abstract arguments"—regarding the origins and the development of human rights that abound amongst activists, lawyers, and political theorists (Cmiel 2004, 120), they actually transcribe and reproduce them into a historical register. Ironically, they buttress ahistorical claims with historically induced professions (Moyn 2014b, xiii; Mazower 2009, 6–7). Exploring the contingency of human rights, putting into question their alleged deep temporal roots, or daring to see them as something novel would presumably undermine human rights' claims to universality, perhaps reducing their persuasiveness and contemporary power. It is their historical momentum that seemingly accounts for human rights' contemporary moral authority. This is history *for* rather than *of* human rights.

Consequently, what much human rights historiography has given us, maintains Moyn, are the repeated historical sightings of an alleged self-same moral principle or truth linked together by the thinnest of historical threads (see Afshari 2007). Equated to an inextinguishable moral flame, the task for historians has been to detect human rights' flickering glow in all manner of texts, episodes of human redemption, or in the actions of visionary heroes.[21] Contemporary human rights are understood as the luminous coming into being of their historical predecessors. There are, however, shortcomings to such an approach: "if the past is read as a preparation for a surprising recent event, both are distorted. The past is treated as if it were simply the future waiting to happen. And the surprising recent event is treated as less surprising than it really is" (Moyn 2010, 11).

A Thin Postwar Narrative

It is precisely this logic that underwrites much of the contemporary understanding of the relationship between the immediate post-World War period and the current dominance of human rights. Human rights are assumed to be a response to the devastation of World War II and its genocidal barbarism, most notably, but not exclusively, in the case of the Shoah (Ishay 2004, 218; Cohen 2012, 53–54; Lauren 1998, 291; Morsink 1999, 37–38; Anderson 2003, 36). This generated a moral germplasm that found fertile ground in what was claimed to be an unprecedented and striking global consensus. In the words of Lauren, it "struck a chord among the peoples of the world and rapidly began to take on a life of its own" (Lauren 1998, 232).[22] Favourable conditions broadcast human rights through an assertive American internationalism, announcing the future harvest of *A New Deal for the World* (Borgwardt 2007). Human rights equally seeded the emerging post-colonial third world. The latter not only contributed to the development of human rights, but, more importantly, human rights landed in the furrows ploughed by anti-colonial consciousness (Burke 2011).

Despite such overwhelmingly propitious growing conditions, alas human rights were not to germinate. A dramatic shift in the world political climate—the Cold War's "deep freeze" (Lauren 1998, 280)—forced them into dormancy. Decades later, however, awoken by the Cold War thaw they blossomed as they would have in the postwar had it not been for the unfortunate obstacle of the East-West geopolitical alignments. They grew true to their postwar seed. No question that the human rights of the 1990s might be a new variety or cultivar, let alone a new species![23] Contemporary human rights represent the unfolding of the potential with which they were coded in the postwar period, nothing especially new or surprising here.

Indeed, in the 1990s even the idea of human rights' postwar dormancy was buried from sight: "it became common to assume that, ever since their birth in a moment of postgenocidal revulsion and wisdom [in 1948], human rights had become embedded slowly but steadily in human consciousness in what amounted to a revolution of moral life" (Moyn 2014b, 72). However, recent historical research suggests that it was not the Holocaust that made human rights salient in the immediate postwar, "but belated memories of it in new circumstances" (Moyn 2014b, 87; Borgwardt 2007, 86; Keys 2014, 11; Mazower 2004, 381). It is perhaps difficult to grasp, but the Holocaust was not as central a frame of understanding in the immediate post-World War II period as our current sensibilities might lead us to believe. Strikingly, this is not only true in the US (Novick 2000; Stein 2014; Alexander 2003, 27–84; Dubiel 2003), but also in Germany and Israel (Dubiel 2003).

In Germany, the assumption of collective responsibility was for a long time evaded, as was the possibility of grasping the real dimensions of the Shoah; in fact, "the intensification of references to the 'German Nation' and the ignorance of the genocide were still traceable in the 1980s" (Dubiel 2003, 63). Amongst other reasons, this is because "in the first decades after the war the overwhelming majority of Germans cast themselves in the role of primary victims – of Hitler and of the war", and it was not until 1985 that a "representative of German government [Richard Weitzsaecker] officially acknowledged and took responsibility for the Holocaust" (Dubiel 2003, 63–64). "Mass anti-Nazi revulsion", argues Moishe Postone, did not arise in the postwar horizon. Instead,

> the goal was "normalcy" at all costs – one to be achieved without dealing with the past [...] A kind of collective somnambulism resulted, with the majority of the population sleep-walking its way through the Cold War, the 'economic miracle,' the re-emergence of politics with the student revolt, repressing the past. (Postone 1980, 100)[24]

In Israel, it was not until Eichmann's trial, in 1961, that the Shoah took on a prominent role in public life, and this despite the fact that at its founding, at least half of its citizens were survivors (Dubiel 2003, 63; Porat 2004; Shapira 1998). Dubiel contends,

> It was much more important to the founding generation of Israelis, for political reasons, to represent the Israeli state as the work of those individuals and groups who had actively opposed the Nazis. That is why in the first years after the foundation of the state more attention was lavished on the insurrection in the Warsaw ghetto than to the mass murder in the death camps. (Dubiel 2003, 63)

In the postwar US, the Shoah was not seen as a central aspect of the war, not even in the context of the Nuremberg process, in part, because it was "normalized" as an extreme form of a familiar phenomenon, that is, racism (Dubiel 2003, 65; see Novick 2000; Stein 2014; Alexander 2003, 27–84).

Recently, Hasia Diner has forcefully critiqued the myth of silence amongst American Jews after the Holocaust (2010). She has drawn attention to the stunning claim accepted by a broad array of historians, social scientists, literary critics, and informed commentators that

> [h]owever universal the urge to memorialize communal catastrophes and however deeply Jewish culture embedded such collective remembering, American Jews in the years after World War II, according to most later observers, behaved very differently when it came to the brutal deaths of six million Jews. As regards them, a very different story has been told and has become accepted as the truth (H. Diner 2010, 4).

She sets herself the task of dislodging this conception by exploring "the ways in which a group of women and men, Jews of the United States, went about the process of shaping, from the ground up, a memorial culture" (Diner 2010, 9). This she does, and in doing so she shows how

> by putting words on paper, conveying emotions, facts, and ideas through oratory and sermons, crafting liturgies for synagogues and homes they [American Jews] constructed a vast unorganized spontaneous project that sought to keep alive the image of Europe's murdered Jews (2010, 11).

Diner continuously reiterates the decentralized and explorative nature of this endeavour, as well as the variety of practices that embodied this memorial work.

This repertoire of memorialization was undertaken in a broader political and social context that provided little support, namely, discrimination, anti-communism, a conception of liberalism that had little room for group claims, and the absence of existing models to follow (2010, 16). Consequently, the memorialization of the Holocaust unfolded chronologically dispersed across a multitude of spaces and practices, "evolving, changing and developing over time" (2010, 17). The key point with respect to human rights is not the presence or absence of memorialization amongst American Jewish communities, whose absence given the magnitude of the tragedy would have be astonishing, but rather whether the memorialization took a form with which broader American society could identify.

Diner provides historical evidence for the claim, explored below, made by Alexander (2003, 27–84) that, in the immediate postwar, cultural structures enabling such identification were lacking. This is perhaps why many assumed that memorialization had not taken place and postwar Holocaust consciousness non-existent. The memorialization of the moral trauma of the Shoah, as Diner shows, certainly did exist amongst Jewish Americans; it just did not resonate more broadly in American society until the 1960s and 1970s, when it contingently intersected with human rights.

This dynamic is illustrated forcefully in Arlene Stein's study of the children of Holocaust survivors: "If their parents saw Holocaust storytelling as *mainly a private affair*, their children were part of a cohort that *transformed private pains into public stories*, and claimed a sense of victimhood" (Stein 2014, 5 my emphasis). Similarly, while Daniel Cohen has suggested the need to find a middle ground between the over- and underestimates of the moral consensus that revulsion to the Holocaust generated (2012), the evidence that he presents as Moyn points out is "found in 'private memory' and Jewish subcultures" (2014b, 90). This goes a long way towards illustrating that it could have little influence on the emergence of human rights in the postwar period.

Alexander, as telegraphed above, argues that the cultural structures that would have enabled the broader US public to identify with the victims of the Holocaust were not available. This is because, notwithstanding the fact that Nazism had been culturally coded as evil, this occurred against the background of a progressive narrative in which said evil could and was eventually overcome through the allied victory and visions of a new world order (Alexander 2003, 37; Novick 2000, 112). Consequently,

> while the 1945 revelations confirmed the Jewish mass murder, they did not create a trauma for the postwar audience. Victory and the Nuremberg war trials would put an end to Nazism and alleviate its effects. Postwar redemption depended on putting mass murder "behind us," moving on and getting on with the construction of the new world. (Alexander 2003, 41)

Subsequently, the erosion of the progressive narrative, in the late 1960s, enabled a more ambivalent, even tragic reading of the Holocaust, which gradually became coded as an event that could not be, that indeed had not been, left behind: "The horrific trauma of the Jews became the trauma of all humankind" (Alexander 2003, 57). Elements including, but not limited to, the national political realignments of the American Jewish community, and the broader geopolitical conjuncture (Novick 2000), as well as the coming of age of the children of Holocaust survivors (Stein 2014) intersected with the emerging tragic narrative, and the collapse of postwar utopias (Moyn 2010). This intertwined the twin threads of Holocaust consciousness and human rights that remain woven into our contemporary moral fibre (Moyn 2014b, 96).

Similar patterns of marginality in the immediate postwar era can be found. For instance, as late as 1979, the Holocaust scholar Yehuda Bauer could claim that "in Britain nothing at all has been done" to promote remembrance of the Shoah (Bauer cited in Pearce 2008, 72). Equally, there is a seminal view that the revulsion towards the Holocaust prepared the moral ground for the founding of a united Europe, providing the latter with a unifying memory (Diner 1997, 2003; Levy and Sznaider 2010). Historical evidence, however, suggests that "when the first steps of the EU were set up, the eradication of European Jews was scarcely a point of reference at all. At that time the collective memory in Europe was, above all, determined by two concepts: Anti-nazism and Antifascism" (Probst 2003, 54; see Duranti 2012, 2016). Nor was the Holocaust a significant point of reference in discussions relating to the future of the European project in the period between 1950 and 1989 according to Lothar Probst (2003, 54).[25] In like manner, despite the assumed covalent bond between the Holocaust and the rise of human rights in Europe, crystallizing in the European Convention on Human Rights, the cast of characters who played a role in the process suggests that honouring the victims of the Shoah was not the primary goal of the convention (Moyn 2014b, 91).[26]

Christian Human Rights

Recently, Samuel Moyn has very persuasively shown that more important than the absence of the Holocaust acting as a moral lighting rod in the development of postwar European human rights was the presence of a religious and spiritual substrate that nurtured the development of "human rights" in Europe, namely, personalism (Moyn 2015). Personalism, whose intellectual fortune owed much to the French Catholic thinker Emmanuel Mounier, highlighted the dignity of the person and his or her self-realization in a community of believers as a shield against their twin debasement in modernity, to wit the atomism and chaotic radical individualism of bourgeois liberalism and the collectivism of socialism (Moyn 2015, 71; cf. Meunier 2007; Bengtsson 2006).[27] The subsequent personalist vision of human rights represented an attempt to reformulate Christian conservatism, after more authoritarian forms of European conservatism had failed or degenerated into right-wing state terror.

Personalism's goal, however, was "moral constraint" and "not human emancipation or individual liberation" (Moyn 2015, 10). Consequently the European Convention on Human Rights, strongly inflected with personalist principles (Moyn 2010, 78), was a statement of Christian moral values, "rather than any genuine transformation of regional governance. (That has waited our time)" (Moyn 2015, 15; Duranti 2016, 193). It also stood as a rampart against "domestic socialism, in an era when the popular and ideological appeal of social democratic ideals and communist ones were rising to new height" (Moyn 2015, 159), and provided the "spiritual union" of Western Christian culture against "Eastern criminality" (Moyn 2015, 159) and the secular communist threat (Moyn 2015, 163).

Personalism flourished in the postwar *Weltanschauung* of European Christian Democracy (Kersbergen and Verbeek 1994, 224; Kaiser 2007, 10), giving substantive content to European human rights (Moyn 2015, 65–100). Its influence however flowed further, circulating amongst post-colonial elites intent on ploughing a middle way between communism and the excesses of Western materialism (Moyn 2015, 91). Such was the case of Charles Malik, a Lebanese Christian diplomat with personalist tendencies, who was one of the UDHR's key drafters (Moyn 2015, 125), and responsible for the introduction of the language of the "human person" in the declaration (Moyn 2010, 65, 2015, 148).[28] One of Malik's core concerns was that of religious freedom (Moyn 2015, 125). This united him with another constituency that had rallied to the call of human rights, namely, as I will show below, North American Protestants.

Today, much is made of Roosevelt's Four Freedoms address, delivered to Congress in 1941, considered by many the clarion call of the human rights era, not least because it appeared to conjugate the "freedoms"—freedom of expression and religion, and freedom from want and fear—with the claim that "Freedom means the supremacy of human rights everywhere" (Borgwardt 2007, 21; Glendon 2002, 10; Lauren 1998, 137). However, it is far from clear that the term "human rights" then had the meaning that we attribute it today. Introduced in a final revision, it is unlikely, Moyn contends, that it was a means to interject something radically new (Moyn 2010, 49).[29] Indeed, the term is best understood as a war slogan mobilizing support for the anti-Nazi war effort (Moyn 2010, 49), as Elizabeth Borgwardt shows, "his [FDR's] intent was specifically anti-Nazi, not broadly anti-totalitarian, as some commentators have recently suggested" (Borgwardt 2007, 21).[30]

Although the expression "human rights" had been in circulation prior to its capsular role in Roosevelt's speech, its meaning was highly ambiguous, "the phrase meant different things to different people from the beginning. And therefore, it meant nothing specific as various parties tried to give it sense" (Moyn 2010, 50; Borgwardt 2007, 59; Mazower 2009, 9). In the 1940s, human rights had very little traction, outside of an insular community within the United Nations. Tellingly, in the US, the term was not taken up as a political vernacular nor did it fuel any broader movements (Moyn 2014b, 73), with one notable exception.

American Protestants, argues Moyn, were the only constituency to seriously rally behind Roosevelt's "human rights". Conceiving religious freedom metonymically as freedom, groups such as the Federal Council of Churches of Christ (FCC) and its Commission of Churches on

International Affairs (CCIA) contributed to the dissemination of the notion of religious freedom as a fundamental right. They were instrumental in getting the language of human rights into the United Nations Charter in San Francisco and, subsequently, religious freedom into the UDHR (Moyn 2015, 148–49). Contra the often-repeated refrain that the Cold War froze human rights in their tracks, it is worth noting that communism or rather Christian anti-communism was the fuel that gave life to human rights in the US, the UN, and in Europe in the immediate postwar (Moyn 2015, 150; Duranti 2016, Chap. 7), not as a universalistic global ethic but as a religious prophylactic against a secular foe.[31] Human rights they might have been called, but they had little to do with the conception of human rights that resonate today.

In drawing attention to Moyn's pivotal contribution, the fact that in the 1940s the most viable rendition of human rights took the form of an anti-communist Christian worldview (Moyn 2015), my intention is not to argue against contemporary human rights, claiming that today they are inescapably stained due to their religious origin.[32] Instead, it is to reiterate Moyn's compelling claim that events in the 1940s provide significantly less insight into the contemporary dominance of human rights than is usually presumed (Moyn 2014b, 74; Keys 2014; Mazower 2009). In part, this is because the broader social, political, and economic environment, at the time, was inhospitable to what we understand to be key features of contemporary human rights, namely, an international consensus on the morality, legitimacy, and legality of holding sovereign states, and increasingly other powerful actors, accountable for violating the rights of citizens.

The Postwar New Deal

Capacious contemporary readings to the contrary, the UDHR did not put in question the notion of state sovereignty that had been entrenched in the UN's founding Charter (Moyn 2010, 45). Article 2(7) of the Charter leaves no doubt about the incontestability of national sovereignty (Keys 2014, 20). Indeed, as Mark Mazower notes,

> many left the founding conference at San Francisco in 1945 believing that the world body they were being asked to sign up to was shot through with hypocrisy. They saw its universal rhetoric of freedom and rights as all to partial – a veil masking the consolidation of a great power directorate that was not as different from the Axis powers, in its imperious attitude to how the world's weak and poor should be governed. (2009, 7)

Moreover, it is incontrovertibly true that human rights were invoked in the context of decolonization and the movement of non-aligned nations, as ably demonstrated by the work of Roland Burke (2011). They, however, were typically summoned in the name of self-determination with the avowed purpose of curbing neo-colonial incursions rather than ceding sovereignty for the sake of a new international moral consensus, or legal architecture (Moyn 2010, 84, 2012). As Moyn perspicaciously points out, anti-colonialism has to be understood as "the agent of the greatest dissemination of sovereignty in world history, not of its qualification" (2012, 161). What is more, it is too easy to forget that "anticolonialism and anti-racism [frequently associated with human rights] quickly lost their radical edge once states won independence – at that point they often turned into defenders of the status quo and the Indian government was to resist UN intervention in its internal affairs as South Africans had done earlier" (Mazower 2009, 27; Afshari 2007, 51; Keys 2014, 75–76).

Today, it is economic, social, and cultural human rights that appear most difficult to envisage and secure in contrast to civil and political human rights. Ironically, in the postwar period, a broad consensus prevailed regarding the centrality of these rights, understood as citizenship rather than human rights, epitomized by Roosevelt's freedom from want. Economic and social rights, however, were not grounded in the emergence of novel international instruments nor a global ethic, but by the then evolving welfare states that many decolonized nations hoped to imitate (Moyn 2010, 73). The experience of the economic instability of the 1930s, successful worker's organization, the immensity of the national sacrifice of the World War II effort, and the state's increased ability to plan and organize the war economy and society meant that some type of postwar social citizenship contract was on the agenda. However, it would be wrong to overly generalize. For instance, in Western Europe, as seen above, commitment to welfare policies had more to do with the preservation of core Christian values combined with a mildly interventionist yet better tooled state (Kaiser 2007, 168–69) against the background of anti-communism.

When seen from the present, such was the resonance of postwar citizenship social rights that the historian Elizabeth Borgwardt has cleverly and suggestively written a compelling account of the period in which the American idiom for social citizenship, the New Deal, becomes the organizing principle underpinning American postwar multilateral internationalism (2007). Encoded in New Deal thinking, she argues, was "the duty of governments to use the combined resources of the nation to prevent distress and to promote the general welfare of all people" and to do so by drawing on the efficiencies of planning (Borgwardt 2007, 6).

In the same manner that the New Deal had expanded the idea of "security" to include economic and social security (Borgwardt 2007, 7), the Atlantic Charter, the nucleus of the New Deal for the World, envisioned "a wider and permanent system of general security" (Borgwardt 2007, 27). The insights of the New Deal—namely, that economic security supported political stability and that a modicum of economic security could be ensured through careful policy development—were to be stretched on to the world polity (Borgwardt 2007, 11, 61, 109). Consequently, for Borgwardt, postwar international multilateral milestones such as the United Nations, the Bretton Woods agreements, and the Nuremberg Charter represent the institutional maturation of the ideas inherent in the Atlantic Charter, engendered by New Deal thinking (2007, 286). What is more, in the same manner that the New Deal endowed individuals with dignity arising from a broader conception of economic justice, the human rights cautiously announced in the Four Freedoms address, projected this dignity to all individuals throughout the world (Borgwardt 2007, 285).

Borgwardt is at pains to argue that too much work on human rights relies on unexamined assumptions and normative discussions far divorced from the actual historical terrain. The latter is significantly messier and more unruly than many present-day accounts would have us believe (2007, 57–58). Consequently, "as contemporary scholars of human rights ransack the past for early expressions of familiar-sounding political concepts, they often distort ideas by divorcing them from context" (Borgwardt 2007, 58–59). Borgwardt offers her analysis as an example of what a more detailed historically contextualized analysis can provide, making an important contribution to the scholarship of the postwar period.

However, if she successfully shows that American multilateral internationalism in the period can plausibly be understood as a transposition of the ideals of the New Deal onto the world stage, her contention that human rights are part of this package is far less convincing. Much hangs on her suggestion that Roosevelt's internationalism, and universalist language, as crystallized in his Four Freedoms address and in the negotiation of the Atlantic Charter, succeeded in internationalizing New Deal "human rights". In other words, she claims that domestic civil, political, and economic rights that were inherent to the New Deal became, through the prism of Roosevelt's internationalism, global human rights. Moreover, even though she admits that the very notion of "human rights" was probably introduced as part of a rhetorical flourish, she suggests that this was a consequential and fateful oratorical choice (Borgwardt 2007, 56).

The claim that human rights had some currency as a way of symbolizing the freedoms for which the allies were fighting (Borgwardt 2007, 53) is indubitable. That New Deal thinking impacted American postwar multilateralism is convincingly argued.[33] However, that postwar multilateralism and its international institutional architecture should be read as an attempt to institutionalize human rights (Borgwardt 2007, 133–34) is significantly more contentious and less convincing. It relies on establishing an equivalence between internationalism, universalism, and humanity with human rights in the postwar period. I think this is implausible given the marginality and the semantic narrowness of human rights at the time, as discussed above (see Keys 2014, 15–31). If human rights had such little traction in the US, how could they provide the springboard for their launch into the international arena?

The putative equivalence speaks more to the manner in which, at present, human rights have colonized these terms—that is, internationalism, universalism, and humanity—than to the historical genesis of contemporary human rights. As a result, it blots out one of the most significant variants of internationalism in the postwar period: the alternative internationalism engendered by "subaltern national liberation". The goal of the latter was an unorthodox model of economic development that owed more to the realities of neo-colonial relationships, and in some cases socialist ideals, than to the idiom of human rights that it sometimes instrumentally invoked (Moyn 2010, 85–86; see Afshari 2007).

The alleged continuity between American internationalism in the postwar period and contemporary human rights similarly ignores the distinctiveness of both, making illegible the extent to which human rights in the 1970s represented a break with "Cold War verities that had guided policy-making since the late 1940s" (Keys 2014, 7). The equivalence also obfuscates the extent to which the governance institutions fostered by postwar internationalism were divorced from human rights. To take one example, the Food and Agricultural Organization (FAO) makes no mention of human rights in its founding constitution in 1945, tellingly delaying serious engagement with the language of human rights until the mid-1990s (López 2015). Much the same could be said regarding other institutions, such as the World Bank (Staples 2006). Significantly, in Borgwardt's discussion of the Bretton Woods agreements, human rights virtually do no explanatory work (2007, 114–41).

The human rights idiom was certainly heard in the halls of the UN in the postwar. However, it does not follow that all UN activity in the period should be understood as an instantiation of human rights work. In fact, by the late 1960s, UN advocacy of human rights was generally seen as having borne little fruit, as evidenced by the lacklustre of the 1968 Teheran Conference meant to commemorate the 20th anniversary of the UDHR (Moyn 2010, 126–27; Keys 2014, 6). Moreover, until fairly recently, it has been possible to write the history of American internationalism without reference to human rights (Moyn 2014b), which should not have been the case if human rights had truly been central. Equally, the human rights currency that flowed in postwar Europe was pegged, as seen above and explored further in Chap. 6, to an altogether different suite of political and moral values from those associated with New Deal internationalism. What is more, the take-off of human rights in the

1970s was largely the product of social movements that initially circumvented the UN (Moyn 2010, 129; Keck and Sikkink 1998).

Subsequently, social movements in the so-called global south that rallied around economic, cultural, and social human rights in the 1990s did so precisely in opposition to the postwar internationalist organizations that Borgwardt claims had institutionalized human right values (see Nelson and Dorsey 2008). Moyn argues that scholar such as Borgwardt (2007) and Sunstein (2009), intent on framing US postwar internationalism in terms of contemporary understandings of human rights, "select and single out what now look like milestones, because of the retroactive importance, but fail to grasp their marginality in their own period, from which no broad-gauge international movement emerged" (2014b, 146). Additionally, the impetus for such work is indissociable from attempts to unearth a usable American internationalism to act as a foil against the disdain for multilateralism and the UN evidenced by American foreign policy at the turn of the twenty-first century (Mazower 2009, 5–6). This is aptly illustrated by the arguments Borgwardt develops in her concluding chapter.

Thickening the Human Rights Historical Narrative

If not the immediate postwar, where does one, then, look for the origins of contemporary human rights? In the conclusion to a recent collection of studies, the historian Mark Philip Bradley writes, "[i]f pieces of the puzzle of global human rights history in the 1970s and beyond are now being put into place in an increasingly sophisticated scholarship, we still don't know where the ubiquitous presence of human rights talk in this period really came from" (Bradley 2012, 232). He goes on to note that there are a number of suggestive contributions.

Key amongst these is Moyn's persuasive and game-changing argument that human rights are best understood as the contingent emergence of a form of anti-politics, developed in the 1970s in the ashes of the grand political utopias of the twentieth century, namely, liberal capitalism, state socialism, and the nationalisms and internationalisms of post-colonial states. The moral power of these postwar utopias had been consumed by the flames of their outright failures and inner contradictions, as well as by the extraordinarily high cost they had exacted in human suffering. Dissident groups in the Soviet Bloc, groups grappling with repression in Latin America, and the fledging organizational forms developed by organizations such as Amnesty International, via different trajectories and for different reasons, converged around a rejection of grand political projects. Instead, they nurtured a highly moralistic form of anti-politics whose surprising pragmatism sought to transcend politics itself. As a result, contends Moyn,

> It was the crisis of other utopias that allowed the very neutrality that had made "human rights" wholly peripheral to the aftermath of the World War II – when taking sides in a contest of programmatic visions seemed so pressing – to become the conditions of their success [...] human rights could breakthrough in the era [the 1970s] because the ideological climate was ripe for claims to make a difference not through political vision but by transcending politics. Morality, global in its potential scope, could become the aspiration of mankind. (2010, 213)

More recently, Moyn has further thickened his historical analysis. As discussed above, he has done so by unearthing the consequential Christian roots of human rights both in Europe and the UN in the postwar (Moyn 2015). Another thick reading of the emergence of human rights in the US intersects with and contributes to Moyn's fruitful focus on the 1970s. Barbara Keys argues that the growth of human rights has to be located in the context of "a struggle for the soul of the country" against the backdrop of the loss of the Vietnam War that served not "as a means of coming to terms with the Vietnam War but as a means of moving past it. Human rights became a way to heal the country by taming the legacy of Vietnam" (2014, 3).

Human Rights and American Virtue

Read alongside the work of Moyn (2010, 2014b), Keys' careful study of US politics in the postwar era (2012, 2014) dispels the notion that human rights were incubated during said period and that they were to play a significant role in the civil rights movement. Insofar as human rights as a term surfaced in political discourse, it was understood as a synonym for domestic civil rights, that is, as remedy for racism and discrimination (Keys 2014, 32–47). In the US vernacular, human rights indexed the rights guaranteed by the US constitution rather than the exogenous international rights of UDHR (Keys 2014, 39).[34] Tellingly, Keys notes that the kinds of violence that would be a lightning rod for outrage in the name of human rights in the 1970s—to wit torture, mass killings, and wrongful imprisonment—occurred in the early 1960s, and before for that matter, but did not eventuate into collective international action before 1967 (2014, 40). In addition, she maintains, "to the extent that US diplomacy aligned itself with anticolonialism, self-determination, and antiracism, it did so not as part of an overt scheme to promote human rights but to promote friendly relations with newly independent African countries" (2014, 43). In fact, it was only when civil rights receded from "the national agenda" that a space would open up for human rights. Crucially, when contemporary human rights finally burst on to the scene, the overriding objective was not to broaden the struggles from the sixties, but rather to engage in an altogether new project: slaying "foreign rather than home-grown monsters" (2014, 47).

If the decentring of the civil rights movement from federal politics was one of the factors that enabled the rise of human rights, the other was the end of the Vietnam War (Keys 2014, 49). Despite the multifarious nature of the moral vocabularies deployed to criticize the war—ranging from anti-imperialism to religious and utilitarian critiques—human rights was strikingly absent (Keys 2014, 51–55). Amnesty International successfully publicized the coup in Greece in 1967 and the subsequent *Regime of the Colonels*, and the issue of torture, in particular, got a considerable amount of traction in the US (Keys 2012, 2014, 84–88). However, as long as US involvement in the Vietnam War persisted, writes Keys, "Americans found the type of human rights activism peddled by Amnesty International to be almost totally irrelevant, and no one as yet had thought to offer human rights as panacea for America's foreign policy dilemmas" (2014, 103).[35]

A fateful consequence of the Vietnam War, for the story of human rights in the US, is the ideological rift it created in the Democratic Party between anti-communist Cold War warriors and liberals.[36] The former exemplified by Senator Henry M. "Scoop" Jackson (WA)[37] energetically reacted against leftist and liberal critiques of American foreign policy. In particular the democratic hawks were outraged by the sense of shame and culpability promulgated by the 1972 McGovern presidential campaign, which produced a stunning landslide defeat for democrats. Decrying accusations of imperialism and loss of a moral compass, Jackson seized on the incipient dissident and the *refusenik*[38] movement in the USSR to align a defence of American values with human rights in a critique of Soviet totalitarianism, the true evil in the world. Jacksonian Democrats, moreover, held that Nixon and Ford were conceding too much, even imperilling America's anti-communist democratic global mission, in efforts to achieve détente with the Soviet Union. Despite drawing on the universalist language of human rights, the latter "for Jackson, meant the liberties abrogated by the Soviet Union and its allies, not the abuses committed by anti-communist governments" (Keys 2014, 124).

The liberal espousal of human rights as antidote to the moral malaise engendered by the Vietnam War had a number of dimensions. The trauma of the war left liberal democrats without a moral compass with which to plot a course for US foreign policy in the post-Vietnam War era. What is more, McGovern's decisive defeat made clear that shame and guilt had not worked as a national frame for overcoming the sense of ethical listlessness produced by the war (Keys 2014, 74). In 1976, however, Jimmy Carter would succeed in combining a sense of moral purpose with a balm to soothe the ethical lacerations produced by the Vietnam War, telling "voters that he hoped to make the American government as good and kind and decent as the American people already were" (Keys 2012, 74). This would require neither contrition nor self-flagellation. "International human rights promotion" would not entail abandoning American values, but a turn towards them: "Our nation should always derive its character directly from the people and let this be the strength and the image to be represented to the world – the character of the American people" (Carter in Keys 2014, 240).

Given Jimmy Carter's association with the pivot towards human rights in American foreign policy, it is striking to realize that he did not in fact seriously embrace human rights until the final two months of the 1976 presidential campaign, motivated, it appears, by promising polling numbers (Keys 2014, 236). By this time, Amnesty International and other groups had begun to secure some traction in the US and in Congress. This was in part made possible by the "Insurgency on Capitol Hill", coinciding with the end of the US' participation in Vietnam War (Keys 2014, 153–77). The insurgency however was not necessarily fuelled by a principled promotion of human rights as a way to change the world rather it was, Keys argues, "an almost accidental tool picked up to fight other battles" (2014, 155). These other battles included attempts to secure a voice for the legislature in foreign policy—which the Secretary of State Henry Kissinger vigorously tried to prevent, reorganizing foreign aid, and decreasing military expenditure and arms sales (Keys 2014, 155). Human rights appeared to provide liberal democrats moral catharsis in the field of foreign policy, giving them voice in a policy area where they had struggled to speak as a result of the trauma of the Vietnam War. Moreover, as Keys writes, "the new agenda was an outlet for moral indignation and a program for virtue without cost. Least of all was it a method to effect change in the rest of the world" (2014, 156).

What is more, by the early 1970s, liberal democrats began to recognize the conceit that had powered the grand modernization and development projects of the postwar era (Staples 2006). Consequently, more modest efforts to alleviate human suffering and address more pressing humanitarian causes rose to the top of their agenda. Accepting that they could not change the world, they focused instead on "not abetting evil" (Keys 2014, 160).[39] They did so, as Keys' historical reconstruction shows by using hearings to draw attention to human rights abuses, slashing aid to "friendly but strategically expendable governments",[40] and requiring the State Department to gather and disseminate information on human rights abuses and cooperate with human rights organizations (2014, 176). This gave the activities of non-governmental organizations a significant stimulus, securing them a space in the US political field (Keys 2014, 184).

Assessments of Carter's human rights foreign policy are varied, depending on whether one makes a minimalist or maximalist reading of the administration's human rights tack (Keys 2014, 242–67). Most would claim it was more "rhetoric than reality" (Stohl et al. 1984; Carleton and Stohl 1985; Apodaca and Stohl 1999). In other words, rhetorically it greatly contributed to the spread of human rights as a new international idiom, in reality "the correlations with both military and economic aid [were], at best, very small [...] Over the course of the four years Carter was in office, security assistance was cut off in only eight cases: Argentina, Bolivia, El Salvador, Guatemala, Haiti, Nicaragua, Paraguay and Uruguay" (Carleton and Stohl 1985, 215–16). Its most significant achievement, Keys argues, is perhaps domestic rather international insofar as it enabled Americans to link their country with a worthy international cause in the post-Vietnam War era (Keys 2014, 267), "reclaiming American virtue".[41]

Ronald Reagan, famously campaigned against the Carter human rights policy, denouncing it as "morally unsound, ineffective, and threatening to United States' security interests" (Carleton and Stohl 1985, 205). Indeed, Reagan's Secretary of State, William Haig, in his first interview, announced that "[i]nternational terrorism will take the place of human rights in our concern, because it is the ultimate abuse of human rights" (Haig in Carleton and Stohl 1985, 208),[42] which he of course linked to an international terror network under the Machiavellian control of the Soviet Union (Carleton and Stohl 1985, 208). Reagan also proposed Ernest Lefever as the Assistant Secretary of State for Human Rights; the latter "opposed all efforts to make human rights a concern of US foreign policy. As his post existed to carry out laws adopted in the mid-1970s that required the promotion of human rights, he was a preposterous choice to fill it" (Neier 2012, 207).

Aryeh Neier, one of the founding members of Helsinki Watch, which would later become Human Rights Watch, in his history of the human rights movement, recounts that the organization took a key role in organizing opposition to the nomination, which was defeated in the Senate Foreign Relations Committee by a vote of thirteen to four (2012, 207).[43]

Pressured by NGOs, the pro-human rights legislation enacted by Congress in the 1970s, in the context of the aforementioned insurgency, a Congress under Democratic control, and the State Department's enhanced capacity for monitoring human rights, the Reagan administration's performance on human rights, on some measures, does not differ markedly from that of the Carter administration's (Apodaca and Stohl 1999, 194). As Clair Apodaca and Michael Stohl conclude, in their analysis of the relationship between human rights and foreign assistance from Carter to Clinton, "the differences between Carter and Reagan's human rights policies were not as great as their critics, or champions, like to claim" (1999, 194).[44]

Still, the introduction of human rights as a foreign policy tool in the US, rhetorical or otherwise, has contributed to the current worldwide legitimacy of human rights. As world culture scholars have repeatedly noted, few countries, in the contemporary world, would position themselves explicitly as being against human rights (Meyer et al. 1997). The purpose of this brief excursus into human rights historiography is obviously not to settle the historical debate once and for all. In a very significant sense, it has just begun. I find Moyn, Keys, Mazower, Afshari, Probst, and Duranti's critical readings of the human rights historiography compelling and highly suggestive. As these more recent contributions take hold, they will no doubt stimulate new debates, consensus, and dissension. For instance, scholars who agree with Moyn's focus on the centrality of the 1970s do not necessarily concur with his substantive conclusions (Eckel and Moyn 2014). However, I think that it is possible to use this historical discussion to sharpen the distinction between thin and thick historical narratives so as to clarify what would constitute a thick versus a thin conception of human rights in sociology.

Thick Versus Thin

It is essential to realize that "thickness" does not refer to the attempt to intensively mine the past in order to collect ever earlier, or more plentiful, examples of "expressions of familiar-sounding political concepts" (Borgwardt 2007, 59). Although such efforts appear to thicken, in reality and counter-intuitively, they thin historical accounts. A thin historical account, in the context of human rights, refers to a narrative in which the latter are stripped down and reduced to some essential moral idea or principle, a trans-historical self-generating normative disposition crystallized in specific texts, for example, the UDHR. In this type of account, though buffeted by different historical currents, human rights always appear to retain their identity as they move promiscuously towards the present, slipping in and out of myriad historical events radiating historical episodes and their actors with meaning as they are incorporated into a "metanarrativity" (Somers 1994a, 619) of moral development.

A thick historical account, in contrast, begins with the realization that moral ideas or principles, such as those associated with the human rights semantic universe, are not inevitably blown forward by the winds of time. Though their normative power often relies on their timeless and transcendent self-presentation, human rights are socially, politically, economically, and culturally dense. Absent these, their meaning would cease, and they would be incapable of circulating socially or historically and enacting the types of affect to which Alexander (2006) alludes. Human rights, like all forms of social normativity, are made possible by particular forms of contingent yet relatively stable patterned behaviour, stitching normative dispositions to broader meaning-making cultural practices, interpellating subjects as particular types of individuals, and nurturing specific organizational forms (López 2009). Human rights' ability to participate in the co-production of meaning and affect, and the potentially extensive nature of both, is indissolubly tied to the way they connect, or not, with broader semiotic and non-semiotic social processes.

The mere historical appearance of human rights in texts, or of expressions and acts that invoke them, should not be taken as evidence that these are precursors to contemporary understandings of human rights. The dense social, political, cultural, and economic relations that embed political or normative ideals overdetermine their meaning, be these broadly circulating political vernaculars or more restricted idioms. Human rights and the meaning they denote or connote and the social action they make (im)possible are no different.

Their ability to circulate, to be meaningful, to be socially efficacious, or to recover the language of performativity discussed above, to be successfully performed depends on how they are enmeshed in what Margaret Somers in another context calls a "relational setting": that is to say, "a pattern of relationships among institutions, public narratives, and social practices" that function as a "relational matrix", or a "social network" (Somers 1994a, 626). It is this relational matrix that historical and sociological analyses need to identify and explore. It is true that at different moments in time, all manner of actors and different modalities of texts have invoked rights, the rights of man, the rights of citizens, the rights of members of religious or kin communities, natural rights, social justice, and indeed human rights. A thin historical account, subtly or not, collapses some or all of these into an instantiation of the same ineradicable moral disposition—surely, a *desideratum* rather than a reality!

Whatever the substantive limitations of the critical histories of human rights discussed above, and these will surely emerge as a result of scholarly debate, they all decisively contribute to breaking the widely experienced mesmerism that human rights have engendered. Transfixed by their considerable normative power, all too many have come uncritically to accept that human rights are self-propelled and a natural response to human injustice or barbarism, as when Ignatieff, as cited above, claims that human rights are constituted by "the basic intuition that what is pain and humiliation for you is bound to be pain and humiliation for me" (2001, 91).[45] Such a perspective suggests that all we need to do to understand human rights and their potential is track the historical locations where this natural inclination has materialized.[46]

The lessons that sociologists should glean from this critical historiography are that there are far too many unexamined assumptions of what human rights are, where they come from, how they travel socially and historically, and the nature of their social efficacy. Sociologists, I will show especially in the next chapter, but also throughout the book, frequently, unwittingly perhaps, weave too much of their sociological analyses of human rights with a thin historical thread. In an attempt to dislodge human rights' near hypnotic normative hold, in the next sections I introduce and develop the model of human rights as political imaginary. A model that not only begins with a thick conception of human rights, but also one that is hopefully sufficiently capacious to incorporate the significant sociological contributions to the study of human rights explored throughout this book.

Human Rights as Public Narratives

One of the key conclusions to draw from the discussion of thick and thin conceptions of human rights is the centrality of meaning, understood not in an abstract sense, but, rather, as the densely embedded, structured, and relational processes by which individuals intersubjectively make sense of their world, themselves, and others. To say that individuals make sense of the world, however, is not to suggest that meaning is individual, dyadic, triadic—a mere aggregate of monads. Although meaning-making, or semiosis, certainly "presupposes embodied, intentional, practically-skilled social actors", it also, and crucially, entails the existence of "social relations, material objects and spatio-temporality" (Fairclough et al. 2002, 4). Meaning, as Alexander rightly points out, in his highly stylized framework, is contingent on successful performance that calls not only for an actor and an audience but also for systems of collective representation, means of symbolic production, and a *mise-en-scène*, all of which are indissociable from social power (2011, 28–43).

Such performances enact what Somers has called "public narratives". The latter are "attached to cultural and institutional formations larger than the single individual, to intersubjective networks or institutions, however local or grand, micro or macro" (1994b, 619). Public narratives are "social" and "interpersonal" (Somers 1994a, 118) and are key sites for understanding the "practices of social and historical actors, their collective actions, their modes and meanings of institution-building and group-formations, and their apparent incoherencies" (Somers 1994a, 118). Sociologically speaking, then, what is absent from thin historical and sociological accounts of human rights is precisely an analysis of the public narratives and the relational matrices in which and through which they have been and continue to be meaningful to actors.

Moreover, as seen in the discussion of the critical historiography of human rights above, insofar as public narratives of human rights did circulate in the postwar, they did so in a relational context that differed significantly from that found in the 1970s. The public narratives that materialized in this latter setting resonate conspicuously with those that continue to do so today—that is to say, the moral legitimacy of infringing on the sovereignty of nation-states, in some contexts, in order to hold them to account for a minimally beneficent treatment of their citizens.

In the postwar, as authors such as Moyn, Mazower, and Keys have shown, not only were human rights not cast in this role in the public narratives of the period, the public narratives that drew on human rights were marginal and easily overtaken by broader postwar public narratives: namely, political projects such as liberal capitalism or liberal internationalism, Christian democracy, state socialism, post-colonialism, and the movements of non-aligned states. For instance, insofar as human rights were invoked in the context of post-colonialism, they came to mean freedom from colonial interference—arguably, the opposite of what they signify today. Where human rights public narratives were able to establish some traction as in the case of Western Europe, amongst the Protestants in the US and in the UN, they became attached to, and were reproduced in, relational networks that differed markedly from the ones that developed in the 1970s, and with which *mutatis mutandi* contemporary human rights still resonate.

Drawing inspiration from Margaret Somers' conceptualization of public narratives and relational settings (Somers 1993, 1994a, 1997), and the work of Bob Jessop and his colleagues in the cultural political economy approach (Jessop 2004, 2010, 2013; Jessop and Oosterlynck 2008; Jessop and Sum 2006; Sum and Jessop 2013), I want to propose a model of human rights as political imaginary. This model attempts to capture the most salient features of the broad public narrative and relational settings in which human rights emerged in the 1970s, and through which they have gained enormous social and political traction, if not always efficacy. Here, I provide an initial sketch of the framework, which I will develop in subsequent chapters as I proceed with my sympathetic, yet critical, survey of the sociological scholarship on human rights.

To be clear, my goal is not to provide a historical account of the emergence of human rights, though I will continue to draw on the critical historiography summarized above for reasons I hope are clear at this stage in my argument. Equally, I do not aim to comprehensively describe all the sociological dimensions of human rights. Instead my intent is more modest. It is to move back and forth between the existing sociological scholarship on human rights and the political imaginary model. I want to articulate a framework that is able to incorporate what, to my mind, are the most important insights of this scholarship, and the manner in which such insights might be put together to develop a more robust model for sociologically understanding and researching human rights.

As I noted in the introduction to the book, in the archipelago of the sociology of human rights, a broad attempt to bring together the range of contributions has yet not been undertaken. This book endeavours to begin to fill this lacuna. Finally, my objective is not to provide the definite explanation of what "human rights" are, but to fashion tools that can be used to conceptually and empirically engage with human rights sociologically.[47] In other words, I consider this model as a starting point, a sensitizing tool, rather than a terminus.

Human Rights as Political Imaginary

As indicated above, my use of the term political imaginary differs from a number of well-known usages, namely, Castoriadis (1998), Lacan (1977), Laclau and Mouffe (1985), and Taylor (2002). Instead, it draws on the concept of an "economic imaginary" as developed by Bob Jessop and his colleagues, in their work on cultural political economy. The latter is concerned with integrating semiotic and non-semiotic analyses of social formations. More concretely, cultural political economy's objective is the incorporation of culture—understood as meaning-making or semiosis—into economic analysis where it has overwhelming been epiphenomenal, without, however, falling into the trap of producing "a soft economic sociology that focuses on the similarities between economic and other socio-cultural activities at the expense of the specificity of the economic" (Jessop and Oosterlynck 2008, 1155; López 2016).

Jessop defines imaginaries as "semiotic systems that frame individual subjects' lived experience of an inordinately complex world and/or inform collective calculation about the world" (Jessop 2010, 344). Put in terms of Somers' conceptual vocabulary, "[o]ntological narratives are used to define who we *are*, this in turn can be a precondition for knowing *what to do* [...] People act, or do not act, in part according to how they understand their place in any number of given narratives" (Somers 1994b, 618). In other words, imaginaries or narratives serve to represent "the imaginary relationship of individuals to their real conditions of existence" (Althusser 1971, 109).[48] This capacitates them to act skilfully in the world. Imaginaries align individuals with the world by enabling them to, more or less, coherently grasp the world so that it is infused with meanings. Consequently, imaginaries equip individuals with possible modes of acting and interacting.

Imaginaries or narratives are not one-to-one representations of "the world" because the complexity of what they are trying to grasp (Bhaskar 1978) necessarily eludes them. They thus focus on some aspects of reality to the exclusion of others (Jessop 2010, 345, 2013, 236). Nonetheless, to the extent that imaginaries or narratives organize, but do not determine, intervention and interaction in the world, they cannot be entirely arbitrary or willed: "they must have some significant, albeit necessarily partial, fit with real material interdependencies" (Jessop 2013, 236), social practices, organizational forms, and semiotic networks.

Although I completely concur with Somers that narrativity plays a crucial role in meaning-making, and in the insertion of individuals in intercutting relational matrices, to my mind, narrativity does not exhaust semiosis. Thus, I use the broader term *discursive representations* to refer to the first dimension of an imaginary, which includes narrativity but also other aspects of semiosis such as discourses, genres, and styles (Jessop 2010, 344; Fairclough et al. 2002; Fairclough 2003). The second dimension arises from fact that imaginaries do not merely represent, they also orientate actors towards the world. Consequently imaginaries licence specific forms of individual and collective *subjectivity and agency*. Additionally, if imaginaries are to steer specific ways of seeing and being in the world, they cannot be restricted to "meaning-making"; they must also coordinate "actions within and across specific personal interactions, organizations and networks, and institutional orders" (Jessop 2010, 339). Consequently the third dimension of an imaginary refers to the *social technologies* that are capable of patterning and indeed also disciplining social interaction distributed across heterogeneous spatial and temporal locales (Jessop 2010, 339). The last dimension of the political imaginary refers to the manner in which it materializes in and becomes dependent, even antagonistically, on concrete *organizational forms*.

To sum up, an imaginary is a more or less stable heterogeneous assemblage that brings together discursive representations of the world (i.e., How the world is?), modalities of individual and collective subjectivity and agency (i.e., How should we act on it?), social technologies, and organizational forms (i.e., What enables our action?). What is more, to the extent that an imaginary is concerned with describing and/or achieving determinate forms of solidaristic collective life, it can be called a political imaginary. In order to begin to sketch the contours of human rights as a political imaginary, I am going to add some details to the models for illustrative purposes. I do so with the caveat that this is a preliminary sketch that will be thickened as I work through the sociology of human rights scholarship in subsequent chapters.

Discursive representations not only "represent the world as it is (or rather as it is seen to be)", they also represent "possible worlds which are different from the actual world, and tied in to projects to change the world in particular directions" (Fairclough 2003, 124). In the context of the political imaginary of human rights, key dimensions of their representational dynamics can be identified. First, as amply demonstrated in the discussion above, I note the primacy of the historical narrative of the genesis of human rights qua norms and principles and the subsequent continuity in their development as an indisputable horizon of understanding. What I mean here is the idea of the historical continuity of human rights since 1948, if not before. Second, as I will show in Chaps. 3 and 4, is the highly schematic, pragmatic, and prescriptive rendering of situations of injustice as instances of violations. Obligations are known, duties defined, and remedies available. Actors are unequivocally assigned to the categories of victims, witnesses, or perpetrators with the irrefutable obligations of claiming their human rights, advocating for human rights, and introducing appropriate remedies, respectively (López 2015, 13).

Social technologies refer to those socially constituted practices of calculating, representing, and categorizing that contribute to the social patterning of interactions. In the sphere of human rights, they signify, for instance, modes of bearing witness, documenting atrocities, or representing human rights violations and the deployment of legal rationalities (Hopgood 2006; López 2015; Moon 2012; Wilson 2009). Subjectivity and agency capture both the lived experience of the human rights imaginary and how they are expressed in individual or collective social action mediated by practices. In the case of the former, it can take the form of individual or collective modes of self-understanding as subjects of human rights, witnesses of violations, and/or as membership in the human family (Slaughter 2009; Fassin 2012; Douzinas 2007, 34–50; Kurasawa 2007, 23–55). In the case of the latter, it is manifested in the selectivity of persuasion over force as a genus of political action, political minimalism, forms of advocacy such as letter writing and the sharing of information through networks, and recourse to judicial methods of action (Keck and Sikkink 1998; Hopgood 2006). Finally, organizational forms or structures denote the crystallization and institutionalization of specific organizational configurations, such as international agreements and covenants, transnational and regional human rights bodies, NGOS and INGOs, and human rights advocacy networks.

Human rights, as I conceptualise them, following Woodiwiss, are not understood as being based on unquestioned moral principles or a natural normative disposition against injustice and barbarism (2003, 2005). They are the contingent fusing together of representational practices, modes of subjectivity and agency, social technologies, and organizational forms. It is precisely the ability to analytically distinguish amongst these elements and to explore their independent and/or conjoined variation and interconnection that provides the political imaginary model with its explanatory potential.

Imaginaries in Action

Because an imaginary is not a social representation, as such, but a socially enabled attempt to apprehend the world as it is, and as it might be, imaginaries always have a normative valence. They register the world in particular kinds of ways, focusing on some things and not others. In addition, imaginaries also distinguish between how the world is, always partially of course, and how it might be. Actors act to reproduce certain features that are desirable and to transform others that are not. In acting, they draw on existing resources that are frequently activated by particular practices or through social technologies that are spatially and chronologically organized by different organizations. Actions can reinforce certain tendencies serving to further sediment specific representations, social technologies, subjectivities and modes of actions, and organizational arrangements, or they can serve to draw out inconsistencies, tensions, or obstacles that may appear insurmountable. For instance, the fact that in the US, as we will see in Chap. 6, commitment to human rights is oriented towards foreign rather than domestic policy.

Imaginaries have properties that are almost systemic in nature; they are the effect of representations that are coherent and provide the grounds for successful action in and cognition of the world. On this level they have features that Luhmann associates with autopoetic systems (1995); to wit, they seemingly provide a code for interpreting and making sense of some aspect of social life that is, to a certain extent, internal to the operation of the imaginary itself. These representations can be reinforced by specific social technologies, modes of action, and institutional anchors, creating a sense of stability. However social imaginaries are a complex assemblage of disparate elements. They are best thought of as an "instituted process", that is to say as "a matrix of institutional relationships, technologies, political idioms, and rights-claiming practices that are always dynamic and contingent" (Somers 2008, 35). Coherence and stability cannot be guaranteed. They are not quite systems in the Luhmannian sense. Centrifugal forces abound because the social world is complexly patterned, chaotic, and subject to unforeseen eventualities. Reiterations, repetitions of patterned behaviour, as Butler (2011) and Deleuze (1994; see DeLanda 2002) have shown, are always capable of producing the new, and changing the parameters and functioning of a system. Thus, imaginaries in reproducing themselves are equally always in the process of potentially changing and evolving through variation, selection, and retention (Jessop 2010, 340), some willed, most probably not.

A political imaginary is a project. Project, the origin of which is the Latin *pro* meaning forth and *jacere* meaning to throw, conveys both as a verb and a noun the meaning of throwing forth or forward. A political imaginary as a project has a dual temporal sense, indexing the immediate present as well as the future. To project on to the social world is to throw onto the social world a particular understanding that is underwritten by subjectivities and modulated actions, and to introduce a second metaphor, to see how it bounces back. It is however also to throw forth a design to be realized at some point in the future. As Douzinas notes, "confounding the real and the ideal is a characteristic of human rights" (2007, 10).

Given the diversity, scale, and geographical spread of the different components of an imaginary, the prospect that the components may enter in conflict with one another can certainly not be discounted. What is more, it just might be that the very efforts to encourage consistency through the specific social technologies that modulate the human rights political imaginary might be responsible for engendering friction or discord. For instance, an immutable protocol for documenting human rights violations and generating remedies will certainly contribute to establishing the facticity of the violations and the observer's neutrality. However, by placing "social and political conditions that will determine the meaning a right has in particular contexts" in the background, it could just as easily "render the even-handed pursuit of 'rights' vulnerable to all sorts of distorted outcomes" (Kennedy 2005, 12).

Conversely, the effort to embed elements from the human rights political imaginary in local custom or tradition, what Ignatieff labels "going global by going local" (2001, 7), Merry (2006) "vernacularizing", and Woodiwiss (2012, 966) "provincializing", can be equally disruptive insofar as it has the potential of undermining the perceived impartiality that sustains human rights' ability to circulate as a socio-discourse. Paradoxically, then, it might be useful to think of the human rights political imaginary as a field of dispersion,[49] in which irregularities occur not because of the absence of attempts to modulate, regulate, and make human rights calculable and predictable, but precisely because of such efforts. There is no surer way to produce difference than by treating things that should be treated differently the same.

Conclusion

Contemporary human rights have graded the political and moral terrain such that the true source of their legitimacy and of their persuasiveness can be difficult to discern. There is a generalized expectation that progressive scholars should put their disciplinary tools at the service of human rights, removing obstacles towards their realization, defending human rights' normative stands, and adopting their modes of legal reasoning, tropes, and narrative strategies. Associated with a historical or trans-historical moral reflex against human cruelty, barbarism, and injustice that any reasonable moral actor, individual or collective, should accept, human rights have achieved an almost axiomatic status in contemporary moral and political discourse.

This powerful normative position, supported by what appears to be deep historical roots, has encouraged scholars to welcome and nurture rather than critically explore their contemporary (lack of) success. Thinly conceived, it is their moral irrefutability and their long historical genesis that would seem to account for their contemporary predominance. However, it is precisely because of human rights' almost axiomatic status that sociologists should engage with them critically: not out of cynicism or puerile contrarianism. But because undertaking the process of scientific objectivation is an ineradicable first step into the knowledge terrain that sociological analysis makes possible. The failure to do so, argues Bourdieu, "leaves the crucial operations of scientific construction the choice of the problem, the elaboration of concepts and analytical categories – to the social world *as it is*, to the established order, and thus it fulfills, if only by default, a quintessentially conservative function of ratification of *doxa*" (1992, 246). As Mikael Rask Madsen persuasively argues, if we cannot maintain "a certain analytical distance" from the normative whirlpool generated by human rights' infectious normativity, we run the "real risk of philosophically depoliticizing and de-socializing human rights" (2011a, 267).

In this chapter, I have attempted to show that a first step in establishing some objective[50] sociological distance with respect to human rights is to question the appropriateness of the thin renditions, both historical and sociological, through which they are frequently defined. Thin narratives conceive of human rights as moral values or dispositions whose principled soundness provide them with the legs they need to travel synchronically across social space and diachronically across historical time. In contrast, I have argued for the need to conceptualize human rights as being embedded in dense historical, social, political, cultural, and economic relational networks. It is precisely because of these relational networks, and the public narratives, that weave them together that they are capable of being meaningful to individuals and of circulating socially. Moreover, and crucially, it is because of this that it does not make sense to locate the origins of contemporary human rights in the 1940s, as much thin historiography and sociology attempt to do.

Further, I have developed the notion of relational networks in terms of a political imaginary that is made up of four components: discursive representations, modes of subjectivity and agency, social technologies, and organizational forms. My goal in sociologically thickening them in this manner is not to disavow the fact that human rights are powerfully embodied as "feelings, convictions, and actions of multitudes of individuals" (Hunt 2007, 213), but rather to try to conceptualize the social and cultural "infrastructure" that enables them to be experienced in this manner. Before starting to add more detail to the political imaginary mode in Chap. 4, in the next chapter, I want to elaborate on a claim made in this chapter, namely, that sociologists tend to weave their accounts of human rights with a thin historical thread. In particular I want to explore the work of sociologists that use a thin conception of human rights to weave a strong normative sociological defence for human rights.

Notes

1. On the notion of legal and rights consciousness, see Scheingold (2004, xvii–xvlii). For an overview of the emergence and subsequent development of legal consciousness in sociolegal studies, see Silbey (2005). For examples of substantive empirical explorations of legal consciousness, see Ewick and Silbey (1998), Engel and Munger (2003), and Sarat and

Kearns (2009). For a critique of the legal consciousness research programme, see Valverde (2003a, b).

2. One of the iconic drafters of the UDHR, René Cassin, noted, in its effort to achieve consensus, the committee tasked with drafting the document sidestepped "metaphysical controversies [...] on the origins of human rights" (cited in Slaughter 2009, 47).
3. Amongst the critics of human rights' thinness, some argue, as I will show in the next chapter, for the need to develop a more combative conception, as Blau and Moncada do when they insist on the need to go beyond "the liberal vision" (2005). Others claim that the apparent austerity of human rights as a moral language is belied by an unspoken political project (liberalism) whose hegemony allows it to remain unmarked qua political project (Brown 2004).
4. Charles Beitz (2011), a political philosopher, whose work I discuss in more detail in Chap. 4, develops a thoughtful critique of contemporary attempts to ground human right's normativity. He opts instead for grasping the normative valence of human rights by framing them as the product of an emergent practice that provides agents with reasons for action, specifically with the goal of protecting "important individual interests against predictable threats and to deter societies from developing certain features that might cause their government to pursue policies that threaten international order" (2011, 131).
5. This of course does not entail denying the social and causal efficacy or the "epistemological privilege" of particular "ideational regimes" (Somers and Block 2005). Rather it draws attention to fact that even though a moral order might originate "in an explicit doctrine or theory [...] the process through which it penetrates and takes hold of a social imaginary is slow and complex" (Gaonkar 2002, 11).
6. For a fascinating attempt to show the possibility of universalizing local human rights cultures, see Gregg (2011). Interesting as this account is, it is a prospective one that does not explain the contemporary global currency of human rights, but posits how such a vision might plausibly be extended.
7. This of course is also a dilemma faced by political anthropologists, "So we are left with either a philosophically rich but phenomenologically thin set of explanations for social life on the one hand, or on the other, a set of general ideas of real importance that are nevertheless kept frustratingly incipient – social theory that dare not speak its name" (Goodale 2009, 7).

8. Not surprisingly the analysis of human rights intercultural dialogue is the bailiwick of cultural anthropologists (An-Na'im 2010; Eberhard 2001).
9. For Habermas, "the legitimacy of the rule of law depends, rather, on the institutionalization of those procedural norms, through which the private individual is recognized, not just as a bearer of fundamental rights but also as a potential contributor to those discursive processes through which the idea of the common good gains legal sanction" (Johnson 2001, 45). Concretely, the procedural norms that Habermas has in mind are those that "guarantee the discursive mode by means of which generation and application of legislative programs are to proceed within the parameters of rational debate. This implies the institutionalization of legal procedures that guarantee an approximate fulfillment of the demanding preconditions of communication required for fair negotiations and free debates. These idealizing preconditions demand the complete inclusion of all parties that might be affected, their equality, free and easy interaction, no restrictions of topic and topical contributions, the possibility of revising the outcomes, etc. In this context the legal procedures serve to uphold within an empirically existing community of communication the spatial, temporal, and substantive constraints on choices that are operative within a presumed ideal one" (Habermas 1992, 449). For a range of responses to Habermas' critical theory, see Meehan (2013).
10. Alexander's is not a jejune vision of civil society. From the start he concedes that justice is a possibility that is "devilishly difficult to obtain" because of the contradictions of institutionalization but most fundamentally "because meaning is relational and relative" and "the civility of the self always articulates itself in language about the incivility of the other" (2006, 50).
11. For the purposes of theoretically locating the strong programme, Alexander and his collaborators divide sociological analyses of culture into two camps: the sociology of culture and cultural sociology. The latter is reserved for the strong programme, while the former is used to refer to all those approaches, the majority in sociology according to Alexander and Smith, that understand culture as an effect of social structure, thus depriving culture of any real autonomy. Social structure refers to the social processes whereby individuals are differentially distributed in social space leading to identity, interest and group formation, in different

spheres and at different scales (e.g., gender, class, nation). Social structure is also conjoined with material factors (Alexander and Smith 2003, 11). A cultural sociology, in contrast to a sociology of culture, should be able to identify cultural determinants that function as an "independent variable" identifying "inputs every bit as vital as more material or instrumental forces" (Alexander and Smith 2003, 12). Although this first step is heuristically very useful in opening up a conceptual space for the autonomy of culture, collapsing the totality of the sociology of culture, cultural studies, and Foucauldian analyses under the rubric the sociology of culture cuts the strong programme off from many explanatory elements and mechanisms that could potentially enrich its analysis.

12. I am not discounting the important explanatory power of these elements; I believe they alone do not suffice.
13. In practical conceptual terms, this is accomplished by opposing affect and meaning, which Alexander and Smith see as being generated by the deep structures of culture, with purely instrumental, coerced, or reflexive action. Moreover since culture is transversal to social phenomena, even the most interest-laden action or the most technocratic and rational of bureaucracies are not devoid of the horizon of meaning and affect that culture enables (Alexander and Smith 2003, 12). Thus it is possible to distil the cultural structure that provides any social phenomenon with meaning by "bracketing-out" social relations that are non-symbolic (Alexander and Smith 2003, 14).
14. Somers is referring to the structural or normative autonomy of social institutions. Mention of the relational materialism of science studies is particularly apropos because as Alexander and Smith note, the designation of "strong" is taken from the strong programme in science and technology studies, which they understand to mean the "radical uncoupling of cognitive content from natural determination". Translated into the cultural sphere this requires, they contend, an uncoupling of social structure and cultural structure (2003, 13). I am not convinced that this is a felicitous translation. A more pertinent uncoupling of meaning and its indetermination by the intransitive domain of reality is to be found in the work of Roy Bhaskar (Bhaskar 1978; see López and Potter 2001).
15. In this respect, Alexander is critical of Gramsci's conception of hegemony, Althusser's notion of interpellation, and Foucault's conflation of power and knowledge. He argues that these authors assume an automaticity that obscures the contingency of performance, going as far as

claiming that they "assume powerful scripts, great actors, compliant audiences, corrupted or brainwashed journalists, and bought-off critics. With a wave of the hand, texts become automatically transformed into successful action. Whether it is law, school books, movies, political campaigns or wars, background representations are assumed to speak, and to speak persuasively" (Alexander 2011, 88). This is, to my mind, an overstatement. After all, Gramsci's theory of hegemony represents an attempt not only to explain the failure of the performance of a socialist script but also to theorize the conditions under which the performance of hegemonic worldviews might equally backfire (Gramsci 1971). Similarly, Foucault's conceptualization of knowledge in the context of fields of dispersion (1972), or in terms of micro-politics (1995), frames social performances as contingent and subject to failure. Finally, with respect to Althusser, the problem is perhaps not due to his conception of interpellation, but to his functionalist understanding of the role of ideology in social reproduction (Hirst 1976). All the same, it is worth remembering that Althusser was keen to displace accounts of the social in terms of expressive totalities, and his theoretical work was oriented towards tooling thought to grasp the complexity of the social (López 2003, 115–37). What is more, Judith Butler, an author whose conception of performativity Alexander cites favourably (2011, 217–18), persuasively claims that Althusser's conception of interpellation remains central for contemporary theories of subject formation and "continues to survive its critique" (Butler 1995, 6).

16. The classic source of performance theory outside of dramaturgical studies is of course cultural anthropology, namely, the work of Victor Turner (1985, 1986; see Gonquergood 1989) and James Clifford (1988), the linguistic theory of John Austin (1962; see Hall 1999), and the work of the philosopher Judith Butler (1988), all of which are acknowledged by Alexander (2011). For overviews of performance theory across the humanities and the social sciences, see Bauman and Briggs (1990), Carlson (2013), and Schechner (2004).
17. Of course the notion of a "successful performance" is difficult to disentangle in the context of human rights. While a human rights performance might resonate as morally meaningful to an audience, this in itself does not guarantee that the resources and capacity will be available to remediate the situation. Indeed as Moyn argues, if worldly success were required to maintain the vitality of human rights, then "their worth will ultimately be open to doubt, sooner or later" (2015, 180). That this

has yet to be the case indicates that performance in this second and fuller sense, namely, as change inducing, has not been heretofore necessary for the "successful" performance of human rights. Said differently, "Why does all the energy and effort going into human rights activism produce such decidedly meager results? How could the rhetoric of human rights be so globally pervasive while the politics of human rights is so utterly weak" (Cmiel 2004, 118)?

18. Of course, it is remarkable only in the context of the claims made regarding human rights' purported long historical pedigree (Ishay 2004; Lauren 1998; Hunt 2007; cf. Moyn 2010, 2014b).
19. This section, as well as my general sociological framing of human rights, draws generously on Moyn's pioneering work (2010, 2012, 2014b, 2015) to which I am greatly indebted.
20. For accounts that stress the long roots of human rights, see Lauren (1998) and Ishay (2004) and Cmiel (2004) for a critical overview. The impact of the eighteenth-century revolutions is dealt with by Hunt (2007), while Glendon (2002) is an excellent exemplar of the visionary genre, and Borgwardt (2007) explores the intersection of human rights and American internationalism. The roots of human rights in the abolitionist movement are detailed in Blackburn (2013), while anti-colonialism is dealt with by Burke (2011). Anderson (2003) addresses the criss-crossing of anti-racism and human rights.
21. As Mark Mazower notes, "soon the protagonists of these accounts turn into visionaries and heroes – inspiration for our drabber and less strenuous times: Eleanor Roosevelt, Raphael Lemkin, René Cassin, and other leading figures in the emergence of the UN and especially of its human rights regime are now routinely invoked as reminders of what individual commitment and activism can accomplish" (2009, 6; cf. Bradley 2012, 330). See, especially, Glendon (2002) and Lauren (1998).
22. Lauren, for instance, cites Eleanor Roosevelt, the chair of the Human Rights Committee that drafted the UDHR, who claimed, "At a time when there are so many issues on which we find it difficult to reach a common basis of agreement, it is a significant fact that …[so many] states have found such large measure of agreement in the complex field of human rights" (cited in Lauren 1998, 280).
23. In horticulture a variety typically occurs in nature and is true to type. A cultivar is a "cultivated variety", the product of human selection and cultivation; it is not necessarily true to type, that is, offspring can differ from parents.

24. I develop this point more fully in my analysis of the development of human rights in Europe in Chap. 6.
25. Probst does not argue that the Holocaust was never mentioned or that it played no role at all, but that it was far from central. This was to change in the 1990s after the fall of the Berlin Wall (2003, 55). Consequently the Holocaust as a founding act of the EU is "only plausible from an ex-post perspective" (Probst 2003, 54).
26. Marco Duranti draws attention to "French right-wing intellectuals such as Alexandre Marc, who had called on Hitler to lead the youth of Europe towards the construction of 'new order' in 1933, and Louis Salleron, who had been instrumental in formulating Vichy corporatist policies [...] In the Congress' political committee, Hélène de Suzannet, one of the most outspoken advocates of amnesty for imprisoned collaborators in France tabled a motion in favour of the right of individuals to petition such a court [a European human rights court], and Reginald Thomas Paget, one of the foremost champions of the rights of accused German war criminals and a seminal figure in the 'Holocaust denial'" (Duranti 2012, 161). Duranti argues that "the heretofore overlooked involvement of such figures in the 'human rights revolution' suggests that the birth of international human rights law cannot be read so directly out of the Jewish genocide and the [French] republican tradition as commonly supposed" (2012, 161).
27. Christian democracy's extraordinary success in shepherding postwar Europe away from authoritarian nationalism and positioning itself as a bulwark against the communist threat through its commitment to market liberalism and parliamentary democracy in part explains its surprising postwar hegemony (Kaiser 2007). However, it is worth remembering that even as recently as the interwar period, Catholics and Christian Democrats were deeply suspicious of parliamentary government, mass democracy, and the market economy (Kaiser 2007, 35), hence their support for more conservative, at times authoritarian, social, and political arrangements. Moyn locates the origin of a personalist-inspired Christian human rights in 1937 and argues that the conception of human dignity and rights underwriting Christian human rights was characterized by its rejection of authoritarianism. However, this disavowal of illiberalism was not only compatible with the conservative moral governance that would flourish in the postwar, such governance was in fact the telos of Christian Human Rights (Moyn 2015, 15; see Duranti 2016).

28. Another notable post-colonial elite committed to Christian human rights is Mark Romulo, the Philippines delegate to the United Nations, who made important contributions to the General Assembly debate on the UDHR (Moyn 2015, 92). Moyn also draws attention to the work of Jacques Maritain, the French Catholic philosopher, whose trajectory towards human rights through personalism is a complex one, as it was for the Catholic Church (2015, 73–89). It required breaking with antecedent authoritarian positions and renouncing critical dismissals of formal rights that had echoed those made by Mounier (2015, 86). Following this, he was to become the "main publicist of Christian personalism" in the UN and beyond, giving it a broader resonance (Moyn 2010, 64).
29. Borgwardt (2007) argues that this being so, the rhetorical shift introduced by the incorporation of the term human rights proved nonetheless to be consequential.
30. Borgwardt notes that when Norman Rockwell, the American illustrator, set out to represent the Four Freedoms that subsequently reappeared in the Atlantic Charter, which "went on to become some of the most enduring icons of the war years form many Americans on the home front", the internationalist hue of the freedoms was replaced with an exclusively domestic home front palate (2007, 47).
31. Moyn draws attention to the novelty of the right to change religions in Article 18 of the UDHR. This was motivated by the perception that missionary activities might be under threat and pushed several Muslim states to abstain in the General Assembly (Moyn 2015, 152).
32. Origin may not be destiny, but origin can in some case produce structural selectivity. In this context, it is worth mentioning Moyn's discussion of recent headscarf jurisprudence in the EU. Whereas many commentators critical of the jurisprudence suggest that decisions supporting headscarf bans arise from excessive secularism and Islamophobia, Moyn reflecting on religious freedom's original anti-communist rationale draws different conclusions. He writes, the "doctrinal basis on which the cases ultimately rest had nothing originally to do with religion in general or Islam in particular. Instead its source lies in Cold War anxiety that secularist communism would topple Christian democracy. If so, the secularism of the European Court's headscarf jurisprudence is a recent artifact, primarily following from the collapse of European Christianity in recent memory. Even more ironically [...] the European Court headscarf cases actually owe part of their doctrinal rationale and

perhaps their exclusionary associations not to the secularist associations of religious freedom but to the legacy of religious struggles against communism once feared as secularism incarnate. The Muslim has taken the place of the communist in European imagination – and above all in the history of the religious liberty norm" (2015, 145).

33. It is however worth noting that less sanguine readings of the conjugation of social security and postwar internationalism can be made, see, for instance, Neocleous (2008), as well as significant shortcomings of the Nuremberg trials, see, for instance, Sellars (2002) and Zolo (2009).
34. As historian, political, and legal scholar Mary L. Dudziak shows in her finely researched monograph *Cold War Civil Rights*, leveraging a critique of American racism via the UDHR was blocked to African Americans. This is because "to criticize the nation before an international audience and to air the nation's dirty laundry overseas was to reinforce the negative impact of American racism on the nation's standing as a world leader. It was seen, therefore, as a great breach of loyalty. As a result, just as the House Committee on Un-American Activities and the government's loyalty security programme silenced progressive voices within the United States, through passport restrictions and international negotiations the long arm of US government red-baiting silenced critics of US racism overseas" (2011, 12). Dudziak's work compelling shows how an understanding of the national civil rights reforms necessitates putting them in an international context. Insofar, as the US sought to position itself as a world leader in the Cold War, accusations of racism and racial violence tarnished its image, affecting its foreign relations strategies. One could think here about the US state's concerns to prevent newly independent countries in the global south from falling into the Soviet sphere of influence. Consequently, argues Dudziak, "[t]he Cold War created a constraining environment for domestic politics. It also gave rise to new opportunities for those who could exploit Cold War anxieties, while yet remaining within the bounds of acceptable 'Americanism'" (2011, 15). Ironically, the attempt to introduce a human rights logic to the civil rights struggles, under the banner of anti-imperialism and colonialism, undertaken by more radical figures such as Malcolm X in the late 1960s (Dudziak 2011, 224–25), occurred at a conjuncture when the Vietnam War would replace civil rights as the issue defining US prestige abroad, after which civil rights would become peripheral to US foreign affairs (Dudziak 2011, 248). Moreover, as explored in Chap. 6, it was precisely

the link between human rights and anti-colonialism that made lawyers allergic to human rights.

35. Parenthetically, Keys notes Amnesty International in the US "was saddled, too, with a name that for most Americans immediately conjured up the deeply polarizing issue of amnesty for Vietnam War draft resisters. In the early 1970s AI USA staff feared its mail was being sabotaged by postal workers who misconstrued the amnesty in its title" (2014, 89).
36. The following paragraphs draw extensively from Keys' analysis (2014, 103–213).
37. Scoop, as he was known, assembled a group of political operators such as Richard Perle, Douglas Feith, Elliott Abrams, Donald Rumsfeld, and Paul Wolfowitz who would become key players in the rise of neoconservatism (Keys 2014, 103; Boot 2004; Vaïsse 2010).
38. Term used to describe Soviet Jews who were "refused" permission to emigrate to Israel; see Peretz (2017).
39. This, of course, chimed with the retreat from grand utopian projects of social transformation and the minimalist and moralized politics that had provided fertile ground for the emergence of contemporary human rights, as discussed above.
40. A strategic site of intervention, as Keys documents, was the foreign aid authorization bill. While liberals denounced foreign aid for supporting oppressive regimes, conservatives lambasted its ballooning cost and status as overly generous hand-out. This meant that bipartisan support could be secured for efforts to reduce aid to undemocratic regimes. In addition, because this was a bill that came around every year, the bill became a magnet for all manner of amendments (Keys 2014, 139).
41. As Keys (2014, 264–66) and others have argued, most notably Snyder (2011), more consequential for transnational human rights organizing would be the impact of the Helsinki Final Act, signed during the presidency of Gerald Ford. Sarah B. Snyder argues that "the Helsinki process was one factor that shaped Gorbachev's thinking about human rights, self-determination and nonviolence, all of which contributed to the demise of communism in Eastern Europe and the collapse of the Soviet Union" (2011, 217).
42. It is interesting to note that "Ronald Reagan, William Haig and William Casey, and other high officials read and praised Claire Sterling's book *The Terror Network*, only to later discover to their embarrassment that it was based essentially on CIA disinformation 'blown back'" (Zulaika and

Douglass 1996, 14). Nonetheless, "[i]n general, during the 1980s, counterterrorism became a surrogate for earlier efforts to fight Communist subversion abroad, whereas at home it became 'the talisman' the FBI needed to conduct investigations of those in opposition to the Reagan administration's policies in Central America'" (Zulaika and Douglass 1996, 15).

43. Robert L. Bernstein created Helsinki Watch in 1978, with Orville Schell Jr., an elite New York lawyer, and Aryeh Neier who was finishing his tenure as the director of the American Civil Liberties Union. Bernstein, chairman and CEO of Random House, had become concerned with the situation of dissident writers during a visit to the Soviet Union (Neier 2012, 205). Funded first by the Ford and subsequently by the MacArthur Foundations, Helsinki Watch focused its attention on the Soviet Union and Eastern Europe. The election of Ronald Reagan, who first attempted to dismiss human rights and then co-opt them for anti-communism, forced the organization to widen its mandate: "The Leaders of Helsinki Watch were concerned that in such circumstances, an American organization that denounced abuses of human rights by the Soviet Unions and the states it controlled, but did not also deal with abuses of human rights regimes aligned with Washington would lose credibility. It would be seen simply as a mouthpiece for an administration that had made clear its intention to use accounts of human rights abuse as a stick to belabor its enemies while serving as an apologist for severe abuses by its friends" (Neier 2012, 206–7). This eventuated in the America's Watch Committee (Neier 2012, 207).

Neier argues that the competitive advantage that Helsinki Watch, and then Human Rights Watch, had over Amnesty International in the 1980s in the US was due to the latter's initial narrow focus on prisoners of conscience (Neier 2012, 204). Freedom Watch, which would also become a key player in the field of human rights, "emphasized to its donors that it had no ties to Amnesty and privately criticized its rival for focusing on the effects rather than the causes of repression and for 'emphasiz[ing] the most aberrational acts of violence by the government'" (Keys 2014, 213). Helsinki Watch, on the other hand, expanded its mandates to new areas such as the violations of the laws of war, was more streamlined and could react more quickly to changing conditions as a result of its non-reliance on membership funding, and was openly engaged in the practice of trying to steer US foreign policy in the direction of human rights promotion (Neier 2012, 202–5). This said, as Keys careful analysis shows, Amnesty International had more of an impact on US foreign policy than it first appears (2014, 206–12).

44. Overall the authors conclude, "we find that human rights do play a role in the decision of who receives US bilateral foreign assistance, and how much aid they are allotted. But other national security interests play a more prominent role. Countries perceived to be of vital importance to US national security, as measured by the presence of military personnel, along with Latin America, receive aid regardless of their human rights records" (Apodaca and Stohl 1999, 196). This is telling, as Latin America was a key focus of human rights activism during the Carter and Reagan administrations.
45. This self-evidence as I will show in the next chapter is the product of the human rights political imaginary. Consequently its conditions of possibility need to be investigated rather than taken at face value.
46. Consequently, although to my mind, Borgwardt may not show how human rights were internationalized, she nonetheless convincingly shows how the values of the New Deal were. She accomplishes this by outlining the semiotic, political, cultural, and economic relational matrix that overdetermined their internationalization. Consequently her historical account by no means constitutes a thin account.
47. My approach to sociological explanation does not prioritize theory over empirical work. In fact, as noted in the book's introduction, the political imaginary framework was developed in the context of my empirical historical research on the emergence of the human right to food (López 2015), from which the discussion that follows draws.
48. Of course, this corresponds to Althusser's definition of ideology. Admittedly it has shortfalls as a theory of ideology; nonetheless it has been very productive as a theory of subjectivation (Butler 1995; López 2003, 133–37). What is more, Althusser's inability to develop a tenable distinction between ideology and science does not mean that the concept of ideology should be abolished; for a powerful defence of the pertinence of ideology as an analytical category in the context of the cultural turn, see Purvis and Hunt (1993).
49. The field of dispersion is of course of Foucauldian provenance, from his work on the archaeology of knowledge (1972).
50. I address my own standpoint on objectivity in sociological practice in the next chapter.

Bibliography

Afshari, Reza. 2007. "On Historiography of Human Rights Reflections on Paul Gordon Lauren's The Evolution of International Human Rights: Visions Seen." *Human Rights Quarterly* 29 (1):1–67.

Ake, Claude. 1987. "The African Context of Human Rights." *Africa Today* 34 (1/2):5–12.

Alexander, Jeffrey C. 2003. *The Meanings of Social Life: A Cultural Sociology*. Oxford and New York: Oxford University Press.

Alexander, Jeffrey C. 2006. *The Civil Sphere*. Oxford and New York: Oxford University Press.

Alexander, Jeffrey C. 2011. *Performance and Power*. Cambridge and Malden, MA: Polity.

Alexander, Jeffrey C., and Pjillip Smith. 2003. "The Strong Program in Cultural Sociology: Elements of a Structural Hermeneutics." In *The Meanings of Social Life: A Cultural Sociology*, edited by Jeffrey C. Alexander, 11–26. New York and Oxford: Oxford University Press.

Althusser, Louis. 1971. *Lenin and Philosophy*, Trans. Ben Brewster. New York: Monthly Review Press.

Anderson, Carol Elaine. 2003. *Eyes off the Prize: The United Nations and the African American Struggle for Human Rights, 1944–1955*. Cambridge and New York: Cambridge University Press.

Anleu, Sharyn Roach. 1999. "Sociologists Confront Human Rights: The Problem of Universalism." *Journal of Sociology* 35 (2):198–212.

An-Na'im, Abdullahi Ahmed, ed. 2010. *Human Rights in Cross-Cultural Perspectives: A Quest for Consensus*. Philadelphia: University of Pennsylvania Press.

Apodaca, Clair, and Michael Stohl. 1999. "United States Human Rights Policy and Foreign Assistance." *International Studies Quarterly* 43 (1):185–198.

Armaline, William T., Davita S. Glasberg, and Bandana Purkayastha. 2015. *The Human Rights Enterprise: Political Sociology, State Power, and Social Movements*. Cambridge and Malden, MA: Polity.

Austin, John. 1962. *How to Do Things with Words*. Oxford and New York: Oxford University Press.

Bauman, Richard, and Charles L. Briggs. 1990. "Poetics and Performance as Critical Perspectives on Language and Social Life." *Annual Review of Anthropology* 19:59–88.

Baxi, Upendra. 1998. "Voices of Suffering and the Future of Human Rights." *Transnational Law and Contemporary Problems* 8:125–169.

Beitz, Charles R. 2011. *The Idea of Human Rights*. Oxford and New York: Oxford University Press.

Bell, Daniel A. 2000. *East Meets West: Human Rights and Democracy in East Asia*. Princeton, NJ: Princeton University Press.

Bengtsson, Jan Olof. 2006. *The Worldview of Personalism: Origins and Early Development*. Oxford and New York: Oxford University Press.

Bhaskar, Roy. 1978. *A Realist Theory of Science, Brighton*. Brighton: Harvester Press.

Blackburn, Robin. 2013. *The American Crucible: Slavery, Emancipation and Human Rights*. London: Verso.

Blau, Judith R., and Alberto Moncada. 2005. *Human Rights: Beyond the Liberal Vision*. Lanham, MD and New York: Rowman & Littlefield.

Boot, Max. 2004. "Neocons." *Foreign Policy* 140:20–28.

Borgwardt, Elizabeth. 2007. *A New Deal for the World*. Cambridge, MA: Harvard University Press.

Bourdieu, Pierre. 1992. "The Paris Workshop". In *An Invitation to Reflexive Sociology*, edited by Pierre Bourdieu and Loïc JD Wacquant, 218–260. Chicago: University of Chicago press.

Bradley, Mark Philip. 2012. "Approaching the Universal Declaration of Human Rights." In *The Human Rights Revolution: An International History*, edited by Akara Iriye, Petra Goedde, and William I. Hitchcock, 327–344. Oxford: Oxford University Press.

Bricmont, Jean. 2006. *Humanitarian Imperialism: Using Human Rights to Sell War*. New York: NYU Press.

Brown, Wendy. 2004. "' The Most We Can Hope For...': Human Rights and the Politics of Fatalism." *The South Atlantic Quarterly* 103 (2):451–463.

Burke, Roland. 2011. *Decolonization and the Evolution of International Human Rights*. Philadelphia: University of Pennsylvania Press.

Butler, Judith. 1988. "Performative Acts and Gender Constitution: An Essay in Phenomenology and Feminist Theory." *Theatre Journal* 40 (4):519–531.

Butler, Judith. 1995. "Conscience Doth Make Subjects of Us All." *Yale French Studies* 88:6–26.

Butler, Judith. 2011. *Bodies That Matter: On the Discursive Limits of Sex*. London and New York: Routledge.

Carleton, David, and Michael Stohl. 1985. "The Foreign Policy of Human Rights: Rhetoric and Reality from Jimmy Carter to Ronald Reagan." *Human Rights Quarterly*, 205–229.

Carlson, Marvin. 2013. *Performance: A Critical Introduction*. London and New York: Routledge.

Castoriadis, Cornelius. 1998. *The Imaginary Institution of Society*. Cambridge, MA: MIT Press.
Clifford, James. 1988. *The Predicament of Culture: Twentieth-Century Ethnography, Literature and Art*. Cambridge, MA: Harvard University Press.
Cmiel, Kenneth. 2004. "The Recent History of Human Rights." *The American Historical Review* 109 (1):117–135.
Cobbah, Josiah A.M. 1987. "African Values and the Human Rights Debate: An African Perspective." *Human Rights Quarterly* 9 (3):309–331.
Cohen, G. Daniel. 2012. "The Holocaust and the 'Human Rights Revolution': A Reassessment." In *The Human Rights Revolution: An International History*, edited by Akara Iriye, Petra Goedde, and William I. Hitchcock, 53–72. Oxford: Oxford University Press.
De Sousa Santos, Boaventure. 2008. "Human Rights as an Emancipatory Script: Cultural and Political Conditions." In *Another Knowledge Is Possible*, edited by Boaventura De Sousa Santos, 3–40. London: Verso.
DeLanda, Manuel. 2002. *Intensive Science and Virtual Philosophy*. London: Athlone Press.
Deleuze, Gilles. 1994. *Difference and Repetition*. New York: Columbia University Press.
Diner, Dan. 1997. "On Guilt Discourse and Other Narratives: Epistemological Observations Regarding the Holocaust." *History and Memory* 9 (1/2):301–320.
Diner, Dan. 2003. "Restitution and Memory: The Holocaust in European Political Cultures." *New German Critique* 90:36–44.
Diner, Hasia. 2010. *We Remember with Reverence and Love: American Jews and the Myth of Silence After the Holocaust, 1945–1962*. New York: NYU Press.
Donnelly, Jack. 1984. "Cultural Relativism and Universal Human Rights." *Human Rights Quarterly* 6:400–419.
Douzinas, Costas. 2007. *Human Rights and Empire: The Political Philosophy of Cosmopolitanism*. London and New York: Routledge.
Dubiel, Helmut. 2003. "The Remembrance of the Holocaust as a Catalyst for a Transnational Ethic?" *New German Critique* 90:59–70.
Dudziak, Mary L. 2011. *Cold War Civil Rights: Race and the Image of American Democracy*. Princeton, NJ: Princeton University Press.
Duranti, Marco. 2012. "The Holocaust, the Legacy of 1789 and the Birth of International Human Rights Law: Revisiting the Foundation Myth." *Journal of Genocide Research* 14 (2):159–186.
Duranti, Marco. 2016. *The Conservative Human Rights Revolution: European Identity, Transnational Politics, and the Origins of the European Convention*. Oxford: Oxford University Press.

Eberhard, Christoph. 2001. "Towards an Intercultural Legal Theory: The Dialogical Challenge." *Social & Legal Studies* 10 (2):171–201.
Eckel, Jan, and Samuel Moyn, ed. 2014. *The Breakthrough: Human Rights in the 1970s*. Philadelphia: University of Pennsylvania Press.
Emirbayer, Mustafa. 2004. "The Alexander School of Cultural Sociology." *Thesis Eleven* 79 (1):5–15.
Engel, David M., and Frank W. Munger. 2003. *Rights of Inclusion: Law and Identity in the Life Stories of Americans with Disabilities*. Chicago and London: University of Chicago Press.
Ewick, Patricia, and Susan S. Silbey. 1998. *The Common Place of Law: Stories from Everyday Life*. Chicago and London: University of Chicago Press.
Fairclough, Norman. 2003. *Analysing Discourse: Textual Analysis for Social Research*. London: Routledge.
Fairclough, Norman, Bob Jessop, and Andrew Sayer. 2002. "Critical Realism and Semiosis." *Alethia* 5 (1):2–10.
Fassin, Didier. 2012. *Humanitarian Reason: A Moral History of the Present*. Berkeley, CA: University of California Press.
Foucault, Michel. 1972. *The Archaeology of Knowledge*. New York: Pantheon Books.
Foucault, Michel. 1995. *Discipline and Punish*. New York: Vintage Books.
Freeman, Michael. 1994. "The Philosophical Foundations of Human Rights." *Human Rights Quarterly* 16:491–514.
Gaonkar, Dilip Parameshwar. 2002. "Toward New Imaginaries: An Introduction." *Public Culture* 14 (1):1–19.
Glendon, Mary Ann. 2002. *A World Made New: Eleanor Roosevelt and the Universal Declaration of Human Rights*. New York: Random House.
Gonquergood, Dwight. 1989. "Poetics, Play, Process, and Power: The Performative Turn in Anthropology." *Text and Performance Quarterly* 9 (1):82–88.
Goodale, Mark. 2009. *Surrendering to Utopia: An Anthropology of Human Rights*. Stanford, CA: Stanford University Press.
Gramsci, Antonio. 1971. *Selections Form the Prison Notebooks. Edited and Translated by Q.Hoare & GN Smith*. New York: International Publishers.
Gregg, Benjamin. 2011. *Human Rights as Social Construction*. Cambridge and New York: Cambridge University Press.
Habermas, Jürgen. 1992. "Further Reflections on the Public Sphere." In *Habermas and the Public Sphere*, edited by Craig J. Calhoun, 421–461. Cambridge, MA: MIT Press.
Habermas, Jürgen. 2012. "The Concept of Human Dignity and the Realistic Utopia of Human Rights." *Metaphilosophy* 41 (4):464–480.

Hall, Kita. 1999. "Performativity." *Journal of Linguistic Anthropology* 9 (1/2):184–187.
Hirst, Paul. 1976. "Althusser and the Theory of Ideology." *Economy and Society* 4 (5):385–412.
Hopgood, Stephen. 2006. *Keepers of the Flame. Understanding Amnesty International.* Ithaca, NY: Cornell University Press.
Hunt, Lynn Avery. 2007. *Inventing Human Rights: A History*. New York and London: W. W. Norton & Company.
Hynes, Patricia, Michele Lamb, Damien Short, and Matthew Waites. 2012. "The Sociology of Human Rights: Editorial Foreword." *Sociology* 46 (5):787–796.
Ignatieff, Michael. 2001. *Human Rights as Politics and Human Rights as Idolatry*. Princeton, NJ: Princeton University Press.
Ishay, Micheline R. 2004. *The History of Human Rights*. Berkeley and London: University of California Press.
Jessop, Bob. 2004. "Critical Semiotic Analysis and Cultural Political Economy." *Critical Discourse Studies* 1 (2):159–174.
Jessop, Bob. 2010. "Cultural Political Economy and Critical Policy Studies." *Critical Policy Studies* 3 (3–4):336–356.
Jessop, Bob. 2013. "Recovered Imaginaries, Imagined Recoveries: A Cultural Political Economy of Crisis Construals and Crisis Management in the North Atlantic Financial Crisis." In *Before and Beyond the Global Economics Crisis: Economics, Politics and Settlement*, edited by Mats Brenner, 234–254. Cheltenham: Edward Elgar Publishing.
Jessop, Bob, and Stijn Oosterlynck. 2008. "Cultural Political Economy: On Making the Cultural Turn Without Falling into Soft Economic Sociology." *Geoforum* 39 (3):1155–1169.
Jessop, Bob, and Ngai-Ling Sum. 2006. "Towards a Cultural International Political Economy: Poststructuralism and the Italian School." In *International Political Economy and Poststructural Politics*, 157–176. Springer.
Johnson, Pauline. 2001. "Distorted Communications Feminism's Dispute with Habermas." *Philosophy & Social Criticism* 27 (1):39–62.
Kaiser, Wolfram. 2007. *Christian Democracy and the Origins of European Union*. Cambridge and New York: Cambridge University Press.
Kausikan, Bilahari. 1993. "Asia's Different Standard." *Foreign Policy* 92:24–41.
Keck, Margaret E., and Kathryn Sikkink. 1998. *Activists Beyond Borders: Advocacy Networks in International Politics*. Ithaca, NY and London: Cornell University Press.

Kennedy, David. 2005. *The Dark Sides of Virtue: Reassessing International Humanitarianism*. Princeton, NJ: Princeton University Press.

Kersbergen, Kees van, and Bertjan Verbeek. 1994. "The Politics of Subsidiarity in the European Union." *JCMS: Journal of Common Market Studies* 32 (2):215–236.

Keys, Barbara J. 2012. "Anti-Torture Politics: Amnesty International, the Greek Junta, and the Origins of the Human Rights Boom in the United States." In *The Human Rights Revolution: An International History*, edited by Akara Iriye, Petra Goedde, and William I. Hitchcock, 201–222. Oxford and New York: Oxford University Press.

Keys, Barbara J. 2014. *Reclaiming American Virtue*. Cambridge, MA: Harvard University Press.

Kurasawa, Fuyuki. 2007. *The Work of Global Justice: Human Rights as Practices*. Cambridge and New York: Cambridge University Press.

Lacan, Jacques. 1977. *Ecrits: A Selection*. New York: W. W. Norton & Company.

Laclau, Ernesto, and Chantal Mouffe. 1985. *Hegemony and Socialist Strategy: Towards a Radical Democratic Politics*. London: Verso.

Latour, Bruno. 1987. *Science in Action: How to Follow Scientists and Engineers Through Society*. Cambridge, MA: Harvard University Press.

Lauren, Paul Gordon. 1998. *The Evolution of International Human Rights: Visions Seen*. Philadelphia: University of Pennsylvania Press.

Levy, Daniel, and Natan Sznaider. 2010. *Human Rights and Memory*. Philadelphia: Penn State Press.

López, José Julián. 2003. *Society and Its Metaphors: Language, Social Theory and Social Structure*. London: Continuum Books.

López, José Julián. 2009. "Par-Delà L'éthique: Vers Une Sociologie Des Pratiques Éthiques Contemporaines." *Cahiers de Recherche Sociologique* 48:27–44.

López, José Julián. 2015. "The Human Right to Food as Political Imaginary." *Journal of Historical Sociology* 30 (2): 239–261.

López, José Julián. 2016. "Disembedding the Embedded/Disembedded Opposition." In *Markets, Communities and Nostalgai*, edited by Christian Karner and Bernhard Weicht, 223–247. London and New York: Palgrave Macmillan.

López, José, and Garry Potter, eds. 2001. *After Postmodernism: An Introduction to Critical Realism*. London: Athlone Press.

Luhmann, Niklas. 1995. *Social Systems*. Stanford, CA: Stanford University Press.

Madsen, Mikael Rask. 2011a. "Reflexivity and the Construction of the International Object: The Case of Human Rights." *International Political Sociology* 5 (3):259–275.

Mauzy, Diane K. 1997. "The Human Rights and 'Asian Values' Debate in Southeast Asia: Trying to Clarify the Key Issues." *The Pacific Review* 10 (2):210–236.
Mazower, Mark. 2004. "The Strange Triumph of Human Rights, 1933–1950." *The Historical Journal* 47 (2):379–398.
Mazower, Mark. 2009. *No Enchanted Palace: The End of Empire and the Ideological Origins of the United Nations*. Princeton, NJ: Princeton University Press.
Meehan, Johanna. 2013. *Feminists Read Habermas (RLE Feminist Theory): Gendering the Subject of Discourse*. London and New York: Routledge.
Merry, Sally Engle. 2006. "Transnational Human Rights and Local Activism: Mapping the Middle." *American Anthropologist* 108 (1):38–51.
Meunier, E-Martin. 2007. *Le Pari Personnaliste: Modernité et Catholicisme Au XXe Siècle: Essai*. Montreal: Les Editions Fides.
Meyer, John W., John Boli, George M. Thomas, and Francisco O. Ramirez. 1997. "World Society and the Nation-State." *American Journal of Sociology* 103 (1):144–181.
Moon, Claire. 2012. "What One Sees and How One Files Seeing: Human Rights Reporting, Representation and Action." *Sociology* 46 (5):876–890.
Morris, Lydia. 2013. *Human Rights and Social Theory*. New York: Palgrave Macmillan.
Morsink, Johannes. 1999. *The Universal Declaration of Human Rights: Origins, Drafting, and Intent*. Philadelphia: University of Pennsylvania Press.
Moyn, Samuel. 2010. *The Last Utopia*. Cambridge, MA: Harvard University Press.
Moyn, Samuel. 2012. "Imperialism, Self-Determination, and the Rise of Human Rights." In *The Human Rights Revolution: An International History*, edited by Akara Iriye, Petra Goedde, and William I. Hitchcock, 159–178. Oxford and New York: Oxford University Press.
Moyn, Samuel. 2014b. *Human Rights and the Uses of History*. London: Verso.
Moyn, Samuel. 2015. *Christian Human Rights*. Philadelphia: University of Pennsylvania Press: Philadelphia.
Mutua, Makau W. 2001. "Savages, Victims, and Saviors: The Metaphor of Human Rights." *Harvard International Law Journal* 42 (1):201–245.
Nash, Kate. 2009. *The Cultural Politics of Human Rights*. Cambridge and New York: Cambridge University Press.
Neier, Aryeh. 2012. *The International Human Rights Movement: A History*. Princeton, NJ and Oxford: Princeton University Press.
Nelson, Paul J., and Ellen Dorsey. 2008. *New Rights Advocacy: Changing Strategies of Development and Human Rights NGOs*. Washington, DC: Georgetown University Press.

Neocleous, Mark. 2003. *Imagining the State*. Maidenhead and Philadelphia: Open University Press.
Neocleous, Mark. 2008. *Critique of Security*. Edinburgh: Edinburgh University Press.
Nickel, James W. 1987. *Making Sense of Human Rights: Philosophical Reflections on the Universal Declaration of Human Rights*. Berkeley and London: University of California Press.
Normand, Roger, and Sarah Zaidi. 2008. *Human Rights at the UN: The Political History of Universal Justice*. Bloomington and Indianapolis: Indiana University Press.
Novick, Peter. 2000. *The Holocaust in American Life*. Boston and New York: Houghton Mifflin Harcourt.
Oxford University Press. 2003. *Oxford English Dictionary*. Oxford University Press.
Pearce, Andy. 2008. "The Development of Holocaust Consciousness in Contemporary Britain, 1979–2001." *Holocaust Studies* 14 (2):71–94.
Peck, James. 2011. *Ideal Illusions: How the US Government Co-opted Human Rights*. New York: Macmillan.
Peretz, Pauline. 2017. *Let My People Go: The Transnational Politics of Soviet Jewish Emigration During the Cold War*. London and New York: Routledge.
Porat, Dan A. 2004. "From the Scandal to the Holocaust in Israeli Education." *Journal of Contemporary History* 39 (4):619–636.
Postone, Moishe. 1980. "Anti-Semitism and National Socialism: Notes on the German Reaction to 'Holocaust.'" *New German Critique* 19:97–115.
Probst, Lothar. 2003. "Founding Myths in Europe and the Role of the Holocaust." *New German Critique* 90:45–58.
Purvis, Trevor, and Alan Hunt. 1993. "Discourse, Ideology, Discourse, Ideology, Discourse, Ideology…" *British Journal of Sociology* 44 (3): 473–499.
Sarat, Austin, and Thomas R. Kearns. 2009. *Law in Everyday Life*. Book, Edited. Ann Arbor: University of Michigan Press.
Schechner, Richard. 2004. *Performance Theory*. London and New York: Routledge.
Scheingold, Stuart A. 2004. *The Politics of Rights: Lawyers, Public Policy, and Political Change*. 2nd ed. Ann Arbor: University of Michigan Press.
Sellars, Kirsten. 2002. *The Rise and Rise of Human Rights*. Stroud: Sutton Pub Limited.
Shapira, Anita. 1998. "The Holocaust: Private Memories, Public Memory." *Jewish Social Studies* 4 (2):40–58.
Shestack, Jerome J. 1998. "The Philosophic Foundations of Human Rights." *Human Rights Quarterly* 20 (2):201–234.

Silbey, Susan S. 2005. "After Legal Consciousness." *Annual Review of Law and Social Science* 1:323–368.
Sismondo, Sergio. 2011. *An Introduction to Science and Technology Studies*. Chichester: John Wiley & Sons.
Slaughter, Joseph. 2009. *Human Rights, Inc: The World Novel, Narrative Form, and International Law*. New York: Fordham University Press.
Snyder, Sarah B. 2011. *Human Rights Activism and the End of the Cold War: A Transnational History of the Helsinki Network*. Cambridge and New York: Cambridge University Press.
Somers, Margaret R. 1993. "Citizenship and the Place of the Public Sphere: Law, Community, and Political Culture in the Transition to Democracy." *American Sociological Review* 58 (5):587–620.
Somers, Margaret R. 1994a. "Rights, Relationality, and Membership: Rethinking the Making and Meaning of Citizenship." *Law & Social Inquiry* 19 (1):63–114.
Somers, Margaret R. 1994b. "The Narrative Constitution of Identity: A Relational and Network Approach." *Theory and Society* 23 (5):605–649.
Somers, Margaret R. 1997. "Deconstructing and Reconstructing Class Formation Theory: Narrativity, Relational Analysis and Social Theory." In *Reworking Class*, edited by R. John Hall, 73–106. Ithaca and London: Cornell University Press.
Somers, Margaret R. 2008. *Genealogies of Citizenship*. Cambridge and New York: Cambridge University Press.
Somers, Margaret R., and Fred Block. 2005. "From Poverty to Perversity: Ideas, Markets, and Institutions over 200 Years of Welfare Debate." *American Sociological Review* 70 (2):260–287.
Staples, Amy L. S. 2006. *The Birth of Development: How the World Bank, Food and Agriculture Organization, and World Health Organization Changed the World, 1945–1965*. Kent, OH: Kent State University Press.
Stein, Arlene. 2014. *Reluctant Witnesses: Survivors, Their Children, and the Rise of Holocaust Consciousness*. Oxford and New York: Oxford University Press.
Stohl, Michael, David Carleton, and Steven E. Johnson. 1984. "Human Rights and US Foreign Assistance from Nixon to Carter." *Journal of Peace Research* 21 (3):215–226.
Sum, Ngai-Ling, and Bob Jessop. 2013. *Towards a Cultural Political Economy: Putting Culture in Its Place in Political Economy*. Cheltenham: Edward Elgar Publishing.
Sunstein, Cass. 2009. *The Second Bill of Rights: FDR's Unfinished Revolution – And Why We Need It More Than Ever*. New York: Basic Books.

Taylor, Charles. 2002. "Modern Social Imaginaries." *Public Culture* 14 (1):91–124.
Teeple, Gary. 2005. *The Riddle of Human Rights*. Toronto: University of Toronto Press.
Turner, Victor. 1985. *On the Edge of the Bush: Anthropology as Experience*. Tuscon: University of Arizona Press.
Turner, Victor. 1986. *The Anthropology of Performance*. New York: PAJ Publications.
Vaïsse, Justin. 2010. *Neoconservatism: The Biography of a Movement*. Cambridge, MA: Harvard University Press.
Valverde, Mariana. 2003a. "'Which Side Are You On?' Uses of the Everyday in Sociolegal Scholarship." *PoLAR: Political and Legal Anthropology Review* 26 (1):86–98.
Valverde, Mariana. 2003b. *Law's Dream of a Common Knowledge*. Princeton and Oxford: Princeton University Press.
Waters, Malcolm. 1996. "Human Rights and the Universalization of Interests: Towards a Social Constructionist Approach." *Sociology* 30 (3):593–600.
Wellman, Carl. 2010. *The Moral Dimensions of Human Rights*. Oxford: Oxford University Press.
Wilson, Richard A. 2009. "Representing Human Rights Violations: Social Contexts and Subjectivities." In *Human Rights: An Anthropological Reader*, edited by Mark Goodale, 134–160. Oxford and New York: Wiley Blackwell.
Woodiwiss, Anthony. 2003. *Making Human Rights Work Globally*. London: The Glass House Press.
Woodiwiss, Anthony. 2005. *Human Rights*. London and New York: Routledge.
Woodiwiss, Anthony. 2012. "Asia, Enforceable Benevolence and the Future of Human Rights." *Sociology* 46 (5):966–981.
Žižek, Slavoj. 2005. "Against Human Rights." *New Left Review* 34 (July–August):115–131.
Zolo, Danilo. 2009. *Victors' Justice: From Nuremberg to Baghdad*. London: Verso Books.
Zulaika, Joseba, and William A. Douglass. 1996. *Terror and Taboo: The Follies, Fables, and Faces of Terrorism*. London and New York: Routledge.

3

Sociological Foundationalism for Human Rights?

Introduction

In his discussion of human rights, the legal theorist Costas Douzinas notes that human rights' reach is extensive. It includes at least the sometimes conflicting discourses and practices that follow:

> a diverse group of constitutional, legal, judicial, academic and popular text commentaries; legal, political and cultural institutions and practices of domestic, regional and international level using human rights as their organising principle; government and non-governmental agencies working around human rights; the personnel working in these institutions; diverse campaigns, groups and organisations at various levels; the people involved in them; multiple situations, events and people who use the term in order to describe or evaluate these situations. (2007, 9)

Despite the multitudinous ways in which human rights might be invoked, enacted, and put to work, the distinctiveness of contemporary human rights as a political imaginary is to be found in the manner in which it generates a normative reflex whose self-evidence appears incontestable. This, of course, does not mean that human rights have acquired the social

J. Julián López, *Human Rights as Political Imaginary*,
https://doi.org/10.1007/978-3-319-74274-8_3

power to actually compel actors to refrain from committing human rights violations or to provide remedies once these have taken place. It equally does not mean that all claims couched in the language of human rights are able to mobilize the seemingly automatic normative persuasive power of successful human rights claims or performances, as I will show in Chap. 4.

Indeed, as Hafner-Burton and Tsutsui (2005; Hafner-Burton 2013) convincingly show, there is no clear correlation between state signature of international human rights instruments and a decline in human rights abuses. A more recent assessment of what human rights have thus far achieved in an effort to optimistically propel them into the future (Simmons 2009), when scrutinized more critically, reveals that beneath the hopeful patina one finds a "nearly phobic avoidance of any grandiose assurance that human rights politics might fundamentally transform international politics soon or ever" (Moyn 2012, 333; see Kennedy 2005). Consequently, it is virtually obligatory for any scholar writing on the stunning rise of human rights in the preceding decades to add the caveat that this does not imply that human rights violations are decreasing. Fingers crossed, this might, could, or should happen in the future.

While not devoid of the capacity, under specific circumstances, to cajole, shame, obligate, or force actors to behave in ways that are protective of individuals, human rights' broader social power lies more firmly in the contemporary irrefutability of the normative judgement that they yield and in the immediacy of the response that they demand. Human rights act as a moral shorthand for determining what is acceptable, but more powerfully what is not acceptable in the treatment of individuals. As Alain Badiou unsympathetically[1] but, to my mind, accurately claims,

> We are supposed to assume the existence of universally recognizable human subject possessing "rights" that are in some sense natural: the right to live, to avoid abusive treatment, to enjoy "fundamental" liberties…These rights are held to be self-evident, and the result of a wide consensus. "Ethics" is a matter of busying ourselves with these rights of making sure that they are respected. (2001, 4)

Faced with the moral persuasiveness of human rights and the empirical evidence of ongoing violence against human beings, the sociologists discussed in this chapter argue in favour of aligning the discipline of sociology normatively with human rights. However, the notion of normativity is both a slippery and an intractable one for sociologists. Thus before presenting the arguments developed by the authors advocating a human rights-based normative turn, I want to first explore why the normative dimension is such a salient feature of contemporary human rights. Following this, I will briefly examine the manner in which normative concerns have intersected with the development of sociology more broadly. This will enable me to pinpoint the novelty of the normative stance taken by the sociologists who are advocating a turn towards human rights. Finally, my concluding remarks will draw attention to some of the slippages that occur as these authors argue for sociological engagement with normative questions while simultaneously making human rights the only possible normative position for sociology.

Human Rights' Normative Reflex

Linguistically, the ethical imperative elicited by the utterance of a human rights claim can be understood as the quintessential speech act,[2] an utterance that not only creates meaning but in so doing carries the illocutionary force for listeners to act. In the case of human rights, the imperative is that the listener must undertake to remedy the situation referenced by the speech act. Although the perlocutionary force of a human rights speech act—that is, the state of affairs that it actually brings about—may not correspond with the desired change, it nonetheless at the very least forcefully instantiates the normative necessity and urgency of such a change. When a human rights claim is distilled to its basic moral and social logic, the pithy assertion "It is wrong!" is irrevocably conjoined to a terse and insistent command: "Stop it!" The illocutionary force of a human rights plea, its ability to convince us that we must act, is strongest when it is able to fuse together the "normative power of the factual" (Hopgood 2013, 39) with the notion of "innocent suffering" (Hopgood 2006, 6).

Factually veridical depictions of torture, unlawful imprisonment and other forms of unconscionable violence against vulnerable and blameless individuals are most likely to trigger the "cultural emotions" (Hopgood 2013, 28) that sustain human rights' contemporary power as a normative language for talking about and acting on injustice. Doubts about the veracity or neutrality of the claim, or the guiltlessness of the victims, weaken the performance of the radical unacceptability of the injustice and the immediate need for remedy. This is why human rights organizations have developed social technologies—routines and practices—that seek to communicate their radical impartiality and the unquestionable objectivity of their work. So important is this public narrative that an identifiable genre of human rights reporting has emerged. This genre is characterized by tightly orchestrated modes of reporting that draw on modes of legal reasoning, statistics, and testimonials to certify the "accuracy", "objectivity", "transparency", "credibility", and "efficacy" of the findings (Moon 2012, 878; Wilson 2009; López 2015).

Moreover, the close association of "rights" with legal instruments, as I will show in Chap. 6, seemingly, sharpens the teeth of the moral claims with the social force of the law. Bourdieu argues that law's social authority does not merely reside in the potential of triggering the state's enforcement capacity to force compliance, which in many instances in the context of human rights is not even available. Instead, the force of the law in contemporary society arises from the juridical field and the practices therein that appear "to partake both of the positive logic of science and the normative logic of morality and to be capable of compelling universal acceptance through an inevitability which is simultaneously logical and ethical" (Bourdieu 1986, 197).

It would, of course, be ill advised to deny that a crucial dimension of the contemporary value of the moral tender of human rights rests on the fact that they are expressed, transmitted, and to a certain extent travel as a normative cri de coeur in legal form. Evidently, all legal forms aim to induce compliance through moral commitment to the law when not by dint of the threat of punishment. A particularity of human rights all the same is that it is most often their moral indisputability that makes them legally persuasive rather than being morally obligatory as a result of their force as law.[3] As Douzinas notes, "human rights are moral rights or claims by individuals, which may or may not have been recognized by a particular legal system" (2007, 9). Consequently, the "right" in human rights assertions frequently does not

> [r]efer to an existing legal entitlement but to a claim about what morality (or ideology, or international law or some other higher source) demands. It is the statement of aspiration against the current state of law or a call to arms for the reform of the political and legal system. (Douzinas 2007, 10)

This is why, despite the frequent allusion to human rights as codified legal obligations if push comes to shove, the staunchest defenders of human rights will assert that human rights principles "exist prior to law" (Clément 2008, 6): they are the "highest moral rights" that "regulate the fundamental structures and practices of political life, and in ordinary circumstances they take priority over other moral, legal and political claims" (Donnelly cited in Clément 2008, 5). In this sense, declarations, treaties, and human rights law are understood as merely formalizing what everyone already takes, or should take, as self-evident: "[h]uman rights law legislates as if its common sense were already commonsensical thereby transforming its tautological propositions into teleological projections of a time when everyone will know what everyone should know" (Slaughter 2009, 26).

It is this quality of manifest moral obviousness with which contemporary human rights have been invested that makes them an expedient way of staking out an advantageous moral ground in contemporary social struggles. Indeed, today human rights appear to have become the essential substrate for all manner of claims made in the name of social justice. As Moyn has persuasively contended, "human rights have come to define the most elevated aspirations of both social movements and political entities – they evoke hope and provoke action" (2010, 1). Consequently, for many amongst the diverse array of actors that invoke them, human rights come with the promissory note that progressive social and political claims will be reinforced, or at the very least not hindered, if framed by them.

A sure indicator of the strength of the normative persuasive power that contemporary human rights radiate is the fact that those scholars who have most vehemently argued that sociology turn its attention to human rights have posited with equal vigour the need for the discipline to change as a *sine qua non* of such an engagement (Blau and Moncada 2005; Blau and Frezzo 2012b; Burawoy 2006; Hynes 2010; Hynes et al. 2012a, b; Somers and Roberts 2008; Turner 1993, 2006).[4] More concretely, as I will unpack in detail in this chapter, they have asserted the need for a fundamental normative turn. As a first approximation, what this means is that sociologists should not limit themselves to developing a theoretically informed empirical understanding of the reality of social life and the social mechanisms and processes through which it is reproduced and transformed. They should, in addition, explicitly develop normative arguments about the necessity of certain forms of social life and organization.

Invoking the inherent sociality of individuals as a normative foundation, sociologists, it is argued, should describe which types of social institutions or social arrangements are compatible with or perhaps even inherent in the flourishing of individuals, and how such arrangements might be realized, maintained, and defended. Rather than merely describe "what is", sociologists should also gear their work towards explaining "what ought to be", leveraging their work in order to contribute to bringing about the desired state of affairs. What is more, because the catalyst for this disciplinary normative turn is the contemporary dominance of human rights as a universal moral *lingua franca*, or pidgin, it is claimed, be it implicitly or explicitly, that sociology's normative turn must be compatible with the normative universe associated with human rights. This in effect is an attempt to position the discipline vis-à-vis human rights as *a sociology for* rather than *a sociology of* human rights.

What a call for a normative turn in sociology might encompass can best be grasped if we begin by looking at the intersection of sociology as a discipline with normative concerns. I want to discuss three such meetings of sociology and normativity. The first, however, is perhaps more accurately categorized as an intentional non-meeting. It refers to the manner in which sociology's legitimacy has been tied up with its empirical character precisely by eschewing a normative stance. The second draws attention to the inescapable normative nature of sociological practice, hence the need to moderate or perhaps even abandon the ideal of a value-free sociology. The third draws attention to the significance of normativity in social life, making imperative the analysis of normative practices. I elaborate on each of these in turn, and then try to clarify what I think the current plea for a human rights-centred normative turn in sociology seems to require.

Escaping Normativity Through Sociology

The significance of the plea that sociologists incorporate normative argumentation to their existing repertoire of analytical and empirical explanatory tools has to be gauged against the fact that historically sociology emerged understanding itself as an empirical discipline. This came about in opposition to modes of reasoning in which the social was apprehended through normative analysis, as was the case in moral and political philosophy and in religious thought. Therefore sociology's identity became tied up with differentiating its empirical attitude from existing normative stances.

This is clear in the case of Durkheim for whom the study of moral phenomena is a central task for sociology. However, unlike normative approaches that "construct a new morality, a morality differing in essential points from that followed by their contemporaries or by their predecessors" (Durkheim 1974, 75), sociology or "the science of morals and law" is concerned with understanding the social basis of moral life, the facticity of the law providing a good proxy for morality. Equally, in opposing *Science as a Vocation* to *Politics as a Vocation*, Max Weber sought to shield sociology from the temptation to weigh in on the desirability of specific value orientations: "[s]cientific pleading is meaningless in principle because the various value spheres of the world stand in irreconcilable conflict with each other" (Weber 2009, 147). Insofar as sociology was a science, the vocation of the sociologists should be to labour in

> the service of self-clarification and knowledge of interrelated facts. It is not the gift of grace of seers and prophets dispensing sacred values and revelations, nor does it partake of the contemplation of sages and philosophers about the meaning of the universe. This, to be sure, is the inescapable

condition of our historical situation. We cannot evade it so long as we remain true to ourselves. (Weber 2009, 152)

To complete the tour of the conventional founding trio, even Marx, whose political partisanship and critical attitude towards capitalism sit awkwardly with the notion of value-free social analysis, did not adopt normative argument as an explanatory strategy. Utopian socialists were to Marx what moral philosophers were to Durkheim. Social analysis of values did not entail asserting competing social values based on some abstract or desired notion of justice. The task instead was to identify the social relations underpinning existing social values in order to gauge the prospect of changing both social relations and values. This is powerfully demonstrated by the seriousness with which Marx read political economy and the immanent critique to which he subjects this body of thought in *Capital* and elsewhere.

In the US, during the interwar period, there was a significant project, objectivism, to craft a scientific sociology that would be concerned with facts, rather than with passing moral judgements or with setting up "ethical standards for human conduct" (Bannister 1987, 3).[5] Although the vision was not unanimously embraced and would decline in the late 1930s, "empiricism, quantification and value neutrality continued to find defenders and practitioners in the postwar years", further enhanced by the introduction of "European traditions of quantitative work" via Paul Lazarsfeld and his colleagues (Bannister 1987, 231). In the 1970s, it would be powerfully invoked in an effort to reclaim the discipline's prestige believed to have diminished by its association with radicalism in the 1960s and evidenced by the decline in undergraduate and graduate student enrolments and the closing of sociology programmes (Agger 2007, 14). In an attempt to restore the discipline's legitimacy, methodological rigour, through increasingly sophisticated quantitative methods, was used as a lever to professionalize sociology "making it appear like the natural sciences in its methodology and the professional disciplines in its utilitarian contribution to society" (Agger 2007, 14).[6] Agger (2007) contends that this is the model that is currently dominant in American professional sociology, institutionalized in the discipline's top journals, in its graduate programmes, and in the writing practices of its most prestigious scholars.

The Inescapable Normativity of Sociology

Despite the centrality of the opposition between value-free empirical and normative analysis in the policing of sociology's disciplinary boundary, the reality is that the border has always been porous. As Bryan Turner, amongst others, has argued, those founding figures that most forcefully asserted the centrality of value neutrality did not unequivocally live up to its ideal. For instance, "Durkheim's major sociological studies carried an implicit and often explicit pay-load of philosophical inquiry into the nature of religion and individual behaviour, legal theory, morality and so forth" (Turner 1993, 491). Two competing interpretations come to mind regarding the failure to achieve the aspired value neutrality.

One, they underestimated the difficulty of doing so in the natural science let alone in the social sciences. Alternatively, the one to which I am partial, they had a strong intuitive understanding of the difficulties involved, and this is precisely why they put so much effort into devising strategies that would mitigate the impact of value commitments and normative theorizing. Be this as it may, today, few sociologists would assert that value neutrality is easily achieved through theoretical or methodological inoculations alone. The border between the empirical and the normative, which has defined sociology's raison d'être, is not as easy to secure as once believed. This suggests that if normative argumentation is not granted full-fledged sociological citizenship, then, at the very least, it might be issued temporary visas.

Indeed despite attempts to dispel the spectre of normativity via methodological sophistication, value neutrality has remained an intractable problem for the discipline. Reacting to the ferment of the social movements in the 1960s and 1970s, and the reality of the social divisions and the powerful social dynamics that reproduced them, some sociologists contended that sociological explanation was not endangered by abandoning the paragon of value-free science. Quite the contrary it was the "myth of value free sociology" that was detrimental (Gouldner 1962).

"Taking sides", according to Howard Becker's (1967) seminal paper, was compatible with theoretically and empirically valid social research:

> We take sides as our personal and political commitments dictate, use our theoretical and technical resources to avoid the distortions that might introduce into our work, limit our conclusions carefully, recognize the hierarchy of credibility for what it is, and field as best we can the accusations and doubts that will surely be our fate. (1967, 247)

Further, it is sometimes argued that to the degree that taking sides leads to the introduction of experiences and viewpoints that have previously been excluded, it holds the prospect of improving our understanding of the social world. The standpoints of different actors—for example, women, racialized groups, LGBT, children—positioned at the intersection (Davis 2008; Harding 1992) of the diverse social dynamics that produce injustice and inequality provide important explanatory perspectives that would otherwise be irretrievable.

Here, over and above, the explanatory gains that might be accrued and the normative logic of taking sides, there is an additional normative imperative to which sociologist should commit. That of giving voice and representational agency to actors that have previously been represented as objects of knowledge by "value-free" sociology or altogether ignored. To take two examples, Charles Lemert argues that the manifest failure of "professional or practical sociology" to portray the significance of the experiences of exclusion is fortunately mitigated by a plethora of "extra-sociological sociologists" who can[7]:

> They do not speak as one voice. But each of them and others of like experience with histories of exclusion are, in a most definite way, writing the sociologies of our time. To a large extent these are the sociologists who tell the story of the world as it is. Each tells a different story thus to affirm the necessary recognition of the unstructured and unstructurable differences of a world wherein the power of inclusion slips behind the authority of those excluded. That each tells a different story does not, however, mean there is no story of the world as such to tell. It only means that, as has been said many times, the story is not the story of one world progressing toward a better day when all men will be free and good. (1995, 209)

Similarly, Dorothy Smith contends that

> a sociology for women, for people, seeking a knowledge of how our lives and relations (direct and indirect) are shaped, directs us towards a knowledge community beyond our discipline. Discovering and uncovering how our societies are put together must embrace in its cooperative growing those who have formerly been the objects of our study and must now be, in a new sense, its subjects, its knowers. (1999, 69)

A third response in the same normative register necessitates reconceptualizing sociology so that it might become a genre of normative narrative that would open up opportunities for a moral reimagining of the social, in effect making sociology primarily a normative rather than an empirical discourse:

> Moral analysis would become a part of an elaborated social reason. Theorists would become advocates, abandoning the increasingly cynical, unbelievable guise of objective, value neutral scientists. We would become advocates, but not narrow partisans or activists. Our broader social significance would lie in encouraging unencumbered open public moral and social debate and in deepening the notion of public discourse. We would be a catalyst for the public to think seriously about moral and social concerns. (Seidman 1991, 144)

The responses discussed in this section are all premised on the assumption that the value-free sociology yardstick is irremediably broken, leading to the normative desirability, permissibility, or inevitability of taking sides, giving voice, or making sociology a moral discourse. However the most widespread response to the value-freedom quandary has not involved abandoning value neutrality as such. Instead, it has been to supplement value neutrality by the potentially demanding requirement of reflexivity, which accepts that sociologists as social actors cannot remove themselves by fiat from the social world they study (Bourdieu and Wacquant 1992).

In consequence, sociologists must vigilantly engage in self-observation with the goal of taking into account the myriad ways normative commitments and other social interests insinuate themselves into sociological analysis.[8] In its weaker form, reflexivity, Woodiwiss contends, can easily morph into solipsism, understood "simply as looking inward at one's abstract assumptions, and, à la Jacques Derrida, one's prior reading" (Woodiwiss 2005b, 100). Woodiwiss, however, argues that a more sustained

> reflexive practice is essential if we wish to become critically aware not simply of our own assumptions and preoccupations but also of their interrelationships between knowledge and power that obtain in our fields of interests and expertise, let alone incorporate their insights and outsights into our practice – if, in sum, we wish to be able to avoid confusing the thoughts that are in our minds with our thoughts. (Woodiwiss 2005b, 100; Bourdieu and Wacquant 1992)[9]

The Inescapability of Normative Practices

I now turn to the third manner in which we might think about sociology intersecting with normative concerns. Curiously, despite the fact that in its early years sociology embarked on the project of developing empirical approaches to explaining the normative organization of social life, contemporary sociologists, except those who unambiguously assert that sociology should be reconstructed as a normative enterprise, share a certain unease with normative issues. This does not just arise from the perception that value neutrality, in its idealized or reflexive forms, is required to underwrite the legitimacy of sociology's theoretical and empirical findings. It also derives from the central role that normativity played in Parsonian sociology and the ensuing counter reaction it elicited (López 2009; Wrong 1961).

For Parsons, normative integration via shared expectations and commitment to socially patterned values explained the basis of patterned social interaction (Parsons 1967). As Shilling and Mellor have noted, Parsonian sociology elaborated a "bold depiction of modernity as a normative social system in which apparently divided social groups are actually united by shared value systems" (2001, 16). While it is undeniably true that Parsons significantly overplayed the normative card, the regulatory work that shared normative values perform is difficult for sociologists entirely to discount no matter their feelings towards Parsonian sociology.[10] In fact, on some readings of the sociological tradition, the distinctiveness of sociology as a mode of apprehending social life is closely tied to its attempt to conjoin the social and the normative, or to use Shilling and Mellor's felicitous phrase, to uncover "the elementary forms of social and moral life" (2001; Levine 1995).

Naturally, this does not obviate the considerable debate regarding precisely how the normative patterning of social life should be conceptualized (Shilling and Mellor 2001), for example, its relationship to consensus and/or conflict (Oberschall 1978), or the actual social mechanisms that produce and reproduce specific normative orientations. The tendency in the latter case has been to ignore the specificity of normativity as a lived experience: "[i]nsofar as sociologists have been interested in lay normativity, they have emphasized its social differentiation, that is how it is both sensitive to and influenced by social position" (Sayer 2005, 951; Alexander 2006). Bourdieu's conception of habitus is an instructive example.

Habitus refers to a series of embodied dispositions that actors acquire as a result of their social location in particular social fields. These dispositions grounded in "classificatory schemes, principles of classification and principles of vision and division" modulate particular social practices that correspond with actors' social positions—for example, eating, leisure activities, labour market trajectories, and political opinions. More often implicitly rather than explicitly, this social classificatory apparatus also generates judgements of worth and value by establishing "distinctions between what is good and what is bad, between what is right and what is wrong, between what is distinguished and what is vulgar, and so forth" (Bourdieu 1998a, 8).

The particularity of the normative sphere—"what is right and what is wrong"—however, is lost to the extent that it is folded into other distinctions such as those pertaining to aesthetic judgements or class distinction. Sayer, on the contrary, argues that individuals are normative beings concerned "about the world and the well being of what we value in it" (Sayer 2005, 949). Consequently normative questions attach themselves to "things that people *care* about deeply" (Sayer 2005, 949), and a failure to sociologically come to terms with this class of social phenomena will produce "an anodyne and alienated account of subjectivity that renders our evident concern about what we do and what happens to us incomprehensible" (Sayer 2005, 950).[11]

Sociology and the Alchemy of Human Rights

Having briefly explored the manner in which normative concerns intersect with sociology, it is now possible to identify at least four ways in which the plea for a human rights-centred normative turn for sociology might be interpreted: (1) that sociologists become conscious of and modulate their normative commitments through reflexivity, (2) that sociologists abandon the ideal of value-free sociology, (3) that sociologists supplement their empirical analyses with normative argument, and (4) that sociologists seriously undertake the study of normative practices. I begin by briefly advancing in summary form what will be argued and illustrated in more detail below.

To begin with the last of the four aspects, the sociologists who advocate for a human rights-based normative turn unquestionably draw attention to the importance of normativity—deeply held notions of what is right and wrong, what is and what ought to be—in the patterning of social life, not least because they hope to draw on its social power to promote social change. That said, on my reading, their concern is not to identify the actual functioning of normative mechanisms, be they societal or individual, as does, for instance, Alexander (2006) in the context of the civil sphere or Sayer (2005) in his exploration of normative concerns in everyday life. Instead, it is to gauge how the normativity that is particular to human rights might be used to criticize and contribute to modifying existing social relations of oppression and inequality and provide the social conditions for human flourishing. In this sense, human rights' normative power is presupposed and black boxed rather than explained.

Although the authors promoting a human rights-based normative turn make reference to the illusory boundary between the empirical and the normative, the sociological project that they propose neither entails a taking of sides as such in the manner advocated by Howard Becker, nor an obligation to involve excluded groups in the representational practices of the discipline as promoted by Dorothy Smith. Instead, the normative turn describes the manner in which human rights make available to sociologists the moral alchemy through which objective and empirical analyses of social situations, involving injustice and inequality, can be transformed into normative imperatives capable of potentially giving rise to social change, or at the very least the morally justified demand for such change.[12]

Consequently, in terms of the four possibilities outlined above, at first blush it is the third one—that is, supplementing empirical with normative argument—that best seems to capture the crux of the human rights-based normative turn. I would argue that the movement from empirical to normative, however, is alchemic in nature because what enables the "is" to "ought" transformation remains unclear, or what is the same it remains unquestionably clear thus beyond question. This is because those sociologists arguing for human rights' capacity to transmute empirical claims into normative ones reproduce the discursive representations found elsewhere in the human rights political imaginary, to wit, the self-evidence of human rights and, given the right conditions, their ensuing normative or legal force. This entails accepting human rights discourse, in its own terms, without submitting it to sociological scrutiny. Put in the context of my discussion in the first chapter, these sociologists perform human rights rather than attempt to elucidate what the conditions of possibility of their performance are.

Sociologists, who advocate for a human rights-based normative shift, contribute to reinforcing the self-evidence and alchemic nature of human rights. They do so by attempting to anchor human rights within sociology, through foundational and/or empirical sociological arguments. In the case of the former, these generally make reference to some universal defining feature of human beings, such as their vulnerability, their inherent sociality, and/or the inescapable moral foundation of all human societies. In the case of the latter, the empirical arguments, reference is made to some conjunctural urgency such as the need to defend society against neoliberalism, modern warfare, or new forms of violence.

In both cases—that is, foundational and empirical arguments—human rights' alchemic power is sustained by positioning human rights as the indispensable response. As a result, though empirical inquiry remains a crucial component of a human rights-engendered normative sociology, the latter also partakes of Seidman's conception of sociology as a moral reimagining of social life, but one whose language is derived from the normative syntax of human rights, thus overlapping with the second possibility identified above—that is, abandoning the ideal of value-free sociology and envisioning sociology as a normative practice *tout court.*

In terms of the first option—reflexivity—it appears marginal. This is particularly surprising given the contemporary currency of reflexivity in the discipline. This is conceivably the result of the forcefulness of human rights' self-evidence for which there is no automatic sociological immunity. This is a point to which I will return in the conclusion of this chapter. It is now time to explore Bryan S. Turner's contributions to the sociology of human rights. He is indisputably a pioneer both in terms of drawing the discipline's attention to the growing significance of human rights as a decisive contemporary social phenomena, and creatively spearheading the plea for a human rights-based normative reorientation of sociology.

Sociology's Allergy to and Allegory for Human Rights

Turner maintains that the growth of universal human rights is the "most significant institutional revolution of the twentieth century" (2006, 6). He equally contends that sociology has for the most part not been able to engage with human rights as a result of its aversion to normative modes of analysis (Turner 1993, 2006, 2009). Specifically, the two concrete obstacles that have blocked sociology's entry into the field of human rights are its positivism and relativism. For Turner, sociology's commitment to positivism and its scepticism towards rights is rooted in, and illustrated by, the explanatory strategies the discipline's founding figures devised to account for legal phenomena, to which rights are inextricably linked.

In Durkheim's case, the need to ensure the emerging discipline's autonomy, in relation to philosophy, meant that Durkheim could not entertain the notion that sociology would make judgements about the just or unjustness of law or juridical sanctions. Verdicts regarding justice and fairness were normative in nature, hence within philosophy's explanatory terrain. In contrast, sociology's bailiwick would be consolidated around the observation and explanation of social facts as things (Turner 1993, 492). Marx's hostility towards rights and "the normative analysis of the legal institutions" is, according to Turner, in no small part responsible for sociology's dismissive reception of rights. Because Marx conceptualized "rights" in capitalist society as "merely a façade to hide or mask fundamental economic and social inequalities" (Turner 1993, 492), the received tradition in sociology has been that rights are "individual [...] partial, ineffective and superficial" (Turner 1993, 492).

Despite the non-negligible impact of Durkheim's positivism and Marx's contemptuous attitude towards rights, it is Weber's sociology of law and its legacy that has, claims Turner, most contributed to blocking sociology's ability to engage in normative analysis of modern law and rights. This is because his analysis of the evolution of modern secular law leads Weber to the conclusion that there can be no transcendent normative basis for the law, opening the door to a positivistic, in the legal sense of the black letter of the law, and a relativistic understanding of legal phenomena.[13]

Turner's argument draws on three coiled conceptual strands from Weber's sociology—that is, rationalization, the clash between substantive and formal conceptions of justice, and inter-group conflict—that have tied sociologists in a positivist and relativist knot, from which they must free themselves if they are to undertake the type of normative sociology that Turner endorses. First, the rationalization of the law through processes such as codification, professionalization, formalization of legal reasoning, and the decline of natural law, contributed to the secularization of the normative foundation of the law. It grounded the legitimacy of the law in the legal rationality of the state, leaving legal positivism as the only viable mode of analysis.

Second, the tension between substantive and formal conceptions of justice introduced incompatible and irresolvable demands that engendered relativistic tendencies. Third, these tendencies were further amplified by the manner in which social groups sought to harness the social power of the law, rights, and the state to protect or advance their interests. In consequence, Turner concludes, "The implication of Weber's arguments is that, in the absence of a moral framework like natural law, might is right. Whoever happens de facto to be in power will enjoy de jure control" (Turner 1993, 495).

Turner thinks that the objections and hurdles introduced by the three founding figures, and the manner in which they have subsequently been maintained in sociological thought, are not insurmountable. For instance, value neutrality is a chimera that serves to obscure the value positions that sociologist irremediably take, not to mention the fact that value neutrality is in itself a value position (Turner 1993, 492). Marx's repudiation of rights as a bourgeois ideological charade rested on a narrow individualistic conception of rights and a facile caricature of the liberal tradition (Turner 1993, 492). Finally, Turner contends that the philosopher Leo Strauss has adequately critiqued Weber's conventionalism or relativism—the notion that truth and justice are socially defined rather than transcendent categories (Turner 1993, 493).

Turner's counter-arguments are broad and surprisingly underdeveloped. For example, as seen above, the intractability of the value-freedom question need not lead to its abandonment; it can be addressed to some extent by strong forms of reflexivity.[14] However, if Turner develops a summary rebuttal of the arguments against sociology's adoption of a normative stance, this is perhaps because he believes that the field of citizenship studies categorically demonstrates not only that normative arguments in defence of rights are possible in sociology but also more importantly that sociologists have unwittingly been making them.

For Turner, the sociology of citizenship has operated as a covert sociology of rights. Requiring neither explicit moral nor normative commitments, sociologists have formulated the category of citizenship in terms of a bundle of historically evolving institutionalized rights, in the context of the modern nation-state and its associated welfare practices. Because rights have a time and place of origin in Western societies, and are conceptualized via their embeddedness in concrete social relations and power struggles, the sociological study of citizenship rights has been amenable to the types of sociological explanatory horizons inaugurated by sociology's founding figures. What is more, circumscribed by the territorial boundaries of the nation-state, disciplinary aliens such as universal norms or humanity have been successfully denied entry in the field of citizenship studies. However not all is at it seems. Sociology's borders, like all borders, are porous: "While 'citizenship' functions as a description of certain institutions, it covertly carries the implication that they *ought* to exist in the interest of social harmony" (Turner 1993, 496). Consequently, the sociology of citizenship has functioned as an allegory for sociological normativity.

The light thus shed on sociology's clandestine normative commitments to rights in the field of citizenship studies, Turner draws two conclusions. One, given that sociologists do take normative stances, it would be desirable to do so explicitly and to develop them in the open. The other, despite the fact that citizenship is the cradle where normative arguments have been surreptitiously nurtured, sociological conceptions of citizenship rights, and citizenship rights themselves, do not provide an adequate basis for developing a normative position for justice. This is so for the very reasons that sociological accounts of citizenship have been able to pass as non-normative analyses, namely, their filiation to the institutions of the nation-state.

First, given the Western origin of citizenship, its normative structure is unlikely to be of use in societies with different historical trajectories. Second, as a consequence of global developments and the transformation of the nation-state, it is not clear that the latter should or will remain the referent for rights. Third, and last, because citizenship has been conceptualized by sociology as resulting from the historical and contingent institutionalization of specific bundles of rights, the theory of rights that citizenship might be able to ground is likely to account for them in an arbitrary and fortuitous manner, making for a weak normative defence of rights (Turner 1993, 498).

The terrain cleared for the erection of a normative approach in sociology, but judging the existing submerged foundations in the sociology of citizenship shaky, Turner argues that human rights can contribute to uncovering a sturdier substructure:

> by contrast with the discourse of citizenship, "human rights" appears to be more universal (because they are articulated by many nations through the United Nations charters), more contemporary (because they are not tied to the nation-state) and more progressive (because they are not related to the management of people by the state). If sociology is the study of the transformation of *gemeinschaft* (organic and particularistic values and institutions) into *gesellschaft* (associations which are more universalistic in their definition of social membership) as a consequence of modernization, we can conceptualise human-rights solidarity as a historical stage beyond citizenship solidarity. (Turner 1993, 498)

Precisely how Turner builds a normative foundation for sociology in which human rights signal the development of a more advanced and inclusive form of social solidarity is the topic to which I now turn to in the next section.

Grounding Human Rights in Human Vulnerability

Turner identifies in Michael Ignatieff's "thin" defence of human rights (Ignatieff 2001) an overlooked opportunity to develop a thicker and more robust justification. He notes that Ignatieff advocates for "a minimalist liberal theory of human rights"—limited to the protection of human dignity and agency—in order to secure the conditions for human rights' universal acceptance by avoiding contentious metaphysical entanglements. Turner believes that Ignatieff's allusion to the universality of the experience of pain and humiliation, however, suggests the possibility of a more resilient defence for human rights. This is to be achieved by grounding them in "our common vulnerability":

> There is a foundation to human rights – namely, our common vulnerability. Human beings experience pain and humiliation because they are vulnerable. While humans may not share a common culture, they are bound together by the risks and perturbations that arise from their vulnerability. Because we have a common ontological condition as vulnerable, intelligent

beings, human happiness is diverse, but misery is common and uniform. (Turner 2006, 9)

What makes Turner's argument particularly innovative, as I will elaborate below, is the manner in which he draws on strands from both human and social ontology to weave a series of normative arguments that are mutually reinforcing. The vulnerability of both humans and social institutions creates the normative necessity for the protection that human rights are believed to be able to provide in the contemporary world.

In accord with the philosophical anthropology of Arnold Gehlen and Helmuth Plessner, Turner, following Peter Berger (Berger 1969), argues that "human beings 'are not fully complete animals'" (Turner 1993, 500; Berger 1969, 1–5). The implications of this Nietzschean-inspired affirmation are various. First, humans are "'prematurely' brought into this world, as an accident of their evolution towards an upright posture, and are therefore socially dependent on society and culture for a long period during maturation" (Turner 1993, 501). Second, lacking an invariant instinctual apparatus attaching them narrowly to a specific environment, human beings are characterized by their "world openness" and social-cultural plasticity, necessitating the guidance, nurturing, and protection of social institutions (1993, 501).

Finally, owing to the prevalence and the rapidity of institutional change in modern society, human "'character' has been replaced by a fluid 'personality' which corresponds to an equally uncertain, deinstitutionalized social reality" (Turner 1993, 501). Turner avoids Gehlen's conservative and pessimistic rendition of modernity, drawing two conclusions. The first is the ontological frailty of humans, which ensues from the fact that human "lives are finite, because they typically exists in conditions of scarcity, disease and danger, and because they are constrained by physical processes of ageing and decay" (Turner 1993, 501). The second is the precariousness of social arrangements and institutions (Turner 1993, 501).

On the one hand, "in order to protect themselves from the uncertainties of the everyday world, they [human beings] must build institutions (especially political, familial and cultural institutions) that come to constitute what we call society" (Turner 2006, 26). Accordingly, broad ontological features of social life, such as the need for particular types of protective institutions, are rooted in the exigencies of human ontology. On the other hand, as noted above, humans are subject to a second category of vulnerability, arising from the precariousness of social institutions. Such precariousness comprises

> the inability of political institutions to protect and secure the interests of individuals, the failure of social institutions to manage social change, the incapacity of social institutions to reconcile the conflict of collective and individual interests, and, finally, the difficulty of delivering equity in generational exchanges. (Turner 2006, 31)

For Turner, it is precisely the shared double bind of human vulnerability, that is, ontological and social, that generates patterns of "dependency and connectedness". It is, also, the source of "sympathy, empathy, and trust, without which society would not be possible" leading to a "delicate balance between scarcity, solidarity and security [that] characterizes all social life" (2006, 26). Moreover, in Durkheimian mode, he adds that social and human rights express in law the essence of human sociality, namely, the solidarity that arises from the universal human experience of ontological vulnerability and institutional precariousness (Turner 2006, 27).

Much of Turner's argument, summarized immediately above, parallels that developed by Berger in *The Sacred Canopy*: not surprisingly, he riffs on the latter's title to argue that social and human rights should be understood as components of a "juridical canopy" (Turner 2006, 29). For Berger, the biological incompleteness of human beings—the lack of the highly specialized and firmly directed drives of non-human animals—dictates that they must engage in world-building activity (Berger 1969, 5), with the goal of creating a "*nomos*", a "meaningful order" (Berger 1969, 19). The absence of such a nomos, which functions as a "shield against terror", would lead to the "nightmare" of "disorder", "senselessness", and "madness" (Berger 1969, 22). Similarly, the ontological frailty of human beings means that they must construct, and depend on, social institutions. While social institutions can and do mitigate the ineluctable vulnerability of being human and nurture solidarity, they are ultimately uncertain. For Berger, the most historically widespread institution hedging against the threat of meaningless is religion. *The Sacred Canopy* inserts social order, and its attached meaning, "within a sacred and cosmic frame of reference" (Berger 1969, 33), thus positioning it "beyond the contingencies of human meaning and activity" (Berger 1969, 32).

In a similar manner, Turner contends, legal institutions provide a "juridical shield" against the double vulnerability of ontological frailty and institutional precariousness (Turner 2006, 29). Indeed, Turner claims that from his "basic philosophical account of the ontological incompleteness of humans, we can derive the elementary forms of a juridical canopy of law, habeas corpus, civil liberties, and rights" to which human rights can be added (Turner 2006, 29). More importantly, however, is that the legitimacy of the elementary forms of juridical protection does not necessitate an otherworldly anchor; it is moored in a bare social solidarity that is this-worldly, ineradicably tied to vulnerability and precariousness. What is more, such a normative anchoring circumvents the need for a transcendent natural law to ground human rights.

Here, according to Turner, is human rights' foundation excavated with a normative sociological spade. Its bedrock is not frailty or precariousness as such, but the shared universal experience of both. Upon the later, we find the accumulation of different layers of institutional patterns building on social solidarity. When institutions function, they, imperfectly no doubt, insulate human beings from the bare bedrock experience of being human, namely, vulnerability and uncertainty. However institutions can be disturbed, broken up, and eroded. When this happens, it is human rights in the form of a juridical shield, ranging from a bare social solidarity to a deeper empathy, that expresses our common vulnerability providing the moral basis for human sociality. Human and social rights potentially safeguard us when all else fails and equally, in principle, provide the bedrock upon which more resilient forms of social solidarity can be developed.

In addition to establishing the universal normative basis for human rights in human and social ontology, Turner further buttresses his defence of human rights by identifying a number of contemporary processes that are either beyond the scope of, or have eroded, the types of social institutions that in an earlier epoch were protective of many, but certainly not all individuals. In this latter respect, Turner argues that sexual and reproductive rights must be secured through human rights because of the nation-states', or subnational actors', inherent interest in regulating the family, fertility, and in some instances, the sexual preference of their populations, not to mention the vulnerabilities created in the context of new reproductive technologies and new modes of domination over women such as "patrism" (Turner 2006, 69–74).[15]

Similarly, insofar as social rights have typically been legitimately accessed via the contributions made by "citizens" through paid work, war service, or parenting, this has curbed the social rights of those not capable of, or prevented from, fulfilling their contributory obligations. Human rights, however, overcome this restraint because entitlements arise from shared humanness (Turner 2006, 3). Turner, also, notes that if in the heyday of the welfare state, marginalized and subordinated groups were not able to fully secure their citizenship entitlements, then the contemporary dilution of social rights means that these groups' claims "are perhaps more appropriately couched in the language of human rights rather than the language of national citizenship rights" (Turner 2006, 90).

Given human rights' transnational aspirations, it is not surprising that many of the contemporary empirical figurations that contribute to making human rights urgently necessary are the product of processes with a global span. For instance, the reality of the movement of peoples and of cultural practices across national boundaries, facilitated by global communication and travel infrastructures, means that the monocultures long nurtured by national states are no longer viable. They require "transnational claims to cultural rights from the perspective of universal human rights" (Turner 2006, 45). Particular attention is given to the emergence of new wars: typically fought by subnational or private actors that can include private contractors, insurgents, criminal organizations, and terrorist organizations habitually targeting non-combatants (Turner 2006, 18).

These conflicts frequently lead to population displacement, state failure, epidemics, starvation, and an escalation of violence against women (Turner 2006, 18). Other forms of contemporary global instability include global financial markets, global exposure of populations to disease, environmental degradation and disasters, new forms of insecurity arising from the globalization of slavery, organized crime, and the trafficking of narcotics (Turner 2006, 32). At a more abstract level, drawing on the work of Ulrich Beck (2000b), Turner links many of these developments to the risks inherent in modernization and globalization, risks for which human rights are the best foil (Turner 2006, 32).

On the face of it, Turner's normative case for human rights appears quite compelling, and it is frequently cited with approval by many sociologists working on human rights (Armaline et al. 2015; Blau and Moncada 2007, 2009a, b; Frezzo 2012, 5; Kurasawa 2007, 164 n; Levy and Sznaider 2010, 38; Morris 2013, 136; Sjoberg et al. 2001, 25; Somers and Roberts 2008, 408; Toussaint 2011, 51; Woodiwiss 2005a, 129). Some sociological scholars, nonetheless, do question the attempt to commit sociology to human rights (Anleu 1999), or the wisdom of tacking towards normative foundationalism (Hynes 2010, 817; Nash 2012, 445; Waters 1996).

In the next section, I draw attention to what, I believe, are significant shortcomings in Turner's plea for a normative turn towards human rights in sociology. In particular, I want to focus on a number of easily overlooked argumentative feints that are the product of an unreflective incorporation, or penetration, of the human rights political imaginary into sociological discourse. As such they provide us with insight into the functioning of human rights as a political imaginary, a point I develop further in the conclusion of this chapter.

Sociology *of* or *for* Human Rights?

On my reading, Turner's commitment to the adequacy of human rights, as the endpoint of his sociologically informed normative analysis, relies excessively on their taken-for-granted nature. In places, Turner frames the tenor of his intervention in terms of developing a sociological practice that is capable of engaging in normative debate on fundamental questions such as justice and inequality (Turner 1993, 491). In contrast, I would like to suggest that the effect produced by his arguments is to make human rights the unexamined point of departure.

Accordingly, due to the indisputability of human rights as a normative horizon for sociology, the task Turner entrusts sociology is to make the discipline's tools work for human rights.

The manner in which he proceeds corresponds to the *modi operandi* I identified above for encouraging a human rights-based normative turn. These include shoring up human rights' normative foundation by grounding them in a sociologically derived ontology of human beings, human beings' sociality and interdependence, and the moral nature of social life. Complementing these invariant grounds are also normative pleas whose persuasive powers derive from the urgency of the need to protect and assist individuals subject to new forms of violence and inequality, arising from contemporary political, economic, and social configurations with a global reach.

That Turner's foundationalism rests on the self-evidence of human rights can be established in a variety of ways. First, a close reading of Turner's argument reveals a bait and switch. The argument about the need to overcome sociology's perennial dismissal of normative modes of reasoning provides the bait. If accepted, the switch follows: human rights are introduced as *the* normative rather than *a* normative position. In other words, under the guise of arguing for the necessity of adopting normative modes of analysis, a human rights stance is introduced as the only available normative position, eclipsing other potential normative positions—for example, one grounded in a Marxist critique of capitalism.

Furthermore, it is important to attend to the implicature inherent in Turner's overall framing of the hitherto perceived clash between sociological analysis and human rights. It is not that sociologists do not have the tools to study human rights empirically, rather it is that "a positivistic tradition in social science, which attempts to avoid any engagement with normative debate by aiming at a causal analysis or descriptive account of values, is unlikely to approach problems of justice within a framework of human rights discourse" (1993, 491). The implicature is that human rights are fundamentally defined by their normativity and cannot be accessed in any other way; thus the task for sociology must be to justify rather than to explain them—a position that is justly criticized by Kate Nash (2012, 445).

Above, I summarized Turner's argument to the effect that the sociology of citizenship has operated as a covert normative sociology of citizenship insofar as scholars have been able to focus their analysis on the institutional and historical configurations underpinning citizenship rights. The fact that, according to Turner, human rights cannot be sociologically grasped in this manner, and must be approached via a normative register, might plausibly be explained not as arising from the privileged normative status of human rights. It might, instead, be due to their institutional underdevelopment when compared to citizenship rights (Bosniak 2000). In the context of citizenship rights, rights exist in a plethora of institutions and practices, what Somers designates an "instituted process" (2008, 35). Such constellations of institutions, practices, meanings, and processes are crystallized in durable, yet changeable, social forms such as universal education (Meyer 1977), national identity (Smith 1991), and territory (Meyer 1977; Smith 1991; Brenner et al. 2008; Neocleous 2003) and depend on concrete social technologies such as health, unemployment, and social security insurance, to mention but a few (Rose and Miller 1992; Esping-Andersen 1998).

These different elements operate at different scales and are interwoven in complex historically contingent trajectories (Jessop 1999; Somers 1993). Part of their power is indeed the normative claims that they underwrite, and certainly sociologists have surreptitiously or even in some instances explicitly invoked them. All the same, these normative claims have been synchronized to the kinds of effects that citizenship rights, as social processes and institutional complexes, have been able to produce. Thus to take just one example that *mutatis mutandi* stands for many others, the processes through which citizenship practices have been en*gendere*d has meant that they have time and again failed to develop the institutional mechanisms and processes that would have adequately included and recognized specific categories of citizens, i.e., women (Christie 2000).

Moreover, despite the fact that Turner is certainly right to underscore that sociologists in explaining and describing the emergence of citizenship rights have frequently implicitly argued that they ought to exist, citizenship rights have not necessarily constituted a common taken-for-granted normative horizon for sociologists. Witness the extensive literature critiquing citizenship rights and the welfare state when citizenship rights were thought to be secure (Somers 2008, 400; cf. Gough 1975; Offe 1972; Piven 1971; Poulantzas 1978). What is more, if now, amongst sociologists, there is a more sanguine reading of citizenship rights, seemingly providing some kind of a common normative horizon, this is conceivably due to the unforeseen but terrifyingly effective erosion of citizenship rights in the post-1980s period (Somers 2008; Mishra 2014).

This is not to dismiss in toto the arguments developed by Turner in his effort to quarry down to the bedrock of vulnerability, reciprocity, and morality to lay bare a common and durable source of human interdependence and resultant sympathy. In his endeavour, he develops elegant and compelling analyses of the centrality of normativity in social relations, expanding upon what was a central insight of nineteenth- and early twentieth-century sociology (Shilling and Mellor 2001; Levine 1995) and crucially updating it to include areas of sexuality, gender, culture, identity, and disability. But truth be told, he fails to demonstrate that human rights are the necessary response to the normative potential associated with shared ontological vulnerability or an effective shield, now or ever, against institutional precariousness. As Lydia Morris argues, "the bond of mutual sympathy which may follow from our common frailty requires active engagement and cultivation" (Morris 2013, 3) as demonstrated by Jeffrey Alexander's attempt to understand the manner in which the civil sphere, often precariously, provides the social and moral basis for solidarity (2006).

An understanding of how this potential sympathy fuels, is refined, and transformed by specific instituted processes would open up avenues for exploring the adequacy of human rights that Turner so passionately asserts. This, in turn, would require grasping the historical emergence of and the institutional mechanisms through which human rights have acquired the normative persuasive power that they currently wield. In other words, what can human rights as networks of social relations and public narratives do? What remains obscured by Turner's account is the manner in which societies have dealt with frailty and precariousness in the past, and what different political and social projects have been imagined as well as the manner in which they differ from human rights.

In a fashion that merely reiterates a central representational feature of human rights' political imaginary, human rights for Turner have a thin decontextualized quality, transcribed into sociological discourse almost exclusively as norms upon which "we can agree" (Turner 2006, 23), that "are designed" (Turner 2006, 36), and from which "we can derive" particular modalities of protection (Turner 2006, 29). In referring to the UDHR, Turner cites pertinent articles (Turner 2006, 7, 36, 49, 79) and, as seen above, claims that they "appear more universal", "are more contemporary", and "more progressive" (Turner 1993, 498). This hardly gives us a sense of the source of their efficacy and their potential social power; it does not provide an account of how human rights engage and cultivate human social dispositions of "care and respect" (Turner 2006, 23) or the type of ethico-political labour (Kurasawa 2007, 4) that they enable and entail.

Turner does not entirely ignore the space between the normative bedrock and human rights ideals, that is, contextualized historical institutions and practices. He does, for instance, point out that human rights are habitually not available to those who need them the most (Turner 2006, 19). He equally observes somewhat faintly that absent "economic reform", and "structural changes", they will have limited social efficacy (Turner 2006, 42). Yet, even the floundering of human right institutions does not incite Turner to explore the specificity of the limits of the social efficacy of human rights. Instead, he folds human rights' institutional failure into a broader and decontextualized account of institutional precariousness that in turn becomes the motor of human rights development:

> The dynamic and dialectical relationship between institutional precariousness and ontological vulnerability drives the evolution of human rights legislation and culture. Institutions need to be continuously repaired and redesigned, and human rights need to be constantly reviewed in the light of their misapplication, misappropriation, and failures. (Turner 2006, 32)

In other words, we are provided with an abstract decontextualized social reflex, something akin to Polanyi's double movement, where social breakdown provokes a protective countermovement (Polanyi 1957; López 2016), rather than an examination of the possible shortcomings of human rights themselves, and the modes through which they have been instituted. Human rights are beyond dispute. Consequently, the failure of human rights law requires more law and better designed institutions. Unwittingly perhaps, Turner adopts simultaneously the posture of the "politico-legal institutionalist" and of the "philosophical normativist" that, as the two hegemonic forms of understanding the contemporary development of human rights (Risse et al. 1999, 2013), "treat global justice as a question of redesigning the world system in accordance with international human rights procedures and cosmopolitan principles", respectively (Kurasawa 2007, 5).

All of the above is not to deny that human rights merit serious sociological analysis in the diverse modalities through which they are socially instantiated: for example, "normative moral aspiration", "codification and doctrine", and "mechanisms and institutions of enforcement" (Somers and Roberts 2008, 488), perhaps even contributing to making each more coherent and/or more efficacious. Neither is to foreclose the possibility that "law is the rough draft of social theory" (Scheppele cited in Somers and Roberts 2008, 389) and the insights that such a strategy delivers, as evidenced in nineteenth-century European sociology (Scheppele 1994; Thornhill 2011, 1–7).

However, as Kim Scheppele shows, the most fruitful avenues for writing social theory with a legal plume require understanding the distinct range of each; the converse is equally true (Scheppele 1994, 384). Paraphrasing Scheppele, one could say that the fact legal theorists go to authoritative legal texts, such as the UDHR, to mine normative principles and construct their intertextually linked arguments is to the legal scholar as "unremarkable as gravity" (1994, 384). Indubitably, "the ways in which legal theorists think about legal doctrine may be of more than a passing interest to sociologist who are thinking through cultural formations" (Scheppele 1994, 384). However, necessarily what is unremarkable to the legal theorist must surely be so to the social theorist, and vice versa.

Whereas legal scholars can point to the UDHR and the cascade of legal instruments subsequently engendered as a fruitful avenue for engaging with human rights, sociologists must surely not follow them. Instead, they should attempt to elucidate the social processes that give legal reasoning, in the sphere of human rights, its social traction, and efficacy.

That Turner does not, as I will reiterate in the conclusion to this chapter, is due to the fact that human rights are the point of departure for his normative analysis rather than its conclusion. Consequently the merits of Turner's normative analysis, which are significant, have to be understood in the context of a sociology *for* as opposed to a sociology *of* human rights. Something similar can be said of the authors to whom I now turn in the next section.

Channelling the Global Human Rights Revolution

If Turner is the undisputed pioneer in the sociology of human rights in the frontier sense of clearing a path through a sociological wilderness hostile to human rights, then Judith Blau and Alberto Moncada are pioneers in the ecological sense: endeavouring to create an environment that can support the flourishing of human rights in the academy and in broader society. Equally, while Turner attempts to insert sociology within the logic of the human rights political imaginary by insisting on the *sine qua non* of a normative turn for sociology, Blau and Moncada do this and more. Averring that the normative turn is already afoot in the sciences (Blau and Moncada 2009b; Blau and Frezzo 2012a), they argue for a pivot towards activism, which they themselves undertake through their participation in a human rights NGO, Sociologists Without Borders/*Sociologos Sin Fronteras*. The latter is "committed to advancing human rights through practice and in solidarity with those who lack basic rights such as sufficient food, jobs and a decent wage" (Blau and Moncada 2005, xiii).

The emphasis on human rights activism, found in Blau and Moncada's work, is more likely than not derived from their understanding of the contemporary "human rights revolution" as a global political response to the ravages of neoliberalism (Blau and Moncada 2009a, 502). It is not, as in Turner's case, a component in a juridical canopy to mitigate institutional precariousness. Turner's addressees are fellow sociologists or social scientists whose discipline induced relativism and/or positivism inhibit engagement with human rights in normative terms. Blau and Moncada's addressees are potential members of global civil society. Consequently, the authors are less concerned to facilitate sociology's reception of or engagement with human rights, focusing instead on how sociology might contribute to dislodging the blockages that prevent human rights from being realized in everyday social relations. Despite these differences in their understanding of human rights, Turner and Blau and Moncada share a surprising amount of common ground in their normative approach to human rights. This is so despite the fact that their inaugural publication (Blau and Moncada 2005) makes no mention of Turner's (1993) trailblazing paper.[16]

For instance, in both, human rights are grounded normatively (pace Nash 2012, 445) as a consequence of a shared human ontology and a concomitant universal social ethic of interdependence and solidarity. For Turner, as seen above, the common denominator in human and social ontology is vulnerability, arising from human beings' unfinished nature at birth. In contrast, Blau and Moncada ground rights in a deep instinctual mechanism that humans share with their primate cousins:

> Humans share with baboons, chimps and gorillas the capacity to symbolically represent their rights, to communicate them to others, and to defend them. All primates are elaborately hardwired to manage their own and others' rights for food, water, territory, social status and sexual partners, both cooperatively and competitively within collectivities. It is similar with respect to duties. Humans and all other primates have elaborate instincts and socially evolved rules for caring for others, particularly the young, the old, and the infirm, and for distributing resources. (Blau and Moncada 2005, 137)

Despite one grounding human rights in the absence and the others in the presence of a strong instinctual mechanism, either choice is fateful. For Turner, the lack of a strong instinctual drive makes humans reliant on institutions that nurture social solidarity, that, expressed in the juridical canopy, take the form of rights or human rights. The latter potentially safeguard individuals when institutions fail and/or when social solidarity contracts as they are wont to do. For Blau and Moncada, the instinctual pull towards working out rights and duties in collectivities means that "rights are dynamically embedded in society and therefore that people's identities are expressed positively through their social and other group memberships" (Blau and Moncada 2005, 6), which, they claim, reverberates with human rights' ethical core (Blau and Moncada 2005, 27). Finally, both, Turner and Blau and Moncada, argue that the contemporary normative demand for human rights arises most urgently from current global processes that undermine the fabric of society as well as imperil the safety, freedom, and, in extreme cases, the lives of its constituents. For Turner the referent for these processes is a heterogeneous mix of risk in an increasingly globalized postnational world, while for Blau and Moncada it is neoliberalism or advanced global capitalism.

Above, I noted that Blau and Moncada's addressees are potential members of a justice-seeking global civil society. However in their earlier publication, they focus on the US' outlier status vis-à-vis human rights, claiming that outside of the US "human rights are commonly discussed [...] and increasingly help to shape other government's policies" (Blau and Moncada 2005, xviii). One plausible reason, they argue, is the US' role in promoting neoliberalism, an economic ideology that "stands in stark opposition" to "the logic of human rights" (Blau and Moncada 2009a, 497). Although neoliberalism is by no means solely the progeny of American capitalism, nor is its capitalist class its exclusive beneficiary, the US has nonetheless played a dominant role in diffusing neoliberal norms and practices and assuring compliance (Blau and Moncada 2005, xvi, 2009a, 502; Mirowski 2013; Panitch and Gindin 2012), perhaps explaining the US' unwillingness to host human rights.

Notwithstanding the power of neoliberalism as an influential economic and political ideology, Blau and Moncada contend that neoliberalism alone is not sufficient to explain human rights' inability to root in US soil (Blau and Moncada 2005, xvii). After all, the global dispersion and seeding of neoliberal norms and practices and the resultant highly unequal concentration of wealth have elicited a protective response around the globe in the form of countervailing human rights claims (Blau and Moncada 2005, xvii). Moreover, though the US has most certainly not been immune to the economic ills generated by neoliberalism in the form of "high rates of poverty, job loss, homelessness, unemployment and underemployment", it has been remarkably allergic to human rights as a prospective antidote (Blau and Moncada 2005, xvi–xvii).

Consequently, there is, according to the authors, a more intractable obstacle preventing human rights claims from taking root in the US—crystallized in the pithy phrase "there is no free lunch!"—namely, liberalism (Blau and Moncada 2005, xvii). While not disregarding the broader Western liberal tradition, the authors claim that the US variant must have distinctive traits (Blau and Moncada 2005, xiii). Otherwise how to make sense of the embrace of human rights in other countries that draw from the common fund of Western liberalism, Europe, for instance (Blau and Moncada 2008, 234)?[17]

For Blau and Moncada, the "no-free-lunch syndrome" is rooted in a "complex system of American values centering on political freedoms and liberties", enshrined in the constitution (Blau and Moncada 2005, xvii), and made robust through the "nineteenth- and early twentieth-century experiences of immigrant mobility in a vast country overflowing with opportunities" (Blau and Moncada 2005, 4). Western liberalism's constitutionalization conjoined with a particular historical conjuncture has contributed to a "*weltanschauung*" or "consciousness" with deep roots in American society. This has eventuated in the tenacity of a negative conception of freedom as "freedom *from*" rather than "freedom *to*", making autonomy the central motif of American life (Blau and Moncada 2005, 2–3).

The triumvirate of individual achievement, self-reliance, and hard work not only captures the core of American liberalism, it also inexorably yokes individualism to economic success insofar as "the wealthy appear almost to validate Americans' views that inequalities are the fair outcomes of individual competition", making the accumulation of wealth "a right that accompanies all other rights and liberties", obviating the inequalities thus produced (Blau and Moncada 2005, 9). As a result, free markets and individual political freedoms and liberties become intertwined epistemologically and normatively in a mutually reinforcing recursive loop (Blau and Moncada 2005, 12).[18]

Blau and Moncada parry the thrust of liberalism by invoking Adam Smith, if only to remind free market liberals that even their undisputed champion conceded that the sovereignty of the economy should ultimately be subject to the social system and the principles of mutual regard (Blau and Moncada 2005, 14). Less surprisingly, they also conjure Polanyi's conception of the need to "embed" the economy (Blau and Moncada 2005, 13), a frustratingly ambiguous concept that is much in vogue of late amongst neoliberalism's detractors (Dale 2010a, b, 2011, 2012; López 2016). However, Blau and Moncada's most forceful critique of American (market) liberalism builds on what they understand to be its radical opposite: to wit, human rights. Whereas liberalism's *weltanschauung* is articulated around a strong sense of independence and autonomy, human rights' worldview is premised on people's shared humanity and reciprocity (Blau and Moncada 2005, 24).

Drawing on the work of the economist Amartya Sen (1999) on the right to development, they argue

> by connecting the rights of each person to those of all others and linking the developmental goals of persons with those of societies and nations, human rights harmonize practices and practical objectives from one place to another and through the many layers of communities, institutions, society and government. (Blau and Moncada 2005, 23)

This is in contradistinction to liberalism that, in their view, promotes economic, political, and military practices that enshrine individual political and property rights at the expense of other rights, especially in its contemporary neoliberal form (Blau and Moncada 2005, 25). Moreover, because human rights reach beyond the nationally grounded political and economic rights of liberalism, they embody the premise of "universal equality with respect to social worthiness, economic needs and creative drives" (Blau and Moncada 2005, 25).

Another pivotal distinction between the two rival worldviews is their framing of equality and difference. Whereas liberalism understands difference merely as the outcome of individual achievement, the human rights perspective additionally interprets difference as arising from cultural tradition and group membership. Insofar as these attachments foster the development of desired identities in a context of political participation, fairness, and choice, such differences are encouraged and supported. Within a human rights universe, difference does not promote the social closure of groups; instead, the logic of human rights nurtures attitudes that seek to unveil points in common while not effacing diversity: "What do we share", "How do we achieve solidarities with those who are different from us" (Blau and Moncada 2005, 27; cf. De Sousa Santos 2008)?

Seen from the authors' perspective, human rights "relate to the particularities of the human condition" (Blau and Moncada 2005, 4). Human rights substantively foster and enable the innate normative and social inclinations, as seen above, with which humans are hardwired. Human beings are not seen as the locus of abstract economic or formal political rights. Consequently, a society structured by human rights is akin to Marx's sketch of a post-capitalist society: "Men [sic], not as abstractions, but as real, living, particular individuals, are this community" (Marx cited in Blau and Moncada 2005, 28). Human rights empower agents to "enlarge the spaces of cooperation and collaboration" and "enhance popular democracy and economic fairness" (Blau and Moncada 2005, 28). The logic of human rights is "liberating", fostering "individual embeddedness in groups and communities", and sustaining "a dialogical process that entails ongoing recognition of the other" (Blau and Moncada 2005, 28–29).

Given the stark nature of the antithesis between human and liberal rights, and the dominance of the latter in the US, what is the prospect that human rights might bloom on the latter's soil? Blau and Moncada divine a number of signs that augur well. First, they discuss two factors with the potential of being turned from being "rights destructive" to "rights restorative" (Woodiwiss 2011, 135), namely, communications media and neoliberal-led globalization. In the case of the former, under the not too subtle chapter title of "Bread and Circuses", Blau and Moncada include a discussion of the news and the media, the media industry, advertising, and cultural imperialism. The gist of their discussion is to substantiate that "Americans cannot easily access accurate news accounts, owing to the spin of government officials put on stories, the control that advertisers have, and government's classification of documents" (Blau and Moncada 2005, 70). However, increasing access to decentralizing communications technology such as the internet is enabling the circulation of messages that the US and other governments cannot bend to their will, providing the basis for new forms of global consciousness, anchored in the principles of the UDHR (Blau and Moncada 2005, 80, 2009a).

Much of the vitality fuelling this global consciousness has been fostered by "the proliferation of social networks among people worldwide who are determined to fundamentally change the nature of capitalism" (Blau and Moncada 2005, 109). Thus, neoliberal globalization in ploughing global furrows of inequality, in conjunction with the spread of communications technology, has seeded networks of resistance devoted to the promoition of human rights and global justice. Moreover, Blau and Moncada claim,

> a widely and multinationally connected world will not tolerate a single country's [the US'] pre-empting the global stage in pursuit of its own national interests, nor will such a world allow economic actors to chase the globe in pursuit of the cheapest workers and natural resources. (Blau and Moncada 2005, 109–10)

Evidence for the emerging global struggle is provided via discussions of what are now the usual suspects that the global left showcases to claim "another world is possible". These include the World Social Forum, human rights NGOs and INGOs, regional alliances, transnational coalitions, cooperativism, fair trade, sweat-free campaigns, living-wage campaigns, multipartnership supply chains, and responsible investments (Blau and Moncada 2005, 161–76, 2009b, 146–48).

In addition Blau and Moncada point to a number of auspicious epistemological shifts. The first, the ethical turn in philosophy and its consequential foregrounding of responsibility for the "other" as a normative imperative (Blau and Moncada 2005, 30, 2009a, 504–5, b, 148–50), is corroborated by the growing significance of cosmopolitanism and mutuality in philosophy and the social sciences (Blau and Moncada 2009b, 149). Another is the normative shift in sociology towards human rights epitomized by the resurgence in the US of the sociologist as a public intellectual embracing human rights (Blau and Moncada 2009a, 507–8). This is particularly significant, they argue, given the manner in which American social science had been interpellated by liberal values as demonstrated by its commitment to positivism, empiricism, and rationalism (Blau and Moncada 2005, 20–21, fn. 30). More recently Blau has gone further, suggesting that the normative shift has been amplified beyond the social sciences to encompass the sciences more broadly claiming, "It can be stressed here that a scientific revolution is now under way that posits that the realization of human rights is the objective (*telos*) of any scientific endeavour" (Blau and Frezzo 2012a, 278).

The last portent of the blooming of a world structured by the logic of human rights can be found in the seeding of national constitutions with human rights concepts, which emphasize the equal moral worth and dignity of human beings (Blau and Moncada 2005). The constitutional embedding of human rights concepts has broadened the horizon of what citizens can legitimately demand and for which they can struggle (Blau 2012, 144–45). Though certainly not a guarantee that demands will be met, they enable civil society groups to put pressure on governments, and, in some instances, to reach out to INGOs, who in turn can attempt to push governments to change domestic behaviour (Blau 2012, 145), in what has been referred to as the "boomerang effect" (Keck and Sikkink 1998, 36).

Such boomeranging however is not an option in the US, saddled as it is with an eighteenth-century constitution, entrenching individual rights, (Blau and Moncada 2005, 138), that has not been updated to reflect the global human rights revolution (Blau and Moncada 2005, 155). Accordingly, sociological advocates of human rights and their allies should work towards promoting "a comprehensive revision of the US constitution (1787) to reflect recent innovations in civil and political rights, economic and social rights". "The adoption of new conceptions of human rights represents the key to the deepening of democracy in the United States", writes Blau's co-editor Mark Frezzo (2012, 6), in the introduction to their volume that probes how such constitutional revision might be undertaken (Blau and Frezzo 2012b; Blau and Smith 2006; Blau et al. 2008).

Blau and Moncada, and the scholars who have joined their quest to develop a normative sociology for human rights, paint a disturbing portrait of the scope and intensity of social injustice, rights violation, and inequality in the US and around the globe. Their concern should be our own. They accurately register the extent to which, since the mid-1990s, human rights has become the political and moral vernacular for a broad range of neoliberal resistance and social justice movements in both hemispheres, but markedly so in the global south. Consequently, that human rights is not common parlance when addressing domestic issues in the US is certainly intriguing and worth exploring, an issue I address in Chap. 6. In addition, they are equally right to see constitutions as open to contest and modifiable because, in the words of Chris Thornhill, constitutions are best seized sociologically as attempts "to construct the rule of law and the public regulation of governmental power as expressions of societal, rather than deductive prescriptive" norms (Thornhill 2011, 4). Moreover, given the role of the American constitution in symbolically, politically, and judicially entrenching individual rights, and Blau and Moncada's diagnosis of the incompatibility of human rights with the American variant of liberalism, exploration of the scope of constitutional change is comprehensible.

For all this, I would argue that Blau and Moncada conduct, as a metal conducts electricity, the moral and normative current of the so-called global human rights revolution via sociological filaments rather than analyse or explain it. Like Turner, they make a compelling normative argument for an ethic of solidarity, mutual respect, and interdependence, but they do not, to my mind, succeed in showing sociologically that human rights must be the outcome of this normative demand or that it is an adequate institutional response. Human rights are the unquestioned point of origin of their analysis. I suspect that this is perhaps due to the exigencies of advocacy, which privileges action over reflection and certainty over doubt. As a result, Blau and Moncada fail to explore what gives human rights their alleged social efficacy or power and what the limits of that power might be. In other words, they do not address how human rights are performed, the energy that feeds them, or the relational networks through which they travel. Theirs is a normatively thick, but sociologically thin conception of human rights. Again as with Turner's arguments, it is not the engagement with normative argument per se that is the problem, rather, as I explore in the next section, it is their avowal that the normative shift in sociology must be written in the ink of the human rights political imaginary.

Reflecting or Reflecting Upon Human Rights?

To the extent that Blau and Moncada reflect human rights onto a sociological plane, they mirror the representations generated by the human rights political imaginary. Crystallized in the UDHR and the cascade of subsequent international instruments, human rights are presented by Blau and Moncada in a descriptive discussion of pertinent norms, principles, and intertextual linkages (Blau and Moncada 2005, 30–63). There is no need for them to energetically enquire into their origin because they have always been present. In fact, Blau and Moncada push the roots of human rights back even further to humanity's pre-history since a disposition towards proto-rights is the product of our biological hardwiring.

Thus the universalism of human rights is not only synchronic, meaning that they apply to all humans, but also diachronic—they have in some manner always existed. Indeed, Blau and Moncada claim, "all people everywhere and at all times – probably since humans began to talk – have recognized human rights within their circles of kin and friends. What is new is recognizing the human rights of all others. We might say that Kant's moral imperative has been universalized and globalized" (Blau and Moncada 2005, 157). This surprising claim distils human rights to a perennial reflex that provides the bedrock on which their normative claim stands: human rights realize in us our ontologically defined potential as biological and social beings! As seen above, human rights correspond, Blau and Moncada contend, to the "peculiarities of our human condition". However, the dialectic of the always existing, but equally the frequently denied nature of human rights, makes it difficult to understand what are the historical and social conditions through which human rights have become institutionalized and have acquired their social efficacy and normative persuasiveness. If all social situations that have enabled individuals to flourish in communities are equated to the realization of human rights, then there is nothing in particular to be grasped in contemporary human rights. The new is not so new after all.

For instance, one of their central empirical claims is that the global human rights revolution is a response to neoliberalism (Blau and Moncada 2005, 24). Does this mean that human rights were secure in the context of earlier variants of postwar capitalism or pre-capitalist formations? Surely not. Equally, they also argue, "People in any poor, underdeveloped country can maintain communities and societies and live by human rights tenets so long as conditions are stable, just as people did in pre-industrial America" (Blau and Moncada 2005, 24). This suggests that absent outside perturbation, that is, neoliberal globalization, human rights will be secured. This, I would argue is doubtful. The claim that human rights have always been "recognized" amongst family and kin and that the contemporary challenge is to expand them to a global community glosses over a variety of social dynamics and processes that have not been conducive to what we now call human rights in the past or the present, for instance, patriarchy. Equally it ignores the extent to which "social cohesion" is compatible with inequalities based on ascriptive status systems (Howard 1995a, 2). This is not to exclude the possibility that different historical or current social forms are protective of what we currently designate as human rights, but it fails to provide us with an understanding of the actual social dynamics and processes, and the particularity of the normative claims, that are rights protective.

What is at work here is a variant of the bait and switch I identified in Turner's argument, which as in Turner's case is likely unintended. The bait is the sociologically defensible claim that human groupings, communities, or societies are inherently based on forms of socially mediated interdependence. Members have different forms of obligation to each other, frequently expressed in normative terms that may under certain conditions foster a sense of solidarity. The switch, however, is to equate this arguably trans-historical dimension of sociality with human rights themselves. This is not only anachronistic in the sense that it obviates, as I argued in the previous chapter, the recent emergence of human rights, but it also blurs levels of analysis by linking normative analysis with a specific contingent historical development, to wit, the contemporary centrality of human rights as moral and political vernacular. It normatively deduces rather than sociologically explains human rights.

Said differently, to claim that human societies are founded on a logic of interdependence and solidarity, and that under certain conditions this moral bond enables individuals to flourish in conditions of equality, cannot lead to the conclusion that human rights actualize this potential merely because the logic of human rights allegedly discursively echoes this basic normative insight. As with Turner, this claim renders unnecessary an analysis of the variety of social dynamics and processes that have been rights protective across time and space. Perhaps more significantly, it does not enable an understanding of the specificity of human rights claims. In what ways are they an advance over previous forms of social protection? In what ways might they be a retreat?[19]

In addition there is a second, probably equally unintended, evasive manoeuvre in the manner in which they set up their argument. Blau and Moncada oppose liberalism and human rights as two competing worldviews. In each case they provide an analysis of the normative implications of both, and the type of societies that each of them ideally imagines. One of them, liberalism, however, is at odds with the proposed normative essence of society, namely, interdependence and mutuality. However, whereas their discussion of liberalism locates it historically and identifies a number of social processes and institutions that have allowed it to flourish, including its global proliferation under neoliberal globalization, this is not the case with human rights. Aside from a descriptive discussion of the international instruments, illustrations of contemporary human rights advocacy, and an enumeration of human rights concepts enshrined in constitutions, there is no attempt to explain the institutional and historical context that has given rise to human rights. Said simply, they are not comparing like with like. The closest they come to explaining the dynamics of the genesis of human rights is when they claim, "human rights are advanced through human struggles. They have been formalized largely in response to these struggles, but only afterwards when people can reflect on their significance" (Blau and Moncada 2005, 63). In equating human rights to "human struggles" more generally, they make human rights synonymous with all progressive struggles, foreclosing the possibility of grasping the specificity of human rights as a form of struggle or even a normative ideal.[20]

This is perhaps why they can claim, as seen above, that human rights facilitate cooperation and collaboration and contribute to strengthening democracy and encouraging economic fairness (Blau and Moncada 2005, 28), or that the logic of human rights is liberating, embeds individuals in their communities, and sustains dialogical processes of recognition (Blau and Moncada 2005, 28–29). Because human rights are framed as a normative principle, a logic, an ethic, or in some cases an idealized legal responsibility (Blau and Moncada 2007), Blau and Moncada do not need to take into account the myriad ways in which human rights have been institutionalized by governments and NGOs, or taken up by social movements. However, "passionately pursued by individuals" driven by the "impulse to make the world more just, more secure, more fair – more humane in short", human rights have, as the human rights lawyer and legal scholar David Kennedy reminds us, a dark side (2005, 327). Contrary to what Blau and Moncada claim, Kennedy notes that reframing "emancipatory objectives in human rights terms" can actually discourage political engagement, or encourage human rights to pursue unrealizable results (2005, 24). Soberly, he claims,

> Aspiring to good, humanitarians too often mute awareness that their best ideas can have bad consequences. When things do go wrong, rather than facing the darker consequences of humanitarian work, we too often simply redouble our efforts and intensify our condemnation of whatever other forces we can find to hold responsible. (2005, 327)[21]

Kennedy's intent, or mine, is not to savage human rights or to caricature them as a ruse that obfuscates the operation of neoliberal globalization, as do the likes of Žižek (2005) or Teeple (2005). Kennedy insists that the human rights impulse "survives exposures" to its dark sides (2005, 327). This is a claim made by other scholars who see the simultaneous presence of progressive and regressive aspects in human rights activism, such as Upendra Baxi through his distinction between "desire-in dominance" and "desire-in-insurrection" politics (1998, 129) or Neil Stammers focus on the "paradox of institutionalization" (2009), not to mention Woodiwiss' broader analysis that uses the metaphor of human sacrifice as his epistemological entry into rights (2005a, 9). The ability to gauge the efficacy of human rights depends crucially, as I will show in the next chapter, on being able to conceptualize how human rights become embodied and mobilized in concrete social practices, and the broader historical and social contexts in which this occurs.

To briefly take an example, Blau and Moncada are certainly right to highlight the importance of the emergence of a human rights vernacular in the global south in the 1990s. However, rather than understanding this phenomenon as an instantiation of a historically ongoing struggle against social injustice, in this case against neoliberalism, the "new [human] rights advocacy" is better grasped as the contingent outcome of the intersection of significant changes in both the organizational fields of human rights and international development with the emergence of a number of social justice and environmental movements in the global south, which coalesced around the language of human rights, of course, against the backdrop of neoliberal globalization (Nelson and Dorsey 2008).

Why and how these movements converged around and leveraged the social and normative power of human rights is, I would argue, a sociologically more effectual way of engaging with human rights. Similarly, in my work on the emergence of the human right to food, the prospect of describing hunger as a human right violation did not only hinge on the soaring of activism on behalf of civil and political human rights in the 1970s. It also, and crucially, rested on the weakening of the postwar imaginaries that had dominated thinking on hunger, that is, humanitarianism and modernist developmentalism, and on the ability to repurpose the social technologies of the human rights political imaginary that had been developed to deal with violations of civil and political human rights (López 2015, 13).

As I argued in Chap. 2, we cannot ignore the social power of the idealism, moral conviction, and normative persuasion attached to contemporary human rights. Equally, however, we would be derelict in our duty as sociologists, or activists, to think of ideals, moral convictions, or normative persuasiveness as operating through some kind of mind ether. Ideas and norms travel socially in cultural forms (Alexander 2006) through relational networks. Normative ideals move across social space and are causally efficacious insofar as they can be stabilized in institutionalized settings, and enacted in performances. Understood in terms of a political imaginary, they are structured by particular representational forms that provide the scaffolding of meaning, are attached to social technologies and modes of agency and subjectivity that pattern behaviour, and are subject to specific organizational conditions.

Much the same could be said regarding constitutions. Though a key object of analysis of nineteenth-century sociological thought, interest in them subsequently waned throughout the twentieth century (Thornhill 2011). Even though the social legitimacy of constitutions requires that they be read in terms of hierarchies of principles and norms, this does not mean they are wholly the product of normative deduction or that it is normative inference that makes them causally efficacious. As recent research in the area of constitutional ethnography and the sociology of constitutions reveals, the work that constitutions do cannot be understood outside of the social, cultural, and political practices that structure their deployment. In other words, it is socially and culturally embodied and enabled normative labour rather than abstract and disembodied normative work (Scheppele 2004; Thornhill 2011; Alexander 2006, 151–92). This is not to argue against amending constitutions and attempting to bend them towards more democratic arrangements, but, instead, to highlight that the labour human rights concepts might do in constitutions cannot be grasped exclusively in terms of human rights' normative resonance, as is implicit in Blau and Moncada's advocacy for constitutional change.

Ultimately, I believe Blau and Moncada reflect in their analysis the moral conviction that is sparked by the contemporary human rights political imaginary as they attempt to inflect it sociologically. This is a point to which I will return in the conclusion of this chapter. The extent to which this is so is, to my mind, revealed by their desire to embody or represent human rights action, not only by incorporating its normative mode of persuasion but by actually seeking to develop a sociological variant of human rights agency or advocacy—for example, NGOs, campaigns for constitutional reform, and the professional sociologist as a public intellectual advocating for human rights. They do not, I believe, reflect upon human rights with the critical spirit that is sociology's most formidable attribute. A critical spirit that does not arise from cynicism but from the recognition that sociologists are social beings always and inevitably at risk of reproducing society's representations rather than explaining them.[22] In other words, like Turner they engage in a sociology *for* rather than a sociology *of* human rights. Before concluding, in the next section I more briefly describe three further frequently noted efforts to conscript sociology to the cause of human rights.

Grounding Human Rights in Their Contemporary Necessity

Both Turner and Blau and Moncada deep mine human and social ontology in an effort to lay bare the bedrock upon which human rights might be grounded. In so doing they mimic, albeit in a different register, the search for deep historical roots so integral to the human rights political imaginary. However for some sociologists, advocating a normative turn towards human rights, it is sufficient to demonstrate that human rights' moral, ethical, or political necessity originates in current social arrangements, an approach, as already seen, that Turner and Blau and Moncada conjoin with their more deep-rooted ontological explorations.

In this section, I review the arguments of three contributions that adopt this strategy. I begin with the work of another pioneer in the field of the sociology of human rights, Rhoda Howard-Hassmann,[23] for whom the contemporary indispensability of human rights originates in the exigencies of social modernization. This is followed by a discussion of Gideon Sjoberg, Elizabeth Gill and Norma William's analysis that frames human rights as a moral standard required to constrain the power of increasingly complex and global organizations. I conclude this section with a discussion of Michael Burawoy's influential Polanyi-inspired call for a public sociology for human rights.

Howard-Hassmann not only eschews the normative ontological spelunking undertaken by Turner and Blau and Moncada, she insists that efforts to ground human rights in empirical or normative accounts of the universality of human wants or needs are bound to prove insufficient. Whether it be the basic rights approach spearheaded by Henry Shue

(1980; see Beitz and Goodin 2009), R. J. Vincent's enumeration of basic human rights (1986), or comparable initiatives, all use human nature to extrapolate human wants, desire, and needs or to define what constitutes a dignified life (Howard 1995b, 14–15). The problem, Howard-Hassmann contends, is that human nature is variable. Though not uncoupled from biological needs, human nature is importantly defined by norms, values, and the desires acquired through socialization and the manner in which this process is modulated by competing cultural ideals. Consequently, "there are no basic human needs, human desires or human rights separate from what human thought considers to be basic" (Howard 1995b, 15). Instead, citing Jack Donnelly, Howard-Hassmann maintains that human rights are best grasped as social constructs. Neither God-given nor physically determined, "human rights arise from human action and represent the choice of a particular moral vision of human potentiality and the institutions for realising that vision" (Donnelly cited in Howard 1995b, 15).

Howard-Hassmann claims that a sociologically framed analysis shows that human rights "are absolutely necessary in the modern world" (Howard 1995b, 8). Coinciding with the rise of the bourgeoisie, the evolution of capitalist social relations required the state "to honor not only a man's property but also his life, his liberty and his opinions" (Howard 1995b, 29). For her, unlike for Blau and Moncada, human rights are not merely compatible with liberalism but are inseparable from it. In a more fundamental sense, she understands human rights as a key dimension of the transition from *gemeinschaft* to *gesellschaft*, from a thick to a thin community. In the latter, individuals frequently leave primary attachments behind to associate with strangers; an individual can choose "one's occupation, place of residence, and marriage partners. Ties to primary kin, place of origin, and church are loose and may be cut off entirely" (Howard 1995b, 25–26).

As a result, human rights become the axis around which a new social moral order is articulated, in which "human dignity consists not of acquiescence to hierarchical order but of equality and assertion of one's claim to respect" (Howard 1995b, 27). Moreover, insofar as "the individual is presumed to have a strong need for separation from the community" in the context of modernization (Howard 1995b, 29), then liberal human rights, understood as freedom from social, cultural, and political intimidation and respect for an individual's property and privacy, become the human armour necessary to protect the nascent ethos of liberal society in capitalist Europe. This, according to Howard-Hassmann, makes human rights "a social fact" (Howard 1995b, 16).

Despite their acknowledged Western European origin and their non-equivalence with generalized conceptions of justice (Howard 1995b, 19), human rights are well on their way to becoming globalized. This is not merely because of their moral persuasiveness, which Howard-Hassmann is at pains to demonstrate, or their coercive enforcement, but because the same process that triggered their development, that is, social modernization, is being extended throughout the globe:

> Modernization appears to be an unavoidable social phenomenon. It is difficult for any society to resist the impact of an international division of labor, of world information flows, of the social model of individuation and freedom. As the world converges into one, ideals of human rights affect the otherwise quiescent underclasses of many societies. Modernization brings openness, opportunity, the merit principle. It permits individuals to leave repressive families and closed communities, and to challenge the authority of established elders. (Howard 1995b, 129)

What is more, her awareness of the abuses associated with the processes of modernization does not diminish her enthusiasm for human rights, quite the contrary: both the inevitability of modernization and its potential for harm make human rights all the more relevant (Howard 1995b, 129).

It is for this reason that an important aspect of her sociology for human rights involves developing arguments against moral or normative positions that to her mind threaten human rights. She identifies five: traditionalism, radical conservatism, left-collectivism, status radicalism, and radical capitalism. The first rejects the universalism of human rights and maintains that the preservation of traditional cultural values offers suitable protection for individuals, making permissible the violation of liberal human rights, for instance, in the case of Asian or African values (Howard 1995b, 4).

Radical conservatism, or right communitarianism, faults liberal human rights with the excesses of contemporary individual freedom that are said to be undermining community, tradition, and consequently social order (Howard 1995b, 4). Left-collectivism is a "third world" challenge that opposes the imperialism of Western liberal human rights through its defence of national sovereignty and the primacy of group over individual rights (Howard 1995b, 4). While, status radicalism maps onto the terrain of identity politics and its indictment of the universality of liberal individual human rights. It is claimed that the latter provides cover for the reproduction of the privilege of particular social and political subjects, typically wealthy white men (Howard 1995b, 5). The first four challenges are united in their dependence on a communitarian ethos and their suspicion of the individualism allegedly championed by a liberal conception of human rights. The last, radical capitalism, or "social minimalism", resonates with Blau and Moncada's critique of liberalism: the acceptance of autonomy and freedom while rejecting correlative social obligations, namely, economic rights (Howard 1995b, 3).

At times, Howard-Hassmann's argument is nuanced and insightful as when she draws attention to the tendency, amongst those that espouse variants of the communitarian critique, to romanticize community and obviate entrenched injustice and social inequality (Howard 1995b, 8). Yet she can, also, be frustratingly ideological as when she dispatches left-collectivism by asserting, "the left collectivist position can tolerate extreme state terror and even genocidal practices", or that it denies "rights to the rich" (Howard 1995a, 3), setting the stage to crown her minimalist rendering of social democracy as the political system capable of accommodating all human rights (Howard 1995b, 199). Ultimately, no matter the particular normative argument put forward, her defence of liberal human rights relies on an always already existing normative identity between modernization, individualism, and human rights:

> Modernized society is inhabited by individuals. As individuals, they sometimes identify themselves as members of groups or collectivities but not necessarily in a predictable or static manner. The liberal stress on individual rights therefore remain the appropriate basis for the entire conception of human rights. (Howard 1995b, 217)

Howard-Hassmann's attempt to normatively derive liberal human rights from the evolution of modernity is, at first blush, plausible. However, by broadly locating the origin of human rights in the evolution of modernity, she obviates the need to address the institutional specificity of human rights. The problem is not that she locates the origin of human rights in bourgeois property rights as such, but that she develops a teleological normative defence of their existence rather than a sociological analysis of the contingency of their development, as in the case of Anthony Woodiwiss' reading of the evolution of broader categories of rights from property rights (2005a).

In arguing that human rights are a social fact, and that indeed so are modernity (Howard 1995b, 19) and global modernization (Howard 1995b, 130), she transforms human rights' real existence as social-relational entities, and their concomitant power to pattern the behaviour of individuals or groups under certain conditions, into an absolute normative necessity. In other words, just as with Turner, human rights provide a taken-for-granted normative point of departure and not the conclusion of an open-ended normative sociological analysis. Sociological normativity, in the context of modernity, *ipso facto* equals human rights. In Howard-Hassmann's interpretation, human rights exist as principles, a normative orientation, or as legal instruments but never as social relations or mechanisms. Their ability to operate in the social world, or the manner in which they interpellate social beings, is not discussed because human rights are presupposed by social modernization itself. It is a process of discovering a predetermined truth about modernity.

Insofar as modernization fails to live up to human rights ideals, this is not due to any deficiency on the part of human rights, or tensions between human rights and modernization or between human rights and capitalism, but to the fact that human rights have not yet been fully realized. They are, to quote Costas Douzinas' allusion to Bloch, the "promise of the 'not yet'" (2000, 308), or in the words of Slaughter, human rights are represented through the literary trope of "an inherency-in-becoming that anticipates the day when human rights law's common sense will become the public culture of an international human rights order" (2009, 80). Consequently, radical capitalism/social minimalism is sustained because it is "a philosophy attractive to successful individuals"; however, "when citizens are possessed of all of their human rights", presumably at some point in the future, "they can act to better not only their own lives, but also the lives of others" (Howard 1995b, 222), withering away the stark antagonisms of capitalism.

Indeed, if in the words of one her critics, Howard-Hassmann is committed to "capitalism-prosperity-democracy-human rights, as an all-in-one package" (O'Connell 2009, 140), this is because she understands, to draw on Althusser's lexicon, modernization as "an expressive totality" (Althusser and Balibar 1970), where human rights express the normative essence of modernization. It is plausibly for this reason that she claims that "human rights represents modern human thought about the nature of justice" (Howard 1995b, 12) or that "the doctrine of human rights reflects the theoretical positions that many individuals have derived independently, the world over, whatever their cultures are claimed to dictate" (Howard 1995b, 16). Equally, it would account for why as a result of the global spread of modernization "there is now an international community of modern men and women who are increasingly capable, no matter how poor or oppressed they are, of recognizing when their human rights are violated" (Howard 1995b, 129). The telos of modernization if read correctly is human rights. Sociological analysis is used to normatively rationalize human rights rather than to explain their origin, development, or contemporary social traction.

Sjoberg et al. (2001) equally inscribe the development of human rights in a broader rights tradition. They trace it back to the pivotal figure of John Locke who "advanced the view that commoners had the right to life, liberty and property" rooted in the claim that "'man' had possessed these rights in the pre-social state, or state of nature" (2001, 17; cf. Woodiwiss 2005a). However, rather than equate human rights with the logic of social modernization like Howard-Hassmann, they, following a historical chronology of the rights doctrine in US history, conclude "the issue of rights emerged within the cauldron of major struggles over power". Consequently, rights condense "concern with power relationships within the social order", and are ultimately invoked in attempts to "restructure past social arrangements" (Sjoberg et al. 2001, 20). For sociology, the value added of human rights is twofold: normative and empirical, which I now discuss in turn.

Disputing the value-neutrality position adopted by sociological positivists, they claim, "moral inquiry has a fundamental place in sociological investigation" (Sjoberg et al. 2001, 14). Amidst the moral positions available to contemporary sociology, they find the communitarian and utilitarian positions unsatisfactory due, amongst other reasons, to their inability to accommodate minority claims and their inherent majoritarianism. Equally, they deem strong forms of relativism "inherently flawed" (2001, 15). However, insofar as human rights posit the need to contain and redirect "the employment of social power by the state and other powerful organizations [...] bent on undermining human dignity in a systematic manner", it provides a more persuasive moral standard upon which to anchor sociological analysis (Sjoberg et al. 2001, 12).

Moreover, it does so in such a way as to invert the polarity between duties and rights typically encoded in citizenship rights. Implicit in the rights associated with citizenship is an "ethicist" approach whereby it is through "the performance of duties [that] one comes to acquire rights" (Sjoberg et al. 2001, 16). In contrast, human rights "begin with rights and moves on to duties" (Sjoberg et al. 2001, 16). Threaded by the moral standard of human rights, sociology is not only positioned to explain but also normatively equipped to render judgement on social patterns in which state and non-state actors deploy social power to erode human dignity. Equally, a sociology so woven can insist on the primacy of rights over duties.

For the authors, the normative alignment between sociological explanation and moral judgement is fused to the empirical context in which human rights emerged, magnified by subsequent postwar trends. With respect to the first, they write,

> The Universal Declaration [UDHR] reflected a deep and abiding concern with the abuse of power, which was documented in the starkest possible way by the Holocaust, but was also apparent in the major shifts in political power relationships worldwide. The West was called upon to respond to the challenge to its historic domination of a vast colonial domain. (2001, 20)

Further they contend, "The Universal Declaration vastly expands the scope of the rights debate, and it does so within the framework of an international setting" (Sjoberg et al. 2001, 20). Amplifying the significance of human rights are a number intersecting postwar empirical trends. These include the weakening of state sovereignty, the rise to power of the US state, the spread of capitalism and the ascendance of multinational corporations, the rise of transnational organizations (e.g., IMF, WTO, new intra-national conflicts, regionalisms, and localisms), the spread of democratic ideals, the growth of NGOs and professional associations, and a continued trend towards individuation (Sjoberg et al. 2001, 21–24).

While some of these postwar dynamics underwrite the types of moral claims that human rights enable, other pose significant threats. Not least are the dangers to human dignity posed by both private and public organizations that have extended their scope both within and beyond nations (Sjoberg et al. 2001, 26). In fact, complex organizations, they contend, are centrally implicated in human rights abuses to the extent that the latter typically arise "from the misuse of organizational power, which can arise when human agents act in behalf of organized power relationships" (Sjoberg et al. 2001, 37). They thus claim it was this type of organizational misuse of social power, in Nazi Germany, that contributed to the emergence of human rights in the postwar period as a counterweight.

Sjoberg, Gill, and Williams convincingly show that complex hierarchical organizations, be they public or private, have had and continue to have the potential to be complicit in the denigration of human beings. The normative conclusion they draw, with which it is difficult to disagree, is that we require mechanisms "to control and channel the activities of organized power groups so as to enhance human dignity" (Sjoberg et al. 2001, 42). However, their argument—that human rights provide the ideals and principles to do so—though a creative reading of human rights, is significantly less persuasive. Their assertion that human rights arose as a response to the Nazi atrocities in the Holocaust and as a challenge to empire and colonialism is, as I argued in the previous chapter, not a critical sociological analysis of the conditions of possibility of the emergence of human rights but rather a sociological echo of a key thin narrative that reproduces the contemporary political imaginary without necessarily explaining it.

For all the well-deserved focus that they train on complex organizations, their analysis completely eschews the organizational foundations of human rights. In fact, they go as far as to claim that even if human rights' moral orientation should fail to be institutionalized, some variant of human rights "remains one of the few most viable moral alternatives available for containing" and keeping organizational power in check (Sjoberg et al. 2001, 12). This is not to reduce moral claims to their organizational embodiments, but rather to highlight that organizational figurations and patterned social practices are necessary carriers of moral claims, as intimated by the political imaginary model.

More recently, Sjoberg has argued that more effort should be directed at holding heads of corporations responsible, designating certain profit-making activities elicit, reviewing the legal structure of corporations, and devising new modalities of punishment and compliance, as well as concocting new forms of collective power as an alternative to corporations (Sjoberg 2009, 170–74). Absent is any consideration of how human rights' allegedly potent moral message is made culturally meaningful, how it achieves social traction or is made socially efficacious. The morality of human rights alchemically becomes sociology's normative stone.

Perhaps the most well-known call to normative arms aimed at sociologists is Michael Burawoy's American Sociological Association presidential address in 2004 (2005).[24] Though in his petition for a public sociology, he mentions human rights indirectly only twice (2005, 5, 8), he does align the normative goal of sociology with that of humanity by describing sociology's partisanship with civil society in the struggle to keep both "state despotism and market tyranny" at bay (Burawoy 2005, 24). In his introduction to the *Public Sociologies Reader*, on the other hand, following the path inaugurated by Blau and Moncada, he explicitly links sociology's normative mission to the defence of human rights: "human rights become publicly defensible if they become part of a public sociology" (2006, 6). Burawoy acknowledges the dark side of human rights' virtue by pointing to their political and ideological instrumentalization, not to mention the frequent slow and capricious pace of their implementation as they become entangled in geopolitics. Nonetheless, he maintains that the advantage of the human rights framework is "its widespread appeal" (2006, 5). In order to account for the appeal of human rights, Burawoy builds on his earlier pivot towards Polanyi (Burawoy 2003).[25]

Following Polanyi, Burawoy writes, "markets tend to destroy the very conditions of their existence, and generate a countermovement by society for its self-protection" (2006, 7). The forms that protective societal countermovements take, and the role to which sociology is assigned within them, depend on historical circumstances and the dynamics between state, civil society, and the market. In a Polanyian-inspired narrative, Burawoy identifies three periods. In the first, in mid-nineteenth-century England, the commodification of labour "led to a counterrebellion by society"—for example, labour organizations, cooperatives, and employment legislation. This was followed by differing but equally self-protective movements, in European and North American societies (Burawoy 2006, 7). The sociological component of the societal move to counteract injurious market dynamics took the form of a "strong moral and reformist bent"—a "utopian sociology" intimately linked to the centrality of the "self-organization of society" (Burawoy 2006, 7).

The turn of the twentieth century saw a strong push towards market expansion at the international level, creating the conditions for the second period. By the 1930s, as a result of economic instability, a number of countermovements emerged to contain the destructive nature of international market pressures. While not all progressive, they shared the strategy of subjugating market dynamics to various modalities of state control, for example, fascism, communism in the form of collectivization and planning, the New Deal, and Social Democracy. Burawoy notes, "In Polanyi's view these new forms of state – destroying society or reconstructing it in the image of the state – owed their origins to the overextension of markets" (Burawoy 2006, 8). While sociology disappeared in some countries, for example, Nazi Germany and the Soviet Union, in others, sociology embodied the protective ethos of the era by turning its focus towards policy science, driven by a concern with "social rights", "social inequality", "status attainment", "stability of liberal democracy", "participation in organizations", and "conditions for modernization" (Burawoy 2006, 8). In this context, state and civil society were understood to be allies in the containment of market excesses (Burawoy 2006, 8).

The third period, one that Polanyi did not see, is a response to neoliberal globalization whose "messianism", Burawoy contends, surpasses "the two previous rounds of market idolatry" (2006, 8). Society's countermovement has been to "grope forward from the local and national to a global scale" exemplified by transnational social movements and NGOs, while sociology has been cast in the role of "a *public sociology* concerned to protect distinctively *human rights* of local communities – freedom from the depredations of markets and states, freedom to survive and collectively self-organize" (Burawoy 2006, 8–9 emphasis in original).

Burawoy is careful to note that there is no automaticity in society's protective countermovement, and much militates against it. Consequently, if sociology is to fulfil its part in these potential counterhegemonic movements, it should contribute to developing "a common language through which we can recognize common experiences at different ends of the world order. A public sociology will have to recognize the global character of social issues" (2006, 13). In addition, because the nation-state can no longer be assumed to be a default ally against the excesses of the global market, not least because it is frequently neoliberalism's willing agent, public sociology's primary audience should be the diverse publics that make up "global civil society" (Burawoy 2006, 13).

Burawoy's Polanyian interpretation of human rights is suggestive and, as is the case with Blau and Moncada, it highlights the prevalence of human rights in the political and moral vernacular of the concatenation of social movements challenging neoliberal globalization, a matter not to be ignored. However, attempting to explain the origin, and the contemporary pertinence, of human rights by arguing "the universality of rights is the reaction or countermovement to the universality of markets" (Burawoy 2006, 9) yields modest explanatory gains, not least because as Dale rightly argues, the Polanyian concept of the countermovement is best understood as a general heuristic tool that alone has limited substantive explanatory value (Dale 2010a, 220).

It is possible to follow the path set out by Polanyi and accept that the systematic overreach of the market creates the conditions for societal countermovements. However, deducing from this general heuristic presupposition, via the felicitous homology between the universality of markets and the universality of rights, that human rights are the ethical core of the countermovement and consequently define sociology's role within such movements is itself an instance of indefensible overreach. Yet again as with the previous authors discussed in this chapter, once a normative need is discerned, and Burawoy presents a compelling account of such a need, in the form of a countermovement, human rights are presumed to fill that need. Human rights are the only game in town.

Conclusion

Although the general tenor of my comments in this chapter has been a critical one, I do not mean to imply that a sociology *for*, rather than a sociology *of* human rights, is incapable of producing valuable knowledge. In fact, as I have briefly pointed out with respect to each of the authors, they advance significant arguments regarding a possible normative mission for sociology and develop important sociologically informed normative readings of human rights that might be of use to human rights advocates. My main point of contention has been the striking elision between a normative orientation for sociology and human rights, which wittingly or not, contributes to reproducing human rights folk theories rather than sociologically interrogating them.

Consequently, the manner in which human rights are invoked by the sociologists discussed in this chapter provides us with a window into some of the characteristics of the human rights political imaginary itself. For example, it reveals the enormous persuasive power of both its normative claims and its representation of the world insofar as the aforementioned sociologists eschew the reflexivity that sociological analysis would normally require. Mimesis of human rights' alleged deep historical roots takes the form of planting the seed of human rights in human and social ontology, or in modernity. In this way, the sociologists discussed above strengthen human rights' foundational claims by demonstrating that the social fabric has always, or at least now, depends on the existence of human rights. In some instances, as we have seen, sociologists do not merely mirror normative modes of reasoning; they go as far as calling for organizational forms, that is, NGOs, and advocacy campaigns; practices that are quintessential to the reproduction of the human rights political imaginary.

For the most part, the sociologists discussed here merely translate human rights discourse into sociological language. They also reproduce the modes of discursivity of the broader human rights political imaginary by relying on legal modes of reasoning as witnessed by the invocation of the diverse human rights instruments as sources of binding norms or principles. As noted above, that lawyers and activists should do so is scarcely surprising, but it is startling that sociologists should obviate the need to think about the actual social relations, mechanisms, and processes that enable such norms or principles to circulate socially and to have the social (in)efficacy that they do. Equally, to draw on the language of victims and vulnerability is, as I will argue in Chap. 5, to tether sociology uncritically to one of human rights' key nodal figures.

The sociological accounts of human rights dealt with in this chapter also mimic human rights in another important way. Just as the normative content of human rights tends to be thin to maximize its diffusion, the sociological accounts are equally remarkably thin, not specifying concrete social and institutional arrangements that make human rights social things, conflating human rights with social justice, modernity, human dignity, and countermovements more generally. Normative engagement with a sociological declension can never be separated from an analysis of what particular instituted forms make possible, the source of their social power, and their ability to shepherd sympathy.

Whatever contributions sociology might make to normative analysis, sociologists cannot forsake the critical reflexive distance that enables us to try to understand anew what we already understand. We should not, to paraphrase Alexander, "loose our sociology" (2006, 15). This not because, as some critics argue, human rights do not matter, but precisely because they might. Figuring out how and why they might matter must remain our first task. In the chapter that follows, I review and engage with a number of contributions that draw on a key sociological concept, social practice, to develop analyses of human rights. I build on such accounts to continue developing the model of political imaginary introduced in the previous chapter.

Notes

1. Badiou claims that human rights participate in the conservative project of regulating the misery that exists rather than inaugurating the possibility of an emancipatory project: "The Law (Human rights, etc.) is always *already there*. It regulates judgments and opinions concerning the evil that happens in some variable elsewhere. But there is no question of reconsidering the foundation of this 'Law', of going right back to the conservative identity that sustains it" (Badiou 2001, 33). As Woodiwiss argues, Badiou's position is an exemplar of those who would assert that "a politics grounded in an optimistic view of human nature would be better able to protect individuals than the law since the latter is grounded in a pessimistic view that almost invites victimization" (2005a, xiv). This is a position that as Woodiwiss rightly highlights ignores the protective and moderating effect of legally entrenched rights.
2. On speech acts, see Austin (1962) and Searle (1969).
3. Stephen Hopgood refers to this as an instance of social magic: "in truth the totem [the sacralisation of human suffering] empowered the symbol, which gave moral authority to the law. And now the law is held to be the source of primary authority. This encapsulates the process of constructing moral authority in order to replace an ailing god with human law" (2013, 38).
4. Even in the case where scholars do not explicitly argue for a normative turn, they nonetheless suggest that human rights have the potential to "renew sociology" (Hynes et al. 2012b, 788). Incidentally, this dynamic is visible in other claims in which major social transformations such as globalization (Giddens 1999), second modernity (Beck 2000a), postmodernism (Seidman 1991), new mobilities (Urry 2012), and technoscience (Latour 1987) allegedly require a significant overhaul of some fundamental aspect of the discipline. Of course, as James B. Rule quite convincingly shows in *Theory and Progress in Social Science*, the relentless injunction for the new is frequently driven by unacknowledged aesthetic and normative choices rather than explanatory gains (1997).
5. The roots of American objectivism are found in Comte's positivism and the British empirical tradition of John Stuart Mill and Herbert Spencer (Bannister 1987). On positivism see Bryant (1985). On Tönnies introduction of positivism and empiricism into a German context, see Bond (2009).

6. The comments in this paragraph pertain to American sociology. The emphasis is warranted insofar as the majority of the authors arguing vigorously for a human rights-propelled normative shift are American, by birth or institutional affiliation. The notable exception is of course Bryan Turner. Developments in American sociology are significant further afield insofar as Woodiwiss persuasively argues, "within the context of the Cold War and the signing of the North Atlantic Treaty of 1949, the institutional site wherein sociological thinking developed became Atlantic rather than European in the sense that the United States with its distinctively individualistic culture became the principal locus of sociology's development" (Woodiwiss 2005b, 106). Canadian sociology was significantly impacted by US sociology. In consequence of the paucity of Canadian sociologists, a large number of American-trained PhDs were hired to meet exploding demand in the 1960s. This migration brought a sundry bunch: functionalists, positivists, and sociologists who identified with the New Left (Brym and Saint-Pierre 1997, 545). However, for reasons that cannot be explored here, Canadian sociology has not adopted the US model of privileging quantitative methods. Indeed quite to the contrary, whereas critics of US sociology will draw attention to its over-infatuation with quantitative methods, Canadian along with British sociology is frequently faulted for its underdevelopment of multivariate quantitative methods (Baer 2005, 498; Payne et al. 2004). The quantitative deficit in Canadian sociology may however be more significant than in Britain and other European countries (Baer 2005, 499).
7. His list of extrasociological sociologists included the following: "Gayatri Chakravorty Spivak, Trinh T. Minh-ha, Henry Louis Gates, Toni Morrison, Spike Lee, Patricia Hills Collins, bell hooks, Teresa de Lauretis, Cornel West, Mary Daley, Andrea Dworkin, Kate Millett, Judith Butler, Donna Haraway, Gloria Anzaldúa" (Lemert 1995, 209).
8. It is of course possible that this exercise in reflexivity can eventuate in the conclusion that sociologists have the normative obligation to take sides, give voice, or become catalysts for public moral reasoning. However, it need not.
9. In the spirit of disclosure, this is the stance that informs my own position on the question of value neutrality and normativity.
10. Indeed one might argue that the energy with which Foucault was embraced by sociology is due to the fact that it provided a non-Parsonian

theoretical strategy for thinking about the basis of normativity in social relations.

11. A comparable emphasis on social actors as active normative agents is to be found in the work of Luc Boltanski and Laurent Thévenot (2006) on justification and Alexander's work on the civil sphere (2006) discussed in the previous chapter.
12. In this case, we see sociology reproducing the same streamlined human rights moral logic described above: the facticity of a wrong entails a unanimous commitment to provide remedy.
13. Turner also attributes a relativistic reading of rights to the sociology of knowledge tradition flowing from Adorno and Horkheimer's reading of Mannheim (1993, 493).
14. Equally, it is difficult to resist the temptation to invoke the caricature argument that Turner uses to critique Marx's conception of rights to characterize Turner's own reading of Marx. Marx's reading of the emergence of rights in Capital, while occasionally relying on parody, is a rigorous attempt to understand the emergence of rights in the context of capitalist social relations. Indeed, Anthony Woodiwiss' Marxist-inspired reading of bourgeois and human rights (Woodiwiss 2005a) can be extremely illuminating and while not dismissive of rights as such, quite to the contrary, provides a more nuanced understanding of what human rights might and might not be able to achieve.
15. Turner uses the term "patrism" to refer to attempts to anchor power over women and sexual behaviour in the context of the erosion of institutionalized forms of patriarchy in religion and/or the state (Turner 2006, 87–88).
16. This omission is remedied in later publications (Blau and Moncada 2009a, b). They do cite the work of Rhoda Howard-Hassmann who is one of the first sociologists off the mark in her engagement with human rights (Howard 1995a, b; Howard-Hassmann 2005).
17. In Chap. 6, I contrast the differential manner in which the human rights political imaginary gets entangled with the law in Europe and the US.
18. For a powerful institutionalist account of the epistemological and normative dominance of market fundamentalism, see Somers and Block (2005), Somers (2008), and Block (2007). For a sympathetic critique, see López (2016).
19. This is the same as claiming that democracy can be accounted for sociologically by a normative theory of democracy that echoes the

democratic desire of populations. Important as normative theories of democracy are, as the late Charles Tilly masterfully shows, and contemporary attempts to democratize countries painfully reveal, democracy historically has been a rare and extremely unlikely form of political organization that is best grasped sociologically in terms of a series of contingent institutional changes and processes that cannot be deduced from normative accounts of democracy (2007).

20. This criticism applies to other authors that distil human rights into a trans-historical logic of resistance, for example, Stammers (2009) and Armaline et al. (2015).
21. Kennedy argues that if one defines humanitarianism broadly, as referring to the desire to make the world more just through a variety of projects underwritten by sundry professional and moral vocabularies (2005, 236), then one can detect the presence of human rights talk in virtually all contemporary humanitarian discourse if only "to get in the door before speaking instrumentally, or in more exclusively ethical terms" (2005, 5). This said, as Moyn (2010) and Barnett (2011) argue in their respective analyses of the emergence of human rights and humanitarianism, the manner in which they are currently intertwined should not obfuscate their differing origins or modes of development.
22. This does not exclude the possibility that societal representations in some circumstances provide an adequate account of the social causes of phenomena, nor, as I argued in the previous chapter, that sociologists in some instances, despite their best efforts, contribute to reproducing social doxa instead of interrogating it.
23. Her publications date back to the 1980s, for example, Howard (1986) and Howard and Donnelly (1986).
24. Blau and Moncada claim that this is an exemplar of the normative shift that has taken hold of sociology (2009a, 507). Though favourably received by some, as John Scott notes, it has been subject to a mixed reception (2005), suggesting that the address does not stand synecdochically for the discipline (cf. Brady 2004; Holmwood 2007; Nielsen 2004; Tittle 2004; J. Turner H. 2005).
25. In this article, Burawoy contends that in order to overcome the limitations of both Marx and classical Marxism it is necessary to engage Polanyi and Gramsci dialogically, arguing that counterhegemonic potential is to be found at the interplay between market and society. Startling, Burawoy claims that this move is required due the market's epiphenomenal

position for Marx as a result of his dogged focus on production. While this is an understandable account of Burawoy's previous focus on production, anyone who has ventured beyond the first chapters of Capital volume one and seriously read volumes two and three knows that the market is far from epiphenomenal in Marx's mature work. Surprisingly, Burawoy adopts Polanyi's decidedly analytically weaker but normatively more suggestive conception of the market, glossing over the fact that one of Marx's most perspicacious analytical accomplishments was identifying the specificity of the functioning of markets in capitalist social formations. This, unfortunately, is a broader trend amongst scholars working with the Polanyian concept of embeddedness; see López (2016).

Bibliography

Agger, Ben. 2007. *Public Sociology: From Social Facts to Literary Acts*. Lanham and New York: Rowman & Littlefield.

Alexander, Jeffrey C. 2006. *The Civil Sphere*. Oxford and New York: Oxford University Press.

Althusser, Louis, and Etienne Balibar. 1970. *Reading Capital*, Trans. Ben Brewster. London: NLB.

Anleu, Sharyn Roach. 1999. "Sociologists Confront Human Rights: The Problem of Universalism." *Journal of Sociology* 35 (2):198–212.

Armaline, William T., Davita S. Glasberg, and Bandana Purkayastha. 2015. *The Human Rights Enterprise: Political Sociology, State Power, and Social Movements*. Cambridge and Malden, MA: Polity.

Austin, John. 1962. *How to Do Things with Words*. Oxford and New York: Oxford University Press.

Badiou, Alain. 2001. *Ethics: An Essay on the Understanding of Evil*. London: Verso.

Baer, Douglas Edward. 2005. "On the Crisis in Canadian Sociology: Comment on McLaughlin." *The Canadian Journal of Sociology* 30 (4):491–502.

Bannister, Robert C. 1987. *Sociology and Scientism*. Chapel Hill: University of North Carolina.

Barnett, Michael N. 2011. *Empire of Humanity: A History of Humanitarianism*. Ithaca, NY: Cornell University Press.

Baxi, Upendra. 1998. "Voices of Suffering and the Future of Human Rights." *Transnational Law and Contemporary Problems* 8:125–169.

Beck, Ulrich. 2000a. "The Cosmopolitan Perspective: Sociology of the Second Age of Modernity." *The British Journal of Sociology* 51 (1):79–105.

Beck, Ulrich. 2000b. *What Is Globalization?* Cambridge and Malden, MA: Polity Press.

Becker, Howard S. 1967. "Whose Side Are We on." *Social Problems* 14 (3):239–247.

Beitz, Charles R., and Robert E. Goodin. 2009. *Global Basic Rights*. Oxford and New York: Oxford University Press.

Berger, Peter L. 1969. *The Sacred Canopy: Elements of a Sociological Theory of Religion*. New York: Anchor Books.

Blau, Judith. 2012. "Comparing Constitutions." In *Sociology and Human Rights: A Bill of Rights for the Twenty-First Century*, edited by Judith Blau and Mark Frezzo, 129–152. London and Los Angeles: Sage.

Blau, Judith R., David L. Brunsma, Alberto Moncada, and Catherine Zimmer, eds. 2008. *The Leading Rogue State: The United States and Human Rights*. Boulder and London: Paradigm Books.

Blau, Judith R., and Mark Frezzo, eds. 2012a. "Going Forward." In *Sociology and Human Rights*, 271–280. Los Angeles and London: Sage.

Blau, Judith R., and Mark Frezzo, eds. 2012b. *Sociology and Human Rights: A Bill of Rights for the Twenty-First Century*. Los Angeles and London: Sage.

Blau, Judith R., and Alberto Moncada. 2005. *Human Rights: Beyond the Liberal Vision*. Lanham, MD and New York: Rowman & Littlefield.

Blau, Judith R., and Alberto Moncada. 2007. "It Ought to Be a Crime: Criminalizing Human Rights Violations." *Sociological Forum* 22:364–371.

Blau, Judith R., and Alberto Moncada. 2008. "Freedom and Security." In *The Leading Rogue State: The United States and Human Rights*, edited by Judith R. Blau, David L. Brunsma, Alberto Moncada, and Catherine Zimmer, 233–237. Boulder and London: Paradigm Publishers.

Blau, Judith R., and Alberto Moncada. 2009a. "Sociological Theory and Human Rights: Two Logics, One World." In *The Blackwell Companion to Social Theory*, edited by Bryan S. Turner, 496–512. Oxford: Wiley-Blackwell.

Blau, Judith R., and Alberto Moncada. 2009b. "The New Humanism: Beyond Modernity and Postmodernism." In *Human Rights: Social Science Perspectives*, edited by Rhiannon Morgan and Bryan S. Turner, 147–156. London and New York: Routledge.

Blau, Judith R., and Keri E. Iyall Smith. 2006. *Public Sociologies Reader*. Lanham, MD: Rowman & Littlefield.

Block, Fred. 2007. "Understanding the Diverging Trajectories of the United States and Western Europe: A Neo-Polanyian Analysis." *Politics & Society* 35 (1):3–33.

Boltanski, Luc, and Laurent Thévenot. 2006. *On Justification: Economies of Worth*. Princeton, NJ: Princeton University Press.
Bond, Niall. 2009. "Ferdinand Tönnies and Western European Positivism." *Intellectual History Review* 19 (3):353–370.
Bosniak, Linda. 2000. "Citizenship Denationalized." *Indiana Journal of Global Legal Studies* 7 (2):447–509.
Bourdieu, Pierre. 1986. "Force of Law: Toward a Sociology of the Juridical Field." *The Hastings Law Journal* 38 (Journal Article):805.
Bourdieu, Pierre. 1998a. *Practical Reason: On the Theory of Action*. Stanford: Stanford University Press.
Bourdieu, Pierre. 1998b. *The State Nobility: Elite Schools in the Field of Power*. Cambridge and New York: Polity Press.
Bourdieu, Pierre, and Loïc J.D. Wacquant. 1992. *An Invitation to Reflexive Sociology*. Chicago and London: University of Chicago press.
Brady, David. 2004. "Why Public Sociology May Fail." *Social Forces* 82 (4):1629–1638.
Brenner, Neil, Bob Jessop, Martin Jones, and Gordon Macleod, eds. 2008. *State/Space: A Reader*. Oxford and Malden, MA: Blackwell.
Bryant, Christopher G. A. 1985. *Positivism in Social Theory and Research*. London: Macmillan.
Brym, Robert, and Celine Saint-Pierre. 1997. "Canadian Sociology." *Contemporary Sociology* 26 (5):543–546.
Burawoy, Michael. 2003. "For a Sociological Marxism: The Complementary Convergence of Antonio Gramsci and Karl Polanyi." *Politics & Society* 31 (2):193–261.
Burawoy, Michael. 2005. "For Public Sociology." *American Sociological Review* 70 (1):4–28.
Burawoy, Michael. 2006. "Introduction: A Public Sociology for Human Rights." In *Public Sociologies Reader*, edited by Judith Blau and Keri E. Iyall-Smith, 1–18. Boulder: Rowan and Littlefield.
Christie, Nancy. 2000. *Engendering the State: Family, Work, and Welfare in Canada*. Toronto: University of Toronto Press.
Clément, Dominique. 2008. *Canada's Rights Revolution: Social Movements and Social Change, 1937–82*. Vancouver: UBC Press.
Dale, Gareth. 2010a. *Karl Polanyi: The Limits of the Market*. Book, Whole. Polity.
Dale, Gareth. 2010b. "Social Democracy, Embeddedness and Decommodification: On the Conceptual Innovations and Intellectual Affiliations of Karl Polanyi." *New Political Economy* 15 (3):369–393.

Dale, Gareth. 2011. "Lineages of Embeddedness: On the Antecedents and Successors of a Polanyian Concept." *American Journal of Economics and Sociology* 70 (2):306–339.

Dale, Gareth. 2012. "Double Movements and Pendular Forces: Polanyian Perspectives on the Neoliberal Age." *Current Sociology* 60 (1):3–27.

Davis, Kathy. 2008. "Intersectionality as Buzzword: A Sociology of Science Perspective on What Makes a Feminist Theory Successful." *Feminist Theory* 9 (1):67–85.

De Sousa Santos, Boaventure. 2008. "Human Rights as an Emancipatory Script: Cultural and Political Conditions." In *Another Knowledge Is Possible*, edited by Boaventura De Sousa Santos, 3–40. London: Verso.

Douzinas, Costas. 2000. *The End of Human Rights: Critical Thought at the Turn of the Century*. Oxford and Portland, OR: Hart Publishing

Douzinas, Costas. 2007. *Human Rights and Empire: The Political Philosophy of Cosmopolitanism*. London and New York: Routledge.

Durkheim, Emile. 1974. *Sociology and Philosophy*. Book, Whole. Simon and Schuster.

Esping-Andersen, Gosta. 1998. *The Three Worlds of Welfare Capitalism*. Cambridge: Polity Press.

Frezzo, Mark. 2012. "Introduction." In *Sociology and Human Rights: A Bill of Rights for the Twenty-First Century*, edited by Judith Blau and Mark Frezzo, 3–14. London and New York: Sage Publications.

Giddens, Anthony. 1999. *Runaway World: How Globalization Is Reshaping Our Lives*. London: Profile Books.

Gough, Ian. 1975. "State Expenditure in Advanced Capitalism." *New Left Review* 92:53–92.

Gouldner, Alvin W. 1962. "Anti-Minotaur: The Myth of a Value-Free Sociology." *Social Problems* 9 (3):199–213.

Hafner-Burton, Emilie M. 2013. *Making Human Rights a Reality*. Princeton, NJ: Princeton University Press.

Hafner-Burton, Emilie M., and Kiyoteru Tsutsui. 2005. "Human Rights in a Globalizing World: The Paradox of Empty Promises1." *American Journal of Sociology* 110 (5):1373–1411.

Harding, Sandra. 1992. "Rethinking Standpoint Epistemology: What Is 'Strong Objectivity?'" *The Centennial Review* 36 (3):437–470.

Holmwood, John. 2007. "Sociology as Public Discourse and Professional Practice: A Critique of Michael Burawoy." *Sociological Theory* 25 (1):46–66.

Hopgood, Stephen. 2006. *Keepers of the Flame. Understanding Amnesty International*. Ithaca, NY: Cornell University Press.

Hopgood, Stephen. 2013. *The Endtimes of Human Rights*. Ithaca, NY: Cornell University Press.

Howard, Rhoda E. 1986. *Human Rights in Commonwealth Africa*. Totowa, NJ: Rowan and Littlefield.

Howard, Rhoda E. 1995a. "Human Rights and the Search for Community." *Journal of Peace Research* 32 (1):1–8.

Howard, Rhoda E. 1995b. *Human Rights and the Search for Community*. Boulder, CO: Westview.

Howard, Rhoda E., and Jack Donnelly. 1986. "Human Dignity, Human Rights and Political Regimes." *American Political Science Review* 80 (3):801–817.

Howard-Hassmann, Rhoda E. 2005. "The Second Great Transformation: Human Rights Leapfrogging in the Era of Globalization." *Human Rights Quarterly* 27 (1):1–40.

Hynes, Patricia. 2010. "Global Points of 'Vulnerability': Understanding Processes of the Trafficking of Children and Young People Into, Within and Out of the UK." *The International Journal of Human Rights* 14 (6):952–970.

Hynes, Patricia, Michele Lamb, Damien Short, and Matthew Waites. 2012a. "New Directions in the Sociology of Human Rights: Foreword." *The International Journal of Human Rights* 16 (8):1123–1126.

Hynes, Patricia, Michele Lamb, Damien Short, and Matthew Waites. 2012b. "The Sociology of Human Rights: Editorial Foreword." *Sociology* 46 (5):787–796.

Ignatieff, Michael. 2001. *Human Rights as Politics and Human Rights as Idolatry*. Princeton, NJ: Princeton University Press.

Jessop, Bob. 1999. "The Changing Governance of Welfare: Recent Trends in Its Primary Functions, Scale, and Modes of Coordination." *Social Policy & Administration* 33 (4):348–359.

Keck, Margaret E., and Kathryn Sikkink. 1998. *Activists Beyond Borders: Advocacy Networks in International Politics*. Ithaca, NY and London: Cornell University Press.

Kennedy, David. 2005. *The Dark Sides of Virtue: Reassessing International Humanitarianism*. Princeton, NJ: Princeton University Press.

Kurasawa, Fuyuki. 2007. *The Work of Global Justice: Human Rights as Practices*. Cambridge and New York: Cambridge University Press.

Latour, Bruno. 1987. *Science in Action: How to Follow Scientists and Engineers Through Society*. Cambridge, MA: Harvard University Press.

Lemert, Charles. 1995. *Sociology After the Crisis*. Boulder: Westview Press.

Levine, Donald N. 1995. *Visions of the Sociological Tradition*. Chicago and London: University of Chicago Press.
Levy, Daniel, and Natan Sznaider. 2010. *Human Rights and Memory*. Philadelphia: Penn State Press.
López, José Julián. 2009. "Par-Delà L'éthique: Vers Une Sociologie Des Pratiques Éthiques Contemporaines." *Cahiers de Recherche Sociologique* 48:27–44.
López, José Julián. 2015. "The Human Right to Food as Political Imaginary." *Journal of Historical Sociology* 30 (2): 239–261.
López, José Julián. 2016. "Disembedding the Embedded/Disembedded Opposition." In *Markets, Communities and Nostalgai*, edited by Christian Karner and Bernhard Weicht, 223–247. London and New York: Palgrave Macmillan.
Meyer, John W. 1977. "The Effects of Education as an Institution." *American Journal of Sociology*, Journal Article:55–77.
Mirowski, Philip. 2013. *Never Let a Serious Crisis Go to Waste: How Neoliberalism Survived the Financial Meltdown*. London: Verso Books.
Mishra, Ramesh. 2014. *Welfare State Capitalist Society*. London and New York: Routledge.
Moon, Claire. 2012. "What One Sees and How One Files Seeing: Human Rights Reporting, Representation and Action." *Sociology* 46 (5):876–890.
Morris, Lydia. 2013. *Human Rights and Social Theory*. New York: Palgrave Macmillan.
Moyn, Samuel. 2010. *The Last Utopia*. Cambridge MA: Harvard University Press.
Moyn, Samuel. 2012. "Do Human Rights Treaties Make Enough of a Difference?" In *Cambridge Companion to Human Rights Law*, edited by Conor Gearty and Costas Douzinas, 329–347. Cambridge and New York: Cambridge University Press.
Nash, Kate. 2012. "Towards a Political Sociology of Human Rights." In *The Wiley-Blackwell Companion to Political Sociology*, edited by Kate Nash, Edwin Amenta Scott, and Alan Edwin, 444–454. Malden: Wiley Blackwell.
Nelson, Paul J., and Ellen Dorsey. 2008. *New Rights Advocacy: Changing Strategies of Development and Human Rights NGOs*. Washington, DC: Georgetown University Press.
Neocleous, Mark. 2003. *Imagining the State*. Maidenhead and Philadelphia: Open University Press.
Nielsen, François. 2004. "The Vacant 'We': Remarks on Public Sociology." *Social Forces* 82 (4):1619–1627.
Oberschall, Anthony. 1978. "Theories of Social Conflict." *Annual Review of Sociology*, Journal Article:291–315.

O'Connell, Paul. 2009. "Not Seeing the Forest for the Trees: A Reply to Rhoda Howard-Hassmann." *Human Rights Law Review* 9 (1):135–141.
Offe, Claus. 1972. "Advanced Capitalism and the Welfare State." *Politics & Society* 2 (4):479–488.
Panitch, Leo, and Sam Gindin. 2012. *The Making of Global Capitalism*. London: Verso Books.
Parsons, Talcott, 1902–1967. *Sociological Theory and Modern Society*. New York: New York Free Press.
Payne, Geoff, Malcolm Williams, and Suzanne Chamberlain. 2004. "Methodological Pluralism in British Sociology." *Sociology* 38 (1):153–163.
Piven, Frances Fox. 1971. *Regulating the Poor; the Functions of Public Welfare*. Vol. [1st ed.]. Book, Whole. New York: Pantheon Books.
Polanyi, Karl. 1957. Book, Whole. Beacon Hill, Boston: Beacon Hill.
Poulantzas, Nicos Ar. 1978. *State, Power, Socialism*. London: NLB.
Risse, Thomas, C. Ropp Stephen, and Kathryn Sikkink. 1999. *The Power of Human Rights: International Norms and Domestic Change*. Cambridge and New York: Cambridge University Press.
Risse, Thomas, C. Ropp Stephen, and Kathryn Sikkink. 2013. *The Persistent Power of Human Rights: From Commitment to Compliance*. Cambridge and New York: Cambridge University Press.
Rose, Nikolas, and Peter Miller. 1992. "Political Power Beyond the State: Problematics of Government." *British Journal of Sociology*:173–205.
Rule, James B. 1997. *Theory and Progress in Social Science*. Cambridge and New York: Cambridge University Press.
Sayer, Andrew. 2005. *The Moral Significance of Class*. Book, Whole. Cambridge University Press.
Scheppele, Kim Lane. 1994. "Legal Theory and Social Theory." *Annual Review of Sociology* 20:383–406.
Scheppele, Kim Lane. 2004. "Constitutional Ethnography: An Introduction." *Law & Society Review* 38 (3):389–406.
Scott, John. 2005. "Who Will Speak, and Who Will Listen? Comments on Burawoy and Public Sociology." *The British Journal of Sociology* 56 (3):405–409.
Searle, John R. 1969. *Speech Acts: An Essay in the Philosophy of Language*. Cambridge: Cambridge University Press.
Seidman, Steven. 1991. "The End of Sociological Theory: The Postmodern Hope." *Sociological Theory* 9 (2): 131–146.

Sen, Amartya. 1999. *Development as Freedom*. Oxford and New York: Oxford University Press.
Shilling, Chris, and Philip A. Mellor. 2001. *The Sociological Ambition*. London: Sage.
Shue, Henry. 1980. *Basic Rights: Subsistence, Affluence, and US Foreign Policy*. Princeton, NJ: Princeton University Press.
Simmons, Beth A. 2009. *Mobilizing for Human Rights: International Law in Domestic Politics*. Cambridge and New York: Cambridge University Press.
Sjoberg, Gideon. 2009. "Corporations and Human Rights." In *Interpreting Human Rights: Social Science Perspectives*, edited by S. Turner Bryan and Rhiannon Morgan, 157–176. London: Routledge.
Sjoberg, Gideon, Elizabeth A. Gill, and Norma Williams. 2001. "A Sociology of Human Rights." *Social Problems* 48 (1):11–47.
Slaughter, Joseph. 2009. *Human Rights, Inc: The World Novel, Narrative Form, and International Law*. New York: Fordham University Press.
Smith, Anthony. 1991. *National Identity*. Reno, NV: University of Nevada Press.
Smith, Dorothy E. 1999. *Writing the Social: Critique, Theory, and Investigations*. Toronto: University of Toronto Press.
Somers, Margaret R. 1993. "Citizenship and the Place of the Public Sphere: Law, Community, and Political Culture in the Transition to Democracy." *American Sociological Review* 58 (5):587–620.
Somers, Margaret R. 2008. *Genealogies of Citizenship*. Cambridge and New York: Cambridge University Press.
Somers, Margaret R., and Fred Block. 2005. "From Poverty to Perversity: Ideas, Markets, and Institutions over 200 Years of Welfare Debate." *American Sociological Review* 70 (2):260–287.
Somers, Margaret R., and Christopher N. J. Roberts. 2008. "Toward a New Sociology of Rights: A Genealogy of 'Buried Bodies' of Citizenship and Human Rights." *Annual Review of Law and Social Science* 4:385–425.
Stammers, Neil. 2009. *Human Rights and Social Movements*. London: Pluto Press.
Teeple, Gary. 2005. *The Riddle of Human Rights*. Toronto: University of Toronto Press.
Thornhill, Chris. 2011. *A Sociology of Constitutions: Constitutions and State Legitimacy in Historical-Sociological Perspective*. Cambridge and New York: Cambridge University Press.

Tilly, Charles. 2007. *Democracy*. Cambridge and New York: Cambridge University Press.

Tittle, Charles R. 2004. "The Arrogance of Public Sociology." *Social Forces* 82 (4):1639–1643.

Toussaint, Laura. 2011. "Promoting Cultural Rights." In *Sociology and Human Rights: A Bill of Rights for the Twenty-First Century*, edited by Judith Blau and Mark Frezzo. Los Angeles and London: Sage.

Turner, Bryan S. 1993. "Outline of a Theory of Human Rights." *Sociology* 27 (3):489–512.

Turner, Bryan S. 2006. *Vulnerability and Human Rights*. Philadelphia: Penn State Press.

Turner, Bryan S. 2009. "10 A Sociology of Citizenship and Human Rights." *Interpreting Human Rights: Social Science Perspectives* 47:177.

Turner, Jonathan H. 2005. "Is Public Sociology such a Good Idea?" *The American Sociologist* 36 (3–4):27–45.

Urry, John. 2012. *Sociology Beyond Societies: Mobilities for the Twenty-First Century*. London: Routledge.

Vincent, Raymond John. 1986. *Human Rights and International Relations*. Cambridge and New York: Cambridge University Press.

Waters, Malcolm. 1996. "Human Rights and the Universalization of Interests: Towards a Social Constructionist Approach." *Sociology* 30 (3):593–600.

Weber, Max. 2009. *From Max Weber: Essays in Sociology*. London: Routledge.

Wilson, Richard A. 2009. "Representing Human Rights Violations: Social Contexts and Subjectivities." In *Human Rights: An Anthropological Reader*, edited by Mark Goodale, 134–160. Oxford and New York: Wiley Blackwell.

Woodiwiss, Anthony. 2005a. *Human Rights*. London and New York: Routledge.

Woodiwiss, Anthony. 2005b. *Scoping the Social*. London and New York: McGraw-Hill Education.

Woodiwiss, Anthony. 2011. "Making the Sociology of Human Rights More Sociological." *Development and Society* 40 (1):117–138.

Wrong, Dennis H. 1961. "The Oversocialized Conception of Man in Modern Sociology." *American Sociological Review*, Journal Article:183–193.

Žižek, Slavoj. 2005. "Against Human Rights." *New Left Review* 34 (July–August):115–131.

4

Practising Human Rights

Introduction

In the previous chapter, I illustrated how some sociologists who engage with human rights are subject to its considerable normative pull and accordingly, but to my mind unfortunately, frame sociology's relationship to human rights primarily in normative terms. In this chapter, I survey another mode of engagement, organized around the attempt to seize the sociological significance of human rights, via a concept that has become increasingly important in the social sciences, that of practice. Practice theory introduces the potential of contextualizing and embedding ideas, norms, and principles in patterns of routine behaviour that puts the emphasis on activity and its associated resources and relational contexts. Therefore it contains the potential of thickening our conceptualisation of ideas and norms by drawing attention to their broader social conditions of (im)possibility.

I begin the chapter by looking at the work of Charles R. Beitz (2011), a political philosopher who forcefully argues for the necessity of conceptualizing human rights as an emergent normative practice rather than as an idea. After sketching out his conception of practice, I show that it

J. Julián López, *Human Rights as Political Imaginary*,
https://doi.org/10.1007/978-3-319-74274-8_4

remains too thin and move on to survey sociological attempts to engage with human rights via the category of practice. Surprisingly, a significant number of these sociologists, and some anthropologists, rather than follow Beitz's lead and pose the question of what it means to conceptualize human rights as a practice, instead oppose the notion of practice to the idea of human rights. This means that the analyses of one group, as I illustrate in detail, are geared towards showing how the ideas, norms, laws, and principles of human rights can be made a reality in practice by drawing attention to new sources of violence and injustice. The other group remains concerned with mapping the concrete social-structural obstacles that prevent the ideas, norms, and laws from being put into practice. Although this work is important, it sidesteps what I think is a crucial task for sociologists, namely, thinking about human right as itself a practice.

I then turn to the work of Fuyuki Kurasawa (2007) and Kate Nash (2009b). Both scholars offer a more fruitful manner of conceptualizing human rights as a normative practice. Kurasawa, in particular, draws attention to the ethico-political labour that fuels the normative and political struggles for global justice. Ideas and political will are mobilized, yes. But, they are also embodied and embedded in ongoing patterned efforts to create ethico-political communities where ethico-political claims made by, or on behalf of, distant others are audible ("I am suffering. It is unjust! Help me!"). And, if they are heard perhaps acted upon. Carefully exploring the socially complex and fragile social practice of bearing witness, Kurasawa brings to the foreground the concatenation of social structured practices and relations that, under the right conditions, can generate a sense of ethical and political responsibility for the suffering of distant others.

Nash, equally, draws attention to the fact that the formation of a community where the normative power of human rights claims can be transformed into socially persuasive representations, successful political claims, or judicial decisions cannot be presumed to exist. Community formation and the testing of claims is a product of a cultural politics that is inflected by the authority of the different subfields where the claims circulate, principally, the legal, political, activist, and mediated subfields.

In locating the social power of norms and ideas in the actual cultural and social-political activities of social actors, both Kurasawa and Nash offer important clues regarding how to conceptualize human rights as a normative practice rather than just as a persuasive idea.

I conclude the chapter by further specifying the human rights political imaginary model that I introduced in Chap. 2. I suggest that human rights, as a political imaginary, can be understood as the socially patterned activity that uses social technologies of witnessing (documenting and communicating evidence of violence and injustice, speaking on behalf of others), frequently hosted by human rights organizations, to produce representations of a shared moral and political community where individuals see themselves as having an ethical and/or political responsibility to act. Such acting may take the form of individual indignation or outrage, different forms of patterned political behaviour (lobbying, letter writing, protesting, transnational networking), or, in some cases, the search for legal remedy. In sum, the human rights political imaginary is a social space requiring an ongoing, yet always subvertible, ethico-political labour. This labour is undertaken in the attempt to render visible situations of violence or inequality of distant and/or excluded others with the goal of achieving moral recognition and provoking legal and political remedy.

Idea or Practice?

In a cogent, enlightening, and sympathetic critique of prevailing philosophical and normative conceptions of human rights, Beitz argues that rather than attempting to grasp human rights as a normative idea, or ideal, we should see them as the product of an actually existing, historically situated, and emergent normative practice (2011). This requires, he adds, disavowing two of the dominant ways in which human rights are currently understood, "the idea of human rights as entitlements that belong to people 'by nature' or 'simply in virtue of their humanity' and the distinct idea of human rights as objects of agreement among diverse moral and political cultures" (2011, 10). Beitz contends that the normative force of human rights needs to be understood as being immanent in the actually existing practice and not as an exogenous force.

This does not mean that there is no point in exploring the historical manifestations of different conceptions of "human rights" or cognate terms, as the bevy of human rights' scholars are wont to do. However, he adds, we should not construe this activity as constituting "an investigation of human rights in the sense in which they occur in contemporary public discourse" (Beitz 2011, 11). Beitz argues that despite the current habit of grafting contemporary human rights onto old growth rights vines, the former "differ strikingly from their [alleged] predecessors" (2011, 29) and cannot be persuasively seen as articulating "protections of timeless significance" (2011, 30–31). What then does Beitz mean when he suggests that human rights should be analysed as a novel, emergent, and evolving social practice?

He understands human rights, as a practice, to be both discursive and political, consisting of "a set of norms for the regulation of the behaviour of states together with a set of modes or strategies of action for which violations of the norms may count as reasons" (2011, 8). Human rights stitch together a normative global discursive community where the members accept "the practice's norms as reason-giving and use them in deliberating and arguing about how to act" (2011, 8). This implies "a more-or-less widespread belief that these rules ought to be complied with, and some institutions, quasi-institutions, and informal processes for their propagation and implementation" (2011, 42). Consequently, in situations where human right's norms are judged to apply, designated agents (e.g., states, social movements, NGOs) "regard the rules as providing reasons for action and grounds criticism", as they engage in conduct to coax compliance and discourage defiance, deploying the different registers of action made available through the practice of human rights (2011, 42).

Currently, permissible actions within the human rights' repertoire include fostering accountability; offering inducements and assistance, domestic engagement, and contestation; seeking conformity through compulsion; and adapting the external environment to make it more conducive to compliance (Beitz 2011, 31–42). Nonetheless, due to its status as an emergent social practice, it remains uneven. With relatively weak capacity for enforcement and adjudication (2011, 43), the repertoire continues to be open to contestation on normative, political, and instrumental grounds (2011, 44).

Beitz infers that the normative power of human rights—that is, the ability to provide binding reasons for action within the scope of the practice—is likely to be more persuasive when it is aligned with human rights' endogenously generated aim, which his analysis seeks to reveal. The aim should be considered *sui generis*, rather than "the instantiation of one or another received idea" (2011, 197). This leads him to conclude that human rights are the norms, principles, rules, and actions produced and reproduced by a global practice that has developed "to protect individuals against threats to their most important interests arising from the acts and omissions of their governments (including failures to regulate the conduct of other agents)" (2011, 197). Its distinctive *modus operandi* is to bring "these aspects of the domestic conduct of governments within the scope of legitimate international concern" (2011, 197), triggering one or more of the suite of actions enumerated above.

The actual content of the norms, their applicability in particular instances, and the specific actions that they license are the product of the unfolding of the practice itself and are not exempt from disagreement. Consequently, Beitz maintains that "it is probably a mistake to expect to discover a basis for human rights in one or a few clear moral ideas, to formulate a canonical list of rights, or to devise a single authoritative means for bringing them to bear on practical choices" (2011, 212). He concludes that any theory of human rights "would seek to interpret the normative discipline implicit in the practice"; it would not "stand outside the practice"; instead, "it would be continuous with it" (2011, 212).

In Beitz's hands, the concept of practice achieves much. Not only does it provide a sympathetic and thoughtful critique of the shortcomings in contemporary philosophical and political attempts to represent and ground human rights—that is, naturalistic and agreement theories—it, also, provides a more plausible model for thinking about the normativity specific to human rights, as well as its ontological basis. Human rights are not a timeless trans-historical moral ideal, but the emergence of a particular normative social technology, binding under certain situations, constituted by political-historical relations. Yet for all this, his conceptualization of the notion of practice remains, for our purposes, regrettably narrow. Although Beitz cites approvingly the work of the cultural and legal anthropologist Sally Engle Merry (2009) to argue that human rights can be usefully conceptualized as a cultural practice with the capacity to produce new modalities of cultural understanding and action (2011, 38), his principal interlocutors remain, for the most part, philosophers and political scientists. Instead of providing the tools for thick conceptions of cultural practices, the latter two are more concerned, in the first case, with elucidating the soundness of arguments that rationally ground action and thought, and, in the second, with the institutional arrangements and the inherent, or emergent, rationalities that pattern political calculation and behaviour. These contributions are by no means without value, but they do not contribute to the thick sociological understanding of human rights that the political imaginary model seeks to develop.

Indeed, in sharpening his conception of human rights as a social practice, Beitz argues that human rights share some features associated with international regimes (Beitz 2011, 42–43). The latter are defined as sets of "implicit or explicit principles, norms, rules, and decision-making procedures around which [state] actors' expectations tend to converge" (Krasner cited in Beitz 2011, 43). For my purposes, more important than whether human rights constitute a regime or not, a question that some scholars such as John Donnelly (1986) answer in the affirmative is the significance of Beitz's decision to compare and contrast human rights as a social practice with international regimes. Any useful comparison assumes that the comparators are sufficiently similar for their differences to be informative. Therefore, notwithstanding their differences, the idea of an international regime, as I will show in the next section, tells us something about what Beitz understands a social practice to be.[1]

Seeing Practice Through the Lens of International Regimes

The nature of international regimes is, and has been, a key area of conceptual, theoretical, and empirical debate amongst international relations (IR) scholars (Hasenclever et al. 1996; Checkel 1998). Very broadly, three approaches are distinguished: neoliberal, realist, and cognitivist. Each focuses on different explanatory elements: self-interests, relative power relations, and the social construction of both self-interest and power, respectively (Hasenclever et al. 1996). Since the mid-1990s, strong cognitivists, also known as social constructivists, have sought to moderate the alleged explanatory power of the rationalism espoused by neoliberals and the materialism embraced by realists in the patterning of behaviour amongst states. They have done so by focusing on the importance of "perceptual, ideational and cultural factors" (Checkel 1998, 329).

More specifically, constructivists contest the notion that states are "rational actors whose identities, powers, and fundamental interests are prior to international society and its institutions" (Hasenclever et al. 1996, 205–06). Equally, they are critical "of the static approach to the study of IR", and the positivist bias that obfuscates the manner in which "international social norms work" (Hasenclever et al. 1996, 206). Consequently, it is constructivists who are more likely to see the principles, norms, rules, and decision-making procedures, stabilized in international regimes, as having causal force in the structuring of interactions amongst states and their agents. Norms, rules, and decision-making mechanism are not merely a residue or by-product of strategic calculations in fields of power or of the variable geometries of interests (Checkel 1998, 328). Although Beitz does not specify the variant of regime theory he has in mind as the comparator to human rights practice, given his emphasis on the normative power of human rights as a social practice, it is likely he endorses some variant of the constructivist account.

It is an indubitable advance to introduce analyses of norms, and their social construction, into regime theory. However, seen from a sociological perspective, the scope of regime analysis still remains circumscribed by what one pair of scholars have called the "Westphalian straitjacket" of the IR discipline, that is, "the strong tendency to assume that the model established in the seventeenth century Europe should define what the international system is for all times and places" (Buzan and Little 2001, 25). Indeed, constructivist accounts have tended to be more influential to the extent that they have filed away their critical edges to better blend into the rationalist assumptions and positivist methodologies that continue to constitute the mainstream of the IR discipline in the US (Buzan and Little 2001, 25, 32; Waever 1998, 715).[2] Most significantly, however, is the ongoing centrality, in American IR, of "an individualistic and choice-theoretical ontology [that] is transferred to other primitive units or ontological givens who become the instrumental calculators, be they states, rulers or firms" (Waever 1998, 721–22).

That the interests, or the understanding of the power dynamics at stake, are the product of norms or culture does not by itself displace the centrality of the rational calculator that remains *primus inter pares* in North American IR. And indeed, at the very centre of Beitz's account of human rights as a social practice are the actors for which human rights norms and principles, when made rationally legible through the global practice of human rights, provide normatively good reasons for action, if not always agreement. Interestingly, Beitz does introduce the possibility of distinguishing among the diverse "international and transnational agents that participate in human rights practice", only to set it aside (Beitz 2011, 33). In doing so, he locates the centre of his understanding of the practice around the normative reasons for action. He asks, in a relatively decontextualized manner, under what circumstances and for which actions do human rights give states and other actors reasons (Beitz 2011, 9)?

This cognitivist or "regulist" conception of practice, of which more below, forecloses, or at least does not invite, the possibility of investigating the social technologies and processes that coordinate the activities of these actors, the worldviews that fuel them and make them meaningful, the modes of subjectivity and affect that they nurture, and the divergent organizational forms with which they are associated. To recall Alexander's critique of philosophical approaches to normativity in social life, cited in Chap. 2, they achieve consistency by ignoring the messiness and work required for the production of everyday life (2006, 14). Consequently, despite his espousal of practice theory, Beitz's is a thin conception of human rights, as defined in the second chapter.

In his own words, it is "a realistic conception of the practice at it presents itself in the range of source materials at hand" (Beitz 2011, 107). Consequently, he is not particularly concerned with questioning human rights' self-presentation(s). Instead he attempts to logically tighten human rights' self-understanding without critically interrogating the constituents of this self-understanding, with the notable exception of his thoughtful and compelling critique of naturalist and agreement theories. It comes as no surprise, then, that he reproduces the conventional thin historical narrative of human rights' origins and development (Beitz 2011, 14–27), discussed in Chap. 2.

In suggesting that Beitz's account of social practice remains too thin, I do not want to minimize the significance of his contribution. Within the parameters of the disciplines from which he writes, political science and philosophy, his contribution to the understanding of human rights is enormous. His thoughtful critique of naturalist and agreement foundationalist theories is sharp and elegant, as is the presentation of his practice model. His promotion of a social practice approach shows a grasp of human rights that is in some senses more sociological than that held by some sociologists. As I will show in the next section, the realization that human rights is not an idea but a social practice is curiously more secure in his work than in that of some sociologists and anthropologists working on human rights.

Idea Versus Practice

Beitz's analysis of human rights is written against the teeth of the book's title, *The Idea of Human Rights*, making the compelling argument that human rights are not an idea but a practice. Said differently, human rights exist as an idea only insofar as it emerges from a concrete social practice. The idea of human rights is a visible facet of the contemporary practice of human rights, the former being a synecdoche for the latter. Thus, on my reading, the tenor of his claim is not that human rights as an idea, or ideal, should be contrasted to the reality of their practice, but that the reality of the idea is generated within practice. The distinction is a subtle one, that, as I show in a moment, can too easily be overlooked.

Since the 1970s, practice theory has had a significant conceptual and empirical impact across a number of domains in the humanities and the social sciences (Bourdieu 1977; Ortner 1984; Reckwitz 2002b). Surprisingly, it is only fairly recently that scholars have undertaken the task of systematically elaborating a critical overview of the range of uses to which it has been put (Cetina et al. 2005; Reckwitz 2002b; Rouse 2007; Schatzki 1996).[3] This is perhaps a consequence of a loose common front that has brought together heterogeneous understandings of practice to hold the line against a number of shared theoretical foes.

Amongst other things, this has entrenched a defence of the interpretive and cultural turn in social theory, as well as highlighting the significance of the "everyday" and the "life-world" (Reckwitz 2002b, 244). This is evidenced by the family of terms with which practice theory has become interwoven: "praxis, action, interaction, activity, experience and performance" and "agent, actor, person, self, individual, subject" (Ortner 1984, 144), and the Heideggerian and Wittgensteinian philosophical lineages from which it has drawn (Reckwitz 2002b, 144; Rouse 2007, 501; Cetina et al. 2005). Those standing under the banner of practice theory, however differentially conceived (Reckwitz 2002b), have been keen to keep the twin enemies of *homo sociologicus* and *homo economicus* at bay—the subsumption of individuals under the weight of collective norms and to the rational pursuit of self-interest, respectively (Reckwitz 2002b, 245). Practice theory has, also, provided a pragmatic solution to the system/action impasse (Ortner 1984, 148) by proposing a way of reconciling, or in some instances bypassing, the seemingly perennial opposition between structure and agency (Rouse 2007, 504).

At its most general level, practice theory can be understood as a reaction in the social sciences and the humanities against normative and interest-based "regulisms". In the case of the former it constitutes a critique of the notion that equates "the understanding of norms or meanings" to that of "grasping and following rules" (Rouse 2007, 528). In the latter, it rejects that in ascribing rational interests to an action, one has explained it. Against these cognitivist, or regulist, understandings of social activity and meaning, practice theory draws attention to "what practitioners do" rather than the rules they follow or the abstract calculations they allegedly make (Rouse 2007, 528). This "doing" presupposes the coming together of interlinked components that unfold in time and space and which pattern social behaviour. A practice, then,

> is a routinized behaviour which consists of several elements, interconnected to one another: forms of bodily activities, forms of mental activities "things" and their use, a background knowledge in the form of understanding, know-how, states of emotion and motivational knowledge. (Reckwitz 2002b, 249)

Practice theory offers the prospect of providing a more complex and nuanced account of not only why, but, perhaps more importantly, how individuals understand, embody, and reproduce normative commitments. It does not conceptualize such normative commitments principally as the outcome of abstract logically compelling rule-following or as the product of an overarching socialization via shared societal values.[4] Instead, practice theory sees normative commitments as the product of embedded, embodied, embrained, and inthinged[5] behaviour, drawing attention to their messiness, variability, and contingency.

Practice theory has much to offer an understanding of human rights as political imaginary. It draws our attention to the relationships between discursive representations, meanings, embodiment, identity, and modes of action patterned by particular social technologies and material artefacts. It allows us to see that human rights are not self-propelled by their inherent normative winds, nor is their social efficacy secured by international agreements, legislation, or even strong personal commitment. Practice theory instead suggests that human rights depend on different types of patterned bodily and mental activities, regulated by social technologies and relationships. There are many insights from practice theory that can be incorporated into the political imaginary model. However, before doing so, in the next section I want to draw attention to a very important pitfall to be avoided.

Beyond the Abstract Idea/Concrete Practice Opposition

As noted above, practice theory arose as a reaction to conceptions of social life where explanatory weight was put on systems of overarching rules and norms, the calculations of individual preferences, or some variant of the two. Whether the instantiation of norms or the calculus of interests was understood as a conscious mental operation or an internalized unconscious disposition, such conceptions held virtually no purchase on the embodied, embedded, and inthinged unfolding of action in time and space. Heuristically, the common-sense expression "theory versus practice" appears to grasp what is at stake in the opposition between regulist and practice-based conceptions of social life: the abstract and coherent ideal versus the concrete, multilayered, messy, and contingent reality. However, it is crucial not to superimpose this critique of regulist explanatory conceptions of social life on to social life itself. Said differently, in the case of human rights, it is important not to argue that human rights as they exist in treaties, covenants, and international agreements are abstract ideals or concepts whose reality can only be understood by analysing how they are used in everyday local practices.

It is undoubtedly true that the legitimacy of human rights is tied to its discursive representation as a moral or normative principle whose self-evidence no reasonable person would contest. Who would deny the rights ensuing from these principles to any human being? Equally, much of the socially visible labour performed by human rights takes the form of the application of abstract norms or legal concepts to concrete situations. This is the case when lawyers or judges invoke legal or normative instruments in their reasoning or adjudications, when Amnesty International documents and reports on human rights violations, when states plot their foreign policy by invoking human rights coordinates, or when activists infuse their political discourse and claims with human rights principles, to give but a few examples. But in all of these cases, the norms, ideals, or principles should be understood as components of a more complexly organized human rights practice that is embedded, embodied, embrained, and inthinged. Seen sociologically, the "idea" or the "ideal" are not found outside of social practices, and should, consequently not be opposed to practice. Human rights as a practice can, of course, be opposed to other practices, such as solidarity or revolutionary practices.

One should resist the momentum underlying the "idea" of human rights, that is, the notion that human rights represent the unfolding of the moral consensus that coalesced in the postwar. Rather than countering the "abstractness" of human rights with the "reality" of its practice, I would argue that it is decisive, for sociologists and other social science scholars, to ask what it is about human rights as a practice that enables them to be perceived and function as a difficult to contest ideal. What social arrangements enable them to travel across heterogeneous locales in contemporary social life? What modulates human rights so that they maintain their stability, making them recognizable to disparate agents?

It is certain that social science scholars who reveal the gap between the coherence of human rights doctrine and the unruly reality of how human rights unfold on the ground contribute much to our understanding of how human rights are reproduced differentially across time and space. They draw attention not only to their plasticity but also to the manner in which human rights fail to achieve their alleged potential, as well as how sometimes they produce effects that run counter to their proposed aims (Englund 2006). They equally reveal how certain ways of practising human rights can be more effective than others at achieving concrete goals, particularly when they become hybridized with local vernaculars (Merry 2006). Yet despite the significant critical and practical insight that can be gleaned from such work, there is a serious drawback. Namely, that in opposing the alleged social reality of the "practice" to the socially disengaged "idea" or "concept" of human rights, it uncritically reproduces a key feature of the commonsense conception of human rights. It accepts that they are an idea, or an ideal, and not a historically contextualized ensemble of practices. This obscures the significance of attending to the complex manner in which even the abstract "idea" of human rights is embedded, embrained, embodied, and inthinged in social life. Or more significantly, what allows human rights to travel globally? What gives them their legs?

As argued in Chap. 2, explicit or implicitly, much contemporary human rights scholarship is threaded with the assumption that human rights ideals are the product of a stunning post-world war moral consensus. Even when the unanimity is recognized as partial, or "truncated" (Moyn 2013a, 190), human rights are understood to have a "greater relevance than they actually do initially, so that if they travel across the globe, it is according to a potential they had from the very beginning" (Moyn 2013a, 190). As those excluded from the original consensus take up human rights and adapt them—for instance, much of the global south—they instantiate the logic of human rights that was already implicit in them, providing a strikingly idealist reading of human rights (Moyn 2013a, 190). Hang on to your hat Hegel! The scenario is one in which "confused actors whose ostensible antagonisms actually works to advance unintended designs, and in its considerable allocation of energy to the built-in destiny of a concept in itself" (Moyn 2013a, 190).

Recent critical historiography suggests that contemporary human rights are best grasped as the product of a series of political practices that gelled into a broader political imaginary circa the 1970s (Eckel and Moyn 2014; Burke 2015). According to Moyn's reading, as seen in Chap. 2, contemporary human rights arose in a context where, for different reasons, the grand political projects—one might say political imaginaries—of the postwar era became increasingly less compelling, to wit, liberal capitalism, state socialism, and the nationalisms and pan-nationalisms of post-colonial states (2010, 8). This opened up a space for an anti-politics that demanded both less and more: less because it was a political imaginary that abandoned the hope of radical structural transformation and more because it demanded a moral commitment to the sanctity of the individual that transcended all political claims.

Contemporary human rights began to emerge around a minimalist politics that was made tangible through the practices of new organizational forms, for which Amnesty International was the exemplar. New modes of representing injustice, conveying the vulnerability of the isolated individual confronted with the overwhelming violence of the state, were narrated in the neutral matter of fact genre of the nascent human rights reporting (Hopgood 2006; McLagan 2006; Moon 2012; Wilson 2009). Moreover,

> Skirting the reform of international governance, it [Amnesty International] sought a direct and public connection with suffering, through lighting candles in a show of solidarity and writing letters to governments pleading for mercy and release. These practical innovations depended in equal parts on a brilliant reading of the fortunes of idealism in the postwar world and a profound understanding of the importance of symbolic gestures. (Moyn 2010, 130)

These and other practices, as captured so elegantly in Stephen Hopgood's institutional ethnography of Amnesty International (2006), gave shape to a durable and transportable conception of human rights that was successfully transplanted via local chapters and national sections (Hopgood 2006, 73–104), or through the institutional mimesis of other organizations that wanted a share of Amnesty International's expanding moral appeal (Moyn 2010, 147). Paradoxically for an institution that today many spontaneously associate with the protection of individual political conscience and freedom, in its early years, "diversity, spontaneity and individuality had all to be constrained in the service of moral authority" (Hopgood 2006, 104). Subsequent attempts to modify the practices of Amnesty International, or expand its mandate, have raised the question of whether Amnesty International can maintain its moral authority in the more competitive contemporary human rights field defined by increasing pragmatism (Hopgood 2006, 221).

Drawing attention to the novelty and the specificity of Amnesty International's practices is crucial because it is all too appealing to cast Amnesty International as a necessary hero in the emplotment of the human rights postwar saga. Stephen Hopgood, after completing the most thorough study of the internal practices of the organization that has been undertaken to date, is unequivocal: "Amnesty has not been the inevitable unfurling of some logic inherent in universal human rights" (2006, 215). He adds, "Amnesty had no preordained historical role to play. Practice came before identity" (2006, 215).

Much the same could be said about the struggles in the two key regions that coincided with human rights' rise to global prominence in the late 1960s and 1970s—namely, in Latin America and the Soviet Union. The centrality of the human rights approach to counter the violence of military dictatorships was neither the result of the legacy of the Inter-American Human Rights system originating in the 1940s, which had played little to no role in the politics of the region (Moyn 2010, 143; Kelly 2014a, 89), nor the development of Catholic human rights in the 1960s, which hardly ignited a human rights movement (Moyn 2010, 144). This is so, notwithstanding the fact that in retrospect, they seem like natural founts feeding the historical course of human rights.

Ironically, Catholic "human rights" in the 1960s resonated more with those human rights, marginal then as they continue to be today, that we currently call economic, cultural, and social rights. The seeds of the latter originated in liberation theology, an altogether distinct political imaginary (Aldunate 1994; Engler 2000; Foroohar 1986; Levine 1988; López 2015; Löwy 1996; Smith 1979). According to Moyn, what was decisive in Latin America, as elsewhere where human rights took root in the 1970s, was the collapse of the belief in, or the realization of the practical unviability of, broader projects of social, economic, and political transformation. The fortuitous availability of a new form of highly moralized political practice that eschewed grand politics via "smaller and more manageable moral acts" (Moyn 2010, 147; Eckel 2014, 258), pioneered by Amnesty International, provided a practicable response that resonated with the political exigencies of the time. It provided a form of social engagement "whose minimalism was its enabling condition and source of power when other post-1968 alternatives were dying" (Moyn 2010, 148).[6]

Moyn equally contends that in the dissidence movements of the USSR and the Eastern European states, human rights did not owe their prominence to the enduring legacy of the human rights "consensus" of the immediate postwar. Instead their increasing influential role expressed the contingent fit between a wider political terrain sterile to grand political projects, but fertile to a minimalist politics sheathed in a morality purporting to transcend politics (2010, 135, 161; Kelly 2014a). This is not to say that having located the emergence of contemporary human rights in a new set of practices of morally infused political minimalism, one has accounted for the spread of human rights. True enough, almost single-handedly Amnesty International "invented grassroots human rights advocacy, and through it drove public awareness of human rights generally" (Moyn 2010, 129). In effect, giving them a political mobility that 1948 human rights never had, the latter predominantly confined to corridors of the UN. Yet, absent the "canonization of human rights in the Helsinki process of the Conference for Security and Cooperation in Europe (CSCE)" followed by "Jimmy Carter's explosive affiliation with the language in 1977, human rights might have remained the preserve of expanding but still minor advocacy groups and their international members and promoters" (Moyn 2010, 149; see Keys 2014; Snyder 2011).

Drawing attention to human right practices and the manner in which they articulate with contingent historical processes adumbrates how little we actually know about how contemporary human rights have actually, as opposed to ideally, travelled historically, how they have circulated and continue to circulate socially. The default understanding of human rights as a moral ideal or abstract logic ignores the question of human rights' ability to travel because every new sighting can always be explained as the unfolding of its inherent logic, whether one sees this logic as liberatory or oppressive. What is more, by contrasting the abstract logic of human right ideals to the messiness of how human rights are practised in "reality", the only critical gesture available to scholars is to chide human rights for their abstractness, for not being made fully concordant with what is happening on the ground in particular localities. While certainly not bereft of insight, this tack sidesteps the question of what might and might not be achievable through human rights—that is, their ability to restructure social relations—introducing the implicature that the only real challenge or obstacle is to make human rights less abstract.

Let me illustrate this through an example. Let's take what is a thoughtful and authoritative overview of an important approach to the anthropology of human rights, provided by a respected scholar in the field, Mark Goodale, in his *Surrendering to Utopia*. In the book, Goodale sets out to develop an anthropological account of human rights that steers a middle course between "intentionally ungrounded and deductive political and social theory on the one hand and intentionally grounded and carefully circumscribed case studies on the other" by wedding the conceptual and the empirical (2009, 9–10). This requires him to differentiate between human rights "universality" and "universalism". The former refers to

> the claims at the core of the modern *idea* of human rights: that everyone at all times is the same because they share a common humanness (which can be usefully thought of as a biological sameness invested with a moral quality); that this common humanness has normative implications; and that these implications take one form among many possibilities – rights. (Goodale 2009, 15 my emphasis)

Human rights universalism, instead, draws our attention to the manner in which human rights claims are entangled "within existing legal, moral, and political *practice*" (Goodale 2009, 15 my emphasis). Such an approach requires that, following Merry, we conceptualize human rights as a "vernacular" (Merry 2006), drawing our attention to "those many sites in which ethical theory and social practice are mutually constitutive" (Goodale 2009, 13).

At first blush, this seems like a promising start. To my mind, however, the promise fades quickly. This is because Goodale goes on to develop a narrative of the development of human rights that is underwritten by the opposition between human rights as an idea, a discourse, or an epistemological view divorced from the reality on the ground, and human rights understood as an everyday embedded cultural practice (2009, 85). The latter, he writes, incubates "an organic, if incipient, expression of the idea of human rights itself" (Goodale 2009, 98). This is already latent in the association of the idea of human rights with universality, and practice with universalism, as emphasized in the definitions above.

As current human rights doxa dictates, Goodale locates the origin of human rights in the 1948 UDHR. He understands the declaration, however, to be a "normative hybrid", in which transnational norms were embedded in an overwhelmingly "international political and legal system" (2009, 95). Thus the human rights system that emerged in the postwar period is one "in which a statement of principles with grander philosophical aspirations is tightly circumscribed by the set of normative and institutional checks and balances that structure other, essentially political, relations between nation states" (Goodale 2009, 98). The carriers of these norms were a vanguard of "cosmopolitan philosopher kings" who "inculcated into the very cell of the global body politic", the ideas of "universal sameness, ethical and legal equality, and human dignity"

(Goodale 2009, 96). As abstract ideas, tethered to the interest of states, human rights could not fulfil their latent transnational potential. However in the post-Cold War period, a different human rights regime emerged. The transnational normative kernel of human rights was released from the hard shell of the international system, enabling the materialization of "a set of relations, or networks, or norms, whose legitimacy, function, and ultimate meaning are radically divorced from the nation-state" (Goodale 2009, 97).[7]

The core of transnational human rights is the "apolitical idea of human rights (and not the logics of international relations)"; the legitimacy of this idea "depends on nothing more complicated than the simple fact of common humanness" (Goodale 2009, 98). The problems become apparent, however, when this "noble" and "essentially speculative idea" is embedded "into the language of social and political practice – as it must necessarily be" (Goodale 2009, 98). It can very well be that the idea of human rights, and its cognates, can become entangled with "a profoundly unorthodox set of moral and legal principles that are firmly rooted in local cultural tradition" (Goodale 2009, 106). In other words, for the idea of human rights to work at all, it must be rendered in local vernaculars (Goodale 2009, 107). Human rights must "remain fluid and essentially plural and depend not on a hypothetical set of principles articulated by a small sliver of the global community but on the social actors for whom human rights come to form part of their contextualized legal, moral, and political practices" (Goodale 2009, 106).

To be sure Goodale's narrative departs from the accounts, discussed in Chap. 2, where the historical and global extension of human rights is understood as the unfolding of an idea that achieved consensus in the immediate postwar. His narrative incorporates a dialectical tension between the logic of international norms and transnational "humanness". Nonetheless, this tension turns out to be the contextual working out in practice of the ideas and abstract principles embedded in the "international human rights system". The latter, however, is not conceptualized as a practice or concatenation of practices with the potential of becoming entangled with geographically disparate and heterogeneous legal, political, and moral practices. Curiously, elsewhere when writing about the arrival of human rights in rural Bolivia, he shows, but perhaps does not acknowledge, how "literate legality" is a key component of how the "idea" of international human rights is practised (Goodale 2002, 598). In other words, "international human rights" are no less the everyday practices of groups of people than are those of transnational human rights networks.[8]

In sum, I am suggesting that it is not productive to oppose abstract human rights to the reality of their practice in the manner in which Goodale, who stands in for many others, does. Instead, we should conceptualize human rights as a concrete practice, which despite being as embodied, embrained, inthinged, and embedded as any other practice is able to represent itself as a disembodied timeless moral ideal. Seen thus, human rights' intersection, or even its hybridization, with other social practices can be explored, as I do in Chap. 6 when I explore the intersection of the human rights political imaginary with the law. It would not be understood as the concretization of an idea, but as the coming together of practices, including *inter alia* ideas, but whose diverse component parts might or might not be aligned.

Human Rights as Practice in Sociology

As seen above, anthropologists articulate the opposition between human rights as an abstract idea and their reality as a practice by drawing attention to the latter's embeddedness in culture. This enables them to circumscribe the purported universality of human rights by reference to the irreducible heterogeneity of culture, as practised in daily life. Numerous sociologists, as I will show in this section, also reproduce the abstract idea/concrete practice opposition. However, as a result of their disciplinary orientation, they focus on social inequality and structured social relations rather than on cultural heterogeneity. They contrast the ideal frictionless abstract legal and normative universe of human rights, as it exists in international declarations, norms, and the letter of the law, with the concrete reality of power and the patterns of structured inequality that constitute the reality of social life (Hynes et al. 2010, 813).

In the allegedly abstract world of human rights norms and laws, all individuals are always already bearers of human rights; violations trigger remedies with an inexorable normative and/or legal logic. However, the actuality of social life is instead littered with the "messy realities of interpretation and implementation" (Hynes et al. 2010, 113). Human rights, when they become entangled in everyday power differentials amongst differently positioned actors or groups, do not have the social, legal, political, and normative efficacy attributed to them by contemporary human rights discourse. Thus a sociological analysis of human rights requires "focusing on the processes, practices and structures of everyday life, [that] can explain why there are political and economic as well as social and cultural barriers to implementing international conventions" (Morrow and Pells 2012, 907).

In this section I draw on a number of contributions published in the context of three special journal issues on the sociology of human rights (Hynes et al. 2010, 2012a, b). Though the individual contributions vary in their subject matter and approach, they are all to some extent framed by the desire to examine "the application of human rights in practice" (Hynes et al. 2012a, 1123). Two broad tendencies can be identified. The first and predominant one is concerned with bringing to light a variety of social phenomena that are not captured, or if captured inadequately so, by contemporary human rights frameworks. The marginalization of these phenomena is the result of enduring historical or contemporary social exclusions (e.g., the rights of children, the rights of indigenous peoples), or arise from the fact that they represent new phenomena that were necessarily unforeseen at the moment of the emergence of contemporary human rights frameworks (e.g., the rights of environmental refugees). Consequently, abstract ideas of human rights are opposed to the actual, yet not visible, practices that produce inequality, and that must become the focus of human rights interventions.

Such phenomena are very wide-ranging: children's human rights in the context of poverty in the global south (Morrow and Pells 2012) or as victims of trafficking (Hynes 2010), the role, or lack thereof, of human rights in buttressing the autonomy, choice, and dignity of those in care (Ferrie 2010), migration and the right to mobility as a human right (Golash-Boza and Menjívar 2012), the international recognition of the cultural genocide of indigenous peoples (Short 2010), genocide and settler colonialism (Rashed and Short 2012), human rights and sexual orientation (Waites 2010), the human rights of women raped in conflict zones (Canning 2010), the implications of the technological transformation of warfare and emerging "geosociological" understandings of territory for human rights (Bhatt 2012), the human rights of soldiers (McGarry et al. 2012), social theoretical contributions to the understanding of torture (Morris 2012), human rights and the challenge of climate change (Skillington 2012), human rights frameworks versus voluntary corporate social responsibilities schemes (Connolly 2012), privacy as a human right (Baghai 2012), cities as the site for human rights advocacy (Grigolo 2010), the framing of diplomacy by human rights (Riga and Kennedy 2012), and food sovereignty and the human right to food (Claeys 2012).

The second approach draws attention to particular social dynamics or processes that act as obstacles to the implementation of human rights. These include the following: the tension between loyalty to community and to human rights principles in the context of the post Northern Ireland Good Friday Agreement of 1998 (Lamb 2010), Asian familialism's challenge to human rights (Woodiwiss 2012), the exigencies of the social construction of human rights in the development sector (Miller 2010), the current limits to using human rights principles to claim social assistance in South Korea (Lee-Gong 2010), the interaction between humanitarian and human rights principles (Hilhorst and Jansen 2012), the balancing of human rights and the promotion of national reconciliation in post-1994 Rwanda (Melvin 2010), and bystander construction of implicatory denial in the context of human rights violations (Seu 2012).

In both approaches, the opposition between the ideal of human rights and their actual practice remains crucial. In the first, decontextualized ideas of human rights are opposed to the actual, yet not visible, practices that produce the authentic inequalities that must become the focus of human rights interventions if human rights are to fulfil their promissory potential. In this second case, the structure of social relations that organize the practices of social life prevents human rights from engendering the potential for equality and social justice, embodied in their ideal form. Consequently, actual human rights practice must take them into account if they are to lead to the desired social transformation.

Bearing Witness in a Sociological Register

Curiously, in the first approach—that is, shedding sociological light on phenomena that currently fall outside the human rights spotlight—human rights themselves play a marginal role in the analysis, functioning instead as a taken-for-granted placeholder for an abstract and decontextualized idea of justice and equity. The texture of the social situations that render individuals vulnerable to new forms of violence and inequality, as well as their socially invisibility, is analysed with all the conceptual and empirical firepower that attentive sociological analysis can muster. However, that human rights properly deployed are the necessary answer to such blatant injustice and inequity is professed rather than demonstrated.

Let me illustrate this point with some examples. In her contribution, Victoria Canning argues that "despite all other differences in the context of conflict, rape is a gendered Crime against Humanity, largely committed by men against women, and is indeed a crime which has historically been marginalised and sidelined legally, academically and politically" (2010, 851). She documents the alarming contemporary scope of this particular form of egregious systematic violence against women. Moreover she not only describes its harrowing effects on women but also draws attention to its broader social consequences:

> when a woman is raped, the effects are seldom experienced by *either* a society *or* a an individual. Society and the individual are interlocked in a complex web of consequences which may be multiplied when violent tactics become even more extreme, such as gang rapes, and when rape and sexual violence occur systematically and en masse. (2010, 852, emphasis in original)

The bulk of her paper is given over to outlining and reviewing the academic literature available to account for the dynamics underpinning this social phenomenon and highlighting three key explanatory dimensions. Concretely, she focuses on masculinity, gang rape, and "fatriarchy" to draw attention to how hypermasculinity, in conflict situations, enables fraternal bonding via the ritualization of gang rapes. The article concludes with a review of the ineffectuality of existing preventive measures, and with the injunction that sociologists acknowledge "the gendered divide in production, implementation and experience of rights on global and localised arenas" (Canning 2010, 860). The sociological arguments regarding the individual and collective conditions leading to gang rape and its contemporary prevalence are depressingly compelling. Canning suggests that human rights have an important role to play in ameliorating this unconscionable situation; she does not, however, explain how or why.

A second paper with a military focus is authored by McGarry et al. on the human rights of British soldiers (2012). In the paper, the authors explore the consequences of British soldiers' "unlimited liability" as inferred from the military covenant, which first appeared in 2000. The covenant "outlines an agreed set of principles of justice for soldiers, veterans and their families that are morally rather than legally binding" (2012, 1184). Unlimited liability refers to the obligation that soldiers have to "forsake their right to life for the good of others" during their service (2012, 1186). This liability however is conditional on the British governments' responsibility to provide soldiers with "'enthusiasm to fight' as 'a product of training, confidence in equipment, effective leadership and management [and] … fair terms of service'" (2012, 1186).

The paper then proceeds to review evidence suggesting a situation of deficiency of both military equipment and training in the context of the Iraq War, and the lack of recourse soldiers and their families have under the law. This is due to the fact that the British Human Rights Act places soldiers' right to life "outside of the judicial process by virtue of their military status, even if their life is forfeited at the expense of inadequate equipment" (2012, 1191). The authors draw attention to a striking and probably little known "state of exception" regarding soldier's rights that certainly should be remedied. As with the preceding article, however, what human rights are and why they would remedy the situation remains undiscussed.

A third article explores how children and young people become vulnerable to trafficking (Hynes 2010). Patricia Hynes convincingly argues that seen sociologically, the deplorable reality of the trafficking of children and young people is better understood as a broader social process rather than as "a one-off event" (2010, 953). Consequently, the focus of the analysis should be on "the contextual and personal 'vulnerabilities' of a child or young person" that makes them susceptible to "being trafficked" (2010, 954). Chief amongst the broader contextual factors are the "dynamics of social exclusion and inclusion [that] lead to inequalities within the global economy and ongoing conflicts across the world [that] create situations whereby children are separated from their families" (Hynes 2010, 955).

The analysis, with sobering acumen, unpacks the situations that are generative of vulnerability: conditions in conflict zones, extreme forms of socio-economic deprivation, state and non-state violence, and insufficient monitoring and resources in countries of destination. What is more, these factors frequently interact recursively intensifying the risk of vulnerability (2010, 959–66). While Hynes claims that this vulnerability "allows for the human rights context within countries of origin to be understood" (2010, 966), the strength of her empirical and theoretical analysis lies in her ability to identify the specific social processes and dynamics that make children and young people susceptible to trafficking. On my reading, human rights themselves play no conceptual or explanatory role in her sociological analysis; human rights is a convenient label rather than an explanatory concept for a complex sociological syndrome associated with violence and inequality.

Much the same can be said regarding three more contributions that I deal with more briefly. Tracey Killington, for instance, shows convincingly that climate change is likely to intensify the unequal struggle for scarce resources, create new waves of climate refugees, and leave some people literally stateless as a result of the actual physical disappearance of the territory on which they reside. What is more, she argues that the now dominant nation-state security-oriented approach is more likely to "promote resource competition and the threat of violence as primary mechanisms regulating relations amongst resources challenged communities in the future" (Skillington 2012, 1200). A more heartening vision of the future, she claims, can be found in the emergence of climate justice coalitions based on "principles of 'global reciprocity' and human rights solidarity" (2012, 1202). Perhaps, but why and how human rights will be able to displace the state-centred realist approach is not explained.

Similarly, in their discussion of the "right to mobility", Tanya Golash-Boza and Cecilia Menjívar argue that the right to mobility "is a fundamental human right, and must be incorporated into human rights doctrine" because state policies are frequently responsible for triggering migrant flows, while receiving countries attempt to discourage or curtail migration (2012). It could be, but the analysis entirely obviates what human rights are or what makes them socially efficacious. Their argument rests on the assumption that enshrining the right to mobility in human rights doctrine would restructure the power relations that organize contemporary migratory patterns. However, no sociological evidence is presented to bolster this assumption.

Finally, Damien Short persuasively shows that a careful reading of Raphael Lemkin's work—the man responsible for coining the term genocide—lends itself to the conclusion that analysing the historical and ongoing encounters of settlers and indigenous peoples through the lens of genocide is justified (2010, 839). He equally argues that the form the *UN Convention on the Prevention and Punishment of the Crime of Genocide* took fell far short of what Lemkin had envisioned (2010, 836). On the one hand, Short's analysis intimates that the kind of exegetical work that his paper undertakes should be mobilized to extend the meaning of genocide so as to include the situation of indigenous peoples. Agreed, but given that Lemkin's original arguments were ignored, it is not clear why contemporary sociologically inspired normative arguments would be more successful, nor that the terminological expansion would provide indigenous peoples with more effective levers with which to pursue their struggles.

Little mention is actually made of human rights in the article: how, why, and when human rights and genocide became entangled is not addressed,[9] a notable omission for an article that aims to position a sociology of genocide within the broader framework of the sociology of human rights. Finally and tellingly, in the closing paragraph, Short argues that sociologists should focus on analysing "continuing settler colonial expansionist projects driven by global capitalism and a 'logic of elimination'" (2010, 844). Once again, the focus is on mobilizing sociology's explanatory capacity to seize the manner in which inequality is produced and reproduced (i.e., capitalism and neo-colonialism!). That human rights provide a manner of overcoming such inequity remains a hopeful yet unexplained assumption.

In all the articles that I have grouped under the first category—that is, that of shedding sociological light on phenomena that contemporary human rights ignore or marginalize, for which the above six constitute exemplars—human rights themselves do no actual sociological explanatory work. Indeed, the logic underpinning the articles is not to interrogate the nature of human rights—the latter are to a large extent taken for granted! They, in effect, function as an abstract idea or fountain of norms used to connote justice and equality. What the different articles do consistently, however, is to deploy the considerable theoretical and empirical tools of sociological analysis to bring to light lamentable forms of inequity and suffering that are the product of unequal structured social relations. The goal of these papers, as I see it, is to make these broader and subtler forms of human suffering legible in the language of human rights.

The exigency of such legibility requires presenting sociological analysis, to invoke the phraseology of human rights, as a mode of bearing witness. Consequently, the commitment to human rights that each of the authors professes, sometimes implicitly, combined with the sobering presentations of the sociological facts of the case is, on my reading, an invocation of the moral alchemy that I analysed in Chap. 3, in my discussion of the normative turn in foundationalist approaches. It is encapsulated by the notion that the presentation of objective empirical analysis of situations of injustice, inequality, and suffering triggers the normative imperative for social change or, at the very least, the morally justified demand for such change.

Though such an approach is reminiscent of the marrying of positivism with ameliorism found in early social policy (Harris 1992), I believe that it is more persuasive to argue that such moral alchemy more closely resonates with the functioning of human rights as a political imaginary. Specifically, it enacts one of human rights' central tropes of representation: to wit, that the factual evidence of a wrong entails a unanimous obligation to provide a remedy. In much the same way that the ethos of human rights campaigns was, and continues to be, to give voice to the voiceless, to amplify the screams of those who cannot be heard, and to shine light on those who suffer in darkness, some sociological proponents of human rights use the tools of the discipline to draw attention to forms of suffering that are generally not seen, heard, or understood by the human rights community.

In doing so, they not only argue for including new and more finely drawn categories of suffering and advancing new human rights that might alleviate them—for example, the right to mobility, rights for women in conflict situations, and the human rights of climate refugees—they, also, identify particular social relations as being the "perpetrators" of suffering and inequality. In effect, they locate responsibility for suffering not in individual or collective perpetrators, central tropes of the human rights political imaginary, but in the "socially-structurally induced 'rights destructive'" currents of social life (Woodiwiss 2011, 135). They purport to bear witness, not to the suffering of particular individuals, the convention in human rights work, but to the specific social arrangements at the root of the suffering.

Powerful as this sociological mode of bearing witness seems, it is remarkably unreflective of the manner in which such sociological presentations of suffering and inequity might be made legible as instances of bearing witness, or the social mechanisms and processes through which bearing witness, in a sociological register, might trigger demands for actual processes of social change. For instance, in the context of what was to become Amnesty International's seminal articulation of bearing witness as a key dimension of the human rights political imaginary, Amnesty International developed and modulated rules, procedures, and doctrines "that maintained moral authority by elevating the idea of impartiality to an organizational imperative" (Hopgood 2006, 60). In doing so, Amnesty International "sought to construct in practical terms the kind of space – above, beyond, outside the world – in which the idea of objective morality, of a kind of universal truth, could be anchored" (Hopgood 2006, 60). It was the ongoing reproduction of such a space that transformed "fact" into the imperative of ethico-political action, through adoptions of prisoners of conscience, and campaigns for their release (Hopgood 2006, 65). Much of the success of these campaigns rested on the naming of both victims and perpetrators.

Today, social technologies of impartiality in factual reporting remain a key dimension of the human rights political imaginary (Moon 2012; Kurasawa 2007, 23–55; McLagan 2006).[10] However, they have to be understood as a component of the broader practice that Fuyuki Kurasawa calls the "ethico-political labour" of bearing witness (2007). Such social labour always confronts perils—that is, silence, incomprehension, indifference, forgetting, and repetition (Kurasawa 2007, 33) as well as the manifold modalities of social denial (Cohen 2001; Seu 2012)—that prevent entry to, or threaten to eject certain forms of suffering from, the human rights political imaginary. Below I explore Kurasawa's important contribution at greater length. Here, I merely invoke him to highlight the fragile link between the facticity of suffering and the moral obligation to remedy such suffering, a link that is fundamental to the efficacy of human rights as a political imaginary.

In other words, it might not necessarily be the case that human rights are inefficacious because they are abstract principles that do not correspond to the social reality of structured power relations on the ground. Instead, certain attempts to remedy suffering and inequality via human rights might fail because the "message in the bottle" (Kurasawa 2007, 12) is never read, or if read not understood as a human rights violation. Sociologists cannot afford to assume that the facticity of social inequality produced by sociological discourse will constitute a "fact" in the human rights imaginary. What is more, even if read and understood, it is perhaps the case that the social, political, and economic levers that would enable the channelling of moral outrage, or ethical responsibility, into social transformation are not available.

To explore such questions, it does not suffice to think about human rights as an idea or an abstract principle that can be concretized or put into practice to fit whatever our social justice needs might be as long as the political will exists. It must be grasped, as a dynamic yet tangible practice, or perhaps better as a set of practices, whose shortcomings might be due, for instance, to the concrete manner in which its representations, social technologies, modes of subjectivity and action, and organizational forms have developed and interact with other social relations and processes. If this is the case, bearing witness, in a sociological register, is not likely to fulfil the hopes with which it has been invested by the sociologists discussed above. Ironically, in their desire to make abstract conceptions of human rights socially concrete, they inadvertently go full circle. By focusing on deploying the empirical tools of sociological analysis to bear witness, rather than to critically interrogate the social conditions of possibility and efficacy of human rights as a structured practice, the aforementioned sociologists, unwittingly to be sure, equate human rights with a highly abstract ideal of justice, equality, and ethico-political action.

Social-Structural Obstacles

In the first set of articles just discussed, the implicit logic is that of bringing abstract ideas into contact with the practical realities of inequality and inequity by bearing witness in a sociological register. In the second set, to be discussed now, the accent is on identifying social-structural configurations that impede the implementation of human rights, or on drawing attention to the need to vernacularize them so that they can interface more effectively with the social relations and practices on the ground to produce social change. These analyses raise important issues with respect to the practices that facilitate or impede social change in the pursuit of justice and equality. The focus of the analyses, however, is on the obstacles that, to my mind, would block most efforts to create more equitable social relations, and not distinctly those faced by human rights. The specificity of human rights themselves is not explored; the implicature being that absent these obstacles, human rights could produce more equitable outcomes. As in all implicatures, that which is implied, in this case, the efficacy of human rights is more difficult to contest because it remains unenunciated. Let me unpack these ideas by reviewing some of the arguments from this second group of articles.

In her piece, Michelle Lamb (2010) identifies a significant obstacle encountered by human rights activists in their effort to introduce the ideas, language, and practices of human rights following the 1998 Northern Ireland Good Friday Agreement, namely, loyalty to ethnonationalist communities. Loyalty, she convincingly shows, is a powerful and layered social attachment that anchors identity and triggers passionate emotive responses that push back against "the introduction of human rights language, principles and practices in both pre- and post-Agreement Northern Ireland" (2010, 1000).

Inspired by the civil rights movement, in the 1960s, Catholics campaigned for "basic civil liberties, equality and non-discrimination"; however, "by the 1970s human rights had moved to the edges of political and social activity" (2010, 1000). Many within the Protestant community hesitated to use the language of human rights insofar as this was understood as veiled criticism of those state actors that constituted a bulwark against republican violence—namely, the Royal Ulster Constabulary and the British military and security apparatus (2010, 1001). Human rights, in Republican communities, were increasingly sidelined as they became associated with a reformist agenda that eschewed what many understood as the main objective, namely, forcing the British to leave, when not considered entirely unable to shield communities from the violence of the British state (2010, 1002).

Human rights resurfaced, argues Lamb, in Northern Ireland in the language of the Good Friday Agreement. Though instrumentalized by political elites for party political purposes, human rights also became available to local communities as a way of framing claims around inequality and poverty. Human rights, also, provided a broader understanding of community, with the potential to overcome the long sedimented ethnonationalist divide (Lamb 2010, 997). Despite evidence of their newfound normative traction, Lamb argues that human rights occupy "a space of liminality" in Northern Ireland: "community activists hover between loyalty and the language, principles and practices of human rights, and between loyalty to their communities and new relationships emerging across the political divide" (2010, 1007).

Lamb skilfully draws on Ann Swidler's (1986) conception of "strategies of action" to convey the complex cultural ecology within which actions unfold: new normative values, ideals, and practices rather than sweeping away existing ones articulate with them in complex ways, frequently generating new vernaculars. Her interview data with human rights activists in Belfast provide a rich illustration of this phenomenon. However, the notion that loyalty acts as an "obstacle" (Lamb 2010, 995) to human rights is premised on the unexplained assertion that the UDHR should be read as containing a "radical vision" for "remaking the world" such that "structure and systems that concretely embody the human rights ideals of respect, dignity and equality all have the power to transform social action" (2010, 994). Consequently, insofar as human rights have not had a more profound impact in the context of Northern Ireland, there must be a social-structural barrier hindering their progress, to wit loyalty to community. What her analysis excludes is the possibility that there might be some inherent limits to human rights' ability to produce the desired change. This is surprising, not least because one of her respondents in fact raises the possibility that human rights practices provide a vision of change that they cannot deliver: "Rights can sometimes create this illusion that things are alright, [that] they are fixable" (Interviewee 4 in Lamb 2010, 1004).

Similarly, Eunna Lee-Gong (2010) frames her analysis of the implementation of the National Basic Livelihood Security System (NBLSS) in South Korea, as an opportunity to explore how rights are affected by the social, political, and economic context in which they emerge (2010, 880). Citing Woodiwiss (2005), she convincingly argues that rights are "constructed in a contingent and variable way according to the specific characteristics of the societies in which they are developed and as a particular outcome of political struggles over interests" (Woodiwiss in Lee-Gong 2010, 880). Consequently, she begins by providing an overview of the broad historical context for the development of social welfare initiatives after South Korea achieved its independence from Japan in 1945. She shows that until 1997 successive governments focused on economic development, drawing on social welfare measures only for the purposes of political legitimacy and social stabilization (2010, 883). Such legitimacy depended, in part, on the elites' successful reworking of the Confucius tradition to foreground values associated with hard work and self-reliance and to stigmatize dependence on state provision (2010, 883–84).

The 1997 Asian Economic Crisis drove a wedge into the hegemonic state discourse that had enabled political and economic elites to rule since the 1940s and opened up space for social welfare movements to advocate for social rights. The election of Kim Dae-jung, "the human rights president",[11] in 1998, accelerated the uptake of human rights discourses in the struggle against poverty and for social justice (Lee-Gong 2010, 886) and contributed to the mobilization in support of the passage of the NBLSS. Despite the efflorescence of new conceptions of social rights, family responsibility and self-reliance remained central to conceptions of welfare in South Korean society (Lee-Gong 2010, 887). It is precisely the prevalence of the latter conjoined with a significant degree of discretion for "street level" welfare officials that has limited the actualization of the rights described in the NBLSS (Lee-Gong 2010, 889). Lee-Gong concludes by arguing that in South Korean society, "where the state had long played the cultural card to justify its lack of financial commitment to social welfare by strategically promoting an individual duty rather than an individual right, advocacy for legal rights and legal reforms to fully guarantee the right to social security is still much needed" (2010, 892).

While Lee-Gong is surely right to point to the political conjuncture that opened up space for the struggle for social rights and the ideologies and political and economic interests that have steered the actualization of the rights enshrined in the NBLSS, the role of human rights in the process is far from clear. How human rights opened up or foreclosed new modes of struggling for social rights is not discussed, nor is the concrete difference that human rights have made in actual practice. Insofar as they have a role in her analysis, human rights have a perfunctory one: a placeholder for a generalized idea of equity and social justice. This is in contrast to the concrete governmental and ideological practices that purportedly thwart their implementation.

Lee-Gong's analysis touches on what Anthony Woodiwiss, in another contribution from this second group of articles, describes as contemporary Asian familialism (2012, 972). However, unlike Lee-Gong for whom familial duty in South Korea constitutes an obstacle to be overcome by human rights (2010, 892), Woodiwiss sees in the social-structural configuration of contemporary familialism the opportunity for a distinctively Asian human rights regime, namely, "enforceable benevolence" (2012). I will discuss Woodiwiss' path-breaking sociological work on human rights in greater detail in Chap. 6 and in the book's conclusion. Here I want to briefly summarize his position and how it fits in with the other contributions discussed in this section.

Woodiwiss writes, "for sociologists human rights are nothing special but simply a subset of the much larger set of social relations that produce and enforce behavioural expectations, a subset distinguished by their legal form and their focus on the limitations of abuses of power" (2012, 967). Further, he adds, human rights are "humanly produced assemblies of discursive elements" whose social and normative efficacy rests on their resonance with the social relations in which and through which they circulate. Consequently, on their own, they "do not and cannot carry the whole or even much of the weight, so to speak, of ensuring that the desired social expectations are met" (2012, 967). When and where they are socially efficacious, "they simply reinforce other means of preventing and punishing abuse by making the provisions of certain specific civil, political, economic, social and cultural entitlements and protections legally enforceable" (2012, 967).

Given the centrality of contemporary familialism in many Asian countries, and that contemporary human rights have a historical trajectory defined by the development of European capitalist social relations, Woodiwiss argues that it does not make sociological or practical sense for that matter to try to impose European human rights discourses on East Asian countries. European-inspired human rights, he argues, will "have little or no social resonance in Asian societies except amongst a heroic but eccentric minority" (2012, 969–70). Drawing on his extensive scholarship on the development of labour and human rights in the Pacific Rim, in the US, and the UK (Woodiwiss 1992, 1998, 2003), he argues that whereas in European social formations, protection from power has been sought through its dispersion via liberal modes of government, in Eastern Asian countries, the preferred method has been "the concentration of power in specific and readily identifiable social locations" (2012, 971).

Consequently, rather than attempting to disassemble familialism and replace it with European conceptions of individual freedoms, the goal should be "to see that the duties and obligations central to familialist discourses may be construed in such a way as to be seen as the equivalents of liberties and freedoms in their social consequences" (2012, 972). Woodiwiss' argument is not that Asian familialism as it exists today is sufficient to deliver the kinds of freedoms and protection to which European human rights aspire. Rather it is that a human rights regime different in form and content could deliver equivalent protections from the abuse of power by democratically codifying and legally enforcing the protective potential contained in the prevailing social relations of inequality.

Woodiwiss' analysis of human rights distils the sociological essence of human rights to the following question: What are the concrete legally codified and socially enforceable arrangements that might offer subjects protection from the abuse of power? In European societies, it is the surprising and circuitous development of private property rights and liberal rationalities of government (Woodiwiss 2005), while in East Asia it is the capacity for enforceable benevolence (Woodiwiss 1998, 2003, 2012). Unlike the other authors discussed in this and in the previous section, Woodiwiss, refreshingly, does not equate human rights to an abstract conception of social justice or equality. Indeed he argues that "respect for human rights cannot logically result in the end of inequality since human rights as an idea, let alone a disciplinary practice, is only possible because of the inequalities intrinsic to the existence of the state and capitalism" (Woodiwiss 2005, 11). That said, limited as human rights might be, Woodiwiss maintains that were they absent, we would certainly be worse off (2005, XIV).

Nonetheless, in inserting his analysis of human rights as a tributary of the longer development of social arrangements offering individuals protection from, and remedy for, the abuse of power, he leaves aside, in the article under discussion, the specificity of their emergence and the particularity of their functioning, beyond their legal nature. He sees human rights as the legal codification of protective possibilities—namely, what we today call civil, political, social, economic, and cultural entitlements—contained within specific configurations of social relations that can be tapped and institutionalized through social and political struggle. In this sense, his position provides a more analytically developed conception of Turner's notion of human rights as a "juridical shield" (2006, 29) discussed in Chap. 3. Thus, once human rights have been sociologically demystified, that is to say their social power has been unveiled as protective in nature rather than revolutionary, they are best analysed with the tools of the sociology of law.

Taking human rights' legal nature seriously is important, as is Woodiwiss' sophisticated understanding of human rights as discursive assemblages whose social efficacy is contingent on their resonance with the prevailing social relations, a point that I develop further in Chap. 6 and the book's conclusion. However, Woodiwiss' approach, as I show in greater detail in Chap. 6, unfortunately sidesteps the crucial question of the specificity of human rights' historical emergence and more importantly the particular ways in which they become patterned in what Wilson (1997) calls "the social life of rights", or what I think is more usefully conceptualized in terms of a political imaginary. In other words, his analysis cannot provide an account of the particularity of the representations, social technologies, modes of subjectivity and agency, and organizational forms that steer and limit the types of discursive elements that can be "assembled" as human rights claims, outside of the legal sphere.

To my mind, he does not give sufficient attention to the prospect that there might be something in the practice of human rights that limits its ability to extract more powerful protective measures from social relations. In a certain sense, Woodiwiss condenses human rights to the abstract notion of legally enforceable protective measures, training the force of his very considerable analytical abilities on what types of vernaculars might give them concrete voice, or in his terms "provincialize them" (Woodiwiss 2012, 966), as in the case of enforced benevolence in his analysis of East Asia. The fact that human rights can only offer limited protection is due to the existing relations of power rather than any limitations in human rights themselves.

More briefly now, in her analysis of the promotion of national reconciliation in post-genocide Rwanda, Jennifer Melvin (2010) argues, following Wilson's (2001) study of the Truth and Reconciliation Commission in South Africa (TRC), that the language of human rights can be instrumentalized by state elites for whom reconciliation becomes an expedient lever for promoting state activities and legitimacy. This, she argues, short-circuits the broader social, political, and judicial dynamics that might contribute to a more equitable and democratic post-genocide reconciliation process (2010, 930). After reviewing some key contributions from the flourishing reconciliation literature, Melvin discusses the central features of the reconciliation programme elaborated by the National Unity and Reconciliation Commission (NURC) created in the transitional period. Subsequently inserted in the 2003 constitution, the NURC was tasked with promoting "positive goals related to unity and reconciliation" or eliminating "factors that create divisions or discrimination in society" (Melvin 2010, 937). Given these goals, mass education initiatives became a key component of the NURC programme. Melvin notes, however, that while educational material and activities have certainly promoted the value of "solidarity, unity and reconciliation", they have equally been woven with government-sponsored discourse supporting "legislation limiting civil and political rights of freedom of expression and press", thus contributing to delegitimizing opposition parties and undermining democracy (2010, 946).

Melvin, also, discusses the restorative justice initiatives pursued through the Gacaca[12] programme, which convicted a sizable number of perpetrators and enabled some genocide survivors to access economic support and resources for reconstruction. Despite this, she adds, many survivors received no support at all, as evidenced by their contemporary marginalization and poverty. The latter is particularly striking when compared to the financial assistance received by repatriated ex-combatants who were also generally excluded from the Gacaca procedures (Melvin 2010, 944). Finally, in addition to the ex-combatants, members of the Rwandan Patriotic Front (RPF)[13] have also been exempted from judicial proceedings in the reconciliation processes. This has raised questions regarding the impartiality, hence the fairness of the judicial proceedings.

Melvin's analysis identifies a number of important shortcomings in the reconciliation process as it has unfolded in Rwanda. It correctly points to its fragility and the ease with which it has been made to serve sectional interests. The educational programmes were overwhelmingly geared towards promoting reconciliation rather than launching a more open-ended process.[14] They did not leave space for dissenting voices, a trend that subsequently was intensified through further curtailments of the right of expression, eroding political and civil rights. The reconciliation programme also failed to deal equitably with perpetrators of violence, shielding those associated with the RPF, not to mention its neglect of the economic and social rights of many of the genocide survivors. The overall thrust of the analysis is that the creators of the reconciliation programme instrumentalized human rights discourse. The implicature being, had state actors not instrumentalized human rights, the reconciliation process would have been more successful. What this would have meant in practice, and how precisely human rights would have been mobilized to produce this outcome, is unfortunately not addressed. The focus, as with all the articles discussed in this section, is on the social-structural obstacles rather than with any potential deficiencies of human rights themselves.

Finally Hannah Miller, in her analysis of the deployment of human rights frames by development practitioners, argues that it is crucial to distinguish between "rights-based" (RBA) and "rights-framed approaches" (RFA) (2010). The former, she claims, should be reserved for organizations that use human rights law, treaties, and norms as explicit tools to operationalize, structure, and deliver their programmes (2010, 916–19). While the term RBA is frequently used to designate all development agencies or groups that draw on human rights language, Miller argues that such an approach obscures important differences in the kind of work that human rights perform in the aid sector (2010, 916). Conceptually, she frames her analysis via Wilson's notion of the life of rights. This necessitates distinguishing between "human rights law" and "human rights talk", the former indexing "'positivised rules' in national and international law" and the latter "how people speak about those norms, or aspire to expand or interpret them in new ways" (Miller 2010, 920).

Seen through the analytical prism of rights talk, Miller shows that RFA organizations adopt a strategic approach in their deployment of human rights, using them to advance goals, programmes, campaigns, or strategies whose origins or goals need not be human rights based. The value of human rights in these cases is the legitimacy that they can command when strategically aimed at specific audiences or fora (2010, 920–27). Though she does not use the term, her analysis is an instance of how human rights are vernacularized by different organizational cultures, and it contributes to our understanding of the manifold ways in which human rights are articulated with other social justice discourses. Indeed, to my mind, the strength of Miller's analysis is that it reveals that human rights discourse, though dominant, has not entirely engulfed all other social justice discourses and practices. This draws attention to an assumption that is too frequently held by many contemporary human rights advocates, namely, that human rights and social justice are of a piece.

This said, even though Miller attempts to analyse how human rights are put into practice, what is in fact being put into practice within her analytical framework is an idea: "By focussing on 'rights talk', one of the central aims of the research project was to establish the meanings assigned by social actors as they incorporate and embed ideas of human rights within campaigning activities" (Miller 2010, 920). Whatever constraints human rights might impose on their vernacularization, as a result of their being structured as a practice, remains hidden from view. Once again it is human rights as an idea, ideal, or norm that is being made tangible by being embedded in a concrete practice, rather than two distinct practices coming together—for instance, human rights and another variant of social justice campaigning. This notion is further reinforced by her approving reference to Wilson's contention that human rights talk can be understood in terms of its "ideological promiscuity" (Wilson in Miller 2010, 920), making them available to all manner of ideological projects, to all appearances, virtually with little constraint.

As in the other cases considered in this and the preceding section, with some exceptions, the understanding of human rights as principles, norms, and ideals that is at the centre of contemporary human rights discourse is accepted at face value. What follows from this understanding is ably summarized by Robin Redhead and Nick Turnbull in their study of human rights practitioners: "It requires us to acknowledge that the construction of human rights is driven by the actions of people at an individual level, in different locations, and is not solely derived from philosophical principles nor from human rights conventions" (2011, 174). Moreover, because of the limited purchase of "human rights law", it is the "rhetorical value"—the latter being more malleable—that human rights practitioners often put to work (Redhead and Turnbull 2011, 179). Redhead and Turnbull conclude that it is important to understand the range of practices that are enacted by actors mobilizing human rights discourse because these actors exercise "considerable agency" (2011, 187). The expansive scope of their agency in deploying human rights rhetoric is made possible by the abstractness of the norms, principles, and laws that underpin them.

What if we put aside this understanding of human rights as an abstract and seemingly extremely manipulable, idea, ideal, or norm? What if we understand human rights, instead, as embedded, embodied, embrained, and inthinged, in other words, if we conceptualize them as a practice in and of themselves? It is to this task that I now turn in the following two sections, where I examine promising forays into conceptualizing human rights as a practice, rather than as an abstract idea opposed to the reality of a social practice.

Human Rights as Ethico-Political Practice

At first glance, Kurasawa's position seems destined to take him along the trajectories that I have summarized in the preceding two sections insofar as he begins with the human rights idea/social practice opposition: "this book", he writes,

> is intended as a contribution to a critical and substantive theory of global justice, one that converts the latter from an ideal steeped in noble sentiments and intentions, or a juridified concept enshrined in multilateral declarations, into an ensemble of emancipatory practices constructed through ethico-political labour. (2007, 4)

He succeeds in opening new ground, however, because he introduces a crucial question. One that, for the most part, has not been broached by the authors discussed in this chapter, namely, *what does it mean to define human rights as a social practice, as opposed to defining human rights in opposition to a social practice*? Kurasawa does not assume that the role of sociological analysis is to expand existing conceptions of human rights nor to sociologically bear witness to a range of vulnerabilities and forms of violence not visible in the contemporary human rights regime. Indeed, as I show below, he attempts to understand the sociological basis for the type of witnessing that has become the *sine qua non* of human rights. Neither does he see the role of the sociological analysis of human rights as identifying the structural obstacles whose absence would release the efficacy of human rights. Instead, he singles out the concrete obstacles that human rights as an identifiable type of social practice confronts. The latter is conceived as a "labour" defined by an assemblage of the "belief-systems that groups and individuals hold and the cultural and socio-political rituals they perform" (2007, 8).

He contrasts this to three dominant approaches for analysing human rights: philosophical normativism, politico-legal institutionalism, and global civil society empiricism (2007, 4). He understands the first as the broad and inclusive effort to develop a universalizable cosmopolitan ethics to enable the realization of human rights. The second refers to efforts to understand how the norms and principles enshrined in human rights instruments might induce the "reform or overhaul of existing transnational legal infrastructure and set of multilateral political institutions, in order to increase democratic accountability and socio-economic fairness as well as to tackling problems confronting humankind as a whole" (Kurasawa 2007, 5).[15] Though not without value, both of these approaches, argues Kurasawa, fail to give an account of the complex and stratified ways in which human rights are practised, echoing Alexander's critique of abstract moral argumentation in the context of the civil sphere (2006, 14–15), Kate Nash's emphasis on the centrality of "cultural politics" (2009b), and my own discussion, in Chap. 2, of the need for thick sociological accounts of human rights.

The third approach, global civil society empiricism, as its name suggests, does not suffer from an excess of abstraction. To the contrary, in climbing down from the heights of the formalism of normative syntax, which characterizes the other two modes of apprehending human rights, it produces a thick description of the diverse, distributed, contingent, and interconnected manner through which actors struggle for competing conceptions of human rights in an emerging global civil society (Kurasawa 2007, 8). The problem here, Kurasawa notes, is that this additive manner, through which the unruly variety of NGOs and social movements are catalogued, eschews the task of identifying the specificity of the ethico-politico labour that these diverse actors and their practices share.

Kurasawa offers his conceptualization of "critical substantivism" as a bridge over the impasses associated with the three aforementioned approaches. It begins by turning over the social soil in which the work of global justice is to be seeded, "unpacking and making sense of the social labour of groups and persons implicated in human rights struggles in historically specific socio-cultural contexts", hence the substantivism (2007, 10). The critical declension of the substantivism arises from the simultaneous attempt to "formulate normative reconstructions of what is required ethically and politically of these struggles to advance the work of global justice" (2007, 10). Kurasawa defines global justice very broadly as a solidaristic sensibility, taking root globally,

> the belief that all human beings are entitled to a full spectrum of socio-economic and civil-political rights, and conversely that abuses of such rights ought not be tolerated because of a territorially unbounded sense of mutuality is acquiring an enviable ethical weight in many societies. (Kurasawa 2007, 3)

This moral sense, however, cannot be accounted for by formalism, of the philosophical or institutionalist varieties. Sociologically, human rights are best grasped, Kurasawa convincingly argues, as a social practice, "a pattern of materially and symbolically oriented social action that agents undertake within organized political, cultural and socio-economic fields, and whose main features are recognizable across several temporal and spatial settings" (Kurasawa 2007, 11).

Wanting to guard against voluntaristic conceptions of human rights—the weakness of global civil society empiricism—and to identify the concrete obstacles, or to use his term "perils", that the labour of human rights confronts, Kurasawa writes that "a practice is neither a spontaneous act nor the expression of free will on the part of agents, who would shape the social world outside of any structural constraint and conditions" (2007, 12). Consequently, he introduces the notion of a "mode of practice", which includes not only the practices that define human rights as particular type of ethico-political labour but also encompasses the broader social-political terrain in which these practices do or do not take effect. In other words, a mode of practice also includes "the historically transmitted and socially institutionalized forms of thought and action, discourses and relations of power, which have enabling and constraining effects upon a practice's effectiveness and the range of possibilities within which it operates" (Kurasawa 2007, 12).

Though ethico-political action is always embedded in concrete historical socio-political contexts, the concept of a mode of practice draws attention to "patterns of discourses, ethical principles, and socio-political rituals" that are modular in nature. That is to say, they are transposable to different settings. This means that human rights, conceived as a mode of practice, "are neither singular (containing a unique combination of elements in each context) nor identical (containing exactly the same combination of elements in all contexts)" (Kurasawa 2007, 13). So much for the form, what are the transposable modes of practice that characterize the work of human rights-inspired global justice?

Kurasawa identifies five such modes of practice, bearing witness, forgiveness, foresight, aid, and solidarity (Kurasawa 2007, 17). All five, he argues, not only capture the range of labours in which global justice actors are engaged, but can be equally understood as action-theoretical approximations of civil, political, and socio-economic rights: bearing witness and forgiveness (civil and political rights), aid and solidarity (socio-economic rights), and foresight (a combination of civil and political and socio-economic rights) (2007, 18). Very briefly, bearing witness involves the social practices through which past and present atrocities and structural injustices are recognized, triggering ethico-political actions aimed at remedy and/or structural change. Consequently, this mode of practice provides the ethico-political foundations for the remaining four (Kurasawa 2007, 12).

Forgiveness, which Kurasawa links to the growth of truth commissions, what Claire Moon elsewhere characterizes as the "reconciliation industry" (2008, 2), is the attempt to memorialize and provide redress for past violence and injustice, drawing a fine balance between retributive and restorative justice that aims for the possibility but not the necessity of reconciliation. The third mode of practice is foresight; it strives to "anticipate and prevent future instances of structural and situational violence" (Kurasawa 2007, 20). The next mode of practice is aid, "humanitarian assistance to distant strangers placed in situations of extreme vulnerability and mass suffering" (Kurasawa 2007, 21), while the last is solidarity, a thick mode of transnational solidaristic labour, "a cosmopolitanism from below" (Kurasawa 2007, 22).

What links all five modes of practices are three aspects that, Kurasawa argues, mark the work of global justice. First, intersubjectivity, the five modes of practice presuppose a "dialogic process" where actors, frequently at a distance, come to some shared understanding of the occurrence, or the need for redress or prevention of situations of structural violence or injustice. Second, publicity, the different modes of practice necessitate public spaces in which accounts of injustice can circulate, and ethico-political demands can be made. These spaces draw attention to and publicize global injustices. Third, transnationalism, the modes of practices, though rooted in local circumstances, increasingly circulate and provoke responses beyond the space of the nation-state.

Kurasawa's approach to human rights makes a decisive contribution to the model of human rights as political imaginary about which I will elaborate below. Most importantly, it draws our attention to the necessity of conceptualizing human rights as consisting of modular sets of practices, tying ethical belief and moral and political imperative to meaningful patterned and ritualized activities or performances that actors embody and enact. Such enactment aims at the formation of an imagined moral community (Kurasawa 2007, 43) built on what Jeffrey Alexander, in the context of his analysis of the civil sphere, identifies as a "process of emotional identification and symbolic extension" (2006, 306), or what Nash calls the "authority" to define who is the subject of human rights (2009b, 30). In other words, rather than act on an already constituted moral community, human rights' modular practices contribute to its possible constitution. The purpose of the community is to collectively imagine and instantiate a sphere of political and ethical solidarity where social and political demands have the power of moral imperative that can be potentially translated into social-political action, legal remedy, or redress.

As noted above, Kurasawa rightly argues that bearing witness is the keystone of human rights practice. In the next section, I discuss his analysis of bearing witness and forgiveness and more briefly the remaining three modes of practice, foresight, aid, and solidarity. Though Kurasawa's contribution to our understanding of human rights is noteworthy, ultimately it is limited by its inability, as I will argue below, to distinguish between human rights and global justice more generally.

The Labour of Global Justice

Kurasawa compellingly draws on the figure of the "message in the bottle" to communicate the social and political fragility of bearing witness (2007, 23). The latter's foundational role in the context of global justice is, Kurasawa argues, overdetermined by a number of factors: the successful dissemination of the discourse of human rights inaugurated by the 1948 UDHR; the development of the legal tools and judicial capacity to prosecute crimes against populations and the incorporation of eyewitness accounts in these processes; the central role of testimonies in the plethora of Truth and Reconciliation Commissions; the deployment of testimonial accounts by NGOs to raise awareness of famines, instances of extreme poverty, and atrocities; the intensification and growth of transnational media flows and media providers; the availability and accessibility of virtual recording technologies; and the exacerbation of modern anxiety regarding social forgetting (Kurasawa 2007, 27–28).

Despite favourable conditions that facilitate bearing witness as a key mode of contemporary social understanding, it remains an intersubjective ethico-political labour that can easily eventuate into misunderstanding. If the success of bearing witness depends on voice, making socially audible the experience of suffering and violence, it is inseparable from the complex and multilayered contexts where the power of competing groups and institutions structure the extent to which voices can circulate and be heard in the public sphere (Kurasawa 2007, 31–32). Voice, understood as an individual speaking for herself or through a proxy, such as an NGO, in the absence of a listening and engaged public, is condemned to the "abyss of silence" (Kurasawa 2007, 33). As scholars have persuasively shown, some voices are more likely to be heard than others (Cohen 2001; Englund 2006; Ron et al. 2005; Ramos et al. 2007).

Even when heard, voice must negotiate the social gauntlet of incomprehension; weaving testimonials that resonate across transnational and transcultural spaces is always haunted by the prospect of crises of "referencing and of witnessing" (Hesford 2004, 130). The likelihood of incomprehension is equally sown by the sheer difficulty of capturing something of the singularity of the suffering while communicating it in terms that makes it more broadly comprehensible, gesturing towards the universalizable (Kurasawa 2007, 38–39). Testimonials are inevitably formally mediated—be they through narrative (Schaffer and Smith 2004; Brysk 2013; Dawes 2009; Gandsman 2013), documentary or other visual media (McLagan 2006; W. S. Hesford 2004, 2011; Manzo 2008; Sliwinski 2011), theatre (Rae 2009; Madison 2010), NGO reports (Moon 2012; R. A. Wilson 2009), or acts of public witnessing in Truth and Reconciliation Commissions (Moon 2008; R. Wilson 2001; Melvin 2010). Insofar as they draw on conventional formulae to communicate their content, testimonials risk rendering the experience of suffering inauthentic for both victim and witness, or as James Dawes notes, "the well-told story of suffering can generate as much suspicion and alienation as sympathy and action" (2009, 64).

Still, even when the likelihood of incomprehension is overcome, it is possible that members of the public, shielded by a plethora of socially patterned modalities of denial, might know, but not care (Cohen 2001). Indifference, Kurasawa argues, is the product of myriad overlapping processes: the various psychological and social mechanisms that distance the modern self from the suffering of others, the moral individualism that makes each responsible for their own fate, the outsourcing of morality and care for the other to bureaucratized organizations, the centrality of nationalism and the social-cultural construction of belonging around the axis of sameness, as well as the compassion fatigue that results from the routinization, and I might add in some cases the exploitation (Richey and Ponte 2011), of suffering (Kurasawa 2007, 40–46; Cohen 2001). If bearing witness is able to overcome silence, incomprehension, and the peril of indifference, it might spark a kind of transnational empathy that makes actors able "to open to, engage and grasp the very different plights of remote strangers" (Kurasawa 2007, 46) and invoke the normative, legal, social, and political practices that could eventuate in remedy, redress, or what Alexander in a different context has called "civil repair" (2006).[16]

Although bearing witness is frequently mobilized to construct an imagined moral community through voice, interpretation, and empathy to respond in the present to past and ongoing injustices, it also seeks to thicken this community through "modes of collective remembrance that counteract the effects of mnemonic erosion in the face of global injustices" (Kurasawa 2007, 47; Levy and Sznaider 2010). Through the ongoing patterned labour of memorialization, commemoration, and ritualization, past injustices are re-inscribed in the present, providing a common ground for the ethico-political labour of global justice that can mitigate but never fully overcome the hazard of forgetting. Finally, implicit in the labour of preserving memory and the development of empathy for the suffering of distant and/or excluded others is also the will to avoid the reoccurrence of violence, that is, prevention. "Testimonies often express the hope that cognitive and moral progress can be achieved, that human beings can learn from history by reflecting upon and realizing the tragic costs of denial, complacency, indifference and forgetting" (Kurasawa 2007, 53), and act to reduce the likelihood of avoidable human suffering in the future.

The second mode of practice of global justice is forgiveness, which Kurasawa understands as an ethico-political response to situations of mass atrocities, and systemic injustices. Forgiveness is not about letting bygones be bygones, but rather about engaging perpetrators, beneficiaries, and bystanders in public acts of truth telling with the goal of collectively authoring an account of the past in which both perpetrators and sufferers, if not agree, can locate themselves (Kurasawa 2007, 59). Even then, forgiveness emerges as a mere possibility rather than a certainty. Kurasawa contrasts his analysis of forgiveness, as a mode of practice, with two competing paradigms: the juridico-political and the theological. The juridico-political paradigm refers to the political imposition of forgiveness from above and/or the use of the court system to settle accounts with individuals accused of human rights violations. In this second case, individuals are charged for human rights violations. If they are found guilty, they are given a punishment proportional to the crime, typically in the form of a jail sentence. Upon completion of the latter, individuals are considered to have paid their debt to society and are eligible for forgiveness.

The juridico-political approach fails to capture key aspects of forgiveness, understood as a socially embedded ethico-political labour. First, the legally deduced proportionality between crime and punishment is not likely to correspond with the immensity of the suffering generated by the acts of the perpetrator. Second, the focus on individual responsibility leaves aside the broader structural context of the violence, whose transformation is necessary for forgiveness, and obviates the need, in some instances, for collective forms of responsibility for mass atrocities. Finally, it fails to grasp the bottom-up nature of forgiveness, the enormously intricate labour in the form of claims, debates, deliberations, publicity, and social activism that weaves the possibility of forgiveness into the social fabric. Forgiveness is not something that can be imposed from the top down as a matter of political or judicial expediency (Kurasawa 2007, 61–62).

The theological paradigm, for its part, understands forgiveness as a gift, "where the ethical burden of forgiveness falls squarely upon the shoulders of the forgiving party, who must demonstrate a self-abnegating righteousness toward the former wrongdoers" (Kurasawa 2007, 63). This voluntaristic and overly abstract conceptualization fails to capture the multilayered social practices that prepare the social terrain in the hope that forgiveness might germinate at some future moment.

In opposition to these two approaches, Kurasawa argues that there is no moral commensurability between those requesting to be forgiven, who may be criminally, ethically, or politically responsible, and the victimized groups. In fact, the latter "accept the logic of non-equivalence and refrain from pursuing a response that would be proportional to the violence of the original act" (2007, 66). In other words, there is no legal squaring of the circle. In addition, victimized groups must be free to decide whether to participate in the labour of forgiveness, while reserving the right to forgive or not.

One of the perils that forgiveness, as a social practice, confronts is the possibility of forgetting, be this wilful or not. Thus, a central aspect of the ethico-labour of forgiveness is not only bearing witness but also reconstructing the past. This reconstruction cannot, as a matter of expediency, gloss over difficult questions; it must confront the nature of the violence or the atrocity without flinching. The success of this process depends on it unfolding in a participatory democratic public sphere, which can lead to a better understanding of the breadth of the injustice. Detailed information, often only known by perpetrators, identifying the particular mechanisms that enabled the injustice and violence, as well as the gains thus obtained, must be made public, as must the identities of perpetrators, beneficiaries, and bystanders. The goal, however, is not solely to excavate the details of a hidden past but to produce a "socio-political construction" of the past that is "meaningful for present and future generations" (Kurasawa 2007, 73).

The collective labour of dealing with the past confronts, yet another peril, that of the denial of responsibility. Such denial might take different forms such as alleging ignorance of the extent of the violence, post hoc rationalization or justification of the violence, scapegoating, shifting blame on to faceless bureaucratic structures, deflection through claims of collective "brainwashing", the shedding of "crocodile tears", alleging collective guilt where no one is responsible because everyone is, and where the principled refusal of some to participate in the injustice is not acknowledged (Kurasawa 2007, 74–76). The prospect of further working the social terrain to give forgiveness an opportunity to bud depends on the social capacity, distinct from a judicial or state one, of distinguishing amongst different forms of responsibility and treating each accordingly. First, there is criminal responsibility for those who directly participated in acts of violence. Second, moral responsibility, which refers to bystanders that were passively complicit, lent tacit support, or knew but opted not to speak out or act. Finally there is the political responsibility of those who gained advantage or concessions as a consequence of the violence (Kurasawa 2007, 76). What is crucial here is not the assignment of guilt by court or state, but the acceptance of responsibility because

> parties taking responsibility for massive human rights abuses are asking those who may forgive them to distinguish doer from deed, so that the collective condemnation of these abuses can still leave enough political and normative space to determine that those who committed them are potentially redeemable – and thus deserving of forgiveness. (Kurasawa 2007, 79)

For all that, responsibility will not contribute to the possibility of forgiveness if it leads to impunity or vigilantism. Human rights abuses must be symbolically repaired; those deemed responsible must be sanctioned, and victims must be compensated (Kurasawa 2007, 80). In the case of criminal responsibility, perpetrators must be subject to retributive justice; in the cases of moral and political responsibility, restorative justice is appropriate. This means individual punishment for some, a systemic dismantling of the regime responsible for the violence, the loss of unfairly acquired privileges, and symbolic and material compensation for victims. It is at this point that reconciliation might begin to develop (Kurasawa 2007, 80–85).

Reconciliation, argues Kurasawa, is not a sudden occurrence but a possible outcome of a long thorny process laced with uncertainty and the ever-present prospect of failure. It is the product of deliberative and symbolic practices, rituals, and performances, and it cannot be enacted by state, constitutional, or legal decree. The past must be reconstituted and remembered, but in a way that seeds the prospect of reconciliation; it cannot be a return to a fabled time of harmony (Kurasawa 2007, 86–88). Reconciliation, continues Kurasawa, must be understood on a continuum from thin to thick. In the former case, reconciliation refers to tolerance, a lack of victimization and cruelty. Despite its minimalism, in cases of extreme violence and social polarization, even a thin reconciliation can be considered a noteworthy accomplishment (2007, 90). Closer to the thicker pole of reconciliation, one would find "widespread civil society participation in the invention of historical narratives and collected symbols that commemorate past horrors and injustices, pay tribute to victims, celebrate societal rebirth and reimagine a different present and future", conjoined with significant structural changes to combat discrimination and economic inequalities (Kurasawa 2007, 91).

The third mode of practice, making up the labour of global justice, is foresight. Whereas the previous two modes of practice have a future-oriented component, they remain modes of global justice for dealing with the past. Cosmopolitan foresight builds on the emergence of recent global patterns of prevention, such as the responsibility to protect, concern over climate change and the global spread of contagious disease, and so on (Kurasawa 2007, 98–99). Despite this, the relative novelty of these practices means that Kurasawa's analysis, as he acknowledges, falls between the analytical ordering of empirical phenomena and the construction of a normative framework to guide the development of this emerging mode of practice (Kurasawa 2007, 99). The perils that foresight, as a mode of ethico-labour in the service of global justice, faces are the putative inscrutability of the future, presentism, alarmism, and resignation.

To counter these, Kurasawa draws attention to the ethico-political practices, dispersed and interconnected transnationally, that develop capacity for early warning—in effect illuminating some aspects of the future, farsighted cosmopolitism as mode of escaping the uncritical focus on the immediate future, and norms of precaution and transnational justice against alarmism and dystopian projections (2007, 98–100). As with the, frequently transnational, communities that emerge around bearing witness and forgiveness, one should not presume the pre-existence of the global community; it is precisely the ethico-labour of preventive foresight that constructs the global community, in an attempt to fashion a more equitable and just future (Kurasawa 2007, 99).

The fourth mode of global justice is aid. Here, Kurasawa is able to draw on the plethora of criticisms of twentieth-century humanitarianism and postwar aid to identify the well-rehearsed perils confronted by the ethico-political practices of providing assistance to distant others. These include the status asymmetry between giving and receiving communities, the ensuing socio-economic and moral domination of recipients of aid, as well as the latter's global segregation (2007, 126–33). Building on Seyla Benhabib's work on the ethics of "care toward concrete others" and the ethics of "justice applied to generalized others" (Kurasawa 2007, 132), he provides a normative reconstruction of aid as a key component of the practice of global justice. This involves filing away status asymmetry by implementing and implanting practices of symmetrical reciprocity, loosening the grip of socio-economic and moral domination through practices of egalitarian cooperation, and the structural transformation of the world economic and political order to mitigate the effects of the contemporary "global apartheid" (Kurasawa 2007, 135–54).

Unlike the first two modes of practice where Kurasawa pulls out the normative threads woven in the already existing practices, his analysis of aid, as in the case of foresight, is geared more towards the development of a normative framework to guide ethico-political practices yet to be developed. Thus his focus is less empirical and more normative, not so much a normative exploration regarding existing practices, but a sociologically grounded proposal for an alternative socio-political ethos. Much the same can be said with respect to the last mode of practice, solidarity, which he understands as a "robust and radical sense of cosmopolitan responsibility for the substantive realization of human rights and opposition to structural injustices in all parts of the world" (Kurasawa 2007, 157). Although Kurasawa draws on the alternative globalization movement to anchor his analysis (Kurasawa 2007, 162), on my reading, his normative reconstruction is the result of a critical dialogue with theories of cosmopolitanism from above, namely, normative cosmopolitanism and institutional cosmopolitanism.[17] The former, unrealistically, prescribes the transcendence of local ties in an effort to build a new global cosmopolitan community, shorn of national and local attachments (Kurasawa 2007, 165). While the latter understands cosmopolitanism as a mode of global governance, with an emphasis of legal institutionalization, in which a trickle-down effect is expected (Kurasawa 2007, 165). Kurasawa argues that both approaches miss the laborious socially embedded ethico-political practices conducive to more robust, bottom-up, and networked forms of solidarity.

The perils that haunt the ethico-political labour of cosmopolitan solidarity, namely, cultural assimilation, political fragmentation, and social thinness, must be confronted through practices that are anchored in the recognition of pluralism, the construction of networked affinities, and the creativity of social action (Kurasawa 2007, 192). Such practices are illustrated in his discussion of the alternative globalization movement where he detects the seed of a cosmopolitan solidarity in the form of decentred assemblages of heterogeneous struggles around different issues, at varies scales, that can be pragmatically linked, or unlinked as the case might be, in response to changing contingencies (Kurasawa 2007, 177). It is precisely by the "aggregation of partial and situated knowledges", argues Kurasawa, that a "'big picture'" of the global realities of injustice and inequality can emerge and an understanding of the types of ethical and political commitments required for the achievement of global justice can be developed (2007, 178), providing the basis for a thicker and more robust form of solidarity.

Localizing Global Justice

Ultimately Kurasawa provides us with a forward-looking sociologically informed normative account of global justice. Global justice is a category of practice insofar as it is used by actors themselves engaged in attempts to make sense of and pattern what they are doing when they intervene in social and political processes with an eye to combating global inequality and violence. However in Kurasawa's work, global justice is equally a category of analysis to the extent that he uses it to analytically group together a range of patterned social phenomena, characterized by shared attributes and a certain degree of modularity, his five modes of practice.[18]

It is important to note, however, that the burden of his analytical work is shifted onto the attempt to use these modes of practice as a way of understanding the social processes whereby normative ideas of global justice are produced, communicated, and made efficacious. This implies not only identifying the complex and fragile dynamics through which normative communities are intersubjectively articulated by virtue of the concrete practice of bearing witness to structural inequality and violence. It also addresses the manner in which the moral and political charge that is produced by this foundational mode of practice might ignite collective action aimed at remedying, redressing, or preventing such violence and inequity through forgiveness, foresight, aid, and solidarity. This involves not only an understanding of the practices themselves but also the broader social and historical conditions that enable, impede, or restrict them.

Insofar as Kurasawa attempts to show how normative commitments are embedded (e.g., perils), embodied (e.g., empathy), embrained (e.g., interpretation), and inthinged (e.g., images of suffering) through ethico-political practices, he provides crucial conceptual and empirical tools for understanding human rights as a practice. First and foremost, he makes amply clear that the community of individuals who can make normative claims, or on whose behalf normative claims can be made, and to whom these claims are addressed does not pre-exist the ethico-politico labour of bearing witness. Consequently, making human rights socially efficacious can never just be a question of applying or concretizing norms, rules, procedures, and so on, removing particular social obstacles, and/or shedding light on unseen forms of violence or injustice. The efficacy of any human rights claim presupposes the socially constituted ability to imagine a particular community of individuals where claims can be received and made morally, legally, or politically persuasive. In my terms, it presupposes a political imaginary.

Such an imaginary is not an act of individual will. At the very crux of human rights, understood as a political imaginary, as Kurasawa is surely right to point out when conceptualizing the work of global justice, is the labour of bearing witness. Bearing witness or the attempt to give voice, enable interpretation, generate empathy, foster remembrance, promote prevention, and I would add seek remedy, draw our attention to a series of social-relational effects, and affects, that are constitutive of the normative experience that human rights practices attempt to engender and mobilize. Bearing witness also presupposes, what I call within the political imaginary model, specific social technologies. These include, without being fully exhaustive, neutral modes of factual reporting; stylized representations of victimhood; textual and/or visual narrative testimonial forms; modes of legal reasoning; discursively connecting archives of authoritative textual documents such as declarations, treaties, and international law; and procedures for disseminating information and mobilizing support on behalf of those who have endured human rights' violations.

These social technologies are relatively enduring, though changeable, assemblages of routines of action (e.g., legal reasoning, human rights violation documentation, campaigns to publicize violations), things (e.g., reports, images), and meanings (e.g., victimhood, injustice, human rights violation). Social technologies modulate and pattern particular modes of individual and collective action such as claiming human rights, mounting human rights campaigns, letter-writing drives, or mobilizing political pressure through shaming and naming activities undertaken by state and non-state actors. In turn, patterned modes of action interface with broader representations of the social world and how it ought to be and serve to strengthen individual and collective subjectivities, for example, the victim, the human rights claimant, the human rights advocate. Finally, it is around particular organizational or institutional forms, such as NGOs, civil society groups, transnational organizations, in which these social technologies crystallize.

Kurasawa effectively develops a normative reconstruction of the social-relational effects, and affects, that specific ethico-political practices—that is, bearing witness, forgiveness, aid, foresight, and solidarity—(would) need to fulfil in the pursuit of global justice. Said differently, he is successful with respect to the critical component of his "critical substantivism". Surprisingly, he is less so with respect to his substantivism. This is particularly clear in his discussion of aid, foresight, and solidarity, where the empirical components of his analysis are suggestive of the manner in which philosophers use empirical examples to illustrate and make conceptual distinctions. This is in contradistinction to social scientists' *modus operandi*, to wit, mobilizing concepts to explain empirical social processes. In his analysis of bearing witness and forgiveness, on the other hand, it is his fine sociological study of the social processes underpinning the modes of practices that enable him to reconstruct normative ideals, and link them to patterned modes of embodiment, embrainment, inthingment, and embeddedness.

I would argue that despite its conceptual usefulness in some regards, his category of analysis, global justice, is far from felicitous. This is so because in linking together the range of practices that fall under the umbrella of global justice, Kurasawa erases the differences that might exist amongst them. In fact, throughout the book, Kurasawa uses the term human rights and global justice interchangeably. This is unfortunate because it eschews the necessity of identifying the specificity of human rights as a particular socio-historical ethico-political practice. It obviates what Miller (2010), as noted above, persuasively argues, namely, that human rights is not central to all contemporary projects, or imaginaries, of global justice.[19] Equally, it precludes developing an understanding of what human rights might or might not contribute to the ethico-political labour of global justice. Moreover, as previously mentioned, it is possible, as Woodiwiss (2005, 11) shows, to be committed to human rights while recognizing that respect for them cannot entail the end to the inequalities that are intrinsic to human rights.

To my mind, Kurasawa's contribution does not reside in what he tells us about human rights per se, but in his effort to sociologically conceptualize contemporary global ethico-political practices. While I contest the equivalence between human rights and global justice, established by Kurasawa, there is no doubt that human rights can profitably be conceptualized as an ethico-political practice. Equally, Kurasawa argues that what links together his five modes of practice is their intersubjectivity, public communicative spaces, and their transnationalism. I would counter that the first two are not specific to global justice as such. To my mind, they make reference to the general sociological conditions of possibility of the constitution of a community in which individuals can make normative and ethical claims on one another, as Benedict Anderson (2004) has shown in the context of nationalism in his seminal *Imagined Communities*.

Finally, though Kurasawa argues that bearing witness is *primus inter pares* with the remaining modes of practice, the reality is that bearing witness might best be conceived as a more abstract relational configuration. Along with intersubjectivity and publicity, bearing witness enables normative claims to be floated in particular ethico-political communities. One could go further and claim that bearing witness, understood as "turning to the face of the other", following Emanuel Levinas, constitutes the very bedrock of ethical behaviour and responsibility tout court (Burggraeve 1999).

Ironically given his own critique of philosophical and institutional formalism, Kurasawa's contribution to understanding human rights remains more formal than substantive. True, Kurasawa eschews the abovementioned formalisms, but what he analytically unearths are not so much substantive practices, but what we might call *elementary forms of ethico-political life that can under certain conditions shape concrete substantive practices.* He does this by sketching the kinds of sociological relational effects and affects that are presupposed by an ethical and political responsibility for the care of distant and/or excluded others in the context of structural violence and inequality. It is, perhaps, for this reason, that his unfeigned substantivism fails to drill down into empirical social processes that would enable him to provide a substantive account of the actual social technologies that pattern his modes of practice. His analysis is weighted more heavily towards the critical than the substantive.

Despite this, insofar as he does identify the social structuring of ethico-political practice, even if abstractly, there is much in his analysis that resonates with the political imaginary model and distinguishes him from the authors, discussed above, who draw on the notion practice to conceptualize human rights. Both, Kurasawa's and the political imaginary models, understand the ethical community in which claims for responsibility for the distant and/or excluded other are made as an achievement of practice and not its presupposition. The focus on rituals, performance, and meaning echoes the centrality of representations and modes of individual and collective subjectivity in the political imaginary model. Equally, the notion of modularity, while distinct from, reverberates with the ideas of social technologies and patterned modes of individual and collective action.

An important departure between Kurasawa's conception and the political imaginary model, however, is the former's relative neglect of institutions outside of civil society (Nash 2009b, 1). Indeed, despite the fact that Kurasawa quite clearly states that the modes of practice of global justice have to be understood as unfolding "within organized political, cultural and socio-economic fields" (2007, 11), this aspect of their social embeddedness is not developed in his study. In other words, he does not clearly define the actual social spaces where the ethico-political labour that he analyses takes place. Fortunately, a way forward is indicated by Kate Nash's analysis of the fields in which the cultural politics of human rights are played out (2009b), to which I now turn.

Echoing the general tenor of Kurasawa's analysis and the political imaginary model, Nash understands that one of the fundamental tasks of human rights, conceived as cultural practice rather than as "abstract moral ideals" (2009b, 166), is the imagining of a moral community beyond the nation (2009b, 27). Such imagining is neither the product of individual volition nor the dissemination of an already existing "human rights culture" that can be inferred from existing international agreements (Nash 2009b, 7). Instead, human rights, when understood through the analytical prism of cultural politics, refers to the localized struggle to establish binding definitions of the moral and political responsibility for those subjected to violence and injustice, in which actors are emotionally and intellectually invested (Nash 2009b, 1). Such responsibility can exist in a variety of registers, some more likely to lead to effective social change than others: for instance, as a generalized moral demand, an intersubjectively shared sentiment that one must do more, a national or transnational campaign to name and shame or pressure state officials, a legal claim for recognition or redress, or as a formally institutionalized state policy as when incorporated into national legislation in the case of EU members states or as a foreign policy objective in the US State Department.

The meaning of localized struggle in Nash's framework refers, on my reading, to two analytically important distinctions. First, although human rights obligations are typically conceptualized as arising from international agreements, understood as part and parcel of globalizing processes that undermine the sovereignty of the nation-state, the absence of an executive arm to enforce agreements means that the efficacy of human rights claims, be they moral, political, or legal, requires the participation, and in some cases the transformation, of the national state. This means, it is best to think about human rights, argues Nash, as being "intermestic"—inter~~nationaldo~~mestic. That is to say, they have a hybrid status; we should not conceive of human rights "as a matter of *either* international *or* national law"; the reality is that "they are both international and domestic at the same time" (2009b, 14).

The second distinction refers to the manner in which the cultural struggles to define human rights are localized in particular social spaces, or what Nash conceptualizes taking a cue from Bourdieu, as social fields. Unlike Bourdieu for whom fields are social spaces for the reproduction of hierarchies of inequality, she defines fields around the construction of authority. The latter is understood as the ability to make binding, and within the context of the field, legitimate definitions of social phenomena. In the context of human rights, authority is mobilized in order to define what human rights and who the subjects of human rights are, and to determine how conflicts over human rights are to be decided (Nash 2009b, 16–17). Nash delineates the field of intermestic human rights as being made up of four subfields: the juridical, the governmental, the activist, and the mediated public (2009b, 32). She notes that within each of the subfields, one can identify distinctive modes of struggle "to decide what human rights mean in practice" (Nash 2009b, 32) and particular types of justifications (Nash 2009b, 58–68), adding that competition also takes place across the subfields, most prominently in the juridical and the mediated public fields (2009b, 32).

The juridical field is the socially structured space where the competition for the monopoly to determine the law takes place, "within this field there occurs a confrontation among actors possessing technical competence which is inevitably social and which consists essentially in the socially recognized capacity to *interpret* a corpus of texts sanctifying a correct or legitimized vision of the social world" (Bourdieu 1986, 817). Because one of the ways in which human rights are represented and enacted is through the social practices of the law, courts and legislative processes become privileged sites for the authoritative definition of human rights. As Nash notes, "the stakes of these conflicts are particularly high: a judicial decision which denies that human rights apply, is a serious setback to the project of establishing human rights law, and therefore to the possibilities of realising human rights in practice" (2009b, 34).

Bourdieu argues that the social efficacy of the juridical field, as a socially legitimated mechanism for dispute resolution, depends on its ability to convert "direct conflict between directly concerned parties into juridically regulated debate between professionals acting by proxy [lawyers and judges]" (1986, 831). Such debate presupposes that the proxies "have in common their knowledge and their acceptance of the rules of the legal game, the written and unwritten laws of the field itself" (Bourdieu 1986, 831). However, the intermestic quality of human rights, the uncertain legal status of international human rights agreements, and international customary law generate "acute conflicts in the human rights field about what such law might include or not include, and indeed, over whether it should be considered law at all" (Nash 2009b, 36). Such ambiguity regarding the status of international human rights law, the centrality of national law as a mechanism for dispute resolution, and its ability to impose authoritative visions of and on the social world positions the juridical field as a key site for the authoritative definition of human rights. Consequently, legal modes of reasoning and practice will be key elements of the representations, social technologies, modes of action and subjectivity, and organizational forms of human rights conceived as a political imaginary, as I shall explore more fully in Chap. 6.

Nash understands the struggle in the governmental subfield to revolve, on the one hand, around state officials' attempts to secure access and control over the legitimate means of violence, and on the other hand, the more general forms of social, political, and economic regulation. Such processes, however, cannot be understood without reference to the processes by which political actors struggle to define issues around competing political rationalities, that is, cultural politics (2009b, 40–41). The cultural politics of human rights intersect with the governmental subfield in two ways, according to Nash. First, government officials can contribute to framing the meaning and scope of human rights practices through their participation at international fora and through the stands they take with respect to existing international agreements or their negotiations for new ones, for instance, the decision to ratify or not international covenants (Nash 2009b, 41). Second, "disputes in the governmental subfield involve the authority to decide how far governmental policy should conform to or ignore human rights law" (Nash 2009b, 42), and the manner in which government policy should respond to the moral and political claims raised by activists or other political actors.

The authority of the activist subfield, unlike that of the governmental and the judicial subfields, is not exercised in virtue of state-sanctioned official positions (2009b, 45). The activist subfield, maintains Nash, is made up of human rights organizations whose indirect authority depends on knowledge of human rights law and policy and the ability to interact effectively with state actors and other members of the activist community at the domestic and international level. Their authority is exercised when they are able "to convince judges and politicians to resolve conflicts by adopting their understanding of how human rights should be put in practice" (Nash 2009b, 46). If the language of denunciation of injustice or moral outrage, which frequently fuels human rights claims, is to contribute to remedy or redress beyond a legal context, then human rights, conceived as a practice, must, also, be able to interface with the cultural politics of the governmental subfield. In other words, it must be able to enact representations, subjectivities, modes of actions, and pattern behaviour and develop organizational forms that are congruent or, at least, resonate with the latter.[20]

Nash notes that the activist subfield also exercises authority indirectly in the last subfield, the mediated public, when actors successfully contribute to making visible and framing issues of violence and injustice as instances of human rights violations, that demand legal and/or political remedy or redress (2009b, 49). She conceives of the mediated public in terms of the "commonality of the symbolic space provided by the media" and the journalistic practices that structure this space (2009b, 51). Indeed, "by determining which perspectives on human rights are made visible, which 'voices' are heard, and which are given credibility, journalist and editors set agendas and frame human rights issues in ways that may influence the outcomes of struggles over human rights" (Nash 2009b, 52). Given the centrality of this last subfield in the building of the moral community, which can potentially uphold the claims of distant and/or excluded others, the human rights imaginary must necessarily couple, if awkwardly and not without tension, with the cultural practices that structure the mediated public.

Conclusion

I began this chapter by drawing on the political philosopher Charles Beitz whose work develops a powerful critique of two widely held modes of conceptualizing human rights: one, the notion that human rights are entitlements that individuals have in virtue of being human and, the other, that human rights are the product of a consensus among diverse moral and political cultures. Instead, Beitz proposes that we think of human rights as a historically situated emergent normative practice. The political imaginary model that I am proposing in this book shares both Beitz's diagnosis (the inadequacy of thinking of human rights as an idea) and his proposed remedy (conceiving human rights as an emergent normative practice). Beitz's conceptualization of human rights as a practice, however, conceives them as *normative reasons for action*. This remedy, as I argued above, remains too thin. What is required is a thicker conception of practice, one that sociologists and anthropologists are, in principle, ideally positioned to develop.

Indeed, as I argued above, the concept of practice in the social sciences emerges as an attempt to overcome the reduction of the patterning of social life to the caricatures of either "*homo sociologicus* or *economicus*" (Reckwitz 2002b, 245). In the former, the ongoing flow of social life is understood as the product of rule-following and adherence to norms and, in the latter, to the strategic pursuit of interests. While practice theory does not deny that social actors abide by norms and strategize in the pursuit of their interests, it understands these as interlinked components of a broader category of socially patterned "doing". Thus practice theory not only draws our attention to mental activities—such as rule-following or the pursuit of interests—but to the manner in which such activities are components in routinized and processual behaviour that can be understood as an assemblage of bodily activities, objects and things, knowledges, and emotional states that unfold in time and across social space (Reckwitz 2002b, 249). More epigrammatically, practice theory draws our attention to the manner in which social phenomena are embedded, embodied, embrained, and inthinged.

Given the above, practice theory's potential for the development of sociologically thicker accounts of human rights is significant. Potential however is not an achievement. As I showed earlier in the chapter, many of the sociologists, and some anthropologists, that draw on practice theory to conceptualize human rights do so to oppose practice to the idea of human rights. Consequently they sustain the folk theory that human rights are an idea, ideals, norms, and principles. This leads to two types of stylized analyses that I sketched out above. The first takes the form of sociological accounts that bear witness. This entails deploying the conceptual and empirical tools of sociological analysis to map the range of contemporary situations of ongoing structural violence and injustice to which human rights must respond if they are to deliver on their promise of justice and equity. The problem here is that while this work soberly identifies the sources of contemporary brutality and inequity, it presumes, without evidence or even argument, that human rights once trained on the real sources of such iniquitous phenomena can provide remedy.

The second style of analysis engendered by the practice/idea opposition seeks to identify the types of localized structural obstacles that prevent human rights from fulfilling their promise of mitigating violence and inequality. While such analyses do draw our attention to the types of structural arrangements that impede efforts to create more just and protective social relations, they have little to say about the specificity of human rights as a tool for social change. Their efficacy, absent the structural obstacles, is presumed. In both styles of analysis, unwittingly no doubt, rather than use the category of practice to flesh out the historically situated emergence of human rights as an identifiable normative practice, human rights is used as a placeholder for an abstract and generalized conception of justice and equality.

A more promising effort at developing a practice-based conception of human rights is to be found in the work of Kurasawa, who explicitly renders global justice in practice theoretical terms. His crucial contribution, to my mind, is his conceptualization of global justice as a coming together of different forms of patterned ethico-political labour with the goal of intersubjectively articulating a moral community where the claims of distant and/or excluded others subject to violence and injustice can be received and (potentially) acted upon.[21] In so doing, he draws attention to key dimensions that must be included in the political imaginary model, namely, the importance of representations, social technologies, individual and collective subjectivities, and modes of action. Despite the indebtedness of the political imaginary model to Kurasawa's conception of ethico-political labour, his substantivism, to my mind, does not go far enough. While the notion of ethico-political labour brings into focus the work of global justice as a normative practice, it does not distinguish amongst different and/or competing conceptions of global justice and their concomitant modes of practices.

As a result, the framework is not capable of seizing the specificity of human rights. The implicit synechdochal relationship between human rights and global justice that shapes his argument prevents him from drilling down more substantively into the specificity of human rights, conceptualized as a historically emergent normative practice. Equally, though Kurasawa is careful to identify the perils that each of the modes of practice confronts, he does not consider, what I take to be the real possibility, that different modes of ethico-political practices can be misaligned and work at cross purposes. Finally, another significant shortcoming of Kurasawa's conceptualization is the neglect of the particularity of the social spaces in which the practices are enacted. This is a deficiency that Nash contributes to palliating through her conceptualization of human rights as cultural politics.

Nash, like Kurasawa and the political imaginary model, does not presume the existence of the community that receives the normative claim of distant and/or excluded others. It is precisely the competition to define the community and its responsibility vis-à-vis the claimant(s) that human rights as cultural politics attempts to bring to light. Crucially, Nash shows that such competition can be localized in at least four subfields, the juridical, the governmental, the activist, and the mediated public. Each of the subfields draws on different forms of authority. As a result, part of the work of human rights—that is, establishing a moral community capable of receiving the normative claims of distant and/or excluded others—takes the form of adapting these claims to the rationalities that correspond to the different forms of authority in the subfields. Said differently, the fact that human rights cross-cut these different subfields entails a certain degree of isomorphism with the practices of these fields.

The critical insight embedded in Nash's work, which the political imaginary model seeks to develop more fully, is that human rights can fruitfully be conceptualized as a relatively (un)stable assemblage of practices that make visible the situations of suffering and violence of distant and/or excluded others. This is achieved by mediating such situations as claims for moral recognition, legal and/or political remedy in an imaginary normative community. I return to this point below; first, I want to address why I prefer to conceptualize human rights as a political imaginary rather than a practice.

While the concept of practice is useful, I find political imaginary more valuable for a number of reasons. First, given the way in which practice has been opposed to the idea of human rights, I think that using the notion of political imaginary is an expedient way of avoiding contributing to the ongoing reproduction of this opposition. Second, although the conceptualization of practice incorporates many of the features that I identified as being important in the political imaginary model, there is, I think, inherent in the notion of practice, a certain expectation of the alignment of the cognitive or representational dimensions, the embodiment and embrainment, and the ongoing routines through which they are reproduced. The political imaginary, instead, draws our attention to the possible, and probable, misalignment between representations, technologies, modes of subjectivity and action, and organizational forms. I think such a conceptualization is better equipped to analyse the functioning of human rights across different subfields. In addition, it draws our attention to what Eckel has identified as the "polycentric and fitful process" by which human rights have been constituted (2014, 241). Third, although the idea of practice is certainly not bereft of complexity, the notion of political imaginary draws attention to a variety of practices that it hosts. Put in terms of Nash's analysis, practices are to the political imaginary what the subfields are to the field of human rights. That is to say, thinking of human rights as a political imaginary enables one to discriminate between competing, or, perhaps, merely differing normative, legal, rhetorical, aspirational, political, or, even, new and evolving practices.

In this chapter, I have developed the argument that human rights, conceived as a political imaginary, can be conceptualized as the attempt to make receivable the normative claims of distant and/or excluded others in an imagined normative community. Making receivable should be understood as a continuum ranging from provoking an emotional reaction, a sense of responsibility, diverse modes of individual or collective political action, and/or triggering the authority of the law in the pursuit of redress and remedy. As Nash has shown (2009b), due to the intermestic qualities of human rights, the nation-state remains a key site for robust articulations of community, political, and legal action. In the next chapter I tackle the first two, while in the subsequent chapter I address the entanglement of human rights with law.

Notes

1. Beitz identifies three ways in which human rights differ from international regimes: (1) human rights' lack of sufficiently robust institutional capacity and authoritative dispute settlement mechanisms, (2) unlike international regimes, human rights also incorporate standards of aspiration, and (3) regimes are cooperative mutually beneficial enterprises that are largely advantageous to member states, whereas human rights advances the interests of individuals, against, or rather, than those of states (Beitz 2011, 43). To my mind, none of this variance undermines the central identity between the two, namely, being constellations of structured principles, rules, norms, and decision-making procedures that are reproduced in ongoing interaction.
2. It is important to note that there are significant differences between how IR has developed in the US and in Europe (Waever 1998; Buzan and Little 2001). Equally, in the US, the constructivist paradigm continues to make significant progress in the discipline (Finnemore and Sikkink 2001; Wiener 2003; Wendt 1999); for recent overviews, see Adler (2013) and Checkel (2013).
3. The exception here, of course, is the early analysis provided by Sherry Ortner (1984). Her analysis, however, was restricted to its import to anthropology, the discipline in which practice theory first took hold.
4. As Kurasawa notes, practice theory falls in between "two broad disciplinary traditions: Kantian moral-political philosophy, which views social actions as following and derived from normative principles grounded in human reason (e.g., the categorical imperative); and the Durkheimian sociology of morality, which understands social action as an outcome of institutionally prescribed ideals and structurally enforced and sanctioned rules of conduct" (2007, 11).
5. In introducing this neologism I want to draw attention to the importance of material "artefacts" in the co-production of social life: not as elements outside of the social but as constitutive of social relations. Of course, the fecundity of this insight is associated with the work of Bruno Latour and the numerous scholars working in the field of science studies. As Andreas Reckwitz makes clear, classical sociology understood the "material" in terms of social structure, while much cultural sociology indexed "the material" to "symbolic objects". As I noted in Chap. 2, these twin threads are woven into Jeffrey Alexander's account of the

strong programme in cultural sociology. However in Bruno Latour "symmetric anthropology", the "material" is conceptualized as "artefacts", that is to say, "as 'things' which are necessary components of social networks or 'practices'" (Reckwitz 2002a, 196).

6. This does not obviate other elements crucial for the take-off of human rights in Latin America such as transnational networks whose study was pioneered by Keck and Sikkink (1998) and has received considerable scholarly attention (Cowan, Dembour, and Wilson 2001).
7. Although Goodale argues that the international human rights system is distinct from transnational human rights regime, his historical narrative locates the latency of the latter in the former. For instance, he argues, "it would not be until after 1989 that transnational NGOs would begin to really fulfill the mission envisioned by [Eleanor] Roosevelt [in 1948]" (Goodale 2009, 95).
8. In anthropology, the casting of human rights in terms of the opposition between an abstract idea and concrete practice is not peculiar to Goodale. For instance, it is also visible in the work of Merry, who has contributed enormously to our understanding of how gender violence is regulated by human rights (2009), not to mention her broader analyses of the anthropology of law, and who introduced the notion of human rights as vernacular in her frequently cited article (2006). At times, like Goodale, she conceptually frames international human rights as a practice, "the source of global ideas and institutions is usually another locality that has developed an idea or practice that is translated into a form that circulates globally and is then transplanted into another locality" (2006, 39). Her concern is to identify the work done by those intermediaries, often NGOs, who "interweave practices and discourses from the locality form elsewhere" (2006, 39). She adds that these "translators are not always successful. New ideas and practices may be ignored, rejected or folded into preexisting institutions to create a more hybrid discourse or organization" (2006, 40). However she does not define the components of human rights understood as a practice, and time and again opposes the "idea of human rights" with the concreteness of local institutions, organizations, indigenous cultural categories, and practices. Both Goodale and Merry cannot avoid seeing that international human rights are made up of practices, but this sighting is displaced to the background as the hegemonic notion of human rights as an idea takes priority in their explanatory schemes.

9. To be clear insofar as the human rights imaginary provides the normative grammar whereby contemporary injustice is framed, there is nothing more "natural" than to think about genocide in human rights terms, indeed as the ultimate violation of human rights. That, however, is precisely the issue. As sociologists, I understand our task to entail questioning the manner in which these moral equivalents develop rather than to merely argue for them.
10. For an attempt to bring together social science analysis with the human rights imperative of impartiality, see Landman and Carvalho (2010), where they frame the social science contribution as an effort to improve both the measurement of the human rights standard, and to improve on the standard.
11. Kim Dae-jung was awarded the Nobel Peace Prize in 2000 for his "sunshine policy" towards North Korea and his work as a pro-democracy dissident under conditions of imprisonment, house arrest, kidnapping, and exile ("Kim Dae-Jung - Facts" 2016, accessed December 2016).
12. Melvin notes, "Gacaca was used during the pre-colonial era and again in the 1980s to hear local disputes and solve conflicts related to relationships, land or property. The principal goal of this system is now to try cases of genocide in an effort to reduce the caseload and accelerate justice after the genocide" (2010, 942).
13. The RPF had sparked the civil war in Rwanda in 1990 and was a key member of the Government of National Unity (GNU), subsequently winning the elections in 2003; it has remained in power to the present.
14. As Kurasawa rightly argues, "contra, what many governments assert through strong communitarian discourses, reconciliation need not suspend or hide socio-political pluralism within post-transitional societies in order to bolster ideals of cultural uniformity or inherent unanimity among citizens" (2007, 89).
15. Both of these are examined at greater length in Chap. 5 under the rubric of cosmopolitanism, and in Chap. 6 in my discussion of global legalism, respectively.
16. Luc Boltanski (1999) explores the psychological and social structuring of spectators' reactions to distant suffering. He distinguishes amongst three types of responses, or "topics": denunciation, sentiment, and aesthetic. He notes, "While the topics of denunciation and sentiment are oriented towards collective action, the former by making speech an

instrument of mobilisation against those responsible for the misfortune, the latter by making it a means for bringing together men of good will for beneficent assistance, and thereby open to political investments, the aesthetic topic seems to renounce action and seems only to inspire a purely individual relationship to distance suffering" (Boltanski 1999, 132). Despite this, Boltanski argues that both the left and the right have attempted to politicize the aesthetic topic. However, in the end he concludes that "It is difficult to call upon the aesthetic topic for dealing with the suffering of real weak, anonymous unfortunates – the massacred or starved, the poor of the shanty-towns etc. – and ultimately it is most effective in the domain in which it was born – that of fiction" (1999, 147).

17. Thus, I concur entirely with Kate Nash when she writes, "However, as his frequent use of the words 'can' and 'could' suggest, Kurasawa is more concerned with the theoretical possibilities of the alternative globalisation movement than with the investigation of its empirical success and failures in relation to the aims and claims of actual participants" (2009b, 141).
18. For the distinction between a category of practice and category of analysis, see Brubaker and Cooper (2000).
19. Just as Upendra Baxi argues that there is not one but "many conflicting worlds of human rights" (2002, 5), there are competing and conflicting worlds of global justice.
20. As Keys' analysis of the development of human rights as a foreign policy field, discussed in Chap. 2, documents, it was the congruence between the desires of activists and US politicians that contributed towards making human rights a foreign policy objective.
21. To be clear, Kurasawa speaks of distant others. I understand distant to refer not only to physical but also social spatial distance. It is not clear to me that "distant" has this second connotation in Kurasawa's analysis, which is why I append excluded to make this clear. The rationale for this will be developed more fully in Chap. 5.

Bibliography

Adler, Emanuel. 2013. "Constructivism in International Relations: Sources, Contributions, and Debates." In *Handbook of International Relations*, edited by Walter Carlsnaes, Tomas Risse and Beth A. Simmons, 122–144. London: SAGE.

Aldunate, Jose. 1994. "Human Rights as the Rights of the Poor: The Perspective from Liberation Theology." *Journal of Moral Education* 23 (3):297–303.

Alexander, Jeffrey C. 2006. *The Civil Sphere*. Oxford and New York: Oxford University Press.

Anderson, Benedict. 2004. *Imagined Communities: Reflections on the Origin and Spread of Nationalism*. London: Verso.

Baghai, Katayoun. 2012. "Privacy as a Human Right: A Sociological Theory." *Sociology* 46 (5):951–965.

Baxi, Upendra. 2002. *The Future of Human Rights*. Oxford: Oxford University Press.

Beitz, Charles R. 2011. *The Idea of Human Rights*. Oxford and New York: Oxford University Press.

Bhatt, Chetan. 2012. "Human Rights and the Transformations of War." *Sociology* 46 (5):813–828.

Boltanski, Luc. 1999. *Distant Suffering: Morality, Media and Politics*. Cambridge and New York: Cambridge University Press.

Bourdieu, Pierre. 1977. *Outline of a Theory of Practice*. Cambridge and New York: Cambridge University Press.

Bourdieu, Pierre. 1986. "Force of Law: Toward a Sociology of the Juridical Field." *The Hastings Law Journal* 38:814–853.

Brubaker, Rogers, and Frederick Cooper. 2000. "Beyond 'Identity.'" *Theory and Society* 29 (1):1–47.

Brysk, Alison. 2013. *Speaking Rights to Power: Constructing Political Will*. Oxford and New York: Oxford University Press.

Burggraeve, Roger. 1999. "Violence and the Vulnerable Face of the Other: The Vision of Emmanuel Levinas on Moral Evil and Our Responsibility." *Journal of Social Philosophy* 30 (1):29–45.

Burke, Roland. 2015. "Human Rights Day After the 'Breakthrough': Celebrating the Universal Declaration of Human Rights at the United Nations in 1978 and 1988." *Journal of Global History* 10 (1):147–170.

Buzan, Barry, and Richard Little. 2001. "Why International Relations Has Failed as an Intellectual Project and What to Do About It." *Millennium* 30 (1):19–39.

Canning, Victoria. 2010. "Who's Human? Developing Sociological Understandings of the Rights of Women Raped in Conflict." *The International Journal of Human Rights* 14 (6):849–864.

Cetina, Karin Knorr, Theodore R. Schatzki, and Eike von Savigny, eds. 2005. *The Practice Turn in Contemporary Theory*. London and New York: Routledge.

Checkel, Jeffrey T. 1998. "The Constructive Turn in International Relations Theory." *World Politics* 50 (2):324–348.

Checkel, Jeffrey T. 2013. "Theoretical Pluralisms in IR: Possibilities and Limits." In *Handbook of International Relations*, edited by Walter Carlsnaes, Tomas Risse, and Beth A. Simmons, 220–242. London: Sage.

Claeys, Priscilla. 2012. "The Creation of New Rights by the Food Sovereignty Movement: The Challenge of Institutionalizing Subversion." *Sociology* 46 (5):844–860.

Cohen, Stanly (2001) States of Denial. Cambridge and New York: Polity Press.

Connolly, Nicholas. 2012. "Corporate Social Responsibility: A Duplicitous Distraction?" *The International Journal of Human Rights* 16 (8):1228–1249.

Dawes, James. 2009. *That the World May Know: Bearing Witness to Atrocity*. Cambridge, MA: Harvard University Press.

Donnelly, Jack. 1986. "International Human Rights: A Regime Analysis." *International Organization* 40 (3):599–642.

Eckel, Jan. 2014. "The Rebirth of Politics from the Spirit of Morality: Explaining the Human Rights Revolution of the 1970s." In *The Breakthrough: Human Rights in the 1970s*, edited by Jan Eckel and Samuel Moyn, 226–260. Philadelphia: University of Pennsylvania Press.

Eckel, Jan, and Samuel Moyn. 2014. *The Breakthrough: Human Rights in the 1970s*. eds. Philadelphia: University of Pennsylvania Press.

Engler, Mark. 2000. "Toward the 'Rights of the Poor' Human Rights in Liberation Theology." *Journal of Religious Ethics* 28 (3):339–365.

Englund, Harri. 2006. *Prisoners of Freedom: Human Rights and the African Poor*. Cambridge: Cambridge University Press.

Ferrie, Joanna. 2010. "Sociology and Human Rights: What Have They Got to Say About Care and Dignity?" *The International Journal of Human Rights* 14 (6):865–879.

Finnemore, Martha, and Kathryn Sikkink. 2001. "TAKING STOCK: The Constructivist Research Program in International Relations and Comparative Politics." *Annual Review of Political Science* 4:391–416.
Foroohar, Manzar. 1986. "Liberation Theology: The Response of Latin American Catholics to Socioeconomic Problems." *Latin American Perspectives* 13 (3):37–58.
Gandsman, Ari. 2013. "Narrative, Human Rights and the Ethnographic Reproduction of Conventional Knowledge." *Anthropologica*, 127–140.
Golash-Boza, Tanya, and Cecilia Menjívar. 2012. "Causes and Consequences of International Migration: Sociological Evidence for the Right to Mobility." *The International Journal of Human Rights* 16 (8):1213–1227.
Goodale, Mark. 2002. "The Globalization of Sympathetic Law and Its Consequences." *Law & Social Inquiry* 27 (3):595–608.
Goodale, Mark. 2009. *Surrendering to Utopia: An Anthropology of Human Rights*. Stanford, CA: Stanford University Press.
Grigolo, Michele. 2010. "Human Rights and Cities: The Barcelona Office for Non-Discrimination and Its Work for Migrants." *The International Journal of Human Rights* 14 (6):896–914.
Harris, Jose. 1992. "Political Thought and the Welfare State 1870–1940: An Intellectual Framework for British Social Policy." *Past & Present* 135:116–141.
Hasenclever, Andreas, Peter Mayer, and Volker Rittberger. 1996. "Interests, Power, Knowledge: The Study of International Regimes." *Mershon International Studies Review* 40 (2):177–228.
Hesford, Wendy. 2011. *Spectacular Rhetorics: Human Rights Visions, Recognitions, Feminisms*. Durham, NC: Duke University Press.
Hesford, Wendy S. 2004. "Documenting Violations: Rhetorical Witnessing and the Spectacle of Distant Suffering." *Biography* 27 (1):104–144.
Hilhorst, Dorothea, and Bram J. Jansen. 2012. "Constructing Rights and Wrongs in Humanitarian Action: Contributions from a Sociology of Praxis." *Sociology* 46 (5):891–905.
Hopgood, Stephen. 2006. *Keepers of the Flame. Understanding Amnesty International*. Ithaca, NY: Cornell University Press.
Hynes, Patricia. 2010. "Global Points of 'Vulnerability': Understanding Processes of the Trafficking of Children and Young People Into, Within and Out of the UK." *The International Journal of Human Rights* 14 (6):952–970.
Hynes, Patricia, Michele Lamb, Damien Short, and Matthew Waites. 2010. "Sociology and Human Rights: Confrontations, Evasions and New Engagements." *The International Journal of Human Rights* 14 (6):811–32.

Hynes, Patricia, Michele Lamb, Damien Short, and Matthew Waites. 2012a. "New Directions in the Sociology of Human Rights: Foreword." *The International Journal of Human Rights* 16 (8):1123–1126.

Hynes, Patricia, Michele Lamb, Damien Short, and Matthew Waites. 2012b. "The Sociology of Human Rights: Editorial Foreword." *Sociology* 46 (5):787–796.

Keck, Margaret E., and Kathryn Sikkink. 1998. *Activists Beyond Borders: Advocacy Networks in International Politics*. Ithaca, NY and London: Cornell University Press.

Kelly, Patrick William. 2014a. "'Magic Words': The Advent of Transnational Human Rights Activism in Latin America's Southern Cone in the Long 1970s." In *The Breakthrough: Human Rights in the 1970s*, edited by Jan Eckel and Samuel Moyn, 88–106. Philadelphia: University of Pennsylvania Press.

Kelly, Tobias. 2014b. "Recognizing Torture: Credibility and the Unstable Codification of Victimhood." In *Histories of Victimhood*, edited by Steffen Jensen and Henrik Ronsbo, 144–160. Philadelphia: University of Pennsylvania Press.

Keys, Barbara J. 2014. *Reclaiming American Virtue*. Cambridge, MA: Harvard University Press.

Kurasawa, Fuyuki. 2007. *The Work of Global Justice: Human Rights as Practices*. Cambridge and New York: Cambridge University Press.

Lamb, Michele. 2010. "Loyalty and Human Rights: Liminality and Social Action in a Divided Society." *The International Journal of Human Rights* 14 (6):994–1012.

Landman, Todd, and Edzia Carvahlho. 2010. *Measuring Human Rights*. London and New York: Routledge.

Lee-Gong, Eunna. 2010. "Contestations over Rights: From Establishment to Implementation of the National Basic Livelihood Security System in South Korea." *The International Journal of Human Rights* 14 (6):880–895.

Levine, Daniel H. 1988. "Assessing the Impacts of Liberation Theology in Latin America." *The Review of Politics* 50 (2):241–263.

Levy, Daniel, and Natan Sznaider. 2010. *Human Rights and Memory*. Philadelphia: Penn State Press.

López, José Julián. 2015. "The Human Right to Food as Political Imaginary." *Journal of Historical Sociology* 30 (2): 239–261.

Löwy, Michael. 1996. *The War of Gods: Religion and Politics in Latin America*. London: Verso.

Madison, D. Soyini. 2010. *Acts of Activism: Human Rights as Radical Performance*. Cambridge and New York: Cambridge University Press.
Manzo, Kate. 2008. "Imaging Humanitarianism: NGO Identity and the Iconography of Childhood." *Antipode* 40 (4):632–657.
McGarry, Ross, Gabe Mythen, and Sandra Walklate. 2012. "The Soldier, Human Rights and the Military Covenant: A Permissible State of Exception?" *The International Journal of Human Rights* 16 (8):1183–1195.
McLagan, Meg. 2006. "Introduction: Making Human Rights Claims Public." *American Anthropologist* 108 (1):191–195.
Melvin, Jennifer. 2010. "Reconstructing Rwanda: Balancing Human Rights and the Promotion of National Reconciliation." *The International Journal of Human Rights* 14 (6):932–951.
Merry, Sally Engle. 2006. "Transnational Human Rights and Local Activism: Mapping the Middle." *American Anthropologist* 108 (1):38–51.
Merry, Sally Engle. 2009. *Human Rights and Gender Violence: Translating International Law into Local Justice*. Cambridge and New York: University of Chicago Press.
Miller, Hannah. 2010. "From 'Rights-Based' to 'Rights-Framed' Approaches: A Social Constructionist View of Human Rights Practice." *The International Journal of Human Rights* 14 (6):915–931.
Moon, Claire. 2008. *Narrating Political Reconciliation: South Africa's Truth and Reconciliation Commission*. Plymouth, UK: Lexington Books.
Moon, Claire. 2012. "What One Sees and How One Files Seeing: Human Rights Reporting, Representation and Action." *Sociology* 46 (5):876–890.
Morris, Lydia. 2012. "Understanding Torture: The Strengths and the Limits of Social Theory." *The International Journal of Human Rights* 16 (8):1127–1141.
Morrow, Virginia, and Kirrily Pells. 2012. "Integrating Children's Human Rights and Child Poverty Debates: Examples from Young Lives in Ethiopia and India." *Sociology* 46 (5):906–920.
Moyn, Samuel. 2010. *The Last Utopia*. Harvard University Press.
Moyn, Samuel. 2012. "Imperialism, Self-Determination, and the Rise of Human Rights." In *The Human Rights Revolution: An International History*, edited by Akara Iriye, Petra Goedde, and William I. Hitchcock, 159–178. Oxford and New York: Oxford University Press.
Moyn, Samuel. 2013a. "On the Nonglobalization of Ideas." In *Global Intellectual History*, 187–204. New York: Columbia University Press.
Moyn, Samuel. 2013b. "The Continuing Perplexities of Human Rights." *Qui Parle: Critical Humanities and Social Sciences* 22 (1):95–115.

Nash, Kate. 2009b. *The Cultural Politics of Human Rights*. Cambridge and New York: Cambridge University Press.

Nash, Kate. 2012. "Towards a Political Sociology of Human Rights." In *The Wiley-Blackwell Companion to Political Sociology*, edited by Kate Nash, Edwin Amenta Scott, and Alan Edwin, 444–454. Malden: Wiley Blackwell.

Ortner, Sherry B. 1984. "Theory in Anthropology Since the Sixties." *Comparative Studies in Society and History* 26 (1):126–166.

Rae, Paul. 2009. *Theatre and Human Rights*. London and New York: Palgrave Macmillan.

Ramos, Howard, James Ron, and Oskar N.T. Thoms. 2007. "Shaping the Northern Media's Human Rights Coverage, 1986–2000." *Journal of Peace Research* 44.

Rashed, Haifa, and Damien Short. 2012. "Genocide and Settler Colonialism: Can a Lemkin-Inspired Genocide Perspective Aid Our Understanding of the Palestinian Situation?" *The International Journal of Human Rights* 16 (8):1142–1169.

Reckwitz, Andreas. 2002a. "The Status of the 'Material' in Theories of Culture: From 'Social Structure' to 'Artefacts.'" *Journal for the Theory of Social Behaviour* 32 (2):195–217.

Reckwitz, Andreas. 2002b. "Toward a Theory of Social Practices a Development in Culturalist Theorizing." *European Journal of Social Theory* 5 (2):243–263.

Redhead, Robin, and Nick Turnbull. 2011. "Towards a Study of Human Rights Practitioners." *Human Rights Review* 12 (2):173–189.

Richey, Lisa Ann, and Stefano Ponte. 2011. *Brand Aid: Shopping Well to Save the World*. Minnesota: University of Minnesota Press.

Riga, Liliana, and James Kennedy. 2012. "'Putting Cruelty First': Interpreting War Crimes as Human Rights Atrocities in US Policy in Bosnia and Herzegovina." *Sociology* 46 (5):861–875.

Ron, James, Howard Ramos, and Kathleen Rodgers. 2005. "Transnational Information Politics: NGO Human Rights Reporting, 1986–2000." *International Studies Quarterly* 49 (3):557–588.

Rouse, Joseph. 2007. "Practice Theory" Division I Faculty Publications. Paper 43. http://wescholar.wesleyan.edu/div1facpubs/43.

Schaffer, Kay, and Sidonie Smith. 2004. *Human Rights and Narrated Lives: The Ethics of Recognition*. New York: Palgrave Macmillan.

Schatzki, Theodore R. 1996. *Social Practices: A Wittgensteinian Approach to Human Activity and the Social*. Cambridge and New York: Cambridge University Press.

Seu, Irene Bruna. 2012. "'In Countries like That…' Moral Boundaries and Implicatory Denial in Response to Human Rights Appeals." *The International Journal of Human Rights* 16 (8):1170–1182.

Short, Damien. 2010. "Cultural Genocide and Indigenous Peoples: A Sociological Approach." *The International Journal of Human Rights* 14 (6):833–848.

Skillington, Tracey. 2012. "Climate Change and the Human Rights Challenge: Extending Justice Beyond the Borders of the Nation State." *The International Journal of Human Rights* 16 (8):1196–1212.

Sliwinski, Sharon. 2011. *Human Rights in Camera*. Chicago and London: University of Chicago Press.

Smith, Brian H. 1979. "Churches and Human Rights in Latin America: Recent Trends in the Subcontinent." *Journal of Interamerican Studies and World Affairs* 21 (1):89–127.

Snyder, Sarah B. 2011. *Human Rights Activism and the End of the Cold War: A Transnational History of the Helsinki Network*. Cambridge and New York: Cambridge University Press.

Swidler, Ann. 1986. "Culture in Action: Symbols and Strategies." *American Sociological Review* 51 (2):273–286.

Turner, Bryan S. 2006. *Vulnerability and Human Rights*. Philadelphia: Penn State Press.

Waever, Ole. 1998. "The Sociology of a Not so International Discipline: American and European Developments in International Relations." *International Organization* 52 (4):687–727.

Waites, Matthew. 2010. "Human Rights, Sexual Orientation and the Generation of Childhoods: Analysing the Partial Decriminalization of 'Unnatural Offences' in India." *The International Journal of Human Rights* 14 (6):971–993.

Wendt, Alexander. 1999. *Social Theory of International Politics*. Cambridge and New York: Cambridge University Press.

Wiener, Antje. 2003. "Constructivism: The Limits of Bridging Gaps." *Journal of International Relations and Development* 6 (3):252–275.

Wilson, Richard A. 2001. *The Politics of Truth and Reconciliation in South Africa: Legitimizing the Post-Apartheid State*. Cambridge and New York: Cambridge University Press.

Wilson, Richard A. 1997. "Introduction." In *Human Rights, Culture and Context: Anthropological Perspectives*. London: Pluto Press.

Wilson, Richard A. 2009. "Representing Human Rights Violations: Social Contexts and Subjectivities." In *Human Rights: An Anthropological Reader*, edited by Mark Goodale, 134–160. Oxford and New York: Wiley Blackwell.

Woodiwiss, Anthony. 1992. *Law, Labour and Society in Japan*. London: Routledge.

Woodiwiss, Anthony. 1998. *Globalisation, Human Rights and Labour Law in Pacific Asian*. Cambridge: Cambridge University Press.

Woodiwiss, Anthony. 2003. *Making Human Rights Work Globally*. London: The Glass House Press.

Woodiwiss, Anthony. 2005. *Human Rights*. London and New York: Routledge.

Woodiwiss, Anthony. 2011. "Making the Sociology of Human Rights More Sociological." *Development and Society* 40 (1):117–138.

Woodiwiss, Anthony. 2012. "Asia, Enforceable Benevolence and the Future of Human Rights." *Sociology* 46 (5):966–981.

5

Humanizing the Citizen

Introduction

It is hardly surprising that one of sociologists' privileged points of entry into the phenomenon of human rights should be via citizenship rights. After all, as I noted in Chap. 3, Bryan Turner, a pioneer of the sociology of human rights, argued in his programmatic 1993, and widely cited, paper that it was on the terrain of citizenship rights where sociologists felt less compunction about engaging in normative discussion: precisely because this took place under the cover of the analysis of objective social relations of power between social groups mediated through state institutions (Turner 1993, 496). However, it was not merely that citizenship assuaged sociologists' angsts when engaged in normative incursions. Turner, also, maintained that human rights were the solidaristic counterpart to a modernized and globalized world because they were more universal, contemporary, and progressive than citizenship rights (Turner 1993, 498). In other words, the globalized world had outgrown nationally based citizenship rights. In his words, "whereas citizenship as a doctrine has been a progressive feature of western societies in terms of universalistic values behind the welfare state, human-rights concepts can

J. Julián López, *Human Rights as Political Imaginary*,
https://doi.org/10.1007/978-3-319-74274-8_5

be seen as a progressive paradigm which is relevant to a world system" (Turner 1993, 498).[1]

The notion that globalized human rights represents an *expansion* or a *supersession of* citizenship rights are powerful contemporary tropes in the citizenship literature (Bosniak 2000; Brysk and Shafir 2004; Brysk 2002; Frezzo 2011; Jacobson 1996; Levy and Sznaider 2010; Sassen 2009; Shafir and Brysk 2006; Soysal 1994, 2012; Turner 1993, 2006). Indeed as Randall Hansen has argued, "over the last decade and a half, in a literature otherwise obsessed with citizenship in all its forms [global, ecological, cultural, diasporic, local, sexual, etc.], a broad array of scholars has downplayed, criticized and at times trivialized *national* citizenship" (2009, 1 emphasis added). The efficacy of the aforementioned tropes depends, in part, on the analogical relationship they establish between citizenship and human rights. It is only if the meaning of citizenship and human rights overlap in significant ways that it makes sense to think of the former expanding into, or superseding, the latter.

Much depends on how the relationship between the two constituent nouns in the compound nouns is understood. For instance, in the case of *citizenship* rights and *human* rights, the italicized noun adjuncts can be seen as modifying the same plural noun, what linguists call the head, "rights". In other words, *human* and *citizenship* rights both index particular kinds of rights with shared characteristics such as in the case of a *white* and a *black* board; both are writing surfaces. In linguistics these are called endocentric compounds (Bauer 2008); both *human* rights and *citizenship* rights are subclasses of the plural noun "rights". Another possibility, however, is to read them as exocentric compounds. In the latter case, the meaning cannot be straightforwardly inferred because there is no head being modified by an adjunct noun: a redhead is not a type of "head", nor is a pickpocket a type of "pocket" (Bauer 2008, 61). In this case, *human rights* and *citizenship rights* would semantically refer to two potentially different types of phenomena, rather than two variations of the same phenomenon.

Generally, the scholars discussed in this chapter implicitly view citizenship and human rights as endocentric compounds, which enables them to coherently entertain expansion and supersession as explanatory strategies.[2] I want to suggest that as a further step in the development of the political imaginary model, it is sociologically informative to read citizenship and human rights as being exocentric compounds, instead and to sociologically conceptualize them accordingly.[3] I think this enables one to explore the interaction between the practices of citizenship and human rights rather than to assume that one replaces the other or that what distinguishes human rights and citizenship rights is merely the location where they are imagined, legitimized, and practised, namely, national versus transnational spaces (Bosniak 2000; Sassen 2009). In other words, I want to develop the proposal that it makes sense to think about human rights as a distinct political imaginary that intersects with but is not the same as citizenship. However, before developing this argument further, I first devote the bulk of this chapter to reviewing a number of sociological accounts that understand the relationship between citizenship and human rights as one of expansion or supersession.

I begin by looking at the arguments of a number of scholars who generally understand the relationship between citizenship and human rights in terms of postnationalism, namely, Gershon Shafir and Alison Brysk, Yasemin Soysal, Linda Bosniak, and Saskia Sassen. Broadly speaking, these scholars posit that citizenship rights have been, or are possibly in the process of being, superseded by human rights. I spend a considerable amount of time with Yasemin Soysal's arguments because the notion of postnational citizenship is particularly associated with her work. Overall, I argue that these scholars either rely on an identity between citizenship and human rights—that is, think of them as endocentric compounds—that is asserted, rather than demonstrated, or on an under-theorized conception of human rights.

Next, I turn my attention to scholars who centre their analysis of citizenship and human rights in terms of cosmopolitanism, world citizenship. I review the arguments of Seyla Benhabib, David Held, and Ulrich Beck. Drawing on the impressive sociological analysis of cosmopolitanism put forward by Gavin Kendall, Ian Woodward, and Zlatko Skrbis, I show that human rights, as such, are, despite appearances, surprisingly marginal to the aforementioned authors of contemporary cosmopolitanism.

Finally, I return to my contention that it is heuristically useful to think about citizenship and human rights as exocentric compounds. In order to do so, I discuss Margaret Somers' conceptualization of citizenship and show that if one adopts the same explanatory strategy for human rights, one has to recognize a significant difference between the two. Whereas both citizenship and human rights are political imaginaries oriented towards thinking about membership in a community, in the case of the latter, as a result of its historical and institutional trajectory, it is frequently through the figure of the victim that a claim to membership is made and adjudicated. This, I argue, should make us reconsider the notion that human rights represent an expansion of citizenship rights. Instead, I conclude by suggesting that it is sociologically and politically wiser to understand the two sorts of rights as exocentric compounds, referring to different types of membership. If we really want to gauge what human rights can, may, or probably will never be able to do, we should understand what they share, but also what they do not with citizenship rights.

Expanding Citizenship

Gershon Shafir and Alison Brysk collectively and individually have been strong proponents of the notion that human rights are best understood as a global extension of citizenship rights (Brysk 2002, 2013; Brysk and Shafir 2004; Shafir and Brysk 2006). In their work, as in that of many other human rights scholars (Moyn 2010, 12; cf. Hunt 2007; Blau and Moncada 2016), the overlap between citizenship and human rights is anchored in their historical concurrence in the declaration of the 1789 French *Declaration of the Rights of Man and* Citizen. The declaration signals that human rights were not codified in opposition to citizenship rights, allowing the inference of a shared ontological terrain (Shafir and Brysk 2006, 277). Despite this, Shafir and Brysk note that for historical reasons, citizenship trumped human rights (2006, 478), and consequently, human rights' most recent reappearance must be understood as building on the earlier citizenship rights tradition, not least because the latter has served as "a source of inspiration for the growth of human rights" (2006, 275).

According to the authors, the process of expansion from citizenship to human rights can be best explained by grasping the developmental logic underpinning the historical transformation of citizenship. The latter, understood as the anchoring of rights in "membership in a politically sovereign entity", argue Shafir and Brysk, can be traced back to the classic Greek polis (2006, 277). Nonetheless, the nature of the rights, the individuals eligible for membership, and the political sovereignty underwriting the rights have been subject to historical change. Shafir and Brysk identify three principal modalities of change: (1) "the transfer of citizenship from one political context of sovereignty to another", (2) "through extension to members of new groups and ultimately to all members of the nation-state", (3) and "through the expansion of the content of the rights of citizenship themselves" (Shafir and Brysk 2006, 276). From the medieval city to the nation-state, from propertied to all social classes, and from civil and political to social rights, respectively, constitute examples of the aforementioned historical transformations.

Shafir and Brysk draw on the same transformative mechanisms to account for the expansion from citizenship to human rights, through the emergence of new venues of sovereignty, namely, postnational or global venues, and as an extension of rights to a new class of members, from members of the national to those of the postnational or global community (2006, 277). In order to explain the third modality of expansion, that is, the creation of new rights, they, in turn, identify three types of processes. These include "moral induction", bridging existing frames to new domains, and/or the promotion of new rights by "norm entrepreneurs", networks, or structural diffusion (2006, 280). Moral induction refers to the extension of existing claims to new forms of behaviour. In the context of citizenship this process is exemplified by the democratic broadening of civic membership to political and then social and cultural rights. Upgraded to the transnational context, such moral induction can be detected in the introduction and pursuit of second- and third-generation human rights, economic and cultural human rights, respectively (Shafir and Brysk 2006, 280). Frame bridging denotes the manner in which citizenship level entitlements and freedoms, such as access to healthcare, can be transposed onto a global context as the human right to health.

It is the interplay between moral induction and frame bridging from citizenship rights with actors and networks, empowered by the structural diffusion of globalized human right norms that accounts for the development of new human rights (Shafir and Brysk 2006, 281).[4] For instance, according to the authors, although the "right to development" can be read from the International Covenant on Economic and Social Rights, the earlier source is the welfare state and the "citizenship claim of 'freedom from want'" (2006, 281).[5] Equally, "the recognition of health as a human right" (Shafir and Brysk 2006, 281) is grounded in the interface of global processes with the "citizenship tradition [that] establishes the provision of healthcare as a hallmark of the welfare state and the constitution of the body politic" (Shafir and Brysk 2006, 282).

Naturally, Shafir and Brysk recognize that the expansion from, not to mention the supersession of, citizenship rights is far from complete, not least because two key citizenship rights threads are strongly interwoven within the fabric of the nation-state, existing only loosely in the postnational context, namely, social solidarity and effective enforcement tools (2006, 283). However, the strong identity between citizenship and human rights that structures their analysis is reaffirmed and strengthened when they conclude that it is only with the transformation of "human rights" into "citizenship" that the former will succeed, by which they mean it is only with "the creation of and membership in a global community with its own solidarity, institutions and commensurate ability to provide security and social justice" that human rights will finally be realized (Shafir and Brysk 2006, 285).[6]

To my mind, Shafir and Brysk are right to draw attention to the contemporary entanglement between citizenship and human rights. The discursive resonance between the two, as the authors persuasively argue, is difficult to ignore and is rightfully the focus of social scientific inquiry. Human rights, as we saw in the previous chapter, can be understood as claims to membership in an imagined community from which consequential moral and political claims and entitlements can follow. This is also the case for citizenship rights. However entanglement and overlap do not amount to identity. As elementary set theory suggests, the intersection between two sets constitutes a subset of shared elements and not the union of the two sets.

In other words, the fact that human rights and citizenship rights share a subset of elements is not sufficient reason to unite them conceptually.

However the unity between the two is precisely what Shafir and Brysk's account offers. It is in fact the crux of their analysis. Human rights are understood as the product of the dynamics and practices that have historically powered the transformation and the extension of citizenship rights. As such, read through their explanatory narrative, human rights do not represent anything new with respect to citizenship rights, other than their expansion. Said differently, one may see citizenship rights as the precursors of human rights. The historical and institutional specificity of human rights and their practice do not need to be addressed because they are, after all, fulfilling an inherent potential, namely, that of citizenship writ large.

The Supersession of National Citizenship

Insofar as national citizenship has been conceptualized as membership in a political community territorially defined by the nation-state, the conceptualization of human rights as an extension of citizenship is frequently conjoined with an account of the erosion of state capacity arising from globalizing forces, or from the displacement of political sovereignty from the national to some postnational site. Thus although above, Shafir and Brysk rest the bulk of the explanatory burden on the notion of expansion, elsewhere Brysk has equally argued that "human rights provide a multifaceted ethos of connection, protection and entitlement that substitutes for the increasingly hazy promise of citizenship in an era of shifting identities and weakening states" (2013, 14). In other words, the other side of the coin of citizenship's expansion is the national state's inability to pull the levers that ensure the provision of rights. For instance, to take one example in the realm of cultural rights, Bryan Turner argues that "national citizenship was produced by the growth of nation-states in the nineteenth century (and citizenship involves territorially circumscribed set of rights), but cultural identities are now increasingly transnational and diverse" (2006, 46).

In Chap. 3, I analysed a number of normative sociological justifications of human rights that were rooted in the notion that only human rights could provide global citizens with the leverage to seek security and well-being in the maelstrom of economic, migratory, political, and military conflicts that define the contemporary globalized era. For the scholars analysed in Chap. 3, amongst others, the supersession of national citizenship rights by human rights is understood as being necessitated by the transnational origins of the processes that threaten the rights previously secured, in patch work patterns to be sure, through national citizenship.

However, another explanatory possibility for conceptualizing the supersession of national citizenship by postnational human rights is associated with the displacement of sovereignty from a national to a postnational locus. For instance, David Levy and Natan Sznaider argue that despite the tendency of many scholars to associate the development of human rights with the erosion of state sovereignty, it is better understood as a partial denationalization of the legitimacy of the nation-state, which is reconfiguring the very nature of sovereignty itself (2006, 2010).

Levy and Sznaider draw particular attention to the ongoing contemporary pattern of national attempts to come to terms with their violent pasts. Be they through apologies, inquiries, truth and reconciliation commissions, and/or efforts at reconstructing history and historical memory, "national-building practices based on violence and war-like conduct are being recast as illegitimate practices of human rights violations and ethnic cleansing" (2006, 658). The broader significance of this "post-heroic statehood" (Levy and Sznaider 2006, 658) is that the legitimacy of the contemporary state is no longer exclusively secured through a contract with the nation, but increasingly depends on the latter's adherence to "nation-transcending human right ideals" (2006, 659).

This is particularly salient in the context of historical memory. Whereas, historical memory was once stitched to a narrative of national development, providing what the French historian, Pierre Nora, felicitously called, "our quintessential *milieu de mémoire*" (1989, 9), such narratives, argue Levy and Sznaider, are increasingly being threaded by the "public and frequent ritualistic attention to memories" of "past violation of human rights" (2010, 4). Consequently, "memory politics of human rights has become a new form of political rationality and a prerequisite for state legitimacy" (Levy and Sznaider 2010, 5).

Levy and Sznaider's analysis is concerned with "the emergence of the cosmopolitan memory tropes that challenge nation-state-centered memories in the European context" (2010, 56). Insofar as collective memory has historically been one of the mechanisms through which national identity has been forged, underwriting the legitimacy of the nation-state as the locus of sovereignty (Olick and Robbins 1998, 116), the emergence of a cosmopolitan memory is an interesting index of postnational "ethics" (Kendall et al. 2009, 7; Turner 2006, 141), to which I return below in my discussion of cosmopolitan approaches to human rights. Now, I turn to what is without doubt the sociological contribution that in many ways inaugurated the field of postnational citizenship studies, namely, Yasemin Soysal's *The Limits of Citizenship*.

It is rare to find papers or books addressing the contemporary significance of postnational citizenship that do not obsequiously cite this "agenda setting book" (Hansen 2009, 2). What is more, frequently the citation is to the entire book rather than to any of its substantive arguments or findings. Following Bruno Latour, one might say that this degree of stylization in citation indicates that the claims of the text are part of a tacit understanding (1987, 61), in effect presenting the reality of postnational citizenship as an "incontrovertible black box" (1987, 80).[7] For this very reason, I think it is crucial to pry open the box.

Soysal begins her book by arguing that "a new and more universal concept of citizenship has unfolded in the post-war era, one whose organizing principles are based on universal personhood [human rights] rather than national belonging" (1994, 1). The most compelling evidence for this claim, she argues, is to be found in the manner in which the rights and privileges that were once reserved to the citizens of territorially defined nations have been gradually extended across Europe to guestworkers[8] in the postwar era (1994, 2). For Soysal, this extension of citizenship rights to non-citizen residents is explained by a "transnational discourse and structures celebrating human rights as a world-level organizing principle" (1994, 2). Despite this, on my reading, the bulk of the conceptual and empirical content of her book is concerned with showing how variations in the policies for the incorporation of guestworkers in European countries can be explained as arising from the existence of distinct migrant incorporation regimes. The latter are in turn rooted in differing conceptions of membership in the national community.

Soysal argues, at the time of her writing, that much of the literature that attempts to account for differing patterns of migrant integration does so by emphasizing "the demographic, social or cultural characteristics of migrants as the major explanatory variables", in effect drawing on binaries such as tradition/modernity, religious/secular, and so on (1994, 30). Instead, Soysal suggests that the incorporation institutions of host societies, as opposed to the cultural background of migrants or their individual characteristics, might better account for the divergent patterns of incorporation of guestworkers (1994, 31). Incorporation regimes are structured around different understandings of what it means to belong to a polity, in other words, on different models of membership in the community. These models are crystallized in "prevailing principles, discourses, practices, and organizational structure" and are relatively enduring, persisting over time, and creating path dependency in policy development (1994, 36).

Drawing on the extant literature, she creates a typology along two axes, *Locus of Action and Authority* (State or Society) and *Organizational Configuration* (Centralized or Decentralized) to generate four membership models: corporatist, liberal, statist and fragmental, and a fifth corporatist-statist hybrid (1994, 37). The corporatist regime, exemplified by Sweden and the Netherlands, is centrally organized but relies on individuals being included in corporate groups that "can be defined by occupational, ethnic, religious, or gender identity" (1994, 37). The state enables and supports the existence of these corporate groups, which provide a mediating link with individual citizens or residents. It is through participation in these groups that individuals access rights, pursue their interests, and participate in decision-making (1994, 37–38). This model of membership, concludes Soysal, offers a vertical pattern of incorporation: "migrants are incorporated collectively, through their participation in the intermediary structures of the state. The pattern is one of official incorporation with an emphasis on social and welfare rights" (1994, 38).

The liberal regime, for which Switzerland and Britain are the exemplars, refers to a decentralized and individualized mode of incorporation. Political action and organization is voluntary and associational rather than the products of formalized state structures. Local authorities are largely responsible for developing and implementing welfare programmes. In the absence of formal centralized arrangements, the labour market becomes the prime institutional site for incorporation. Equally, since private and voluntary associations are the vehicles through which new populations pursue their interests, liberal models of membership "generate a horizontal incorporation pattern at the societal level through local voluntary associations, in which migrants are incorporated as individuals" (Soysal 1994, 38).

In contrast to the liberal regime, in the statist, "the state is the main provider and initiator of public services"; it "intervenes actively in societal functions" and is central to the organization of collective action (Soysal 1994, 39). As a result, Soysal argues it is the highly centralized state through its web of categories, programmes, and administrative structures that incorporates individuals. Moreover, when groups organize to pursue collective interests, they do so via social movements, directing claims at the state. France, notes Soysal, best exemplifies the statist regime (1994, 39). Between the statist and the liberal types, Soysal discerns a hybrid regime epitomized by the German case. On the one hand, it relies on corporatist forms of incorporation. On the other hand, the centralizing and organizational role of the state remains significant. This engenders a centralized and bureaucratic public sphere in which "highly centralized semi-public bureaucracies, trade unions, churches, welfare institutions, business organizations, and professional chambers actively take part in formulating public policy, and have strong links to the state" (Soysal 1994, 39).

The last regime, typified by Gulf oil countries, is the fragmental. In this case, the state, the seat of sovereignty, lacks the administrative apparatus and capacity to actively intervene in and organize social life. Consequently it is "'primordial' groups such as the family, clan, and church [that] dominate social and public life" (Soysal 1994, 39). Migrants are partially incorporated via the labour market, but remain outside of the social and institutional arrangements that organize social and public life more broadly (Soysal 1994, 39).

The different incorporation models delineated, Soysal explores the fit with actual migrant incorporation regimes through an analysis of the discourses and instruments of incorporation of the countries corresponding to the four regimes found in the European context, the corporate, liberal, statist, and corporate-statist hybrid (1994, 45–64).[9] She shows that, indeed, the policies and institutional structures of Sweden and the Netherlands envision incorporating migrants as corporate groups, in Switzerland and Britain as individuals, in France as individual migrants via a centralized state apparatus, and in Germany as participants in centrally organized corporate groups.[10] This established, she sets out to see whether the different incorporation models can account for the variation in guestworker incorporation, concluding that they do (1994, 79).

As noted above, incorporation regimes do not merely refer to the processes by which individuals can access the goods associated with citizenship, such as healthcare, education, and so on, but also to the manner in which they organize collectively in the pursuit of their interests. Consequently, the incorporation models, argues Soysal, should also be able to explain variation in the collective patterns of migrant organization (1994, 84). Once again, she finds the explanatory value of her model of incorporation regimes quite promising; her analysis suggests that "much organizational activity arises from interaction with the host society's institutions, and migrant organizations appropriate and mobilize the predominating models" (1994, 110).

Having established the explanatory adequacy of her models of incorporations to account for divergences amongst the different countries, Soysal turns her attention to what she claims are broad similarities in the treatment of non-citizen residents across the different incorporation regimes. The latter in fact constitutes the argument for which she is most frequently cited, namely, the emergence of a new form of postnational membership or citizenship. Here, she adds a number of countries to her sample from Europe and North America, namely, Austria, Belgium, Canada, Denmark, and the US, and finds that "the inventory of noncitizen's rights do not differ significantly from those of citizens, and the rights of noncitizens are increasingly standardized across host polities" (Soysal 1994, 119–20).

While some scholars had accounted for this extension of rights by distinguishing between the rights of denizens (i.e., residents) and citizens (Hammar 1986, 1990; Brubaker 1989a, b), and others by making reference to "the ethos of equality" arising from the "mature" welfare state (Heisler and Heisler 1991), Soysal believes that something more significant has been afoot (1994, 138). Underpinning this movement towards the equalization of rights between citizens and non-citizens, maintains Soysal, is a reconfiguration of citizenship from a particularistic conception based on nationhood to a more universalistic one based on personhood (1994, 137). If the former has taken the form of national rights, the latter now takes the form of universal human rights (Soysal 1994, 142). Consequently, in the emerging postnational configuration, "the rights and claims of individuals are legitimated by ideologies grounded in a transnational community, through international, codes, conventions, and laws on human rights independent of their citizenship in a nation-state" (Soysal 1994, 142). The relationship between citizenship and human rights is one of the latter superseding the former.

In very cursory sweep, Soysal explains this shift in the locus of sovereignty from national to transnational institutions by drawing on the work of John Meyer et al. (1997). She argues that it is a global system of rules, norms, principles, and structures that invest contemporary nation-states with their legitimacy, effectively making them "authorized actors" functioning "concurrently with international and normative structures, ordering and organizing individuals' lives" (1994, 145). The global system is structurally the product of "interdependence and connectedness, intensified world-level interaction and organizing, and the emergence of transnational political structures" (Soysal 1994, 144). The normative content of this global system of rules, the notion of personhood, was crystallized in the 1948 UDHR and has been further disseminated in the succession of related covenants, codes, treaties, agreements, and other global and regional initiatives. The mode of diffusion of this new normative conception of the individual has taken various forms such as "international governmental and non-governmental organisations, legal institutions, networks of experts, and scientific communities" (Soysal 1994, 152).

Soysal concludes by forcefully arguing that her analysis should not be read as signifying the disappearance of the nation-state succeeded by a world state. She insists that the two governing principles to emerge from the postwar global system, which are structuring the current shift towards postnational membership, are national sovereignty and universal human rights (1994, 157). Consequently, despite the fact that claims appeal to normative systems beyond the nation-state, it is the latter that nonetheless remains overwhelmingly charged with receiving and fulfilling those claims. True, its margin of manoeuvre is curtailed by the global system, but "the sovereign nation-state retains the formally and organizationally legitimate form venerated by the ideologies and conventions of transnational reference groups such as the UN, UNESCO, and the like" (Soysal 1994, 157). This of course does not mean that the nation-state and the modes of attachment to the nation-state are not in flux. The nation-state "becomes an implementer of a multitude of, at times conflicting, functions and responsibilities, derived from world-level discourses rather than from its territorialized identity", concomitantly, "the link between the individual and state becomes more instrumental and routine rather than charismatic and sentimental" (Soysal 1994, 165).

Postnational Membership?

When taken in its entirety, one of the striking aspects of Soysal's book is the contrast between the carefulness with which she constructs her analysis of the competing incorporation regimes and the perfunctory nature of her assertion that it is the global human rights normative regime that explains the extension of citizenship rights to non-citizen residents, signalling a tectonic shift away from nationally based rights. For Soysal, human rights, the normative scaffolding of the supersession of citizenship by personhood, is read as the materialization of two postwar principles, to wit, national sovereignty and personhood, not unlike the dialectic between "international norms" and transnational "humanness" that I identified in the work of the anthropologist Mark Goodale in Chap. 4. The self-evidence of the significance of human rights requires little in the way of historical and sociological corroboration in her book. Remarkably, besides briefly and anecdotally alluding to the contemporary prevalence of human rights discourses in different European fora (1994, 146–56), she provides no compelling argument and preciously little empirical evidence to support her claim that human rights is the midwife of a new mode of postnational membership.[11]

In a review essay, exploring contributions to the study of postwar migration in Western Europe, the political scientist Anthony Messina argues that Soysal's account of the alleged human rights-fuelled expansion of rights to non-citizens in Western Europe is far from compelling. He asks whether the "generosity of immigrant policy in Western Europe" might not be more plausibly explained as "a function of mundane foreign policy considerations and/or government anxieties about preserving domestic social peace and harmonious relation" (1996, 147). In a more recent theoretical and empirical study of Western European postwar migration policies, he indicates that "contrary to the assumptions of globalization or postnational membership theorists, the nation-state in Western Europe is the primary reference point for defining citizenship and granting citizenship rights", adding that "while postwar immigration has undeniably transformed Western Europe, its effects do not include a significant diminution in the capacity of states to specify the conditions under or the degree to which immigrants are legally and social incorporated" (2007, 171). Similarly, in a second review essay, the political sociologist John Hall contrasts the excellent sociology of Soysal's book, namely, her analysis of regimes of incorporation, with the exaggerated optimism of her postnationalist membership thesis, noting that Soysal's postnationalist conception "often derives from European arrangements rather than from international society *per se*, and it accordingly behoves us to a ask whether Europe is going to maintain its generosity" (1996, 168).[12]

Indeed, a number of scholars have argued that the passage of time has not been kind to Soysal's human rights-powered postnationalist membership thesis. For instance, Hansen insists that the poor performance in the areas of education, employment, and earnings amongst well-established ethnic minorities in Europe has led not to a diminution of but "to a reassertion of state power of integration and citizenship. Across the EU, *at the member-state level*, the nation-state has reasserted its importance in the lives of Europe's migrant communities" (2009, 15). Similarly, Christian Joppke and Ewa Morawska maintain that an analysis of developments in both state policy and immigrant practices, in the US and in Europe, indicates that "citizenship" has been "reaffirmed as the dominant membership principle", while "non-citizen membership" has been "found either insufficient or explicitly devalued" (2003, 1). Evidence for their claim is sourced in social and political trends dating back to the 1990s that have moved in the direction of a "revaluation of citizenship". In the US, this has taken the form of efforts to limit access to substantive benefits and privileges to citizens, excluding non-citizens, as demonstrated in the welfare reforms of the 1990s (2003, 16–17).[13] In Europe, a different tack has been followed, namely, liberalizing citizenship regimes,[14] "making it easier for long-settled migrants and their children to acquire the citizenship of the host society" (Joppke and Morawska 2003, 17).[15]

Other threads weaving the fabric of the revaluation of national citizenship against the grain of the postnational membership thesis, include the introduction of citizenship integration tests and host language requirements (Goodman 2012; Joppke 2010a, 157; Koopmans 2012, 27; Hansen 2009, 14–17; Mouritsen 2011; Schain 2009), the decline of official multiculturalism (Alexander 2013; Joppke and Morawska 2003, 8; Messina 2007, 186–87; Mouritsen 2011; Triadafilopoulos 2011; Triandafyllidou et al. 2011; Schmidtke 2012, 35) and the use of "human rights" to reinforce national limits on religious expression (Edmunds 2012), the lack of convergence towards similar immigration policies amongst EU countries (Baldi and Goodman 2015; Goodman 2012; Koopmans 2012, 22–27; Koopmans et al. 2012; Messina 2007, 192–93), the neoliberal economic segmentation of "personhood" in Europe (Kofman 2005; Schmidtke 2012), and the underdevelopment of political rights (Banerjee 2014, 24; Hansen 2009, 20).

Recently, Soysal has attempted to address some of the aforementioned concerns raised by her critics (Soysal 2012), in what one of them has called "a brave stand for her theory of postnational rights, even in the face of changed circumstances" (Koopmans 2012, 22). The latter refer to the just mentioned reassertion and revaluation of national citizenship documented by a variety of citizenship scholars, as well as the redefinition of citizenship via a "neoliberal creed", which, postnational membership notwithstanding, has meant that migrants have had to "face renewed struggles for recognition and a re-negotiation of legitimate forms of belonging" (Schmidtke 2012, 38). In other words, whatever role human rights might have had in decoupling access to the rights and privileges of citizenship from national membership, if any at all, seems to have been mitigated by the economic and national redefinitions of citizenship. The supersession of citizenship by human rights either did not take place, or, if it did, was a momentary blip rather than a harbinger of postnational membership wave to come.

Faced with these two challenges, Soysal sets out to imaginatively show how changes in the nature of citizenship in Europe arising from both economic transformation and, seemingly, national revaluations of citizenship can in reality be explained in terms of the ongoing expansion of universalistic human rights. How? With respect to what she calls the "neoliberal turn", she begins by conceding that "neoliberal thinking [...] has had significant consequences for the recalibration of the relationship between the individual and the state, and has recalibrated the purview of the state, since the 1990s" (2012, 13). However, she immediately qualifies her concession by arguing that this is far from a complete picture of what has occurred in Europe (2012, 13). This is due, she argues, to an unnoticed yet crucial transformation that has taken place in what she calls the European social project.

The postwar European social project was built on the national welfare model described by T. H. Marshall (1950). Social cohesion and social solidarity were secured through social citizenship (i.e., access to education, health, social security, etc.) to minimize the inequalities that otherwise would have been produced by the capitalist economy. Consequently, the welfare state embodied and scripted a specific conception of social justice, "evolving as an empowering project for the disadvantaged and excluded classes, for the good of the whole society" (Soysal 2012, 2). She argues, however, that the contemporary welfare state has undergone an important transformation, shifting away from "a system of a 'passive benefits'[16] to 'social investment' in human capital", in its attempt to engender a more participatory and active citizenry (2012, 2). The goal is to create, she argues, citing from the EU's 2000 Lisbon strategy, "the most competitive and dynamic knowledge based economy in the world, capable of sustainable growth with maximized human capital, more and better jobs and great social cohesion" (2012, 4).

The pursuit of this goal is evidenced in a variety of European-wide policy initiatives that aim to create a link between social justice and economic productivity by deregulating labour markets, making benefits conditional on labour market integration, investment in human capital, improving skills training, promoting lifelong learning, developing children's capabilities, and raising standards in STEM (science, technology, engineering, and mathematics) subjects (Soysal 2012, 4). Such changes do not reflect an undermining of the welfare state, she contends, but a shift in its investments in the pursuit of a new repertoire[17] of social citizenship grounded in a different moral logic and language of justice (2012, 5). This novel repertoire dictates that social cohesion is no longer the direct responsibility of the state; it falls on the "increasingly moralized and incentivized individual citizen" (2012, 5).

Soysal recognizes that structural conditions, such as the polarization of labour markets, generate "insiders" and "outsiders" in the context of post-industrial globalized economies and that consequently "upskilling [...] does not guarantee that the low paying and poor quality jobs will disappear" (2012, 7). She equally notes that while some highly skilled migrants can indeed become "insiders",[18] much of them are destined to the low-skilled low-paying jobs "rarely considered part of the competitive economy and are not valued as such" (2012, 7). More generally she quotes research to the effects that a staggering one third of jobs in Europe are "poor quality"—hardly conducive to the type of knowledge-based active transformative citizenship envisioned by the new European social project—and admits that it is women, the young, and migrant workers that are most likely to be ensnared in these marginalizing economic situations (2012, 9). Given this bleak picture, where is the human rights silver lining?

The European project, she contends, "exposes a transformation on the constituent elements of good citizenship and its moral language of justice. What underscores this change is the value assigned to individuality and its transformative capacities, as legitimated in public policy, and scientific discourses" (2012, 12). In policy, in law, in education, amongst other areas, Soysal detects the increased presence of the cultural script of "individual actorhood", linked to ideas of individual dignity, autonomy, and well-being (2012, 14). Consequently, the European social project, with its championing of "the rights-bearing, autonomous, and able individual", is extending the "moral and legal boundaries of participation beyond ascriptive limitations" of the nation-state (2012, 14).

The same holds true with respect to the seeming reassertion and revaluation of national citizenship through language requirements, citizenship tests, and integration courses. Read through the lens of the new European social project, the contents of the tests speak less to the particularities of the nation and more to broadly shared conceptions of democracy and individual rights, while integration and language courses hone in on key aspects of social life and institutions such as "health, education, upbringing of children, social participation and volunteer work, sports and leisure, employment, job search, and basic training", emphasizing "individual freedoms and law-abidance" (Soysal 2012, 11). The goal of such programmes is to draw attention to individual migrant's responsibility to author their own citizenship: "Citizenship or residence is 'earned' on the basis of who is worthy, who can contribute and be productive. Integration requires a new purpose—the purpose of achieving social cohesion in society driven by active, participatory, and productive individuals" (Soysal 2012, 11).

Above, I cited Ruud Koopmans comment regarding Soysal's "brave stand" to shore up her postnationalist thesis in inhospitable circumstances. I disagree. I read Soysal as abandoning a good part of her postnational membership thesis as elaborated in Soysal (1994). What she is "standing for", however, is the centrality of human rights in accounting for the mutations of citizenship today, just as she did back then but was obfuscated by the deployment of what turned out to be a stunningly modish and ambiguous term (Bosniak 2000, 454; Hansen 2009, 2), postnational membership. In Soysal (1994), human rights, or "personhood", a key term, which tellingly she does not use in her most recent elaboration, was used to account for the equalization of rights between citizens and non-citizen residents. Discursively and theoretically, her use of the term "personhood", and the overall thrust of her argument, pointed to the extension and expansion of rights to previously excluded groups (1994, 40–41, 164), incorporating non-citizen residents as productive individuals wherever they resided, and presumably whatever work they did (1994, 31), moving from a particularistic to a universalistic conception of citizenship (1994, 137), and perhaps most significantly, with respect to the most recent iteration of her argument, "rendering differential status unjustifiable within the framework of universalistic personhood"

(1994, 142). In contrast, human rights are now mobilized, if only because of their entanglement with the new European social project and the neoliberal turn, in order to legitimate differences in opportunities amongst individuals, drawing attention to their "particularities", not necessarily as a result of national (non)belonging, but in terms of their capacity to "earn" their "residence" and citizenship status.

Conceptually, it is far from clear that it makes sense to use the term "membership" for a "social project", or a cultural script if one prefers, that is premised on the guaranteed exclusion of so many immigrants in the European community, which is why, I suspect, Soysal has the good sense not to use an expression that epitomized the thrust of Soysal (1994), namely, "postnational membership". Along with "personhood" this is another striking absence. It is for this reason that I think that Koopmans errs in reading Soysal (2012) as an attempt to salvage her early postnational membership thesis. Instead, on my reading, Soysal attempts to maintain the relevance of human rights by highlighting the shared focus of individual capacity, human capital, and autonomy that both the new European social project and human rights allegedly share. Moreover, as in Soysal (1994), in Soysal (2012) this is asserted rather than demonstrated through theoretical argument or empirical evidence. What is more, her linking of human rights with practices colluding in such blatant inequalities surely raises an important normative question with respect to the desirability of (her definition of) human rights as a normative horizon tout court. This is a problem that she does not encounter in Soysal (1994), where she links human rights to the equalization of access to the rights and privileges of citizenship for non-citizen residents.

To be sure, Soysal acknowledges that to date, "the European social project has not promised a satisfactory delivery from the tension between the transformative capacities of individuality and the realization and maintenance of social justice" (2012, 15). What this might mean is far from clear because she does not analytically distinguish between what part human rights, the European social project, the neoliberal turn, or even the nation-state play in the social, political, economic, and cultural relations generating the current situation.[19] Curiously, Soysal cites the work of Margaret Somers (2008) as an example of one of the analyses whose attempt to explain changes in citizenship in terms of a new form of economic ideation is found "wanting" (2012, 2). Somers explores in great detail the empirical and normative consequences of what she calls the "contractualisation of citizenship" in the US:

> In a non-contractual relationship, as long as a citizen meets the required obligations, she is presumed an equal member of equal worth regardless of the market value attached to her citizenly responsibilities. But when citizenship has been contractualized, failing to provide a good or service of equivalent market value in exchange for what is now the *privilege* of citizenship results in a reduction of the moral worth of the citizen. And depending on the degree and frequency and quality of such failures to meet contractual criteria, there will be an increasing refusal to recognize the citizen as deserving of membership altogether in the political and social community. (Somers 2008, 89, emphasis in original)

Ironically, given that the contractualization of citizenship is in evidence in both the US and the EU, and that human rights discourse in the former is marginal (Nash 2009b), Somers' argument, I would suggest, provides a more compelling explanation than does Soysal (2012) of the new European "social project".

To return to one of the analytical themes that I introduced above, ultimately, Soysal's persistence in drawing on human rights as an explanatory factor to account for changes in citizenship regimes, even in circumstances that strikes one as being far from propitious as in Soysal (2012), relies on her thinking about *human* rights and *citizenship* rights as endocentric compounds, that is, two related but varying types of the same thing. In a coda, Soysal asserts that the opposition between citizen and human rights is "untenable" because they have "always been highly entangled" (2012, 16). In other words, it makes sense to explain the supersession of national citizenship rights as arising out of human rights generating "postnational membership" (Soysal 1994) or "individualized citizenship" (Soysal 2012) because essentially citizenship and human rights are the same thing. The origin of the identity between the two is grounded in the world culture model which she invokes in both Soysal (1994) and Soysal (2012), but about which she does not sufficiently elaborate.[20]

Postnational Membership Reconsidered

The question of the significance of the dialectic between national and postnational forms of membership does not lend itself to easy solution, not least because the scope and direction of the dialect are currently unfolding, in a "volatile and obscure" manner (Benhabib 2013a, 96).[21] Nonetheless, I do think it is important to acknowledge that it is possible to productively explore the emergence of new forms of membership both beyond and below the national state, the manner in which they interact with national forms of membership and of course the role(s) that human rights as a political imaginary might play in these processes. My reservations with respect to Soysal's variety of postnational membership have less to do with the possible conceptual and empirical fruitfulness of the term, as well as the phenomena it might index, and more with, to my mind, the weakly supported contention that these phenomena are adequately explained as the product of the emergence of postwar human rights.

Indeed, a similar and lucid critique has been developed by Linda Bosniak (2000), a scholar who has made important contributions to our understanding of postnational membership, and the considerable, yet not insurmountable, challenge non-citizen residents face in demanding rights (2000, 2006). Bosniak argues that much of the discussion around citizenship has been focused on its "substance" (i.e., what makes up citizenship?) or its "subjects" (i.e., who is entitled to the status?). Instead, she suggests that it might be useful to pose the question of its location: where is citizenship practised (2000, 453)? Posing this question enables the exploration of the extent to which "cross-border identities, relationships, and allegiances" constitute the terrain on which new forms of "denationalized citizenship" are developing (Bosniak 2000, 449). This said, Bosniak conceptualizes denationalization as "an aspirational claim, a claim of desire rather than fact", whose desirability needs to be scrutinized rather than asserted (2000, 403).

To evaluate the claims of facticity made on behalf of denationalized citizenship, Bosniak proposes four different conceptions of citizenship that can act as yardsticks: (1) citizenship as legal status, (2) citizenship as rights, (3) citizenship as political activity, and (4) citizenship as identity/solidarity. In the first case, citizenship "refers to formal or nominal membership in an organized political community". Bosniak forcefully argues that in this case, it remains firmly tied to the "territorially-bounded nation-state" (2000, 456). With respect to Soysal's claim that EU citizenship should be understood as a harbinger of a postnational citizenship to come, Bosniak responds that EU citizenship remains subordinated to the national state, and the locus of political power remains firmly entrenched in the latter (2000, 458–59).

What is more, Bosniak notes that there is no indication that the EU model is likely to be extended elsewhere in the foreseeable future; thus it can hardly be presented as a beacon of a postnational membership yet to come (2000, 459).[22] Less convincing still, Bosniak maintains, is Soysal's claim that the extension of rights to non-citizen residents can be explained in terms of the expansion of the international human rights regime, amongst other things because it has nothing to say about the status of such individuals in the US where it is the US constitution that has anchored the rights available to aliens (2000, 460–61). Equally, Bosniak perspicaciously identifies a syllogistic flaw in Soysal's argument, namely, that from the premise that aliens can enjoy some of the benefits of citizenship, it does not follow that the rights of everyone are disarticulated from the national state. Access to some citizenship rights does not change "the formal or nominal legal status" of resident aliens "vis-à-vis the political community in which they reside" (2000, 461).[23] Finally, with respect to the hitching of postnational claims on the growing prominence of dual or multiple citizenships, Bosniak holds that this phenomenon is best characterized as "multinationalization" rather than "postnationalization" (2000, 462–63).

The second yardstick Bosniak proposes to test the claims of denationalized citizenship is that of citizenship as rights. Following T. H. Marshall, amongst others, she understands the latter as being defined by the possession of rights, such that "those who possess the rights are usually presumed thereby to enjoy citizenship" (2000, 464) and are formally recognized as such (2000, 465). The institutional entity responsible for receiving and fulfilling the claims, immunities, powers, and protections advertised by these rights remains overwhelmingly the national state

(2000, 466). Bosniak accepts that the human rights regime, to some extent, "represents an alternative source of rights which transcend the jurisdiction of individual nation-states". She nonetheless argues that "the claim that citizenship is becoming transnationalized" overshoots the extent to which the international human rights regime is actually able to protect individuals (2000, 467), as shown by a growing body of significant empirical evidence (Hafner-Burton 2013; Posner 2014). Bosniak does not dispute, nor do I, that the normative and moral standing of human rights in some instances, makes it possible to engender the moral and political effect of membership in a moral community beyond the state. In this case, however, "citizenship is defined not so much by the existence of the rights themselves as by the universalist sentiment their existence arouses" (2000, 469).[24]

The third gauge of denationalized citizenship, proposed by Bosniak, is citizenship as political activity. Drawing on republican conceptions of political activity, this rendering of citizenship puts the accent on active engagement in the affairs of the community. The locus of this understanding of citizenship has been historically variable, one thinks of the Greek city-state, the Roman Empire, the Italian regional states of the fourteenth and fifteenth centuries. More recently, however, it is the nation-state that has been presumed as the archetype of the political community (Bosniak 2000, 473). Despite this, notes Bosniak, the statist premise of this conception of citizenship has been put in question by developments from below, as in the case of local citizenship where citizens participate in their immediate communities, and from above, in the form of transnational political activity (2000, 473–74). The latter case is characterized by

> the proliferation of transnational political activity in the form of non-governmental organizations (NGOs), grassroots social movements, and other cross-border organizing efforts in the areas, for example, of human rights, the environment, arms control, women's rights, labor rights and the rights of national minorities. (Bosniak 2000, 474)

Such activity can be understood as staking out and contributing to the development of a "global civil society".[25] If one understands that citizenship practices as political engagement at the national level should not be restricted to formal activities within the sphere of the state and are extended "'into a great diversity of (sometimes divisive) decision-making roles' within civil society" (Bosniak 2000, 477), then there is some justification for talking about postnational citizenship in this sense (Bosniak 2000, 479).

The last yardstick proposed as a measure for denationalized citizenship is citizenship as identity/solidarity. This last mode of conceptualizing or practising citizenship draws our attention to the "quality of belonging – the felt aspects of community membership" (2000, 479), which is typically associated with membership in the national community (Bosniak 2000, 480).[26] However a number of scholars have drawn attention to new forms of transnationalized citizenship identities, in the form of euro-consciousness, transnational corporate citizenship, solidarities arising from transnational social movement networks, modes of belonging ensuing from transnational migration, and humanitarian and/or ecological solidarities (Bosniak 2000, 483–85). In these cases, Bosniak claims, it is not "implausible" to speak about a sense of denationalized citizenship (Bosniak 2000, 486).[27]

Bosniak concludes that in some cases there is some justification for claiming that citizenship practices, once strongly moored to the national state, are berthing in transnational spaces (2000, 488). Yet, she equally argues that factual claims of the existence of postnational citizenship must also be read as acts of "political advocacy", demanding "recognition" by drawing attention to "recent transnational political and social practices that have often been overlooked or otherwise neglected in mainstream political and social thought" (2000, 490). Implicit in these demands for recognition is the suggestion that these denationalized social and political practices are the grounds from which political and moral claims might be enunciated, and through which, under certain circumstances, they might be acted upon.

However, if human rights are not the motor of this process, as Soysal claims, how might we understand the emergence of these new forms of postnational citizenship practice? Equally, how might we grasp the role that human rights play in these emerging transnational figurations? Further below, I explore the part that human rights, conceptualized as political imaginary, might perform in this process. First, however, in the next section, I want to build a more complex understanding of the practices and subjectivities associated with postnational citizenship by exploring the work of Saskia Sassen, as well as emerging conceptions of cosmopolitanism and cosmopolitan norms.

Denationalized Citizenship

The contemporary trends towards interpreting changes in the status of national citizenship as evidence of an incipient postnational citizenship (Hansen 2009) are usefully foiled by the valuable conceptual distinction that Saskia Sassen makes between "postnational" and "denationalized citizenship" (2002, 2006, 2009). The former's focus on "the emergence of locations for citizenship outside the confines of the national state" needs to be differentiated from related yet distinct processes which she calls "denationalization" (2002, 277–78). In the latter case, "transformations are not predicated necessarily on a relocating of citizenship components outside the nation state", but on changes that are taking place inside the national state (2002, 278). In putting the emphasis on the denationalization of citizenship, Sassen wants to draw attention to the fact that "some of the major transformations occurring today under the impact of globalization may give citizenship yet another set of features as it continues to respond to the conditions within which it is embedded", adding that "the nationalizing of the institution that took place over the last several centuries may give way to a partial denationalizing" (2006, 283).

Sassen argues that "the rights articulated through the subject of the citizen are of a particular type and cannot be easily generalized to other subjects" (2006, 277). However, notwithstanding the significant degree of formalization that it has achieved (2009, 230), national citizenship, she claims, remains an "incompletely theorized contract between the state and its subjects" (2006, 277). Its incompleteness enables national citizenship to accommodate new types of political claims and practices while retaining existing formal features. This is precisely what Sassen argues is occurring to national states as a result of global processes (2006, 2009). Amongst the global factors "unsettling" the nexus between the citizen and the national state are changes in laws of nationality and residence, the introduction of international legal instruments in national courts, the increased articulation of global and national economies, and the related privatization and shrinking of welfare entitlements (Sassen 2002, 280). The latter, she argues, combined with technological and organizational developments in the practice of warfare are concomitantly leading to a decrease in the intensity of loyalty, once essential for the mobilization of mass conscription armies (2002, 280). Additionally, digitalization, emergent political practices, new modes of mobility, new political constituencies, as well as the "destabilization of national-state centered hierarchies of legitimate power and allegiance" are also contributing to unbundling the relationship between the citizen and the national state (Sassen 2006, 278–79).

The impact of the aforementioned dynamics is clearly legible in some formal changes to the nature of citizenship in the national context, such as the acceptance of dual nationality, citizen access to international normative and legal instruments, and the retrenchment of welfare entitlements. Equally important, however, are unofficial and incipient modes of informal citizenship, such as undocumented long-term residents whose successful integration opens up the prospect of regularizing their presence (Sassen 2009, 234), or the undocumented worker "who can nonetheless function as a bearers of partial rights (e.g., the rights to wages for work done) and, more generally, as part of a larger informal landscape" (Sassen 2009, 235).

Sassen locates the mechanisms for the expansion of informal rights within the logic of citizenship itself. She argues that "citizenship is partly produced by the practices of the excluded" (2009, 241), by which I take her to mean, in the setting of national citizenship, the struggle for the inclusion of individuals present within the national territory but excluded from full citizenship rights, as, for instance, the exclusion of African Americans in the US.[28] In the context of globalization and important migratory movements and settlement patterns, this same logic has also enabled non-citizen documented and undocumented residents to make formal and/or informal claims for inclusion, achieving sundry forms of "informal citizenship". In addition, the retrenchment of the welfare state, the "contractualization of citizenship" (Somers 2008, 89), or if one likes the new repertoires of citizenship associated with the new European social project (Soysal 2012) have fractured the link between legal status and substantive rights: "legal status is no longer enough not only for those who are minoritized socially, but also for the newly vulnerable traditional middle classes" (Sassen 2009, 241). Consequently, claims Sassen, for those with and without formal legal status, "citizenship is now a normative project whereby social membership becomes increasingly comprehensive and open-ended" (2009, 241).

Here we have an account of some of the mechanisms that might plausibly explain the extension of citizenship rights to non-citizen residents identified in Soysal (1994) and even the precarious situation of more recent migrants to Europe as described in Soysal (2012). These are rendered as instances of denationalization—"the transformation of the national, including the national in its condition as foundational for citizenship" (Sassen 2009, 246)—rather than as an emerging postnational citizenship regime fuelled by the expansion of postwar human rights.

While Sassen (1996, 2006, 2009) includes human rights as one of the elements in the repertoire of the processes contributing to the denationalization of citizenship, she is vague regarding their role. She writes of the "increasingly formalized interaction between citizenship rights and human rights" (2009, 234); and that the "global forces that challenge and transform the authority of nation-states may give human rights an expanded role in the normative regulation of politics as politics become more global" (2009, 237); or even that "both globalization and the human rights regime have contributed to destabilizing the existing political hierarchies of legitimate power and allegiance" (2009, 241). Moreover though she recognizes that there are differences between citizenship and human rights (2009, 242), she does not delve into them. Two significant themes appear to resonate in her writing with respect to human rights: one that, along with globalization, they "have contributed to creating formal and informal operational openings for non-state actors to enter international arenas that were once the exclusive domain of national states" (2015, 32); the other that human rights together with capital markets, in different ways, are able to extract accountability from national states (1996, 27–28).

On my reading, Sassen's conceptualization of human rights is a thin one, indexing the global political legal institutions (Kurasawa 2007, 5) claimed to underpin "a new world order" (Slaughter 2004), providing the legal and normative architecture for incipient forms of global democracy (Held 2004). This sociologically slim rendering of human rights is surprising, not least when contrasted to the care with which she has surveyed the transformation of the rights-bearing subject in the transition from the feudal to the national state, and its current denationalization (Sassen 2006). It is not clear to me why her nuanced understanding of the rights-bearing subject that draws attention to the "making of the citizen-subject" through a thoughtful analysis of changes "in the law, in political subjectivities, and in discursive practices" (Sassen 2009, 232) is not extended to the *human rights*-bearing subject, which is precisely the task to which the political imaginary hopes to contribute. It can be plausibly argued that this is perhaps an effect of human rights' status as a "sociological unthought" (Bourdieu and Wacquant 1992, 238) or "pret-à-penser" (Dubois 2007, 128) of which I have rendered account in preceding chapters—in other words, a taken-for-granted and self-evident conception of human rights as ideas, laws, or principles that obviates the need to inquire into their sociological status.

In addition to providing a more empirically and conceptually defensible account of the extension of formal or informal rights to non-citizen residents than Soysal's postnationalist thesis, Sassen also offers an explanation of why Bosniak's first and second conception of citizenship rights—as seen above, legal status and rights, respectively—barely register on the postnationalist meter. Both of these inflections of citizenship still remain within the bailiwick of an undoubtedly transformed yet enduring national state. However, what of the other two, namely, citizenship as political activity and solidarity beyond the national state? These two concerns have been of great interest to scholars who have engaged with cosmopolitanism; might we find in their work a thick sociological account of the role played by human rights in these emerging forms of postnational political practices?

Human Rights and Cosmopolitan Norms

Cosmopolitanism is not an easy term to define due to competing definitions and the wide range of foci which these definitions index.[29] However, as Gavin Kendall, Ian Woodward, and Zlatko Skrbis argue, in their very valuable sociological treatment of the phenomenon, "in most of the literature, cosmopolitanism is understood as primarily a political and cultural manifestation of processes of globalization" (2009, 3). As a political manifestation of globalization, cosmopolitanism and human rights are frequently assumed to be inextricably linked; as Robert Fine has argued, " [c]osmopolitanism imagines a global order in which the idea of human rights is an operative principle of justice, with mechanisms of global governance established specifically for their protection" (2009, 8).

As a cultural manifestation, cosmopolitanism is often understood as an ethico-political orientation "towards selflessness, worldliness and communitarianism" (Kendall et al. 2009, 22) that, to a lesser or greater extent, foregrounds notions of "human rights, human worth and citizenship" (Kendall et al. 2009, 78). However, cosmopolitanism is also defined, more broadly, as an attitude of openness to the world that views "otherness and cultural difference as something desirable", as "a cultural mode of seeing and valuing difference" (Kendall et al. 2009, 105; Delanty 2006). In my terms, it is embedded, embodied, embrained, and inthinged in multiple daily interactions, routines, and practices. In this case, the connection to human rights is frequently more tenuous.

Let me begin by prospecting where we need to dig the least to uncover the link between human rights and cosmopolitanism, namely, cosmopolitanism as a political, and potentially democratic, expression of globalization. Unsurprisingly, cosmopolitanism in this sense crystallizes into notions of global citizenship and its correlative ethical and moral obligations, new forms of transnational sovereignty, and new conceptions of the political. Martha Nussbaum is an outspoken advocate of world citizenship (1996) and of gearing education towards the culturing of world citizens (1998). In an oft-cited essay, she argued that the contemporary world would be well served by commitment to the ideal of cosmopolitanism, where patriotism would be superseded by an allegiance to the "worldwide community of human beings" (1996, 4).

In the essay, she juxtaposes the bare acceptance of the notion that individuals in distant places have basic human rights to a more expansive cultivation of cosmopolitan sentiment (1996, 4). However, elsewhere she clearly links the ideal of liberal education to the unearthing of the universal resonance of the idea of human rights, cross-culturally and cross-historically. While not denying important variations, ultimately the ubiquitous human rights echo arises from a shared humanity (1998, 138). It is precisely an awareness of this shared humanity that is at the centre of her defence of cosmopolitanism. More precisely, drawing on the capabilities approach that both she and Amartya Sen (1995) pioneered, she understands human rights as a response to the fundamental ethico-political question of "What A is actually able to do and be?" (1997, 285) To claim that a person has a human right to something, argues Nussbaum, is to say "that just by virtue of being human, a person has a justified claim to have the capability secured [...] 'human rights' used in this sense lies very close to what I have called 'basic capabilities'" (1997, 293). Human rights are here understood normatively and foundationally, with little interest in uncovering their thicker, variable, historical, and sociological conditions of possibility.

The political philosopher Seyla Benhabib has also forcefully defended the centrality of human rights for the project of cosmopolitanism (2013a). However, she finds Nussbaum's approach wanting: "Nussbaum's method of philosophical deduction, which grounds rights concepts all too narrowly in a philosophical anthropology of human capabilities is problematic" (2013a, 79).[30] Benhabib argues instead that rights, "which are principles", can only be worked on, concretized, and made effective through the "continuous interpretation and articulation of self-governing polities" (2013a, 12), which she refers to as "democratic iterations". The latter are understood as processes of "linguistic, legal, cultural and political repetitions-in-transformation – invocations that are also revocations" (Benhabib 2013a, 112). Such iterative acts, argues Benhabib, enable a democratic community to work on the norms and principles by which they are, and will be, bound, thus enacting their dual status as subjects and authors of the law (Benhabib 2013a, 112).

Pivotal to Benhabib's view is her commitment to discourse ethics as the source of democratic and moral legitimation founded on communicative freedom.[31] Consequently, she understands freedom of expression and of association as

> crucial conditions for the recognition of individuals who live in a political order of whose legitimacy they have been convinced with good reasons. Rights of expression and association that are exercised in democratic iterations undergird the communicative exercise of freedom itself, and therefore, they are basic human rights as well. (2013a, 15)

Benhabib, however, finds it necessary to pose the question of how this mode of democratic politics and generalizing of human interests is possible in context of the "twilight" of state sovereignty arising from globalizing forces and in situations where migrants, refugees, and asylum seekers find themselves in precarious situations or with multiple transnational affiliations across the globe (2013a, 95–96). How might it be possible to "combine the liberal vision of citizenship as entitlement to rights with the republican-democratic vision of membership through full democratic participation" (2013a, 96), upon which her model of democratic iterations depends? In this context, is the project of cosmopolitanism through the spread of human rights norms "Pollyannaish", or insufficiently radical to address changes required to create a more democratic global order? Are there not global processes that thwart the viability of the cosmopolitan norms coded by human rights and their enactment in democratic iterations (2013a, 96)?

Benhabib thinks not. She argues that the normative vectors of different global processes need to be appraised, which entails differentiating cosmopolitan norms, which provide "generalizable human interests and the articulation of public standards of norm justification", from global capitalism. The latter "leads to the privatization and segmentation of interest communities and the weakening of standards of public justification through the rise of private logics of norm generation", thus undercutting state capacity to protect citizens (2013a, 99).

Key features of global capitalism that make the state "more hostage than sovereign" include the rapid movement of capital and commodities, new forms of "multinational zones of sovereignty"—special economic areas where state regulation is reduced and workers are subject to harsh forms of labour discipline, such as the growth triangles identified by Ong (1999) or the *maquiladoras* of Mexico and Central America (Domínguez et al. 2010)—as well as the development, diffusion, and implementation of "*lex mercatoria* [commercial law]", the profusion of self-generating and self-executing transnational standards, regulations, and laws made by private actors (Benhabib 2013a, 25–26).[32] The dissemination of cosmopolitan norms by contrast is underwritten by an entirely different dynamic.

Benhabib differentiates between state and public sovereignty. The first refers to the "capacity of a public body, in this case the modern nation-state, to act as the *final indivisible* seat of authority to wield not only 'monopoly over the means of violence'... but also to distribute socio-economic justice and manage the economy" (Benhabib 2013a, 97). Public sovereignty, instead, draws attention to the notion that it is the people who both make and are bound by law. It involves "representative institutions, the separation of powers, and the guarantee not only of liberty and equality, but of 'equal value' of the liberty of each" (Benhabib 2013a, 98). Before the onset of contemporary globalization, public sovereignty would have aimed at containing and steering state sovereignty through the enactment of democratic practices. However, in a situation of waning state sovereignty, and of the reconstitution of citizenship, where the latter is characterized increasingly by residency, rather than membership, and ties to manifold localities, what is the ground on which popular sovereignty can be practised?

For Benhabib, international law and human rights treaties are creating the conditions for a new form of democratic sovereignty, which she calls "republican federalism" (2013a, 112). The latter refers to the process of "law's migration", that is to say, the mobilizing of treaties, laws, principles, by various actors across borders, at different scales—for example, transnational, national, regional, municipal—in processes of democratic iterations that are framed by cosmopolitan norms and democratically moulded to the political projects of concrete communities. Consequently, "*Popular sovereignty no longer refers to the physical presence of a people gathered in a delimited territory, but rather to the interlocking in global, local and national public spheres of the many processes of democratic iteration in which people learn from one another*" (Benhabib 2013a, 112 emphasis in original). Insofar as these democratic iterations of popular sovereignty are entwined with human right norms, and particularly those grounded in communicative freedom, different but commensurable democratic fabrics can be woven and tailored to hold both sovereign states and transnational actors accountable.

Benhabib's focus is primarily on mapping the political practices and normative terrain to be seeded by popular sovereignty in the context of globalization and the relative decline of national state sovereignty. She cautions that "we need to differentiate between state and popular sovereignty, while exploring their interdependence" (2013a, 115). Arguably, this caveat also applies to the "resurgence of [the global] institutional imagination" (Benhabib 2013a, 115), where activists and political philosophers are imagining new architectures of national state federations, binding regional or world constitutionalism, institutions of world governance, and even a world parliament (Archibugi 2008, 2012; Habermas 2004; Marchetti 2006). The political scientist David Held has equally outlined some of the contours of what cosmopolitanism entails by differentiating amongst different modes of sovereignty. In his analysis, however, cosmopolitan sovereignty is distinguished from classical and liberal international modes (2002).

Underpinning Held's conception of cosmopolitanism is the "view that human well-being is not defined by geographical or cultural locations, that national or ethnic or gendered boundaries should not determine the limits of rights or responsibilities for the satisfaction of basic human needs, and that all human beings require equal moral respect and concern" (Held 2009, 537). While Held acknowledges the continuing relevance of the national state in the pursuit of these normative goals, he insists that it should not be privileged (2010, 67). At the heart of this claim lies the distinctions among classical, liberal international, and cosmopolitan sovereignty.

Held defines sovereignty as "rightful political authority" (2002, 2). He uses law as a heuristic to specify each of the models of sovereignty: classical, liberal international, and cosmopolitan sovereignty are grounded in the law of states, law of states and law of peoples, and law of peoples, respectively (Held 2002, 1). In the case of the classical model, sovereignty "is the undivided and untrammelled power to make and enforce the law, and, as such, it is the defining characteristic of the state" (Held 2002, 3). States have the unquestioned authority to organize their internal affairs and the capacity, insofar as they can defend it, to enter into agreements with other sovereign states. The codification of such agreements in an international legal system was achieved at the end of the eighteenth and early nineteenth centuries, "when territorial sovereignty, the formal equality of states, non-intervention in the domestic affairs of other recognized states, and state consent as the basis of the international legal obligation became the core principles of international society" (Held 2002, 4).

Liberal international sovereignty was seeded by successive waves of democratization, within the context of classical sovereignty, that reconfigured the basis of the legitimacy of the internal exercise of political authority, but whose impact exceeded national boundaries through the spread of democratic ideals or, to draw on Benhabib's vocabulary, through the revolutionary notion of popular sovereignty. Held contends that by the end of World War II, if not earlier, there is clear evidence of efforts to develop international norms and instruments seeking to regulate the external behaviour of sovereign states—through attempts to govern warfare, prosecute war crimes, and incipient efforts to regulate the global environmental commons. Equally visible are forays into some aspects of national domestic sovereignty via international norms and instruments by enshrining self-determination, democracy, and human rights as the basis for the legitimate exercise of political authority (2002, 5). Held concludes his discussion of the extensive catalogue of international and regional human rights instruments by stating that "human rights have placed individuals, governments and nongovernmental organizations under new systems of legal regulation – regulation that, in principle is indifferent to state boundaries" (2002, 11).

The project of liberal international sovereignty, the notion that liberal democratic rule can be projected onto the international society of states,[33] has been successful to the extent that, in the postwar period, it has acted to constrain the exercise of state power externally but also internally. The state's treatment of its citizens, he notes, is no longer merely a state matter (Held 2002, 17); in a significant sense it has become an "international concern" (Beitz 2011, 197). This said, when viewed from the broader perspective of cosmopolitanism—"the equal worth and dignity of all human beings"—there are significant limitations allied to liberal international sovereignty.

First and foremost, the impact of human rights has been extremely variable (Held 2002, 20), often registering in places where violations of human rights and other international norms are least likely to occur and generally absent in contexts where people are most in need of them (Hafner-Burton and Tsutsui 2007; Hafner-Burton 2013; Mueller 2014; Pogge 2008; Snyder and Vinjamuri 2006).[34] Second, liberal international sovereignty has been incapable of overcoming the "political arrogance" arising from the recent yet deeply entrenched notion that legitimacy rests in the national *demos*; consequently national, geopolitical, and economic interests can be bent to the arc of what the *demos* wills or is understood as willing (Held 2002, 21).[35] Third, argues Held, while democratic practices are firmly entrenched in a territorial conception of political community,

> contemporary regional and global forces disrupt any simple correspondence between national territory, sovereignty, political space, and the democratic political community. These forces enable power and resources to flow across, over, and around territorial boundaries and escape mechanisms of national democratic control. (2002, 21)

Fourth, the focus of liberal international sovereignty is on the curtailment and democratization of political power; consequently this model of sovereignty lacks the tools and resources required to democratize economic power. The latter remains a key contributor to contemporary global economic and political inequality, threatening the viability of cosmopolitan sovereign rule (Held 2002, 22–23). For these reasons, amongst others, the liberal international sovereign model is best characterized as allowing the law of peoples to breathe but remains ultimately corseted by the law of states.

The foregoing suggests that the contemporary world cannot be democratically steered by liberal international sovereignty, highlighting the urgent need for a "common framework for political action" (Held 2002, 24). Held proposes eight principles that build on the commitment to universal standards, human rights, and democracy embedded in liberal international sovereignty (2002, 24) as providing the normative framework for cosmopolitan sovereignty: (1) equal worth and dignity, (2) active agency, (3) personal responsibility and accountability, (4) consent, (5) collective decision-making about public matters through voting procedures, (6) inclusiveness and subsidiarity, (7) avoidance of serious harm, and (8) sustainability (Held 2010, 69).[36] Principles one to three provide the deep grammar of the cosmopolitan moral universe, enshrining individual moral worth and equality, autonomy, and the capacity to act. Principles four to six identify the norms that should govern the political processes whereby individual interests are democratically aggregated, or to use Benhabib's felicitous expression drawn from discourse theory, the procedures for the generalizing of human interests. Finally, principle seven is premised on precaution and ameliorating the situation of those who are worse off, and eight introduces the tenet of environmental stewardship (Held 2010, 74–75).

Held's defence of cosmopolitan sovereignty goes beyond arguing for its current necessity and identifying its core principles; he, also, provides some broad brush strokes for the latter's institutionalization in four key areas, namely, legal, political, economic, and cultural cosmopolitanism. For the first, he envisions "a global legal order in which people can enjoy an equality of status with respect to the fundamental institutions of the legal system" (2002, 34). This would involve a thick charter of rights and obligations addressing political, social, and economic power; interrelated legal systems encompassing fundamentals of criminal, commercial, and civil law; acquiescence to the International Court of Justice and the International Criminal court, an international human rights court; and broadening the scope of regional human rights institutions (2002, 34).

Political cosmopolitanism posits the insertion of national political activity in networks of regional and global participatory political mechanisms with the goal of promoting an

> accountable and responsive politics at local and national levels alongside the establishment of representative and deliberative assemblies in the wider global order; that is, a political order of transparent and democratic cities

> and nations as well as regional and global networks within an overarching framework of global justice. (Held 2010, 178)

Economic cosmopolitanism, claims Held, rests on the moral and legal imperative of eliminating the "asymmetrical production and distribution of life-chances" (2002, 35), by creating equitable "conditions for economic competition and cooperation as the background of the particular choices of human agents" (2002, 36). More concretely this would involve refashioning market mechanisms and other foci of economic power, global taxation, and the redistribution of resources to the most vulnerable (2002, 37). Finally, cultural cosmopolitanism is grounded in the capacity to enter into meaningful dialogue with traditions and discourses different from one's own. Facilitated by the scope, intensity, and speed of global cultural communication, it is an attitude of openness towards others—their diversity, hybridity, and difference—that goes beyond mere tolerance and curiosity. It is receptive to agreement and commonality but also willingly accepts dissonance as an opportunity to learn about others, but equally about one's self (Held 2010, 110–12).

The principles and institutional frameworks for cosmopolitan sovereignty are self-reinforcing. Political or economic cosmopolitanism is not viable without the infrastructure of legal cosmopolitanism; similarly cultural cosmopolitanism would be voiceless were it not for its political counterpart. Cosmopolitan sovereignty, like Benhabib's republican federalism, envisions the distribution of political authority, democratic capacity, and rights in overlapping networks of political practices and institutions. Such dispersal may incorporate the national state as a relevant political locus but just as easily bypass it. In this sense, sovereignty resides in the political autonomy of individuals, democratically articulating collective projects. It represents a radicalization of popular sovereignty, or in terms of Held's heuristic, it is political rule based on the law of peoples. One of the consequences of such a conception is that foundational demarcations such as the inside and the outside of the national state lose their significance. It sets up a situation, according to the late sociologist Ulrich Beck, where the logic of "either/or"—for example, either national or international—is replaced by the logic of "both" (2006, 29).

The proposed cognitive stance, the result of our contemporary cosmopolitan condition, requires that we abandon what Beck calls the "territorial prison theory of identity, society and politics" (2006, 7).[37] The diagnosis of the latter is justified, argues Beck, due to five key constitutive elements that characterize the current moment and the foreseeable future. First is the fact that current crises and risks—for example, environmental, economic, political violence, poverty—have engendered a global awareness of their transnational nature, increasingly blurring the distinction between national and international, or between "us" and "them". Second is the Janus-faced nature of the cosmopolitan recognition of difference, which prompts curiosity and rejection, sympathy, and hatred. Related to the second is the third: the capacity for perspective taking that generates empathy and conflict.[38] Fourth is the impossibility of living in a world society, thus the compulsion to redraw borders that will be rickety at best. The last feature is the "*mélange principle*", the interconnection, coalescing, and fusing of levels of politics, culture, and religion summarized by Beck's pithy phrase, "cosmopolitanism without provincialism is empty, provincialism without cosmopolitanism is blind" (2006, 7).

For Beck, the cosmopolitan condition has an ontological quality: "the sole task of sociologists is to understand and interpret reality, which at present means the cosmopolitanization of reality" (Beck 2006, 112).[39] Consequently, he distinguishes normative and political cosmopolitanisms from analytical-empirical cosmopolitanism, which the social sciences have a responsibility to develop. This necessitates a break with their long-wedded attachment to methodological nationalism (2006, 24–32). With respect to philosophical cosmopolitanism, he quips "cosmopolitan interdependence is not a love affair of everyone with everyone" (2006, 23). Cosmopolitanism does not encode a normative attitude with which to overcome conflict. Indeed, for Beck, "cosmopolitanism", understood as a reaction to the cosmopolitanization of reality, arises, as I read him, from the dynamic, chaotic, complex, and national-border-defying nature of contemporary global risks and processes.

Cosmopolitanism, he writes, "generally occurs as an unintended and coerced side effect" (2006, 34). Consequently the logic of his argument parallels that developed in his seminal *Risk Society* (1992), where he argued that the new nature of risk required novel modes of reflexive knowledge and action, that is, "risk consciousness" (1992, 77). In the context of "world risk society" (2006, 22), Beck claims that the only response, willingly chosen or coerced, is a cosmopolitan one insofar as global threats "create an unavoidable pressure to cooperate" (Beck 2006, 23). Cosmopolitanism is not so much a solution to democratic deficits or global risks, but rather a manner of understanding global conundrums and framing responses, which might or might not be effective. Success in one area might produce new types of risks. What Beck wrote for *Risk Society*, "risk consciousness ... does not automatically counteract danger, but it opens up previously closed areas and opportunities for action" (1992, 77), goes for world risk society.[40]

Human Rights as Cosmopolitan's *Pret-à-Penser*

What then is the relationship between cosmopolitanism and human rights? Because the conceptual logic that guides the unfolding of Beck's cosmopolitan framework is that of the extension of the risk society to the world risk society thesis, human rights, as such, are fairly marginal. Beck's account of cosmopolitanism is ontological rather normative. In other words it speaks to the reality of nation-state boundary-transcending crises and processes and the obligatory cosmopolitan responses they elicit. Insofar as most of the scholarship on human rights has taken a normative bent, it is of little use for Beck's analytical-empirical analysis. It is true that, for instance, Beck writes that "the human rights regime is the key example of how the distinction between the national and the international is being superseded and the internal cosmopolitanization of national societies is being promoted, and how the grammar of the social and the political is being rewritten" (2006, 47).[41] But his mention of human rights is episodic and illustrative, falling prey to its broader *pret-à penser* status.

It is astonishing that Beck who argues so passionately for the need of a radical revision of the social science's taken-for-granted conceptual commitments to methodological nationalism should be so *laissez-faire* with the analytical and empirical status of human rights: to my mind, one of the great normative and political unthought of our times! Despite the fact that human rights, within Beck's own framework, appeared at a time, the postwar, when the either/or logic of the national or international was firmly entrenched, he does not attempt to explain how it is that human rights have, empirically and analytically, come to play the different role that he alleges they now play. In part, this is because, as I noted above, cosmopolitanism, in Beck's hands, is an attempt to describe an overarching epochal shift in the conditions of social and political life, "the cosmopolitanization of reality!" However, even authors who pivot their understanding of cosmopolitanism around human rights are remarkably uncritical and unreflexive regarding their origin and the sources of their purported social or political efficacy. This, I believe, is, also, the case with both Held and Benhabib.

Held sees human rights treaties, covenants, and legal instruments as instantiations of cosmopolitan norms. Although Held's normative defence of cosmopolitan institutions is compelling, he provides no clear evidence that human rights, as such, have the capacity to deliver the types of political and social outcomes that he deems, or any decent person would deem, reasonable. In fact, in a certain sense, and not unlike in Beck's case, human rights as an object of knowledge is, in reality, fairly marginal to the development of his cosmopolitan framework, key elements of which had already been identified in his rightly influential *Models of Democracy* (1987). The centrality of individual autonomy and the necessary resources to underwrite it, the melding of the republican and liberal rights democratic traditions, and the demand for economic democracy and for accessible and responsive political institutions are all in evidence in his concluding chapter, where he pans competing theories of democracy in search of democratic gold in his pre-cosmopolitan phase (Held 1987, Chap. 9). Cosmopolitanism, for Held, is an attempt to think the normative and institutional conditions of democracy in a global world. As with Beck, human rights are a handy *pret-à-penser*.

A similar argument could be made regarding Benhabib's cosmopolitan framework. In a sense, Benhabib is adapting her discourse ethics framework (1992), built on her early critique of critical theory (1986), to the context of a globalized world where national state sovereignty is being subject to change. In *Situating the Self*, she had sympathetically parried the critical lunges of communitarians, feminists, and postmodernists to "situate reason and the moral self more decisively in contexts of gender and community, while insisting upon the discursive power of individuals to challenge such situated-ness in the name of universalistic principles, future identities and as yet undiscovered communities" (1992, 8). Elsewhere, she grounded democratic legitimacy in "unconstrained public deliberation", arguing that

> a public sphere of deliberation about matters of mutual concern is essential to the legitimacy of democratic institutions. I define democratic legitimacy as the belief on the part of the citizens that the major institutions of society and the decisions reached by them on behalf of the public are worthy of being obeyed. (1994, 27)

Indeed as she herself claims, she is engaged in a reformulation of "human rights" in terms of communicative ethics to show that "the basic human right to communicative freedom enables us both to justify the *human right to membership* and to interdict *loss of membership* of denaturalization" (2004, 136). The necessity of human rights is conceived endogenously within her normative framework and not as a result of the normative potential associated with the actual historical emergence of human rights. Human rights are the globalized referent of the "egalitarian reciprocity" (Benhabib 1992, 30) that enables the procedural universalization of moral norms and the democratic deliberative production of binding laws that she had previously developed outside of the cosmopolitan framework. As Beck and Held have done, she picks up human rights as a ready-made concept that she shapes to accommodate the normative position she had developed in an earlier stage of her thinking, not seriously exploring whether human rights actually have the social capacity to produce the kind of effects that her normative theory predicts.[42]

Ultimately, as Alexander (2006) and Kurasawa (2007), the latter more specifically in the context of cosmopolitanism, argue, the weaknesses with philosophical normative and institutional approaches to grasping normativity in social relations are that they reduce such normativity to an "ideal or a legal institutional project from above" (Kurasawa 2007, 160). I think this captures the essence of the work that human rights perform in Beck, Held, and Benhabib's differing formulations of cosmopolitanism.

Sociologically speaking, they are working with a thin conception of human rights. Human rights are a normative ideal, principle, or legal project whose historical, social, and political conditions of possibility and efficacy are asserted but not examined. To be clear, my purpose here is not to evaluate or critique cosmopolitanism as such, but to investigate the manner in which human rights have been attached to cosmopolitanism. In the work of Beck, Held, and Benhabib, they are attached opportunistically, commandeered to thinly fill in the place occupied by citizenship or nationally based rights in these scholars' previous works.

They are consequently aligned with much of the contemporary scholarship, surveyed here, that understands human rights as superseding citizenship rights. To return to the terminology introduced at the beginning of this chapter, they see human rights and citizenship rights as endocentric rather than exocentric compounds. In other words, human rights are understood as a variation on citizenship rights, their global extension in fact. When human rights are understood thinly as ideas, norms, or legal principles, the notion of their continuity with citizenship rights seems, at first blush, justified. However, when framed through the perspective of a historically rooted and socially reproduced political imaginary, they are better understood as exocentric compounds, as being two different types of things. I develop this argument in the next section by continuing to construct human rights as political imaginary with the help of Margaret Somers' conceptualization of citizenship. However, before doing so I want to return to the question of how human rights might be understood in a cosmopolitan context.

I think that it is undeniable that the scholars working in the area of cosmopolitanism are right to argue that it is possible to register evidence of an incipient cosmopolitan solidarity. As Kendall, Woodward, and Skrbis argue,

> As a principle of social solidarity cosmopolitan asks members reflexively to reconsider local loyalties as the primary basis for social and cultural interaction. It is founded upon the development of shared connections, material linkages and ethical reflexivities which seek inspiration beyond the local and national, or the restricted and the parochial. The result of such devel-

> opments leads to the acknowledgement of, engagement with and possibly incorporation of social groups previously considered to represent the other. (2009, 149)

There are many contemporary processes and social practices, ranging from the reflexive and idealistic to the banal, that enable contemporary individuals to discover and nurture a cosmopolitan attitude, for example, economic integration, global risks, migratory and residential patterns, cosmopolitan education, cultural consumption, tourism, communications infrastructure, social media, and human rights. Cosmopolitan solidarity is also fostered and institutionalized in transnational movements, NGOs, INGOs, and transnational regional units like EU.[43]

However, Kendall, Woodward, and Skrbis argue, in a manner that resonates with the position I am developing here with respect to human rights, that "overinvesting the concept [cosmopolitanism] with hope and idealism leads to deflating real chances of its having widespread cultural efficacy" (2009, 150). Moreover, further chiming with the political imaginary approach, cosmopolitanism, they argue, is sociologically best grasped "as a type of assemblage or complex where various ethical, cultural and political requirements exist which bring the cosmopolitan subject into being" (2009, 53). Understood thus, cosmopolitan is "less an unfolding global certainty, and more an aspirational ideal" (Kendall et al. 2009, 156).[44] This draws attention to the labour through which it is fuelled:

> cosmopolitan solidarity is, just as importantly, a transnational mode of practice whereby actors construct bonds of mutual commitment and reciprocity across borders through public discourse and socio-political struggle. The crux of the matter lies in grasping the labour of creating and enacting solidarity, the performance of normatively, aesthetically and politically oriented forms of social action that thickens cosmopolitanism from below. (Kurasawa 2007, 160)

Thoughtful as Kurasawa's account of global justice is, as I have argued above, I think he errs in using the terms global justice and cosmopolitanism interchangeably with human rights. That human rights is a contemporary component in the struggle for global justice and cosmopolitanism is, to my mind, unquestionable. More suspect, however, is the notion that human rights should be conceptualized as being coextensive with cosmopolitanism.[45] Opening up an analytical space to explore the specificity of human rights, as a political imaginary, enables us to better gauge how it contributes to, and/or detracts from, cosmopolitan solidarity, an emergent form of solidarity, "where strangers are recognized and incorporated" (Kendall et al. 2009, 157).

Relationality, Membership, and Rights[46]

T. H. Marshall's (1950) account of citizenship has been the foundation stone of contemporary sociological discussions of citizenship. As Margaret Somers has written, "Marshall essentially invented the social approach to citizenship. And once he did so, he became until recently its sole 'owner'" (2008, 152). It is true that Marshall's account of citizenship has been the object of numerous criticisms (Barbalet 1988; Crouch et al. 2000; Fraser and Gordon 1992; Isin and Turner 2007; Lister 2003; Mann 1987; Nash 2009a, Chap. 4; Pakulski 1997; Turner 1990, 1997). These appraisals have identified a number of shortcomings in Marshall's account—generally, its inability to capture empirical variations of differing citizenship regimes and the failure to adequately grasp citizenship as a mechanism of internal exclusion and stratification. But they have left its broad historical premises, that is, that it is an adequate explanation of the British case, and its ontological assumptions, for the most part, largely intact. These premises, argues Somers, include the following: (1) capitalist social forces were the historical motor of citizenship's development; (2) social classes were the agents of change; (3) "citizenship proper" only emerged with the demise of feudalism; (4) modern citizenship is associated with the uniform extension of rights, Marshall's universalism; and (5) citizenship is understood "as the gradual enlargement of individual rights to wider spheres of society through the equality of status" (1994a, 69).[47]

Somers contests each of these five assumptions. To do so, she departs from the largely stylized historical accounts that trace the emergence of civil rights to the rise of the eighteenth-century gentry, political rights to the ascendency of the bourgeoisie, and modern citizenship rights to the institutionalization of working class power in the welfare state, in the twentieth century (1994a, 67–68). She also adopts a historical narrative analysis with a focus on institutions in an attempt to identify the particular types of practices, forms of membership, and institutional contexts that enabled the emergence of citizenship rights. This is particularly important because it reveals the historical contingencies that are effaced when the necessity of citizenship rights is read retrospectively. She defines an institution as being the product of "organisational and symbolic practices that operate within networks of (breakable) rules, (fix and unfixed), structural ties, (often-contested) public narratives, binding and unbound relationships that are embedded in time and space" (1994a, 72). Institutions, in turn, are embedded in "relational settings", namely, "a patterned matrix of institutional relationships among cultural, economic, social and political practices" (1994a, 72).

Somers' nuanced historical narrative analysis challenges each of the five assumptions enumerated above. First, rather than abstract "capitalist social forces", it was a "shifting configuration of political, legal, community and economic institutions at work in the development of a series of national laws and institutions that only contingently could be transformed into specific political cultures of citizenship rights". Second, instead of social classes, it was "as members of contesting institutions" that social groups struggled for citizenship rights. Third, modern citizenship has a developmental path that extends back to medieval legal arrangements, predating the development of capitalism. Fourth, rather than evenly spread amongst the population, citizenship was considerably "more localized and unevenly spatially distributed; there was, moreover, an uneven capacity for and consequences of exercising those rights". And fifth, instead of linking citizenship rights to an abstract conception of "equality of status", they are best understood as hybrid sets of relationships that link individual autonomy to "institutional membership and social attachment" (Somers 1994a, 69). This leads her to framing English citizenship conceptually as "autonomy in membership" or "liberty in embeddedness" (1994a, 78–79).

It is not possible to do justice to the subtlety of Somers' empirical historical analysis here, but it is important to point out that the conception of citizenship that she proposes in Somers (1994a) and, as we shall see, further develops in Somers (2008) provides a powerful sociological conceptualization of citizenship. This can be illustrated if we contrast it with the four competing conceptions of citizenship identified by Bosniak (2000), discussed above, namely, citizenship as legal status, bundle of rights, political activity, and solidarity. Somers understands citizenship, as it emerged historically in the English case, as the dynamic interaction of all four of these conceptions in the context of changing relational settings. More specifically, she argues, "the rights of citizenship comprise a bundle of enforceable claims that are *variably* and *contingently* appropriated by members of small civil societies and differentiated legal cultures – albeit within a territorially defined nation state", concluding that "a citizenship right, like all rights is not a 'thing'; it is a social practice" (1994a, 79 emphasis in original).

More recently, building on her reading of Hannah Arendt, she has argued that citizenship should be understood as being constituted by two types of rights. The first, and more fundamental, right is the "right to have rights".[48] By this, she means the right to political membership and social inclusion, where the latter designates "the [*de jure* and *de facto*] right to *recognition* by others as a moral equal treated by the same standards and values and due the same level of respect and dignity as all other members" (2008, 6 emphasis in original). The second type of rights refers to the specific bundle of civil, political, and social rights, which are open to extension, expansion, and reconfiguration (Somers 2008, 6).[49]

Importantly for my purposes, and as intuited by Turner (1993, 496), Somers demonstrates that citizenship is both a normative and an empirical concept (2008, 23) and, crucially, that one need not forsake the latter in order to attend to the former, as suggested by the sociologists discussed in Chap. 3. Citizenship, in its formulation as "the right to have rights", is analysed as a normative concept. Its empirical nature, on the other hand, is captured through its instantiation as an "instituted process"—a term of Polanyian derivation meant to draw attention to citizenship's temporality and "changing balance of power among institutional sites" (Somers 2008, 35). Building on her historical narrative analysis of the emergence of citizenship in the English case, she defines citizenship as

> a matrix of institutional relationships, technologies, political idioms and rights-claiming practices that are always dynamic and contingent. As an instituted process, it is comprised of membership rules and political cultures shaped by competing narratives of egalitarianism and social inclusionary rights in opposition to both unfettered marketizations and to hyper-securitization by the government. (2008, 35)

In sociological terms, she locates the practices of citizenship as unfolding in civil society, a third space: a site of resistance against the "imperial designs of the market no less than the state" (2008, 30). The civil sphere, argues Somers, as illustrated eloquently by Alexander (2006) is where the normative ideals of citizenship—namely, membership, inclusion, solidarity, and justice—exist as potential but not as a certainty (2008, 30–31).

In addition to analytically distinguishing between citizenship as a normative and an empirical concept, she shows how the power of the former—that is, the ideals of membership, recognition, and justice—can only be socially efficacious in particular relational contexts. These contexts are made up of "political idioms" and "narratives" (representations), "rules" and "technologies" (social technologies), "rights-claiming practices" (modes of agency and subjectivity), and "institutional relationships" (organizational forms). In other words, they roughly, but not precisely, line up with the analytical distinctions of my political imaginary model.[50]

What is more, Somers' exploration of the empirical and relational aspects of citizenship in the context of its emergence in the English case (1994a), and more recently in her thought-provoking analysis of racialized social exclusion in New Orleans in the context of hurricane Katrina (2008, Chap. 2), makes clear that judgements of normative social efficacy, or power, are inseparable from the particular relational processes, rules, technologies, and practices that allow, or prevent, them from being instantiated.[51] Said differently, it is particular historically emergent relational and institutional arrangements that enable individuals to be incorporated as members capable of making rights claims, hence the sequence of relationality, membership, and rights in the section title.

Given this model for thinking about citizenship rights, how does Somers deal with human rights? She argues that "the right to have rights" is "existentially foundational" of any right's claim—that is, "autonomy in membership" (Somers 1994a). The right of political membership, she notes, is no less a human right than it is a citizenship right; what distinguishes the two is the scale, national versus global (2008, 6). Consequently, citizenship and human rights are "*both* rooted in that which endows us with our humanity – recognition that comes only from attachments and inclusion" (2008, 7 emphasis in original). If human rights is understood exclusively in normative turns, then her argument is defensible, as is Benhabib's regarding communicative freedom or Held's with respect to autonomy and democracy in the context of cosmopolitanism. However in arguing thus, she sets aside what she, herself, has identified as a crucial dimension of the study of normative ideals and how they achieve social efficacy, namely, "precisely because it is an ideal and aspiration, the right to have rights is sociologically incomplete unless complemented by institutional foundations, both historical and structural, that can explain the social requirements for its realization" (2008, 8). This she has done compellingly with respect to citizenship but not for human rights.

It is true that elsewhere with Christopher N. J. Roberts she develops a historical, though not an institutional, account of human rights (2008). However, their historical presentation takes the form of the thin stylized chronicle of the emergence and the development of human rights that trace back their development to the normative logic of UDHR, in lieu of the subtle historical narrative analysis exemplified by her survey of the emergence of citizenship in England (Somers 1994a). Surprisingly, though conceptually and theoretically, Somers is well primed to do otherwise; she, like many of the authors considered in this and earlier chapters, derives her conception of human rights normatively from the articles of the UDHR and subsequent legal and normative instruments. In doing so, she obviates the institutional and structural conditions that, to quote her, "explain the social requirements" for the realization of human rights. Moreover, as I argue in the next section, it overlooks some troubling consequences of thinking about human rights as the extension of citizenship rights.

Bearing Sociological Witness to Victimhood

If one reads the UDHR, it is easy to be struck by the similarities between the rights there enumerated and those associated with the citizenship rights of vigorous social-democratic leaning welfare states. This resemblance, I suspect, is frequently taken as incontrovertible evidence that human and citizenship rights are endocentric compounds, bonded by a durable normative glue. Yet, the confluence of citizenship with the rights enumerated in the UDHR, in reality, is not at all surprising. In projecting the ideal situation for citizens in the context of *sovereign states*, a generous welfare system had increasingly become part of the postwar's common sense. As Moyn has written, "in international view, and especially after William Beveridge's report urging a postwar of guaranteed work and higher standards of living, human rights were most often simply synonymous with the central wartime promise of Allied leaders for some sort of social democracy" (2010, 52).[52] Normatively, beyond the messiness and institutional complexities of history and social relations, the line from citizenship rights to human rights, and then back again, is unbroken.

However, as seen in my discussion in Chap. 2, scholars have begun to question the thin postwar historical account of human rights, arguing that no socially efficacious institutional and structural arrangement for human rights coalesced in the postwar era. It is, of course, true that human rights made some institutional incursions in the UN and elsewhere. However, even at the UN International Human Rights Conference, held in Teheran in 1968 to commemorate the 20th anniversary of the UDHR—opened by a dictatorial monarch! (Moyn 2010, 2), it was generally recognized that such institutional arrangements had failed to generate significant support for or engendered human rights-fuelled activism (Moyn 2010, 126–29)—a view that in 1973, the international human rights activist Moses Moskowitz shared in his book, *International Concern with Human Rights*. According to Keys the book was mostly a lament: "Human rights advocacy had not '[lit] a flame of high purpose among the mass of people anywhere' nor 'seize[d] the minds of men'" (2014, 152).

Almost simultaneously though, the rudiments of a new normative and more socially robust and efficacious political imaginary were being cast, best exemplified by the emergence of Amnesty International (Moyn 2010, 129). This new fledgling political imaginary, grounded in a highly moralized and minimalist politics, is much closer, institutionally and social relationally, to our contemporary conception and the actual practice of human rights than the grand universalistic claims of the UDHR. In Chap. 2, I summarized the arguments regarding the centrality of the socio-political context and practices of the 1960s and 1970s made by Moyn and others. Here, I would like to draw attention to one facet that was crucial to the genesis of human rights as a political imaginary then and, arguably, still remains so today, the figure of the victim.

In the previous chapter, building on the work of Kurasawa (2007) and my review of practice approaches to human rights, I concluded that human rights as a political imaginary can be fruitfully understood as an attempt to establish a moral community capable of receiving and, in some cases, acting upon the normative claims of distant and/or excluded others. In other words, actors make public the situation of violence or injustice of an excluded and/or distant other. The goal of such publicity is to trigger an ethico-politico response, a judgement about the unacceptability of the violence and injustice, and a willingness to engage in remedy, be this political pressure, petition signing, public protest, legal action, and so on. This is an extremely fragile activity, as Kurasawa's thoughtful analysis reveals (2007). This process, I have argued, is patterned by the dimensions of human rights as a political imaginary: representations, social technologies, modes of subjectivity and agency, and organizational forms.

I would like to add that it is crucial to realize that this distant and/or excluded other frequently takes the form of a "victim". This, I would like to show, is grounded in the relational institutional context in which human rights developed in the 1960s and 1970s and in which they, *mutatis mutandi,* continue to function today. The centrality of the figure of the victim for institutionalized human rights practices is, to my mind, what undermines the normatively defensible, yet social institutionally and historically suspect, equivalence between human and citizenship rights, which the authors discussed in this chapter posit.

Stephen Hopgood has convincingly traced the centrality of the figure of the victim in the context of the emergence of Amnesty International's formative human rights work (2006), and more broadly in the convergence of human rights and humanitarianism that characterizes the contemporary "Human Rights Imperium" (2013, 4). Born at the confluence of "marginality, internationalism and spirituality" (2006, 57),[53] Amnesty International, argues Hopgood, elaborated a form of ethico-political "action centered on individual conscience not collective protest and social mobilization" (2006, 59). Eschewing grand utopian political projects, spurning classification along a left-right axis (Moyn 2010), Amnesty International's sought to step outside of politics, developing a normative space by institutionalizing a series of modularized practices that produced the effect of an objective morality, a universal truth (Hopgood 2006, 60). Key in securing the normative and social space for this incipient form of minimalist politics was the ability to establish what Hopgood, paraphrasing Georg Jellinek, calls the "normative power of the factual" (2013, 39): the wherewithal to expose wrongs that no moral individual, whatever their political or ethical leanings, could tolerate.[54]

More specifically, as Hopgood shows, this entailed "bearing witness to the private suffering of nonviolent innocents, to demand release on the sole ground that such suffering was unjust, and, it was hoped, to generate a collective sense of purpose among those on the same wavelength" (2006, 62). Such a logic dictated identifying "the most marginal individuals": powerless, voiceless, and forsaken (2006, 53). Amnesty International's role was to bring the light of a flickering candle, the awareness of a nascent moral community, to their plight. The truer the victim's suffering, the more helpless their situation, the more likely that individuals of conscience would respond. They would see the objective moral responsibility to act. Of course, what Amnesty International presented was not so much the victim as such but victimhood; the latter, as Steffen Jensen and Henrik Ronsbo argue, is best understood as a heterogeneous relational assemblage, product of specific social technologies (2014).

Indeed a key dimension of Hopgood's institutional ethnography is his account of the organizational practices and social relations through which Amnesty International was able to accumulate, and bank, the moral authority to become the voice through which true victimhood could be conveyed. These included what Richard Wilson has identified as "unflinching realism" devoid of emotive or political language, absolute political impartiality, a relentless commitment to research and the verification of the "facts", and a draconian implementation of its mandate (Hopgood 2006, 73). All of these crystallized in "a highly centralized and rule bound organization" in which "maintaining external authority required maintaining internal authority. Diversity, spontaneity, and individuality had all to be constrained in the service of moral authority" (Hopgood 2006, 104).

In the second half of his institutional ethnography, Hopgood goes on to explore the centrifugal forces Amnesty International had to confront to maintain its moral authority as new actors and claims entered the field of human rights. However the focus on victimhood has persisted. The success of new claims, to a certain extent, has relied on their being convincingly constructed and recognized as instances of victimhood.[55] Hopgood's most recent work shows that the figure of the victim continues to be part of the broader field of contemporary human rights and humanitarianism (2013),[56] aided by the refinement and the expansion of the social technologies through which the victimhood of individuals or groups are articulated, as discussed in Chap. 4.

Vulnerability and marginality persist as the indispensable marks that identify individuals as victims of human rights violations, "those who are in some way helpless, powerless, unable to make choices for themselves, and forced to endure forms of pain and suffering" (Merry 2007, 195). Diana Meyers distinguishes between pathetic and heroic victims in her analysis of the victimhood paradigms rooted in the human rights institutional practices (2011). The former

> requires claimants to have undergone severe, documentable, humanly inflicted harm that they are not responsible for incurring. The irreproachable innocence of pathetic victims is crucial. Otherwise they can be accused of provoking their own suffering, whether because it is a foreseeable consequence of their actions or because it is a penalty for their wrongdoing. (2011, 258)

The paradigm of heroic victimhood is crystallized in the figure of the superordinary "prisoner of conscience":

> Heroic victims are idealistic and courageous. They take it upon themselves to face off against the police power of the state in the name of a just cause. They may stand up for democracy and human rights, resist the subjugation of a social group singled out for oppression, or protest the misuse of military might. What heroic victims have in common isn't a single political agenda but rather a commitment to peace and justice. (2011, 258–59)

Unlike the pathetic declension of victimhood, agency is central in the heroic case. However, innocence is no less crucial. The agency of the heroic victim must not be "morally compromised": it is the "the nonviolent activism of heroic victims [that] secures their innocence" (Meyers 2011, 259). Why should this crucial role of victimhood in the development of human right, as a political imaginary, matter in the context of the relationship between citizenship and human rights?

First of all, it matters because representations of victimhood (innocence, vulnerability, powerlessness), stabilized by particular social technologies (factual reporting, legal reasoning, political neutrality), have positioned individuals as victims and elicited responses appropriate to their victimhood and have been institutionalized in NGOs, INGOs, courts, and other institutional settings. In other words, victimhood is a crucial relational node in human rights understood as a political imaginary, linking representations, social technologies, modes of subjectivity and action, and organizational structures. Victimhood is, if one likes, one of the key material, relational, and representational practices through which human rights have frequently been institutionalized, travelled, and made themselves available to actors as tools of social change and as remedy for the violence experienced by distant and/or excluded others.

If one holds that our understanding of normative ideals remains deficient unless it is supplemented by the awareness of their "institutional foundations, both historical and structural, that can explain the social requirements" for their realization (Somers 2008, 8), as I have argued we should, then the figure of the victim is crucial. What is striking is the way in which many of the scholars who have traced a normative course between citizenship and human rights have steered clear of the actual trajectory through which human rights have historically and socially made their way towards contemporary actors. Rather, as the crow flies, these scholars have linked human and citizenship rights through the normative logic of the UDHR and subsequent international instruments. In doing so they have disregarded the vagaries of the intervening historical and social contingencies that have made human rights the types of assemblages that they are, and calibrated what they might be able to achieve, and under which conditions. In other words, they have largely been uninterested in mapping the social and the historical terrain that has defined the relational contexts in which the normative idea of human rights has become socially efficacious. Sociologically, however, a focus on this latter mode of analysis is preferable to holding, implicit or explicitly, to the notion that the normative idea of human rights can "norma-form" the social world.

Second, as a result of the centrality of victimhood in the human rights political imaginary, the attempt to frame the latter as an extension of citizenship rights, as many scholars discussed in this chapter do, should give us pause for thought. Not least because victimhood as it has been modulated by human rights is frequently associated with passivity and helplessness. In other words, "victimhood can be a prime way of suspending or attempting to suspend the political through an appeal to something non-agentive and 'beyond' or 'before' politics, such as poverty or suffering" (Jeffery and Candea 2006, 289). What is more, as Merry argues, because victimhood is pivotal to the institutionalized practices of human rights, it encourages individuals who are not passive or helpless, and their advocates, to adopt victimhood as a subjectivity, strategy, and mode of social action (2007, 195). Moreover such a decision is frequently fateful, not least because "to keep the winnings of victimhood, you must play the victim. You must prove that you are less than a full citizen and haven't yet arrived" (Cole 2007, 170). This, in turn, restricts an individual's ability to be seen as anything other than as a victim:

> We know nothing, or almost nothing, of their subjectivity – or – interiority as victims. Survivors of disasters, oppression, and persecution adopt the only person that allows them to be heard – that of the victim. In doing so,

> they tell us less of what they are than of the moral economies of our era in which they find their place. (Fassin and Rechtman 2009)

Given the emphasis that the scholars, discussed in this chapter, place on broadening and enhancing political action (from the local to the global), it is not immediately clear how such an expansive mode of politics can be reconciled with the reality of the frequently depoliticizing institutional and relational practices of victimhood, which are embedded in human rights as political imaginary. What type of citizenship politics is possible when grounded on "'the rights of the absolute victim' or the rights of those who are victims of an "absolute evil" (Gündoğdu 2015, 80)?[57]

Third, as we saw in Chap. 4, the cornerstone of human rights is the attempt to establish an ethico-political community where the ethical and political claims of excluded and/or distant others can be received and acted upon. The mechanism through which these claims are communicated to the potential, and pervasively fragile, moral community is that of bearing witness. The latter is a necessary condition for the possibility of inclusion, eliciting the ethical or political imperative to act, that is, this is wrong; it must be stopped and/or remedied! However "hearing", "seeing", or "knowing about" the situation of the distant and/or excluded other does not guarantee an appropriate, or even an, ethico-political response (Cohen 2001), as revealed by the Kurasawa's analysis of the perils of bearing witness, solidarity, and aid (2007).

When the figure of the distant and/or excluded other takes the form of the victim, as she almost invariably does in the context of human rights, rather than solidarity, she is just as likely to "inspire equal amounts of 'compassion or contemptuous pity'" (Jensen and Ronsbo 2014, 4). And compassion, even in the more secure context of national citizenship rights, has traditionally been characterized by discretion and uncertainty as a result of its association with charity (Merry 2007, 197; Cole 2007). However as Nancy Fraser and Linda Gordon (1992), so eloquently argued, and more recently, disability rights scholars have claimed (Fleischer et al. 2012), charity is antithetical to any decent vision of citizenship. This primarily, because as Fassin shows, the social relation between two agents mediated through compassion, is, regardless of the intent of the agents involved, founded on "a moral sentiment with no possible reciprocity" (2012, 3).

Fourth, victimhood places the victim in the position of the supplicant, in a "truth ordeal" (Fassin 2012, 109). She must demonstrate not only her innocence but also display her wounds. This reduces her to a quantum of suffering, whose plea eliciting the socio-political intervention of the moral community she addresses is dependent on making her wounds, but most frequently her scars, visible and, more importantly, legible. Even in the paradigmatic human rights violation of torture, it is not easy to make scars index suffering (Kelly 2014b). Increasingly, as Didier Fassin and Richard Rechtman have argued, these wounds are expressed within a moral economy of trauma (2009). Despite its claim to objectivity, as a result of its origin in psychiatry, trauma as a credible index of suffering and as a synecdoche for victimhood is relationally determined by the extent to which a moral community is able to identify with victims, and "the distance engendered by" their otherness (Fassin and Rechtman 2009, 282). This means that

> Cultural, social and perhaps even ontological proximity matter; as does the a priori valuation of the validity of the cause, misfortune, or suffering, a valuation that obviously implies a political and often an ethical judgement. Thus trauma, often unbeknownst to those who promote it, reinvents "good" and "bad" victims, or at least a ranking of legitimacy among victims. (Fassin and Rechtman 2009, 282)

This hierarchy of suffering, as Alyson Cole has shown, enshrines the "cult of true victimhood" (2007), the true victim, the deserving victim, the pathetic victim, the superordinary victim.[58] Consequently, suffering, arising from misfortune or from the banality of everyday systemic oppression, is often unheeded:

> They [human rights activists] prefer to concentrate on torture, state crimes, and mass atrocity, building early warning systems and transitional justice mechanisms and spreading lessons learned about preventing genocide and crimes against humanity. Everyday discrimination and violence, that which constitutes 99 percent of oppression people suffer, and where the need is

> greatest, comes a distant second. No one is building a universal court for that. (Hopgood 2013, 173)

The figure of the victim, rather than opening up the space of membership, frequently forecloses it. As Fassin concludes, "Western societies" open "their democratic space as little as possible, while preserving the possibility, as a last resort, of granting consideration to those who succeed in entering our world, but on the basis of humanitarianism rather than as of right" (2012, 253). Might not the normative ideal of democratic iterations crash on the undemocratic iterations of victimhood that have underwritten the social efficacy of human rights since the 1960s?

In drawing attention to the centrality of victimhood in the contemporary human rights political imaginary, I am not adopting an anti-victimist position (Cole 2007) that holds that victimhood should be expunged from our moral or political practices. Victimhood can be articulated to capture the reality of certain contexts where individuals truly are in great need, suffer unspeakable violence, whether systemic or episodic, and with extremely limited agency. However, given the historical and social relations that have wrought victimhood, "it remains unclear how a radical political theory that deploys victimizations as its organizing principle might work" (Cole 2007, 176). Equally, in counterposing the historical and social-relational trajectory of victimhood in the human rights political imaginary to the democratic normative ideals, espoused by many of the scholars discussed in this chapter, I am not rejecting the social efficacy of norms.

Certainly norms matter, as does their coherence. However, it is relational assemblages, which may but rarely do embody pure normative logics, that make norms socially efficacious. Can representations, social technologies, modes of subjectivity and agency, and organizational structures of victimhood be separated from human rights? Perhaps. But for a sociologist this is an empirical question rather than a normative one. It is one that has not been visible in sociology because of the tendency to read human rights exclusively as a normative script rather than a historical and relational assemblage. This is why it is important for sociologists to bear witness to the central role of victimhood in the trajectory, and ongoing instantiations, of human rights as a political imaginary.

Conclusion

Above, I quoted Somers to the effect that Marshall has been until recently the sole owner of the sociological conception of citizenship. However, I would add that even if citizenship is now part of citizenship scholars' "sharing economy", Marshall's underlying proprietary claim has not been extinguished. This is because, despite significant empirical and conceptual critique, the fundamental normative elements that he used to define citizenship continue to provide the matrix for contemporary conceptualizations of (post)citizenship, namely, equality of status (Marshall 1950, 9, 34), membership in (national) community (Marshall 1950, 13, 21, 28–29), and a directionality towards equality (Marshall 1950, 30, 33).

It is important to note that it is the dynamic interrelationship amongst the three elements that continue to thread the contemporary understanding of citizenship, rather than any one of them on their own. Marshall, of course, was quite aware that the equality of status associated with citizenship was also "the architect of legitimate social inequality" (Marshall 1950, 9), and as subsequent scholars have shown, most notably David Lockwood (1996), that citizenship is an institution of social stratification. And yet narratively and normatively, Marshall's account is one where the equality of status has seemingly powered the progressive growth of an expanding national community, hence the temptation to see it as a "Whig version of history" (Halsey 1984, 10).[59]

It is of course true that the universalism, that is, the extension of citizenship status to all members of the national community (Marshall 1950, 18), which Marshall saw as a fait accompli, has been shown to be a work in progress, achieved through conflict as much as consensus. But even then, much of the twentieth century, before the neoliberal turn, can be plotted in terms of the growth of substantive rights and the expansion of the ethico-political community, whether based on recognition and universalism (Alexander 2006) or difference (Young 1989). Indeed it is this foundational matrix that threads narratives of the expansion from citizenship to human rights in the accounts of many of the authors discussed in this chapter. They rely on a stylized history that stages rather than explains human rights—by "stages" I mean both its mise-en-scène in the

UDHR, and as the next "stage" in the global expansion of membership in the human community underwritten by the equality of human status.

However, just as Somers argued that a better understanding of citizenship requires abandoning the stylized historical narrative implicit in Marshall's account (1994a), I have argued that in order to understand what human rights might be able to achieve, we need to stop assuming, without historical reflection, that citizenship and human rights are endocentric compounds. Indeed, turning our attention to human rights' institutional and historical trajectory from the 1960s to the present, that is, framing human rights as a political imaginary fashioned through a social-relational historical terrain rather than an ethereal normative one, suggests that it might be more fruitful to think about them as exocentric compounds instead.

Both citizenship and human rights, as instituted practices, are social-relational spaces where individuals can make ethico-political claims. In the former, those claims are based on membership in a political community made by an individual with an institutionally guaranteed right to social and political recognition.[60] However, in the case of human rights, the social mechanism for making an ethico-political claim is different. The claim is frequently made through the figure of the victim, a victim whose suffering and innocence is the catalyst for the possibility, but not the certainty of ethico-political action activated by compassion. This is not because on normative grounds it is not possible, or desirable, to imagine a global community where all individuals would have access to the institutionalized rights of social and political recognition, but rather because the historical and institutionalized trajectories of human rights are strongly tied to the production and mobilization of victimhood within its political imaginary.

The conceptual and empirical arguments made by many of the authors discussed in this chapter track a form of political activity that takes place above, and sometimes below, the space of the national state. The latter, for some time, had been both the principal site for the practice of politics and the struggle to define and expand citizenship rights. Given this, it makes sense to look for a transnational cognate for citizenship rights, and human rights normatively would appear at first blush to fit the bill. However, when understood as a political imaginary, human rights appear less a transnational cognate, that is, citizenship rights transferred to a global level, and more a fragile claim for inclusion in an ethico-political community. For the moment the more general conception of cosmopolitanism as openness to the other beyond the community of the nation-state seems more promising as way of projecting the claims, protections, and immunities of citizenship transnationally. Our goal, as social scientists, should be to try to understand the institutional processes underpinning the undeniable and empirical nature of this cultural, political, economic, and ethical activity that transcends the state. Sociologists have much to contribute as demonstrated by the work of Kendall, Woodward, and Zlatko (2009). Human rights will maybe play a role, but probably a more modest one than many of the authors discussed in this chapter believe.

My discussion of human rights as political imaginary, in this and in the preceding chapters, has overwhelming looked at the processes by which ethico-politico claims of distant and/or excluded victimized others became, and still remain, attached to the idea of human rights. In doing so, I have had little to say about the legal nature of human rights. In the next and last substantive chapter, I explore the manner in which the human rights political imaginary has become entangled with the law. This is a process that has generally received little attention, mostly likely due to the assumption that human rights have always already been legal rights. It also enables the exploration of the historical intersection of human and citizenship rights that provides the unacknowledged basis for the notion, deeply embedded in the sociology of human rights literature, that the two are endocentric compounds.

Notes

1. One might equally be tempted to argue that the concept of citizenship has been a central concept of sociological analysis, at the very least since its classic formulation by T. H. Marshall (1950). However, as Margaret Somers has observed, "history shows us that citizenship has been only an occasional concern to social analysis, with the strange habit of being discovered, forgotten, and rediscovered yet again" (2008, 148).

2. In Chap. 2, I dealt with a historical version of this narrative of expansion in my discussion of Borgwardt's (2007) *A New Deal for the World.*
3. Strictly speaking, linguists use the distinction between endocentric and exocentric to classify different types of noun compounds (Benczes 2006, 183), though there is not always agreement on the characteristics that distinguish between the two; see, for instance, Bauer (2008). In contemporary English language use, human and citizenship rights would be largely understood as exemplars of endocentric compounds. My suggestion that they might be read as exocentric compounds should be understood as a sociological heuristic, whose utility I hope is demonstrated in the analysis that follows, rather than an instance of linguistic analysis.
4. More recently, Brysk has developed a much more detailed analysis of the communicative conditions of success for the framing of human rights campaigns (2013) that chimes with Kurasawa's conceptualization of the work of global justice discussed in Chap. 4.
5. This is an argument that follows the lineage developed by Borgwardt (2007), discussed in Chap. 2.
6. This is a position that Alison Brysk has reasserted in her recent work (2013, 17).
7. The existence of such stylization in citation is not itself a problem. It merely serves as shorthand, identifying issues around which there is a significant consensus in a field or largely known and/or undisputed facts. This said, it is incumbent on sociologists to critically open these black boxes when these are used to make broad, sweeping, and consequential empirical and conceptual claims, such as the supersession of national by postnational citizenship.
8. Guestworkers were conceived, in the postwar period, as a category of foreign workers that could be attracted in the context of labour shortfalls and expediently made to return to their countries of origin when the demand for their labour ceased. In reality, despite rising unemployment guestworkers became established as communities of "foreigners", in host countries. Lacking formal citizenship, they were nonetheless able to access the rights and advantages traditionally only granted to citizens, as a result providing glimpses of the emergence of a new postnational mode of membership (Soysal 1994, 5).
9. The data for her analysis was collected from documentary research and on-site interviews with individuals from "relevant ministries, municipalities, and other administrative agencies, representatives of pertinent

welfare organizations, trade unions, and the leaders of migrant associations", as well as from participation in the cultural activities of Turkish migrant associations (Soysal 1994, 11).

10. Soysal's analysis only explores the organization and crystallization of the incorporation policy and does not deal with implementation, practice, or actual outcomes (Soysal 1994, 10).
11. A number of earlier reviewers made just this point. For instance, "Soysal supports her argument with correlational reasoning. On the one hand, she notes that normative ideas about citizenship and rights have changed in the post war. On the other hand, she observes that during the same period European states extended more expansive rights to citizens and noncitizens alike and guestworkers organized to demand rights they were denied. While this correlation appears robust, it remains inconclusive, in large part because she does not chart out the causal mechanism(s) by which these changes have taken place" (Yashar 2002, 368). Another noted that Soysal's conclusion that universal discourses of personhood explain the extension of rights to non-citizens "was not warranted by the evidence provided by her analysis" (Klopp 1995, 780), while a third suggested, "it is hard to avoid the impression that Soysal presses her case too far and projects the legal privileges of immigrants beyond a more modest social reality" (Alba 1995, 328). More recently Hansen has noted "though it is undeniable that legal residents in Europe enjoy a greater degree of security than previously, the sources of the security are domestic, not transnational. Socio-economic rights do not derive from the discourse of universal personhood or from international norms, but rather from the institutions of the liberal democratic state, above all the courts, which articulated, through a series of decisions, the rights of residents on the basis of *national* constitutions" (2003, 103).
12. The optimism and utopianism of her analysis are also highlighted by a number of reviewers, for instance, Martiniello (1997, 640), Hintjens (1995, 887), and Lazaridis (1995, 574). Indeed one might ask to what extent the success of Soysal's least substantiated part of her analysis, her human rights-powered postnational membership thesis, was not in part the product of the "millenarian optimism" of the close of the twentieth century: "Nuclear war had been avoided (although the arsenal remained), and the prospects for being internationally minded had radically altered. A new Europe without borders was accompanied by the prophesy of the

'end of history', that is, the resolution of the story of the ideological struggle between capitalism and communism. The promise of new era of permanent, possibly boring peace was in the air. Social scientists invented a new vocabulary to match the more optimistic mode. This time 'postinternationalism' was to reflect the reality in which 'more and more of the interactions that sustain world politics unfold without the direct involvement of nation and states'" (Sluga 2013, 140–41).

13. As Peter Spiro has argued, "The 1996 act rendered even permanent resident aliens ineligible for a variety of federal benefits. Aliens were barred from Medicare and Medicaid unless their state of residence opted for eligibility; with certain minor exceptions, they were counted out of the SSI and food stamp programmes altogether. In the wake of the 1996 act, there were widely voiced fears that citizenship was making a comeback as a tool of deprivation and exclusion. Indeed, the exclusions were sobering and, at least in modern times, without precedent; coupled with intense anti-immigrant sentiments in the mid-1990s, the resident alien ineligibility was understandably perceived as another stage in the circling of the wagons" (2008, 89). Spiro goes on to argue that the worst-case scenario was avoided for many resident aliens, as they were able to access state benefits instead, not so for undocumented aliens deprived of both state- and federal-level safety nets (2008, 90).
14. This statement of course glosses over the significant variation that can be identified at the empirical level (Messina 2007).
15. For readers not familiar with the trajectory of Western European migration in the postwar era, the significance of the liberalization of access to citizenship in some European countries might require some contextualization. Here I briefly draw on Anthony Messina's extremely lucid analysis, where he identifies three overlapping waves of immigration in Western Europe, which correspond to labour migration (1945–1979), family reunification (1973–present), and irregular/forced immigration (1989–present) (Messina 2007, 19). The first wave refers to the movement of surplus labourers from less developed countries in the Mediterranean, Eastern Europe, and subsequently from specific areas in the third world recruited for, or drawn to, the remarkable economic expansion in postwar Europe (2007, 20). These "immigrants" were generally well received, in part because it was believed that they were only temporary workers, thus not raising any concerns with respect to their

long-term integration nor requiring citizenship of the host country as they were expected to return to their country of origin (2007, 53).

In the 1970s as a result of deteriorating economic conditions, active recruitment of foreign workers came to an end and voluntary repatriation schemes were developed (Messina 2007, 25). These schemes were far from successful, in part because foreign workers had established an important beachhead in the advanced industrial economies of Western Europe (2007, 29–30), but also because many of the foreign workers, and their families, did not want to forego access to high-calibre education and social services or their integration in "extensive social networks in host countries" (2007, 34).

What is more, in some cases, Germany, for instance, "as trends toward longer-term residence emerged, belated attempts [...] to curtail its growing migrant population only 'reinforced the process of settlement, sharply limiting back-and-forth migration and prompting a surge of immigration of family members'" (Banerjee 2014, 19). Other countries "reluctantly tolerated high levels of secondary immigration [i.e., family reunification] [...] in order to facilitate the social integration of long-settled foreign workers in the host society" (Messina 2007, 38). These processes created the conditions for the acceleration of the second wave of family reunification immigration (2007, 36) and more generally led to the large populations of long-established non-citizen residents in Western Europe, which for Soysal signalled the frontline of postnational membership.

However, rather than seeing in this a harbinger of a new exogenously imposed form of postnational membership, it is equally, or perhaps more, plausible to conceptualize as states pursuing "a strategic alternative to inclusion in national citizenship (creating a type of *demicitizenship*)" (Goodman 2012, 671 emphasis added). Be this as it may, opening access to citizenship to non-citizen residents in an attempt to integrate them highlights the value of national citizenship, vis-à-vis settlement, in countries where naturalization had not been a key policy tool for immigrant integration (Mollenkopf and Hochschild 2010). Moreover insofar as this opening up of citizenship has entailed a "bevy of formal instruments to measure an applicant's integration, including knowledge tests, language and civic-orientations courses, modules for role-playing society interaction, and naturalization ceremonies" (Goodman 2012, 660), these policies can tenably be read, as Sara Goodman convincingly argues, as processes that fortify rather than undermine national citizenship (2012).

The third wave, composed of "legitimate and illegitimate refugees and asylum seekers and illegal alien workers" (Messina 2007, 39), gained momentum as states attempted to curb the immigration via the channels that had made possible the two previous waves (2007, 40). Nonetheless, economic demand for the labour of undocumented migrants has remained strong (2007, 40), as indicated by the fact that the majority are employed (Chimienti and Solomos 2011, 347). Despite important variations, "undocumented immigrants have very few rights at all, although they may have access to fundamental services such as health care and schooling for their children" (Koopmans et al. 2012, 1209). The rights that they do have depend less on "personhood" than on the intersection of the welfare and citizenship regimes of the individual national states (Sainsbury 2006). Indeed, in some cases, "personhood" provides little protection against "rightlessness" as evidenced by the increased prominence of detention, and in some cases deportation (Gündoğdu 2015, 125), as well as attempts to enforce internal movement controls through new forms of digital surveillance (Broeders 2007), denying noncitizens the foundational European citizenship right of "free movement" (Joppke 2010b, 19). It is perhaps for this reason that these undocumented immigrants are marginal to Soysal's analysis (Schuster and Solomos 2002, 40).

16. Given the contributory nature of the postwar welfare state, the second-class nature, and in some cases the punitive framing of non-contributory benefits, it is surprising that Soysal characterizes the postwar welfare states as being based on "passive benefits"!
17. By repertoire, I have in mind Ann Swidler's notion of a "'tool kit' of habits, skills from which people construct 'strategies of action'" (1986, 273).
18. Even in this context there is fair degree of precariousness as Schmidtke argues "newcomers often face various forms of exclusion from the labour market and end up working in jobs for which they are overqualified" (2012, 33).
19. To my mind, her account of the significance of human rights in the transformation of citizenship remains what Robert Merton characterized as a "post factum sociological interpretation" (1967, 147).
20. Also known as the world polity, or world society school, world culture theory grows out of the work of the Stanford institutionalist sociologist

John W. Meyer. Rooted in a creative neo-institutionalist reading of organizational life, rationalized formal structures are understood as myths that are taken up ceremoniously rather than arising from their efficacy or rationality (Meyer and Rowan 1977).

The framework was subsequently expanded to understand how world "models of legitimate action" (myths in the earlier framework) could explain what he and his colleagues saw as the striking isomorphisms amongst nation-states in the postwar era—for example, educational structure, state apparatus, welfare and citizenship practices, and personhood (Meyer et al. 1997). Meyer and his colleagues were critical of the realist and neorealist models of IR, and the world systems theory of Immanuel Wallerstein, and remained unconvinced by microphenomenological analyses focusing on national culture and interpretive systems. Consequently, they have argued for a macrophenomenological approach that sees "the national state as culturally constructed and embedded rather than as the analyzed rational actor depicted by realists"; understand that the "culture involved is substantially organized on a worldwide basis"; and "see such transnational forces at work throughout Western history, but [...] argue that particular features and processes characteristic of world society since World War II have greatly enhanced the impact of world-institutional development on nation states" (Meyer et al. 1997, 147–48).

The cultural model or script is not expressive; it is cognitive and instrumental. "Agency" is defined as the "legitimate representation of some legitimated principle" rather than the mere pursuit of naked interests (Meyer and Jepperson 2000, 101). The "actorhood of individuals, organisations, and nation states" is understood as "an elaborate system of social *agency* that has a long and continuous and postreligious evolution" (Meyer and Jepperson 2000, 101, emphasis in original). Essentially, the idea is that the transcendental authority that once organized the normative regulation of societies (religious systems or gods) has been relocated; authority has been relocated from "from god to church, from church to state, from church and state to individuals souls and later citizens" (Meyer and Jepperson 2000, 101).

This cultural devolution, from the religious to the social and to the individual, is underwritten by a commitment to science, rationality, and the search for law-like regularities and commonalities in representations of nature and society (Meyer and Jepperson 2000, 103; Drori et al. 2003).

Facilitated by the development of the rationalized professions (Strang and Meyer 1993), education (Schofer and Meyer 2005), rationalized organizations (Boli and Thomas 1999), and the diffusion of isomorphic state identities (Meyer et al. 1997), "modern culture creates an agentic individual managing goals thought to reside in personality or life course … a sovereign state managing goals of a national society. And an organizational structure managing its legitimated interests" (Meyer and Jepperson 2000, 106). In this sense, human rights represents an instantiation of the universalizing and standardizing cultural script underwriting the agency of the modern individual, germinating in the idea of modern citizenship and blossoming in the context of globalization (Meyer 2009). It is for this reason that Soysal understands citizen and human rights as essentially the same thing.

The conceptual and empirical innovations of Meyer and the World Society School are considerable and impressive by any standard. Their contributions to our thinking about world cultural systems, and the diffusion of global ideas and practices, are significant, and their account of standardization and global isomorphism is noteworthy. This said, their conception of modernity is, to my mind, excessively Hegelian, both in its teleological tenor and its idealism. It fails to capture the historical contingency of social life and the plurality of modernisms, internationalisms, rationalisms, and individualisms that have been and still remain possible. Regarding human rights, they have little to say, except that it is the legal and normative expression of their quasi-religious notion of actorhood.

21. In this context it is worth commenting on a recent conversion to the postnationalist citizenship thesis by an erstwhile vocal critic. Christian Joppke has written, "European citizenship is postnational citizenship in its most elaborate form, belatedly vindicating Yasemin Soysal's earlier claim in this respect" (2010b, 21–22). However, he claims that "what past critics of an underwhelming EU citizenship could not know, and what current critics overlook is the activism by the European Court of Justice that has transformed EU citizenship from a derivative status into a free-standing source of rights" (2010b, 22). However, his account of what has made European citizenship postnational—that is, an activist court—cannot be a vindication of Soysal's position, for whom postnational membership arose from the postwar institutionalization of human rights. What is more, the European Court of Justice did not reference

European Human Rights Court case law until 1996 (Douglas-Scott 2006, 660), two years after Soysal had published her book. More generally, Kiran Banerjee argues there is no reason to think that this means that third-country nationals—that is, residents in the EU without the nationality of an EU country—will be extended the rights and benefits of EU citizenship (2014, 22).

22. One might add that the contemporary situation, where important divisions are emerging within the EU, and new ascensions are hardly on the horizon (Barber 2017), has proven Bosniak right.
23. Bosniak's (2006) study of alienage is a thoughtful exploration of why this might be the case.
24. I read Brysk (2013), compared to Shafir and Brysk (2006), as a belated recognition of just this point.
25. On global civil society, see Beck (2006), Boli and Thomas (1999), Iriye (2002), Kaldor (2013), Kumar (2007), Laxer and Halperin (2003).
26. For an interesting philosophical rebuttal of the notion that global solidarity is not possible because "identity" requires an "Other", see Abizadeh (2005).
27. Bosniak does caution however that "talking about the 'feeling of citizenship' in ways that extend it beyond the parameters of the nation-state or other formal political community runs the risk of producing a concept of citizenship that begins to mean very little since it can so readily mean so much" (2000, 487).
28. One can think here about the mechanisms for the expansion of citizenship rights identified by Shafir and Brysk (2006) discussed above.
29. What follows is obviously not a comprehensive engagement with cosmopolitanism, or even the beginnings of a sustained analysis of the manner in which human rights intersect with the field of cosmopolitan studies. Such an undertaking would require a volume of its own. There is a clear resonance between cosmopolitanism and human rights. As Garret Wallace Brown and David Held write in the introduction to their cosmopolitan reader, "[i]n its most basic form, cosmopolitanism maintains that there are moral obligations owed to all human beings based on our humanity alone, without reference to race, gender, nationality, ethnicity culture, religion, political affiliation, state citizenship, or other communal particularities" (2010, 1). This said, cosmopolitanism, whose philosophical and political pedigree extends to antiquity, represents a broader ethical, cultural, and political framework. A careful reading of contributions to

two recent readers edited by key contributors to the field, Brown and Held (2010) and Delanty (2012), shows that though human rights are not absent from the field, they are frequently superseded and overshadowed by more expansive notions such as cosmopolitan law, world citizenship, and cultural cosmopolitanism. Consequently, human rights are less scrutinized within the cosmopolitan framework than one would think. In a word, as in much of the literature discussed in this book, they are taken for granted. They constitute a *pret-à-penser*. Here I attempt to provide a sample of some of the key positions most relevant to sociologists. These include a much cited contributor who proposes a close link between human rights and cosmopolitanism, adopting a normative approach, Seyla Benhabib (2013a); another, David Held who builds on human rights to propose a broader cosmopolitan normative and institutional architecture (2004, 2009, 2010); a sociologist, Ulrich Beck, for whom cosmopolitanism requires a reconsideration of the nature of sociological inquiry (2006); and a sociological overview of cosmopolitanism provided by Kendall, Woodward, and Skrbis (2009). What I want to suggest in this section is that it is not productive to conflate cosmopolitanism and human rights, as does, for instance, Kurasawa (2007, 157).

30. Specifically, Benhabib objects to the fact that "no distinction is made in her [Nussbaum's] account between rights as 'moral principles' and rights as 'legal entitlements' on the one hand, and 'the principle of rights' and 'the schedule of rights' on the other … Moral rights do not dictate the specific content of legal entitlements" (Benhabib 2013a, 79).
31. Discourse ethics links together the idea of democratic legitimacy with practical rationality and deliberation: "The basic idea behind this model is that only those norms, i.e., general rules of action and institutional arrangements, can be said to be valid which would be agreed to by all those affected by their consequences; if such agreement were reached as a consequence of a process of deliberation which had the following features: a. participation in such deliberation is governed by the norms of equality and symmetry; all have the same chances to initiate speech acts, to question, to interrogate, and to open debate; b. all have the right to question the assigned topics of conversation; c. all have the right to initiate reflexive arguments about the very rules of the discourse procedure and the way in which they are applied or carried out" (Benhabib 1994, 31). Despite important overlaps, Benhabib distinguishes her own

approach from Habermas' whom she criticizes for narrowing the scope of procedural discourse ethics to justice in the public realm, that is, politics and the economy, to the exclusion of questions of the "good life" that are located in the domain of the private sphere (Benhabib 1992, 109). Benhabib claims that "if universalism is interpreted procedurally, as it must be, then such a procedure can be applied to test the validity of moral judgments, principles and maxims even in situations which according to Habermas' and Kohlberg's definitions of them, appear to be concerned with 'evaluative questions of the good life' rather than with 'moral matters of justice.' Questions of care are moral issues and can also be dealt with from within a universalist standpoint. Such a universalism supplies the constraints within which the morality of care must operate" (1992, 187). Benhabib's critique of Habermas has been widely accepted as authoritative by feminist scholars (Wright 2004, 48), though some commentators argue that, in reality, the ground separating Habermas and Benhabib is not as significant as appears at first blush (Cohen 1995; Wright 2004).

32. As Dezalay and Garth show, commercial disputes have become "subject to a new *lex mercatoria* – or New York or English law serving as such a universal set of rules – implemented through a transnational private justice system – international commercial arbitration [...] throughout the world there is a proliferation of US-style corporate law firms promoting their expertise in transnational rules and practices for global commerce. New law schools and newly reformed law schools in Asia and Latin America, in addition, have as a major part of their agenda the production of corporate lawyers conversant in these transnational rules and practices" (2012a, 3–4).
33. In effect creating a "New Deal for the World" (Borgwardt 2007). It is important to note that Held's conception of liberal international sovereignty differs from that of liberal internationalism as defined by international relations; see, for instance, Dunne and McDonald (2013).
34. More optimistic, but qualified, readings can be found in Cole (2012), Simmons (2009), and Jo and Simmons (2016). Even in these cases, Eric A. Posner argues, "Understood in the best possible light, these studies suggest that a small number of treaty provisions may have improved a small number of human rights outcomes in a small number of countries by a small, possibly trivial amount. They do not show that the [human right] treaties improved the overall well-being of people in those countries

because it is unknown whether governments complied with treaty obligations by taking resources away from other projects that served the public interest or shifted resources from more visible to less visible means of repression. Realistically, one can have little confidence that the treaties have improved people's lives" (2014, 78).

35. In this sense, Nash's comparative analysis of the mobilization of human rights in the political and legal realms in the US and the UK is interesting (2009b). She shows that "human rights" when framed in terms of national issues, as the will of the *demos*, are more likely to receive traction. This holds despite human rights being significantly institutionalized in the UK as a result of its membership in the EU and as a signatory to the European Convention on Human Rights.
36. In Held (2002), the eighth principle, sustainability, is absent.
37. Beck does not use the expression the "cosmopolitan condition". I use it because his diagnosis of cosmopolitanism resonates with that developed by Jean-Francois Lyotard's *The Postmodern Condition* (1984), albeit in an entirely different register, insofar as it identifies an epochal change requiring a new epistemological understanding of reality, as well as a new mode of politics, a "new grammar of the social and the political" (Beck 2006, 33).
38. Cosmopolitan empathy is not only extended to others in the present; it is equally projected backwards in the "politics of forgiveness" (Levy and Sznaider 2010, 102). As Levy and Sznaider argue, "Cosmopolitan forms of memory, newly emerging institutions of transnational jurisdiction, negotiations about restitution, and the political relevance of universal human rights are all constitutive elements of these developments" (2010, 102).
39. Its existential dimension is signalled by the fact that even those who reject cosmopolitanism as a political or normative project have to operate on the terrain of the reality of cosmopolitanization. Beck illustrates this by contrasting the national-based terrorism of ETA and the deterritorialized terrorism of al-Qaeda (2006, 112–13).
40. As Beck writes, "In world risk society – this is my thesis, at least – the question concerning the causes and agencies of global threats sparks new political conflicts, which in turn promote an institutional cosmopolitanism in struggles over definitions and jurisdictions" (2006, 23).
41. Even here however, his emphasis is not primarily on their normative or political content but rather on the manner in which they are generative

of new forms of tension and conflict: "The key insight is that the human rights regime has a profoundly double-edged impact. It not only makes possible new forms of conflict regulation beyond borders, but it also opens the door to 'humanitarian interventions' in other countries. Like an erupting volcano, it covers the earth with a red-hot lava of military conflicts. Because human rights must overcome national resistance, the promise of pacification and stability through human rights – Kant's 'perpetual peace' – can easily flip over into depacification and destabilization through perpetual war" (Beck 2006, 47).

42. In arguing thus, it is not my intention to downplay the foundational, though to my mind ultimately unconvincing, sociological reflection undertaken by Beck or the serious philosophical labour that underpins Held and Benhabib's work. I do want to draw attention to the limitations of such normative reflection insofar as it sidesteps the broader historical, social, and political conditions of efficacy of normative ideas as political imaginaries. Indeed, this entire book is an argument against reducing human rights to this kind of thinking. A telling example is Benhabib's appraisal of Samuel Moyn's *The Last Utopia* (2013b). Depressingly, she develops a critique of a normative argument that is absent from Moyn's book, but that she nonetheless projects, in the psychoanalytical sense, on to it. Moyn is an intellectual historian, and his book traces the historico-practical trajectory associated with the idea of human rights. Benhabib's engagement with human rights is not historical; this however does not prevent her from making meta-historical claims, such as "Yet the 1948 Universal Declaration, and the era of human rights that has followed it, reflect the moral learning experiences not only Western humanity but of humanity at large. The world wars were fought not only in the European continent but also in the colonies, in Africa and Asia. The national liberation and anti-colonization struggles of the post-World War II period, in turn, inspired principles of self-determination. The public law documents of our world are distillation of such collective struggles, as well as collective learning processes. It may be too utopian to name them steps towards a 'world constitution', but they are more than mere treaties among states" (2013a, 75). Moyn's contribution is precisely an attempt to circumscribe such grandiose historical normative claims through careful historical analysis, raising uncomfortable but necessary questions. One would not know this from Benhabib's assessment because she never engages with any of his historical

claims. What I find disheartening is that the undisputed doyenne of discourse ethics cannot put in practice in her own work, which provides an exceptionally conducive context for communicative freedom, the ideals that she argues should lubricate democratic practices in considerably more complex and contentious iterations of cosmopolitan democracy. See Moyn (2013b) for his excellent and measured rebuttal of Benhabib's criticism.

43. This said, Beck's (2006) warning regarding the darker side of cosmopolitanization should be kept in mind.
44. Moreover, rather than attaching this aspiration to a particular normative commitment or world-institutional architecture, it is perhaps more sociologically defensible to frame cosmopolitanism along the lines of Gerard Delanty's critical cosmopolitanism, "the cosmopolitan imagination occurs when and wherever new relations between self, other and world develop in moments of openness [geared towards] the analysis of cultural modes of mediation by which the social world is shaped and where the emphasis is on moments of world openness created out of the encounter of the local with the global" (Delanty 2006, 27).
45. This is clear from the variety of practices, processes, and dynamics that Kendall, Woodward, and Skrbis identify in their analysis of contemporary cosmopolitanism (2009).
46. This section title is an allusion to the title of Margaret Somers' brilliant article, *Rights, Relationality and Membership: Rethinking the Making and Meaning of Citizenship* (1994a). I have taken the liberty of rearranging the order of appearance of the terms to reflect what I understand to be their theoretical relationship as developed in this section.
47. This last one is particularly noticeable in the context of authors who analogically understand human rights as an extension of citizenship rights.
48. The Arendtian notion of "the right to have rights" has captured the imagination of many scholars; Ayten Gündoğdu's (2015) productive rereading of Hannah Arendt and her significance for contemporary understanding of human rights begins instead with the notion of "statelessness", to which "the right to have rights" was a response.
49. Seyla Benhabib also draws on Hannah Arendt's formulation of "the right to have rights" to distinguish between the foundational rights of communicative freedom and political association and the broader bundle of rights that are the outcome of democratic iterations (2013a, 62). An

important difference between the two is that Benhabib arrives at this through normative deduction, whereas Somers does so through a historical narrative analysis of the emergence of citizenship. From a sociological perspective, which is always inherently empirical, this constitutes a decisive difference.

50. This is not accidental because Somers' "instituted process" model of citizenship is one of the inspirations behind my own political imaginary model!
51. Concluding her analysis of the different elements contributing to the striking situation of New Orleans' racialized "left behind", she writes "Of all the ways in which Hurricane Katrina should strike us as instructive, however, the most notable is how dramatically this one great tragedy illuminates the conditions currently endangering a social inclusive democratic citizenship, conditions that inevitably led to the catastrophe of so many people being abandoned – first by the contractualisation of citizenship, then by a hollow and corrupt federal agency that had been conquered and cronyized by market-driven politics. Most dramatically, thanks to Katrina, we now know what is entailed when an entire segment of civil society has so disintegrated that its people have been robbed of their ontological rights to membership and inclusion, and with it their recognizable humanity – without which no other rights are possible" (2008, 133–114).
52. This is a point to which I return in Chap. 6 following my discussion of Anthony Woodiwiss' analysis of the juridification of human rights at the UN in the 1970s.
53. Hopgood insists that Amnesty International is best understood as a secular religion: "a kind of Free Church, an ecumenical gathering concerned with the earthly relations between human beings rather than between an individual and a god" (2006, 71). He traces both human rights and humanitarianism to the European desire to establish "Moral Authority in a Godless World", to cultivate "a sense of the secular sacred among the new middle classes of rapidly modernizing Europe" (2013, 1).
54. In other words, creating the conditions for what in Chap. 2 I called the "quintessential speech act", an utterance that conveys meaning but also the illocutionary demand for listeners to act.
55. For instance, in my own work on the human right to food, I have shown that its viability as a human rights claim depended on it successfully

being articulated in terms of victimhood, clearly distinguishing between perpetrator and victim (2015).

56. Hopgood tends to conflate human rights with humanitarianism, while other scholars claim that notwithstanding the fact that they share various traits, they are not synonymous (Barnett 2011, 18). However as Daniel Sargent argues, "While human rights are not commensurate with humanitarianism, their rise depended on engagement with suffering human beings, from Biafran infants to Soviet political prisoners" (2014, 142).
57. Gündoğdu is here drawing on the work of Jacques Rancière. A powerful critique of grounding politics in victimhood is developed by Wendy Brown (1995, 52–76).
58. This is most visible today in the precariousness of the status of migrants and refugees (Gündoğdu 2015).
59. Halsey (1984, 10) claims that though prone to the whiggish readings of Hobhouse and Alfred Marshall, there was in T. H. Marshall's work a more nuanced understanding of historical contingency than is often recognized.
60. Of course as Somers (2008) and Bosniak (2006), respectively, show, both formal and informal membership can frequently be precarious.

Bibliography

Abizadeh, Arash. 2005. "Does Collective Identity Presuppose an Other? On the Alleged Incoherence of Global Solidarity." *American Political Science Review* 99 (1):45–60.

Alba, Richard D. 1995. "Review of Limits of Citizenship: Migrants and Postnational Membership in Europe." *Contemporary Sociology* 24 (4):326–329.

Alexander, Jeffrey C. 2006. *The Civil Sphere.* Oxford and New York: Oxford University Press.

Alexander, Jeffrey C. 2013. "Struggling over the Mode of Incorporation: Backlash Against Multiculturalism in Europe." *Ethnic and Racial Studies* 36 (4):531–556.

Archibugi, Daniele. 2008. *The Global Commonwealth of Citizens: Toward Cosmopolitan Democracy.* Princeton, NJ: Princeton University Press.

Archibugi, Daniele. 2012. "Cosmopolitan Democracy: A Restatement." *Cambridge Journal of Education* 42 (1):9–20.
Baldi, Gregory, and Sara Wallace Goodman. 2015. "Migrants into Members: Social Rights, Civic Requirements, and Citizenship in Western Europe." *West European Politics* 38 (6):1152–1173.
Banerjee, Kiran. 2014. "Toward Post-National Membership-Tensions and Transformation in German and EU Citizenship." *Journal of International Law and International Relations* 10:4–30.
Barbalet, Jack M. 1988. *Citizenship: Rights, Struggle, and Class Inequality*. Maidenhead and Philadelphia: Open University Press.
Barber, Tony. 2017. "Europe's New Political Divisions." *Financial Times*. May 14, 2017.https://www.ft.com/content/21138f54-35ab-11e7-bce4-9023f8c0fd2e.
Barnett, Michael N. 2011. *Empire of Humanity: A History of Humanitarianism*. Ithaca, NY: Cornell University Press.
Bauer, Laurie. 2008. "Exocentric Compounds." *Morphology* 18 (1):51–74.
Beck, Ulrich. 1992. *Risk Society: Towards a New Modernity*. London: Sage.
Beck, Ulrich. 2006. *Cosmopolitan Vision*. Cambridge and Malden, MA: Polity.
Beitz, Charles R. 2011. *The Idea of Human Rights*. Oxford and New York: Oxford University Press.
Benczes, Réka. 2006. *Creative Compounding in English*. Amsterdam and Philadelphia: John Benjamins Publishing Company.
Benhabib, Seyla. 1986. *Critique, Norm and Utopia: A Study of the Foundations of Critical Theory*. New York: Columbia University Press.
Benhabib, Seyla. 1992. *Situating the Self: Gender, Community and Postmodernism in Contemporary Ethics*. Cambridge and Malden, MA: Polity Press.
Benhabib, Seyla. 1994. "Deliberative Rationality and Models of Democratic Legitimacy." *Constellations* 1 (1):26–52.
Benhabib, Seyla. 2004. *The Rights of Others: Aliens, Residents, and Citizens*. Cambridge and New York: Cambridge University Press.
Benhabib, Seyla. 2013a. *Dignity in Adversity: Human Rights in Troubled Times*. Cambridge and New York: Polity.
Benhabib, Seyla. 2013b. "Moving Beyond False Binarisms: On Samuel Moyn's The Last Utopia." *Qui Parle: Critical Humanities and Social Sciences* 22 (1):81–93.
Blau, Judith, and Alberto Moncada. 2016. *Human Rights: A Primer*. New York: Routledge.

Boli, John, and George M. Thomas. 1999. *Constructing World Culture: International Nongovernmental Organizations Since 1875*. Stanford: Stanford University Press.
Borgwardt, Elizabeth. 2007. *A New Deal for the World*. Cambridge, MA: Harvard University Press.
Bosniak, Linda. 2000. "Citizenship Denationalized." *Indiana Journal of Global Legal Studies* 7 (2):447–509.
Bosniak, Linda. 2006. *The Citizen and the Alien: Dilemmas of Contemporary Membership*. Princeton, NJ: Princeton University Press.
Bourdieu, Pierre, and Loïc J.D. Wacquant. 1992. *An Invitation to Reflexive Sociology*. Chicago and London: University of Chicago press.
Broeders, Dennis. 2007. "The New Digital Borders of Europe: EU Databases and the Surveillance of Irregular Migrants." *International Sociology* 22 (1):71–92.
Brown, Garrett W., and David Held, eds. 2010. *The Cosmopolitanism Reader*. Cambridge and Malden, MA: Polity Press.
Brown, Wendy. 1995. *States of Injury*. Princeton, NJ: Princeton University Press.
Brubaker, William Rogers. 1989a. "Introduction." In *Immigration and the Politics of Citizenship in Europe and North America*, edited by William Rogers Brubaker, 1–27. Lanham, MD: University Press of America.
Brubaker, William Rogers. 1989b. "Membership Without Citizenship: The Economic and Social Rights of Noncitizens." In *Immigration and the Politics of Citizenship in Europe and North America*, edited by William Rogers Brubaker, 145–181. Lanham, MD: University Press of America.
Brysk, Alison. 2002. *Globalization and Human Rights*. Berkeley, CA. University of California Press.
Brysk, Alison. 2013. *Speaking Rights to Power: Constructing Political Will*. Oxford and New York: Oxford University Press.
Brysk, Alison, and Gershon Shafir. 2004. *People Out of Place: Globalization, Human Rights and the Citizenship Gap*. London: Routledge.
Chimienti, Milena, and John Solomos. 2011. "Social Movements of Irregular Migrants, Recognition, and Citizenship." *Globalizations* 8 (3):343–360.
Cohen, Jean L. 1995. "Critical Social Theory and Feminist Critiques: The Debate with Jurgen Habermas." In *Feminists Read Habermas (RLE Feminist Theory): Gendering the Subject of Discourse*, edited by Johanna Meehan, 57–90. London and New York: Routledge.
Cohen, Stan. 2001. *States of Denial: Knowing About Atrocities and Suffering*. Cambridge and New York: Polity Press.

Cole, Alyson M. 2007. *The Cult of True Victimhood: From the War on Welfare to the War on Terror*. Stanford, CA: Stanford University Press.

Cole, Wade M. 2012. "Human Rights as Myth and Ceremony? Reevaluating the Effectiveness of Human Rights Treaties, 1981–2007 1." *American Journal of Sociology* 117 (4):1131–1171.

Crouch, Colin, Klau Eder, and Damian Tambini. 2000. *Citizenship, Markets, and the State*. Oxford: Oxford University Press.

Delanty, Gerard. 2006. "The Cosmopolitan Imagination: Critical Cosmopolitanism and Social Theory." *The British Journal of Sociology* 57 (1):25–47.

Delanty, Gerard, ed. 2012. *Routledge Handbook of Cosmopolitanism Studies*. London and New York: Routledge.

Dezalay, Yves, and Bryant Garth. 2012a. "Introduction: Constructing Transnational Justice." In *Lawyers and the Construction of Transnational Justice*, edited by Yves Dezalay and Bryant Garth, 3–12. Milton Park and New York: Routledge.

Dezalay, Yves, and Bryant Garth, eds. 2012b. *Lawyers and the Construction of Transnational Justice*. Milton Park and New York: Routledge.

Domínguez, Edmé, Rosalba Icaza, Cirila Quintero, Silvia López, and Åsa Stenman. 2010. "Women Workers in the Maquiladoras and the Debate on Global Labor Standards." *Feminist Economics* 16 (4):185–209.

Douglas-Scott, S. 2006. "A Tale of Two Courts: Luxembourg, Strasbourg and the Growing European Human Rights *Acquis*." *Common Market Law Review* 43 (3):629–665.

Drori, Gili S., John W. Meyer, Francisco O. Ramirez, and Evan Schofer. 2003. "World Society and the Authority and Empowerment of Science." In *Science in the Modern World Polity: Institutionalization and Globalization*, edited by Gili S. Drori, 23–42. Stanford, CA: Stanford University Press.

Dubois, Michel. 2007. "La Construction Métaphorique Du Collectif: Dimensions Implicites Du Prêt-À-Penser Constructiviste et Théorie de L'acteur-Réseau." *L'Année Sociologique* 57 (1):127–150.

Dunne, Tim, and Matt McDonald. 2013. "The Politics of Liberal Internationalism." *International Politics* 50 (1):1–17.

Edmunds, June. 2012. "The Limits of Post-National Citizenship: European Muslims, Human Rights and the Hijab." *Ethnic and Racial Studies* 35 (7):1181–1199.

Fassin, Didier. 2012. *Humanitarian Reason: A Moral History of the Present*. Berkeley, CA: University of California Press.

Fassin, Didier, and Richard Rechtman. 2009. *The Empire of Trauma: An Inquiry into the Condition of Victimhood*. Princeton, NJ: Princeton University Press.

Fine, Robert. 2009. "Cosmopolitanism and Human Rights: Radicalism in a Global Age." *Metaphilosophy* 40 (1):8–23.

Fleischer, Doris Zames, Fleischer Doris Zames, and Frieda Zames. 2012. *The Disability Rights Movement: From Charity to Confrontation*. Philadelphia: Temple University Press.

Fraser, Nancy, and Linda Gordon. 1992. "Contract Versus Charity." *Socialist Review* 22 (3):45–67.

Frezzo, Mark. 2011. "Sociology and Human Rights in the Post-Development Era." *Sociology Compass* 5 (3):203–214.

Goodman, Sara Wallace. 2012. "Fortifying Citizenship: Policy Strategies for Civic Integration in Western Europe." *World Politics* 64 (4):659–698.

Gündoğdu, Ayten. 2015. *Rightlessness in an Agee of Rights: Hannah Arendt and the Contemporary Struggles of Migrants*. Oxford and New York: Oxford University Press.

Habermas, Jürgen. 2004. "Why Europe Needs a Constitution." In *Developing a Constitution for Europe*, edited by Erik O. Eriksen, John E. Fossum, and Augustin J. Menendez, 1:17–33. London and New York: Routledge.

Hafner-Burton, Emilie M. 2013. *Making Human Rights a Reality*. Princeton, NJ: Princeton University Press.

Hafner-Burton, Emilie M., and Kiyoteru Tsutsui. 2007. "Justice Lost! The Failure of International Human Rights Law to Matter Where Needed Most." *Journal of Peace Research* 44 (4):407–425.

Hall, John A. 1996. "How Homogenous Need We Be? Reflections on Nationalism and Liberty." *Sociology* 30 (1):163–171.

Halsey, A. H. 1984. "TH Marshall: Past and Present 1893–1981: President of the British Sociological Association 1964–1969." *Sociology* 18 (1):1–18.

Hammar, Tomas. 1986. "Citizenship: Membership of a Nation and of a State." *International Migration* 24 (4):735–748.

Hammar, Tomas. 1990. *International Migration, Citizenship and Democracy*. Aldershot: Gower.

Hansen, Randall. 2003. "Citizenship and Integration in Europe." In *Toward Assimilation and Citizenship: Immigrants in Liberal Nation-States*, edited by Christian Joppke and Ewa Morawska, 87–109. New York and London: Palgrave Macmillan.

Hansen, Randall. 2009. "The Poverty of Postnationalism: Citizenship, Immigration, and the New Europe." *Theory and Society* 38 (1):1–24.

Heisler, Martin O., and Barbara Schmitter Heisler. 1991. "Citizenship—Old, New and Changing: Inclusion, Exclusion and Limbo for Ethnic Groups and Migrants in the Modern Democratic State." In *Dominant National Cultures and Ethnic Identities*, edited by J. Fijalkowski, H. Merkens and F. Schmidt, 91–128. Berlin: Free University.

Held, David. 1987. *Models of Democracy*. Stanford, CA: Stanford University Press.

Held, David. 2002. "Law of States, Law of Peoples." *Legal Theory* 8 (1):1–44.

Held, David. 2004. *Global Covenant: The Social Democratic Alternative to the Washington Consensus*. Cambridge and Malden, MA: Polity Press.

Held, David. 2009. "Restructuring Global Governance: Cosmopolitanism, Democracy and the Global Order." *Millennium: Journal of International Studies* 37 (3):535–547.

Held, David. 2010. *Cosmopolitanism: Ideals and Realities*. Cambridge and Malden, MA: Polity.

Hintjens, Helen M. 1995. Review of *Review of Limits of Citizenship: Migrants and Postnational Membership in Europe*, by Yasemin Nuhoglu Soysal. *International Affairs (Royal Institute of International Affairs 1944–)* 71 (4):887–888.

Hopgood, Stephen. 2006. *Keepers of the Flame. Understanding Amnesty International*. Ithaca, NY: Cornell University Press.

Hopgood, Stephen. 2013. *The Endtimes of Human Rights*. Ithaca, NY: Cornell University Press.

Hunt, Lynn Avery. 2007. *Inventing Human Rights: A History*. Book, Whole. W. W. Norton & Company.

Iriye, Akira. 2002. *Global Community: The Role of International Organizations in the Making of the Contemporary World*. Berkeley: University of California Press.

Isin, Engin F., and Bryan S. Turner. 2007. "Investigating Citizenship: An Agenda for Citizenship Studies." *Citizenship Studies* 11 (1):5–17.

Jacobson, David. 1996. *Rights Across Borders: Immigration and the Decline of Citizenship*. Baltimore and London: The John Hopkins University Press.

Jeffery, Laura, and Matei Candea. 2006. "The Politics of Victimhood." *History and Anthropology* 17 (4):287–296.

Jensen, Steffen, and Henrik Ronsbo. 2014. "Introduction. Histories of Victimhood: Assemblages, Transactions, and Figures." In *Histories of Victimhood*, edited by Steffen Jensen and Henrik Ronsbo, 1–22. Philadelphia: University of Pennsylvania Press.

Jo, Hyeran, and Beth A. Simmons. 2016. "Can the International Criminal Court Deter Atrocity?" *International Organization* 70 (3):443–475.
Joppke, Christian. 2010a. *Citizenship and Immigration*. Cambridge and Malden, MA: Polity Press.
Joppke, Christian. 2010b. "The Inevitable Lightening of Citizenship." *European Journal of Sociology* 51 (1):9–32.
Joppke, Christian, and Ewa Morawska. 2003. "Integrating Immigrants in Liberal Nation-States: Policies and Practices." In *Toward Assimilation and Citizenship: Immigrants in Liberal Nation-States*, edited by Christian Joppke and Ewa Morawska, 1–36. London and New York: Palgrave Macmillan.
Kaldor, Mary. 2013. *Global Civil Society: An Answer to War*. Cambridge and Malden, MA: Polity.
Klopp, Brett. 1995. Review of *Limits of Citizenship: Migrants and Postnational Membership in Europe*, by Yasemin Nuhoglu Soysal. *American Journal of Sociology* 101 (3):779–781.
Keys, Barbara J. 2014. Reclaiming American Virtue. Cambridge, MA: Harvard University Press.
Kelly, Patrick William. 2014a. "'Magic Words': The Advent of Transnational Human Rights Activism in Latin America's Southern Cone in the Long 1970s." In *The Breakthrough: Human Rights in the 1970s*, edited by Jan Eckel and Samuel Moyn, 88–106. Philadelphia: University of Pennsylvania Press.
Kelly, Tobias. 2014b. "Recognizing Torture: Credibility and the Unstable Codification of Victimhood." In *Histories of Victimhood*, edited by Steffen Jensen and Henrik Ronsbo, 144–160. Philadelphia: University of Pennsylvania Press.
Kendall, Gavin, Ian Woodward, and Zlatko Skrbis. 2009. *The Sociology of Cosmopolitanism: Globalization, Identity, Culture and Government*. New York: Palgrave Macmillan.
Kofman, Eleonore. 2005. "Citizenship, Migration and the Reassertion of National Identity." *Citizenship Studies* 9 (5):453–467.
Koopmans, Ruud. 2012. "The Post-Nationalization of Immigrant Rights: A Theory in Search of Evidence1." *The British Journal of Sociology* 63 (1):22–30.
Koopmans, Ruud, Ines Michalowski, and Stine Waibel. 2012. "Citizenship Rights for Immigrants: National Political Processes and Cross-National Convergence in Western Europe, 1980–2008." *American Journal of Sociology* 117 (4):1202–1245.
Kumar, Krishan. 2007. "Global Civil Society." *European Journal of Sociology / Archives Européennes de Sociologie* 48 (3):413–434.
Kurasawa, Fuyuki. 2007. *The Work of Global Justice: Human Rights as Practices*. Cambridge and New York: Cambridge University Press.

Latour, Bruno. 1987. *Science in Action: How to Follow Scientists and Engineers Through Society*. Cambridge, MA: Harvard University Press.

Laxer, Gordon, and Sandra Halperin. 2003. *Global Civil Society and Its Limits*. New York: Palgrave Macmillan

Lazaridis, Gabriella. 1995. "Reviews – From Aliens to Citizens: Redefining the Status of Immigrants in Europe Edited by Rainer Baubock / Limits of Citizenship: Migrants and Postnational Membership in Europe by Yasemin Nuhoglu Soysal." *Journal of Social Policy* 24:573.

Levy, Daniel, and Natan Sznaider. 2006. "Sovereignty Transformed: A Sociology of Human rights1." *The British Journal of Sociology* 57 (4):657–676.

Levy, Daniel, and Natan Sznaider. 2010. *Human Rights and Memory*. Philadelphia: Penn State Press.

Lister, Ruth, ed. 2003. *Citizenship: Feminist Perspectives*. New York: NYU Press.

Lockwood, David. 1996. "Civic Integration and Class Formation." *British Journal of Sociology*, 531–550.

Lyotard, Jean-François. 1984. *The Postmodern Condition: A Report on Knowledge*. Minnesota: University of Minnesota Press.

Mann, Michael. 1987. "Ruling Class Strategies and Citizenship." *Sociology* 21 (3):339–354.

Marchetti, Raffaele. 2006. "Global Governance or World Federalism? A Cosmopolitan Dispute on Institutional Models." *Global Society* 20 (3):287–305.

Marshall, Thomas H. 1950. *Citizenship and Social Class*. Cambridge: Cambridge University Press.

Martiniello, Marco. 1997. "Citizenship, Ethnicity and Multiculturalism: Post-national Membership Between Utopia and Reality." *Ethnic and Racial Studies* 20 (3):635–641.

Merry, Sally Engle. 2007. "Introduction: Conditions of Vulnerability." In *The Practice of Human Rights: Tracking Law Between the Global and the Local*, edited by Mark Goodale and Sally Engle Merry, 195–203. Cambridge: Cambridge University Press.

Merton, Robert King. 1967. *On Theoretical Sociology: Five Essays, Old and New*. New York: Free Press.

Messina, Anthony M. 1996. "The Not So Silent Revolution: Postwar Migration to Western Europe." *World Politics* 49 (1):130–154.

Messina, Anthony M. 2007. *The Logics and Politics of Post-WWII Migration to Western Europe*. New York: Cambridge University Press.

Meyer, John W. 2009. "World Society, the Welfare State, and the Life Course: An Institutionalist Perspective." In *World Society: The Writings of John*

W. Meyer, edited by Georg Krücken and Gili S. Drori, 280–295. Oxford and New York: OUP.
Meyer, John W., John Boli, George M. Thomas, and Francisco O. Ramirez. 1997. "World Society and the Nation-State." *American Journal of Sociology* 103 (1):144–181.
Meyer, John W., and Ronald L. Jepperson. 2000. "The 'Actors' of Modern Society: The Cultural Construction of Social Agency." *Sociological Theory* 18 (1):100–120.
Meyer, John W., and Brian Rowan. 1977. "Institutionalized Organizations: Formal Structure as Myth and Ceremony." *American Journal of Sociology* 83 (2):340–363.
Meyers, Diana Tietjens. 2011. "Two Victim Paradigms and the Problem of 'Impure' Victims." *Humanity: An International Journal of Human Rights, Humanitarianism, and Development* 2 (2):255–275.
Mollenkopf, John, and Jennifer Hochschild. 2010. "Immigrant Political Incorporation: Comparing Success in the United States and Western Europe." *Ethnic and Racial Studies* 33 (1):19–38.
Mouritsen, Per. 2011. "Beyond Post-National Citizenship. Access, Consequence, Conditionality." In *European Multiculturalisms: Cultural, Religious and Ethnic Challenges*, edited by Anna Triandafyllidou, Tariq Modood, and Nasar Meer, 88–115. Edinburgh: Edinburgh University Press.
Moyn, Samuel. 2010. *The Last Utopia*. Harvard University Press.
Moyn, Samuel. 2013a. "On the Nonglobalization of Ideas." In *Global Intellectual History*, 187–204. New York: Columbia University Press.
Moyn, Samuel. 2013b. "The Continuing Perplexities of Human Rights." *Qui Parle: Critical Humanities and Social Sciences* 22 (1):95–115.
Mueller, Susanne D. 2014. "Kenya and the International Criminal Court (ICC): Politics, the Election and the Law." *Journal of Eastern African Studies* 8 (1):25–42.
Nash, Kate. 2009a. *Contemporary Political Sociology: Globalization, Politics and Power*. Chichester and Malden, MA: John Wiley & Sons.
Nash, Kate. 2009b. *The Cultural Politics of Human Rights*. Cambridge and New York: Cambridge University Press.
Nora, Pierre. 1989. "Between Memory and History: Les Lieux de Mémoire." *Representations* 26:7–24.
Nussbaum, Martha C. 1996. "Patriotism and Cosmopolitanism." In *For Love of Country?* edited by Joshua Cohen, 2–20. Boston, MA: Beacon Press.
Nussbaum, Martha C. 1997. "Capabilities and Human Rights." *Fordham Law Review* 66:273–300.

Nussbaum, Martha C. 1998. *Cultivating Humanity*. Cambridge, MA: Harvard University Press.

Olick, Jeffrey K., and Joyce Robbins. 1998. "Social Memory Studies: From 'Collective Memory' to the Historical Sociology of Mnemonic Practices." *Annual Review of Sociology* 24 (1):105–140.

Ong, Aihwa. 1999. *Flexible Citizenship: The Cultural Logics of Transnationality*. Durham, NC: Duke University Press.

Pakulski, Jan. 1997. "Cultural Citizenship." *Citizenship Studies* 1 (1):73–86.

Pogge, Thomas W. 2008. *World Poverty and Human Rights*. Cambridge and Malden, MA: Polity.

Posner, Eric A. 2014. *The Twilight of Human Rights Law*. Oxford and New York: Oxford University Press.

Sainsbury, Diane. 2006. "Immigrants' Social Rights in Comparative Perspective: Welfare Regimes, Forms in Immigration and Immigration Policy Regimes." *Journal of European Social Policy* 16 (3):229–244.

Sargent, Daniel. 2014. "Oasis in the Desert? America's Human Rights Rediscovery." In *The Breakthrough: Human Rights in the 1970s*, 125–145. Philadelphia, PA: University of Pennsylvania Press.

Sassen, Saskia. 1996. *Losing Control?: Sovereignty in the Age of Globalization*. New York: Columbia University Press.

Sassen, Saskia. 2002. "Towards Post-National and Denationalized Citizenship." *Handbook of Citizenship Studies*, 277–292.

Sassen, Saskia. 2006. *Territory, Authority, Rights: From Medieval to Global Assemblages*. Cambridge and New York: Cambridge University Press.

Sassen, Saskia. 2009. "Incompleteness and the Possibility of Making: Towards Denationalized Citizenship?" In *Political Power and Social Theory* 20:229–258. Emerald Group Publishing Limited.

Sassen, Saskia. 2015. "From National Borders to Embedded Borderings: One Angle into the Question of Territory and Space in a Global Age." In *Crossroads in New Media, Identity and Law: The Shape of Diversity to Come*, edited by Wouter De Been, Arora Payal, and Mireille Hildebrandt, 17–42. London and New York: Palgrave Macmillan.

Schain, Martin A. 2009. "The State Strikes Back: Immigration Policy in the European Union." *European Journal of International Law* 20 (1):93–109.

Schmidtke, Oliver. 2012. "Commodifying Migration: Excluding Migrants in Europe's Emerging Social Model." *The British Journal of Sociology* 63 (1):31–38.

Schofer, Evan, and John W. Meyer. 2005. "The Worldwide Expansion of Higher Education in the Twentieth Century." *American Sociological Review* 70 (6):898–920.

Schuster, Liza, and John Solomos. 2002. "Rights and Wrongs Across European Borders: Migrants, Minorities and Citizenship." *Citizenship Studies* 6 (1):37–54.

Sen, Amartya. 1995. *Inequality Reexamined.* Boston, MA: Harvard University Press.

Shafir, Gershon, and Alison Brysk. 2006. "The Globalization of Rights: From Citizenship to Human Rights." *Citizenship Studies* 10 (3):275–287.

Simmons, Beth A. 2009. *Mobilizing for Human Rights: International Law in Domestic Politics.* Cambridge and New York: Cambridge University Press.

Slaughter, Anne-Marie. 2004. *A New World Order.* Princeton, NJ: Princeton University Press.

Sluga, Glenda. 2013. *Internationalism in the Age of Nationalism.* Philadelphia, PA: University of Pennsylvania Press.

Snyder, Jack, and Leslie Vinjamuri. 2006. "Trials and Errors: Principle and Pragmatism in Strategies of International Justice." *International Security* 28 (3):5–44.

Somers, Margaret R. 1994a. "Rights, Relationality, and Membership: Rethinking the Making and Meaning of Citizenship." *Law & Social Inquiry* 19 (1):63–114.

Somers, Margaret R. 1994b. "The Narrative Constitution of Identity: A Relational and Network Approach." *Theory and Society* 23 (5):605–649.

Somers, Margaret R. 2008. *Genealogies of Citizenship.* Cambridge and New York: Cambridge University Press.

Soysal, Yasemin Nuhoğlu. 1994. *Limits of Citizenship: Migrants and Postnational Membership in Europe.* Chicago and London: University of Chicago Press.

Soysal, Yasemin Nuhoğlu. 2012. "Citizenship, Immigration, and the European Social Project: Rights and Obligations of Individuality." *The British Journal of Sociology* 63 (1):1–21.

Spiro, Peter J. 2008. *Beyond Citizenship: American Identity After Globalization.* Oxford and New York: Oxford University Press.

Strang, David, and John W. Meyer. 1993. "Institutional Conditions for Diffusion." *Theory and Society* 22 (4):487–511.

Swidler, Ann. 1986. "Culture in Action: Symbols and Strategies." *American Sociological Review* 51 (2):273–286.

Triadafilopoulos, Triadafilos. 2011. "Illiberal Means to Liberal Ends? Understanding Recent Immigrant Integration Policies in Europe." *Journal of Ethnic and Migration Studies* 37 (6):861–880.

Triandafyllidou, Anna, Tariq Modood, and Nasar Meer, eds. 2011. *Beyond Post-National Citizenship. Access, Consequence, Conditionality.* Edinburgh: Edinburgh University Press.

Turner, Bryan S. 1990. "Outline of a Theory of Citizenship." *Sociology* 24 (2):189–217.

Turner, Bryan S. 1993. "Outline of a Theory of Human Rights." *Sociology* 27 (3):489–512.

Turner, Bryan S. 1997. "Citizenship Studies: A General Theory." *Citizenship Studies* 1 (1):5–18.

Turner, Bryan S. 2006. *Vulnerability and Human Rights.* Philadelphia: Penn State Press.

Wright, Charles W. 2004. "Particularity and Perspective Taking: On Feminism and Habermas' Discourse Theory of Morality." *Hypatia* 19 (4):47–74.

Yashar, Deborah J. 2002. "Globalization and Collective Action." *Comparative Politics* 34 (3):355–375.

Young, Iris Marion. 1989. "Polity and Group Difference: A Critique of the Ideal of Universal Citizenship." *Ethics* 99 (2):250–274.

6

Beyond Human Rights Law Naïveté

Introduction

If the ethico-political social-relational practices assembled under the umbrella of the human rights political imaginary are premised on the testimony or collective witnessing that publicizes a wrong, inflicted on a distant and/or excluded victimized other, in the hope of building a moral community and securing an ethico-political response, the contemporary remedy or reparation for this wrong is frequently conceptualized in juridical terms. I have left my exploration of the role played by law within the political imaginary to this last substantive chapter because it is all too easy to overestimate the social power of the law. This is frequently the case because, as Stuart Scheingold wrote in his seminal analysis of the *Politics of Rights*, "[t]here is a strong current belief in rights – both constitutional rights and the generality of rights. We believe that politics *is and should be* conducted in accordance with patterns of rights and obligations established under law" (2004, 13, emphasis in original). Scheingold is writing about the US context; however, the current level of social and political investment in human rights, to which I have alluded in previous chapters, suggests that it applies to human rights as well. Such a belief ignores the

J. Julián López, *Human Rights as Political Imaginary*,
https://doi.org/10.1007/978-3-319-74274-8_6

limits of the law as a tool of social change, but more importantly it obviates the need to explore the social conditions necessary for its social efficacy.

There is frequently a naturalized assumption that since human rights are currently tightly associated with the law this has always been the case, at least since the proclamation of the UDHR. The spread of human rights is understood as having been fuelled by the unfolding of human rights law, hence the widely shared practice amongst human rights activists and scholars of the rote enumeration, and linking, of the diverse international legal instruments. This makes it all too easy to yoke the advancement of human rights, not to its success in preventing or remedying human rights abuses (Hafner-Burton 2013; Posner 2014) but to its arterial and even capillary spread across the globe. Seen thus, the existence of ongoing human rights violations is understood as resulting from not enough law, not the right law, faulty implementation of existing law, or the absence of the political will to enforce the law (Posner 2014, 79–122; Hafner-Burton 2013, 116–34). It is only when human rights law will flow unobstructed through the entire world body, the aspiration of many cosmopolitans as seen in the previous chapter, that human rights will have succeeded in its effort to humanize the world. Implicit here is what I call, adapting Posner's expression (2014, 7), a certain human rights law naïveté, in other words, illusory expectations of the social power and efficacy of human rights law that prevents us from understanding how law has become inserted into the human rights political imaginary.

In this chapter, I begin by exploring human rights law naïveté by discussing the work of two scholars who argue that the limited achievements of human rights law to date suggest the need to rethink its role in the promotion of human rights. These scholars draw attention to the lack of correspondence between the relatively anaemic social power of human rights law, in international and transnational settings, and the highly complex and intractable nature of the problems it is expected to address and remedy. While these analyses are undeniably a useful reality check to human rights' more utopian ambitions, they do not interrogate the naturalized assumption, noted above, that human rights and human rights law are one and the same.

To create some conceptual space between human rights and human rights law, adding more detail to the political imaginary model, I show that it is fruitful to conceptualize the manner in which the activity of jurists and the circulation of law in social relationships are premised on specific types of social practices. Briefly drawing on sociolegal scholarship to shed analytical light on these practices, I then go on to illustrate the generalized absence of these types of practices in the postwar period. This, of course, raises the question of how it is that, and under what circumstances, the law has become entangled in the human rights political imaginary. How might we conceptualize this entanglement?

In order to address this question, I discuss, at some length, the work of scholars who have been concerned with understanding the nature of legal investment in human rights in the US and in Europe, and more briefly the entanglement of law and the human rights imaginary in Chile and Canada. In all these cases, I show how the nature of the entanglement is, to use Nash's term, intermestic and structured by the particular cultural politics of these polities. It is the social-relational intersection of the international human rights political imaginary with the legal fields and the latter's embeddedness in their respective polities that allow us to grasp the nature of the human rights' legal entanglements. This is followed by a discussion of Woodiwiss' illuminating conceptualization of rights as "practical means to ethical ends" and his analysis of how human rights became entangled with the law at the UN. This, in turn, enables me to return to the question of the contemporary equation of human and citizenship rights, as advanced in the previous chapter.

Human Rights Law Naïveté

In a stinging, but thoughtful, critique of the sociology of human rights, Mathieu Deflem and Stephen Chicoine draw attention to its "krypto-legalism" (2011, 122), by which they mean the implicit belief that human rights law is invested with some type of (hidden) power that makes it "an efficient instrument to prevent and respond to human rights violations" (2011, 122). Historical evidence to the contrary, this belief, they claim, is nested in the widely held nostrum that existing sociological scholarship has little to contribute to an understanding of rights and human rights. This is a view, as highlighted in Chap. 3, that is common amongst sociologists who argue for a normative turn towards human rights in sociology, a sociology *for* rather than *of* human rights. Were they instead to seriously engage with the extant scholarship in the sociology of law and criminological sociology that "shows the (potential) gap between the objectives and the consequences of law as well as the unintended consequences of criminalization practices" (Deflem and Chicoine 2011, 122), human rights sociology scholars might be better positioned to develop a more finely honed sociological analysis of human rights[1] and, in consequence, a more realistic appraisal of what human rights law might (not) be able to achieve.

The prevalence of human rights krypto-legalism, however, is not restricted to the sociology community. The legal scholar Eric A. Posner provides a different name, from which the chapter and section titles are derived, for what is essentially the same syndrome: "rule naïveté – the view that the good in every country can be reduced to a set of rules that can be impartially enforced". Moreover, he adds, "[r]ule naïveté is in part responsible for the proliferation of human rights, which has made meaningful enforcement impossible" (2014, 7). Finally, the political scientist Emilie M. Hafner-Burton draws attention to another manifestation of human rights law naïveté that presents in the form of "global legalism".

The latter is premised on the idea, dear to many cosmopolitans, that the further extension and institutionalization of human rights law will lead to a situation where "[m]ore people in more countries will come to see these [human rights] obligations as legitimate, and so obey them willingly because they will learn to believe them and trust that law represents the right values. And the culture of law will become a culture of rights" (2013, 66). Unfortunately, she shows, in persuasive empirical detail, that the human rights system's ability to implement norms is "highly uneven and generally low", as is its capacity for coercion and deterrence. In fact, she concludes, "persistent noncompliance and uneven treatment suggests that the legitimacy of the system is low, which probably diminishes the extent to which international human rights leads countries to comply through persuasion" (2013, 114).

Posner argues that the most significant advances in human rights in the twentieth century, by which is frequently meant the protections associated to the welfare state of which more below, occurred before the international human right legal regime began to be put in place in the 1970s, and countries agreed to sign and ratify the treaties (2014, 7). This, he posits, is because these protections would have generally existed in the absence of the subsequent appearance of human rights legal machinery. Not least because human rights did not require developed countries, where most of the alleged human rights gains were made, to do "anything different from what they had done in the past" (2014, 31). What is more, while recognizing that the words of UDHR might perhaps have been inspirational, he nonetheless contends that

> no one believed at the time that they portended a major change in the way international relations would be conducted, nor did they capture the imagination of voters, politicians, intellectuals, leaders of political movements or anyone else who might have exerted political pressure on governments. (2014, 17)

This explains why in the postwar, as I will highlight in the sections that follow, there was so little legal investment in human rights. Sure, he adds, claims were made on behalf of human rights, but these as "everyone understood", at the time, were mere circumlocutions for the real global political stakes of the time, namely, free markets versus state planning, capitalist or proletariat (state) rule (2014, 18).

Posner devotes some time to a discussion of the most significant human rights treaties, the UN committees, the UN Council of Human Rights (formerly the UN Commission on Human Rights), and the Office of the United Nations High Commissioner for Human Rights (OHCHR), only to conclude that while they might have shamed and cajoled some countries into doing some good, the UN human rights system has foundered in its attempt to give content to or specify human rights norms and advance authoritative interpretations of the law (2014, 47).[2] Said differently, it has failed to perform the types of roles fulfilled by domestic courts and their judicial system (Posner 2014, 47). These roles, as I will show below, contribute significantly to the autonomy, social power, and operational capacity of law. One, of course, might argue that the UN is an easy target and that if one looks at regional human right systems or courts, particularly the European Convention on Human Rights (ECHR) and its European Court of Human Rights (ECtHR), discussed in more detail below, it is possible to accommodate a more sanguine reading.

Posner, however, doubts this. He notes that the Court has relatively anaemic powers. It cannot strike down offending legislation and can only order governments to pay relatively small damages, providing remedy to one person, or possibly a group, at a time (2014, 48). Operationally, the ECtHR is dwarfed by its constituency; it caters to 47 states (including Russia, Ukraine, and Turkey) and more than 800 million people (Posner 2014, 48). Consequently, notes Posner, in a typical year the Court will receive between 40,000 and 90,000 applications, declaring the large majority inadmissible and rendering judgement on less than three thousand applications, attaching monetary remedy to less than a thousand (2014, 49).[3] As a consequence, he writes "even the worst human rights abusing countries know that they will never pay in aggregate more than a few million euros per year under the ECHR" (2014, 49). Posner does admit that "states are under pressure to change laws that the Court has deemed in violation of the Convention" (2014, 48); however, even this peer pressure is subject to political negotiation at the Council of Europe[4] (2014, 51).[5] Moreover as Greer notes, "apart from persuasion, suspension of voting rights on the Committee of Ministers, and expulsion – The Council of Europe lacks any direct means of inducing states to improve their Convention violation records" (2006, 278).[6]

Human rights are best conceptualized, argues Posner, as "no more than the vague encouragement to govern well", doubting that such encouragement keeps countries who already do so on the straight and narrow, or brings those who do not into line (2014, 93). What is more, because "the treaties send confusing signals", even a country inclined to be guided by international human rights law would be at a loss when attempting to work out its human rights legal obligations (Posner 2014, 93). For Posner, the arterial or capillary spread of human rights law across the world body does not represent a triumph of human rights; irrigating the world with ever more fluid claims is, he contends, more likely to trigger the system's collapse (2014, 94). In the last instance, the reason for the failure of the international human rights system is the absence of the authoritative structures required for human rights to function as law, which are generally only found in well-established democratic countries (2014, 115). Posner does not argue for isolationism, but suggests more humble and targeted foreign aid efforts aimed at developing countries that are most likely to benefit from them, as well as the difficult recognition that, in many instances, "there is little that developed countries can do" (2014, 148).

A more country-specific focus and non-legal approach is, also, proposed by Emilie M. Hafner-Burton, who argues that "the reality is that law on its own can't achieve ambitious goals to spread human rights protections in many contexts" (2013, 136). This is the conclusion she draws after her review of the scholarly literature evaluating the success of global legalism, which largely chimes with that presented by Posner. Generally, and not surprisingly, most advanced democratic countries do a good job of protecting human rights (2013, 71) and link their national identity to respect for and promotion of human rights. This, however, does not mean that human rights will necessarily supersede national interests in foreign policy (2013, 72). On the other hand, she notes, human rights law will be least effective in countries where human rights are most likely to violated (2013, 73), and ratification of human rights treaties in these contexts does not generally correlate with improvement (2013, 73). In fact she concludes, "[w]hatever the reasons for this poor [...] link between some human rights treaties and actual protections for human rights, the systematic scholarly research paints a dismal picture of the ability of international law to protect human rights among the world's most vulnerable populations" (2013, 76).

More positively, Hafner-Burton reports that there has been a generalized trend towards incorporating human rights law into domestic settings, yet even here the potential benefits have remained meagre as a result of broken legal commitments, "[b]ureacratic backlogs, ambiguity in the norms, and overlapping requirements" (2013, 91). Other shortcomings include insufficient resources, political instrumentalization of human rights, and overlaps and inconsistency (2013, 91–115). She does not discount that advances could be secured through reforms such as improving outreach, streamlining the human rights law system, its professionalization, and investing in its credibility and legitimacy (2013, 127–33). Still, even in the best-case scenarios, global legalism will likely not succeed (2013, 135). What Hafner-Burton proposes, instead, is that states with an interest in promoting human rights adopt a "stewardship" and "triage" approach, that is to say, embrace a commitment to "chang[ing] the calculus that drives abusive behavior" (2013, 136) through a range of foreign policy tools —coercive and persuasive—in contexts where the "greatest return on investments" can be secured (2013, 176), by localizing efforts through NGOs (2013, 151–63) and national human rights institutions (2013, 164–75).

Hafner-Burton, like Posner, ultimately argues that the hopes attached to the expansion of the international human rights legal machinery have been scuttled. Whereas some scholars, as seen in the previous chapter, believe that progress can be made by efforts to develop more cosmopolitan conceptions of law, these two authors conclude that the experience to date strongly indicates that success will elude international law-focused initiatives. In this, they concur with a growing consensus among some legal scholars, "[i]nternational human rights institutions lack the authority and the means to compel states to comply with human rights norms [because] nuanced coercive methods, modelled along domestic law enforcement lines are not available" (Oberleitner 2012, 265–66). Consequently, "[e]nforcing human rights means largely relying on persuasion and appeals to morality and legitimacy, on occasion and inconsistently supported by political and economic incentives, sanctions or pressure" (Oberleitner 2012, 266).

Hafner-Burton and Posner suggest that a more consistent focus be put on the political and economic incentives in lieu of international law promotion. The implicature here is that international law promotion was the original telos of human rights. This, as I insist in the next section, is an assumption that has to be critically interrogated if a fuller understanding of the role of law in the human rights imaginary is to be achieved. In the next section I lay down the scaffolding for such an interrogation by exploring the practices that produce the social effect of law's autonomy. Following this, in the section that follows, I explore how human rights acquired its international legal legs.

Law's Autonomy

In Chap. 5, I highlighted a progressive narrative, linking equality of status with membership in political community. Born of Marshall's conceptualization of citizenship, wedded with a retroactive, or ex-post, normative reading of the UDHR, this account has contributed to the widely held notion that human rights are an extension or supersession of citizenship rights. Normative arguments, which generally tend to touch time and space lightly—if at all—when sufficiently abstract, can be projected back to time almost immemorial. This is the case, for instance, when Micheline Ishay finds normative artefacts of contemporary human rights in ancient civilizations (2004). Lacking the same historical reach, but still transcending centuries, is Neil Stammers' suggestion that human rights can be convincingly traced back almost four centuries (2009, 40) to the emergence of the European natural rights traditions.[7] In order to do so, he conceptualizes human and natural rights as instances of social praxis oriented towards "challenging existing relations and structures of power" (2009, 68).

While such abstractions can be philosophically informative, indispensable for making political arguments, or seemingly crucial for advancing human rights claims, they, by definition, shed little light on the concrete conditions of the social materialization and efficacy of ethico-politico ideas. Sociologically speaking, they are razor thin, yet surprisingly blunt. Thinking about human rights as a political imaginary, the goal of the present book, is an attempt to understand how the normative ideas so crucial to human right are embodied, embrained, inthinged, and embedded. In other words, what are the historical and social contexts and social relations that give human rights social legs?

Not as historically agile a time traveller as normative ideals, human rights conceptualized as laws, legal obligations, or principles can, nonetheless, also appear to effortlessly step backwards in time. However, the space of their travel is not the timeless conceptual expanses ploughed by philosophical, moral, and political reasoning, but rather that which is delimited by "legal texts, precedents or rulings that limit the realm of legal argument" (Luhmann 1991, 1429). The constraints introduced by the corpus of legitimate texts—statutes, case law, civil codes, treaties, and so on, in a word, authoritative legal texts—secure, at least at first blush, the autonomy of legal reasoning and practice (López and Lunau 2012, 84).

Travelling backwards towards such texts, however, is not merely an option for actors engaged in legal modes of action; it is a necessity. This is because legal reasoning is primarily concerned with deciding cases by reference to already existing rules, laws, or precedent, forming a "seamless web" between past and present, "not because it [the law] prescribes in advance the outcome in every case that may arise, but because when a case does arise, however unusual it may be, the outcome is to be found within the law" (Weinreb 2005, 102). As Bourdieu argues, legal practice

> ties the present continuously to the past [...] it provides the guarantee that, in the absence of a revolution which would upset the very foundation of the juridical order, the future will resemble what has gone before, that necessary transformations and adaptations will be conceived and expressed in a language that conforms to the past. (1986, 845)

It is this "closure" that enables law to function as a social mechanism for legitimate dispute resolution, where "direct conflict" is transposed into a "juridically regulated debate between professionals acting by proxy" (Bourdieu 1986, 831). Inescapably eventuating in a decision, the legitimacy of the resolution derives from its rationalized entanglement in a chain of textual legitimation that exorcises the spectre of arbitrariness, a sure sign of the legal field's malfunction (Bourdieu 1986, 824). The normative and epistemological closure produced by the juridical field presumes that legal reasoning is free of external constraint and is guided by the coherent application of the legal principles that exist in a corpus of authoritative texts. It is this that provides law with its social autonomy and indeed a good part of its social power. However, there is a paradox here. As Nash rightly argues, "the law requires interpretation and decision; it is not simply a body of texts that transparently leads practitioners to a single rational outcome" (2009b, 33). Indeed it would not be able to function as a mechanism of dispute resolution were this not the case!

It would lack the limberness required to adapt to unforeseeable new situations.[8]

Insofar as human rights, as a political imaginary, draws on, or is entangled with, the normative and social power of the law, it does not merely avail itself of the law's symbolic legitimacy and tutelary cloak (Arthurs and Kreklewich 1996, 29).[9] It incorporates the practices that are embodied, embrained, inthinged, and embedded in the juridical field, or at least attempts to do so. Just as the normative power of human rights is not merely the product of an idea, but of the particular social practices that stabilize and make that idea persuasive across time and social space, the social power and legitimacy of law is not the outcome of some mysterious transcendent and extra-social legal capacity. It arises from the ongoing social practices and relations of the juridical field and, as I will indicate below, the manner in which the latter are embedded in other fields of power.

Legal subjectivity and repertoires of action, that is, modes of "legal consciousness" (Ewick and Silbey 1998; Silbey 2005), are pervasive in the social and political practices enabled by the human rights political imaginary. Indeed, Woodiwiss argues that by the 1990s, human rights were overwhelmingly juridified (2003, 30–32). In human rights contexts, jurists of course draw on the professional practices of their trade. It could not be otherwise. However, it is not uncommon for non-jurists to deploy the same language and modes of legal reasoning. References to authoritative international, regional, and national legal texts typically, in an effort to invoke a chain of textual legitimation, precede or are intertwined with ethico-political human rights claims. A claim is made, or communicated, on behalf of distant and/or excluded victimized others: This is wrong! And it violates international law! Equally, advocates, who are not putting forward particular human rights claims will also assemble simulacra of legal arguments by drawing on international human rights texts.

The moral responsibility to be open to the suffering of distant and/or excluded victimized others, bearing witness, is the ethical moment of the human rights claim. Legal reason and legality,[10] in turn, draw attention to the political mechanisms and responsibility for remedying the situation, once the legal "truth" of the victimization has been established.[11] Within the human rights political imaginary, bearing witness to the suffering of distant and/or excluded victimized others, in an imaginary ethico-political community, is what potentially triggers the ethico-political duty to act. It is the impartial, and socially recognized truth, of the representation of violence and injustice that compels one, if compel one it does, to react, to make a human rights claim, or participate in the collective demand that human rights be respected.

Bearing witness, if successful, enacts the suffering of distant and/or excluded victimized others as an instance of unmediated truth. For a bystander, to bear witness is to feel the victim's suffering as his or her own and to be irrevocably propelled to act by the unbearable nature of what is witnessed.[12] Law and legality inject another form of impartiality into the human rights claim. It does not, however, ensue from the representation of the experience of the suffering as such, but from the socially enacted autonomy of the law. Established the facts of the case, in the contexts of human rights, the victimization of the claimant and the receivability of the claim, the law offers an inventory of remedies that can be adjudicated objectively.

Consequently, if one wants to understand how law is interwoven into the human rights political imaginary, then it is crucial to further explore the broader social conditions that underwrite the law's claim to autonomy, and contributes to the perception of its autonomy in everyday legality. Bourdieu argues that to do so, it is necessary to think about law as a juridical field of practice,

> [a] site of competition for monopoly of the right to determine the law. Within this field their occurs a confrontation among actors possessing a technical competence which consists essentially in the socially recognized capacity to *interpret* a corpus of texts sanctifying a correct or legitimized vision of the social world. It is essential to recognize this, in order to take account both of the relative autonomy of the law and of the properly symbolic effect of "miscognition" that results from the illusion of the law's absolute autonomy in relation to external pressures.

The coherence and authoritative systematicity, upon which the legitimacy of law rests, is produced, argues Bourdieu, by the division of labour in the juridical field between the legal theorist and the jurist. The former draws on fundamental axioms of justice and a commitment to coherence to render the law as "an autonomous and self sufficient system" (1986, 824). The latter draws on a series of professional routines, knowledges, and modes of reasoning that puts the law to work in the resolution of concrete disputes. Such work enables the "adaptation to reality of a system which would risk closing itself into rigid rationalism if it were left to theorists alone" (Bourdieu 1986, 824). It is this back and forth, between abstract systematization and quasi-casuistic application, that produces the effect of continuity and autonomy in the juridical field. It nurtures the sense that legal decisions are not arbitrary, that they are authoritative and compel obedience.

The plaiting of these two distinct modes of interpretation, one incorporating cases into an axiomatic understanding of justice and the other parsing cases by linking them to past decisions, leads to the "historicization of the norm" (Bourdieu 1986, 826). This two-stranded braid is produced, notes Bourdieu, "by adapting sources to new circumstances, by discovering new possibilities within them, and eliminating what has been superseded or become obsolete" (1986, 826–27). More broadly, it is the legal habitus, arising from legal studies and the practices structuring the legal field that shapes the perception and judgements of its practitioners (Bourdieu 1986, 833). It fosters "the tacit acceptance of the field's fundamental law, an essential tautology which requires that, within the field, conflicts can only be resolved juridically – that is, according to the rules and conventions of the field itself" (Bourdieu 1986, 831).

I do not want to give the impression that Pierre Bourdieu has settled the sociological question of the apparent autonomy of the law. A powerful theoretical competitor is Niklas Luhmann's autopoetic conception of the legal system (Luhmann 1991, 2004).[13] Other scholars, however, question the very notion that the law is characterized by the coherence and normative closure accentuated by both Bourdieu and Luhmann. For instance, Mariana Valverde claims that legal practitioners and institutions "care little about epistemological purity and derive great benefit from being epistemologically creative" (2003b, 26). Consequently, she concludes, "the study of the epistemological creativity and hybridity displayed not only by judges but by both ordinary citizens and lowly officials engaged in the negotiation of legal truths may thus make an indirect contribution to the work of those who take a more normative approach" (2003b, 26).

Indeed a number of scholars aim to show how the apparent autonomy of law is gainsaid by capitalist imperatives (Collins 1982; Fine 2002; Pashukanis 1980, 1983), patriarchal structures of domination (Finley 1989; Fineman and Thomadsen 2013; Snyder 2014; Weisberg 1993), the instrumentalization of the law (Kalman 1986), law's indeterminacy due its embeddedness in social, political, and economic relations of power (Hunt 1985, 1993; Unger 1983), and its racialized nature (Crenshaw 1995; Delgado and Stefancic 2017), to mention but a few. In other words, as Woodiwiss rightly argues, the law is embedded in the power relations that prevail in any given social formation (2005a, 15)

What Bourdieu's conception of the law, as a juridical field, does share with those of the aforementioned sociolegal scholars, despite important and consequential differences, is its non-essentialism. The law is not a reified thing nor is it merely a series of principles, norms, or rules enshrined in texts. It is a social relation, an institutionalized dynamic practice. Thus, it draws our attention to a crucial dimension that the law's seeming autonomy cloaks, namely, the ongoing work of interpretation and adaptation that secures law's authority and contributes to its social (in)efficacy and power.[14]

Human Rights' International Legal Legs

When contemporary human rights practitioners effortlessly draw on the UDHR as an authoritative text to argue that international law is fundamentally concerned with the protection of individualized human rights (Moyn 2010, 176), their ability to do so presupposes, not only the circulation of human rights in everyday legality, but, also, a submerged labour of interpretation and legitimation. The latter is a crucial dimension of the contemporary representations, social technologies, modes of subjectivity and agency, and organizational structures of the human rights political imaginary.

In other words, legal principles, norms, and rules are constituted in and through social relations and practices. Outside of such dynamic and complex relations, they do not travel nor do they have social power. It is the foundational work of lawyers and judges in institutionalized legal settings, or juridical fields, that prime laws, legal norms, and principles to be potentially socially efficacious.[15]

What is surprising, then, in the context of the postwar period, is precisely the near absence of this type of juridical interpretive work by mainstream and international jurists. This suggests human rights lacked legal legs during this period. This is because, as Moyn has argued, "most members of the public international law bar were convinced years before the Universal Declaration of Human Rights confirmed their fears that human rights were not to be more than paper promises of the postwar era" (2010, 178). In fact with the exception of René Cassin and John Humphrey, lawyers made few contributions to the UDHR (Moyn 2010, 186). Moreover, contrary to the received wisdom that the Cold War froze the spread of human rights, it confirmed, argues Moyn, "the lawyerly insight into the persisting realities of power and imperative against excessive utopianism" (2010, 187). This was to be further corroborated by the rise of the realpolitik in international relations, for which law and human rights were relatively inconsequential (Dezalay and Garth 2006, 232) as the prism through which the international sphere was conceptualized, leaving international law by the wayside (Moyn 2010, 187) as a "'a disguise' after the fact" (Moyn 2010, 188).

"Outside of the small college of international lawyers", in the US, human rights law was even more marginal as a result of American Cold War imperatives and the prominence of legal realism in the academy (Moyn 2010, 189).[16] Indeed it was only in the late 1960s, when human rights penetrated public consciousness as a result of the new type of politics and the moral authority exemplified by Amnesty International and later Human Rights Watch, that human rights would become a matter of concern for international lawyers (Moyn 2010, 180).[17]

In Europe, as we saw in Chap. 2, the situation was different. Rooted in the Christian tradition of personalism, human rights were understood as inoculating human dignity against the onslaught of godlessness originating in communism and modern industrial society. "As time passed", notes Moyn, "such personalism more and more simply rephrased anti-communism and Western unity rather than offering a philosophy of global amity" (2010, 191). As Duranti persuasively shows, the human rights revolution in Europe "must be understood as a product of its free-market and social conservative origins" (2016, 391). For reasons that I address later, the European Convention on Human Rights (ECHR) did engender, almost by accident, the kind of legal interpretation that was generally absent elsewhere, but "in the early years there was no serious promotion by European international lawyers of human rights as a wider project, as the European Convention signalled values without bringing a serious legal regime into being" (Moyn 2010, 191).

Back in the US, human rights began to acquire some currency amongst the legal profession in the 1970s. For instance, the first US international human rights casebook was issued in 1973, but it was not exactly received by acclamation by the profession, as Yves Dezalay and Bryant G. Garth report:

> One of the early promoters of the field stated that the leaders of the American Society of International Law had argued that 'human rights is not really law. It was politics.' Even worse, according to the leaders of the foreign policy establishment, concern for human rights represented an impractical idealism that was overstepping the boundaries of the society. (2002, 130)

The dual charge of "politics" and "idealism" probably indexed the manner in which the banner of human rights had been seized by the anti-colonial movement at the UN as a normative justification for self-determination, which scandalized much of the international law community (Moyn 2010, 197). At the UN, a new conception of world order was being gestated, "one premised on the breakup of empire rather than its continuation, on politics rather than law" (Mazower 2009, 185). As the anti-colonial moment waned, however, and human rights became associated to the minimalist political practices and the moral authority attached to Amnesty International and cognate organizations, international lawyers would begin to argue for the legal nature of the UDHR, suggesting that it could be advanced "through custom and opinion"

(Moyn 2010, 200). This, in effect, laid the groundwork of the legal sanction for a phenomenon that had been initially fuelled by moral authority (Moyn 2010, 202; Dezalay and Garth 2006, 234), morality got plugged into to legality.[18]

The notion that the current hegemony of human rights law is the product of the steady development of the UDHR, stretching back to the immediate postwar period, is belied by the virtual marginalization of human rights by lawyers, in the US, up to the period of the late 1960s and early 1970s. The unexpected eruption of human rights within the legal profession during this period is exemplified, argues Moyn, by the trajectory of the American legal scholar Louis Henkin (2010, 201–7). In a *New York Times* obituary, Elisa Massimo, president and CEO of Human Rights First, which Henkin had helped found as the Lawyer's Committee for Human Rights in 1978, was cited as claiming, "It is no exaggeration to say that no American was more instrumental in the development of human rights than Lou [...] He literally and figuratively wrote the book on human rights" (Grimes 2010). Despite this, as Moyn persuasively shows, there is nothing in Henkin's earlier writings, which in fact echoed the prevailing view that human rights were an "idealistic disappointment" as late as the mid-1970s (2010, 203–4), that could explain the manner in which he would completely throw himself into the cause. As a matter of fact, "his inability to imagine an impending novelty is simply testimony of how unpredictable it really was" (Moyn 2010, 204).

Moyn contends that the rise of human rights in international law cannot be explained by endogenous doctrinal developments within the human rights law community, the type of interpretive work that Bourdieu argues is essential for the functioning of a juridical field. Quite the opposite, it was the triumph of human rights, as a mode of moral politics, a minimalist utopia, that enabled a reimagining of the field of international law canonizing human rights as "a professional idea and priority" (2010, 210).[19] Such a re-envisioning of human rights through the prism of legal and judicial interpretation would leave a legal imprimatur on the human rights political imaginary. It is precisely at this point that law becomes entangled with the maturing human rights political imaginary.

In order to understand the nature of this entanglement, I turn to Dezalay and Garth's research (2002, 2006, 2012a, b), which explores the development of human rights in the US and its export to Latin America with a focus on the legal profession. Following this, I discuss Mikael Rask Madsen's analysis of the development of human rights in Europe (2007, 2010; Christoffersen and Madsen 2011), which provides another historical and social-relational context where law becomes entangled with the human rights political imaginary.

US Legal Elites' Investment in Human Rights

Above, I introduced Bourdieu's conceptualization of the two types of interpretive work, normative systematization and quasi-casuistic interpretation, undertaken by legal practitioners. It is the contest between these two competing practices, he argues, that produce the semblance of continuity and neutrality—so crucial to law's social power and the social effect of its autonomy. It is the ability to transpose conflicts and disputes into a juridically regulated bout between legal practitioners, who share the habitus of the juridical field, inexorably culminating in a legitimate decision that makes law such a crucial contemporary social technology. Law's autonomy and its social efficacy, however, are not merely the product of internal competition within the juridical field over the meaning of legal texts and the manner in which such meaning organizes broader social relations in everyday legality. It equally ensues from the position of the juridical field in the broader field of state power. A general understanding of this relationship is necessary in order to explore Dezalay and Garth's analysis of the US legal profession's uptake of human rights in the late 1970s.

In his foreword to Bourdieu's *The State Nobility*, Loïc Wacquant notes that in addition to the legitimate power to tax and resort to violence, the state also, and crucially, "monopolizes legitimate *symbolic* violence" (1998b, xvii–xviii, emphasis in original): understood as the capacity to "construct and impose mental structures, categories of perception and thought, which become institutionalized in social and mental structures, and so present themselves as a matter of fact or even as *natural*" (Madsen and Dezalay 2002, 194, emphasis in original). Consequently, for Bourdieu, the state is not merely the institutionalized power of a "ruling class" or an assemblage of bureaucratized institutions. Instead it is conceptualized as a field of struggle in which the "*dominant principle of domination* and the *legitimate principle of domination*" are at stake (Madsen and Dezalay 2002, 195, emphasis in original). For Bourdieu, this is so because

> [n]o power can be satisfied with existing just as power, that is, as brute force, entirely devoid of justification – in a word, arbitrary – and it must thus justify its existence, as well as the form it takes, or at least ensure that the arbitrary nature of its foundation will be misrecognized and thus that it will be recognized as legitimate. (Bourdieu 1998b, 265)

Summarizing Bourdieu's analysis of the key role of juridical capital within the state, Madsen and Dezalay note that the development of the modern European state was linked to the rise of key elements of the state apparatus, namely, "the police, the justice system and the departments of finance and tax" (2002, 196). Contemporaneously, "*The Science d'État*" emerged as a scholastic field of study in universities, training opportunely positioned individuals to staff essential state departments. This incipient body of state knowledge became rationalized and scientifically formalized, contributing to the emergence of modern law, conceived universalistically, as well as a corporate identity for jurists.

As a result, juridical capital, the power to deliver authoritative legal interpretations, was institutionalized as a potent symbolic capital within the state's fields of power (2002, 196). In turn, because of their role in training jurists to undertake "objective" interpretations of the law, and the manner in which the latter increasingly underpinned the state's legitimacy, law faculties developed a certain degree of autonomy from the state, obscuring their dependence on and complicity with state power (2002, 196). Consequently, on a European level, jurists' range of action remained restricted because of their embeddedness in national fields of state power (2002, 197).

The situation was different in the US context. Institutional boundaries between the state and law were not as clearly defined, enabling legal practitioners to develop more entrepreneurial conducts and enter the fields of politics, business, and even public and civic engagement (Madsen and

Dezalay 2002, 197). Thus, in opposition to its European counterparts, in the US, argue Madsen and Dezalay, "the legal field became a source of legitimacy for the state rather than drawing its legitimacy from the state" (2002, 197). This capacitated lawyers to invest their juridical capital beyond affairs of the state, for instance, in the fields of business and commerce as demonstrated by the strategic institutional links between Wall Street law firms and Ivy League law schools, which, according to Madsen and Dezalay, are constitutive of the US legal field (2002, 197).

It equally entitled members of the profession to trade scholarly for political capital, actively engaging in different roles in the field of politics. This, according to Dezalay and Garth (2002), as will be seen below, is crucial for explaining why some elites in the juridical field would invest in human rights in the late 1970s and throughout the 1980s. One of the consequences of the circulation of juridical capital amongst different fields of power has been a stronger focus on cultivating, institutionalizing, and policing professional values to buttress the profession's autonomy. This has also led to an emphasis on *pro bono* work among elite legal firms, and as a professional ideal more broadly, undertaken in the defence of the poor and disadvantaged, intertwining the juridical field with issues of civic and public advocacy in public interest law (Madsen and Dezalay 2002, 197). In the late 1970s and 1980s, the public interest work that had previously been directed at the civil rights movement would train its focus on human rights instead.[20]

Dezalay and Garth argue that the foreign policy establishment was a key site for the deployment of juridical capital in the 1950s and 1960s: "a small elite of cosmopolitan business lawyers" exercised considerable influence over crucial foreign policy outposts such as the CIA, the State Department, Ivy League Universities, the Council on Foreign Relations, and the Ford, Rockefeller, and Carnegie Foundations (2002, 61–64). Having rendered service during the war effort, pivotal figures from this group subsequently balanced commitments to business with public service in the foreign policy sphere, drawing on networks in institutions that they themselves had contributed to creating—for example, World Bank, CIA, USAID (Dezalay and Garth 2002, 64).

Two objectives were crucial for these establishment lawyers, and the broader foreign policy community, "inoculat[ing] the world against the contagion of Communism and eas[ing] the passage of American foreign policy interests abroad" (Saunders in Dezalay and Garth 2002, 64). An important element in the pursuit of the former objective was the waging of the "cultural cold war" (Dezalay and Garth 2002, 64; Saunders 1999), carried forward with the help of the Liberal Foundations, which mobilized their privileged access to the scholarly world. The Foundations, which had served the Liberal Establishment as key tools for the development and promotion of reformist agendas in the US, targeted regions most exposed to the communist threat (Dezalay and Garth 2002, 65).

All the same, the broader consensus over US foreign policy would begin to unravel by the late 1960s and early 1970s. As discussed in Chap. 2, one of the consequences of the Vietnam War is that it created a rift in the Democratic Party, cleaving conservative Cold War warriors from the liberal wing of the party, leaving the party without a unified voice on foreign policy (Dezalay and Garth 2002, 53). This fracture not only realigned party politics, it also destabilized the foreign policy establishment. However, another seismic force was producing fissures that compounded the threat faced by the liberal elites that had dominated US foreign policy in the postwar. These waves did not originate overseas, but in the homeland. They were the product of a war, but a war fought on the terrain of ideas. It was waged in the name of a conservative counterrevolution (Dezalay and Garth 2002, 127; Blumenthal 2008; Ehrman 1996; Smith 1993).

In the context of the postwar liberal consensus, counter-establishment conservatives were eventually able to position themselves as radicals, "self-described revolutionaries" (Smith 1993, 8), conducting war on the Liberal Establishment. The latter was "comprised of the nation's major foundations, Ivy League Universities, New York publishing houses, research institutions, newspapers, and the broadcast media which maintain[ed] the supremacy of liberal ideas policies" (Smith 1993, 169). The Liberal Establishment, which conservatives believed drew support from both parties, whatever its reality as conceived by conservative counterrevolutionaries, was seen as a formidable opponent. A prominent right-wing ideologue and author of one of its central manifestos—the *Sharon Statement*—M. Stanton Evans wrote, after Barry Goldwater's defeat in the 1964 presidential campaign, "[t]he chief point about the

Liberal Establishment is that it is in control. It is guiding the lives and destinies of the American people. It wields enormous, immeasurable power [...] its control embraces the instruments of public scrutiny. It directs and instructs popular opinion" (M. Stanton Evans in Blumenthal 2008, 2).[21]

Underpinning, the critique of the Liberal Establishment, as James A. Smith has argued, was a profound rejection of "the intellectual basis for American policymaking, including the approaches advanced by progressive reformers: Hoover's technocrats, Roosevelt's New Dealers, Truman's Cold War liberals, and Eisenhower's 'modern' Republicans, as well as Kennedy's New Frontiersmen and the architects of Johnson's Great Society" (1993, 22). Though ostensibly drawing on a commonsense critique of the abstractions of liberal intellectuals, the conservative counterrevolution fielded its own team of intellectuals, mobilizing experts to promote and circulate conservative and free market values.[22] As prominent neoconservative ideologue Irving Kristol noted, "Universities, think tanks, and foundations were the 'idea-germinating' and 'idea legitimizing institutions'. Defenders of the capitalist ethos would have to wage war both by creating their own counterparts and by taking the battle inside the university and, in time, the political bureaucracy" (Smith 1993, 181).[23]

The strategy proved successful: "Their factories of ideology – think tanks, institutes, and journals would win legitimacy for notions that would be translated into policy. The Counter-Establishment was a political elite aspiring to become a governing elite" (Blumenthal 2008, 3). In fact by the early 1980s, "new cadres of policy experts – libertarian and classical liberal economists, traditionalist conservatives, Straussian political philosophers, and 'neoconservatives'" had descended on Washington (Smith 1993, 7). So much so, "that veteran political journalist began to speak of a new 'ideas industry' and to assess the role that conservative think tanks, such as the Hoover Institutions, The American Enterprise Institute, and Heritage Foundation, had played in Reagan's victory" (Smith 1993, 7–8).[24]

A central component of the conservative counterrevolution was the fierce critique of Keynesian economic theory undertaken by the Chicago School of Economics and its advocates. Having accumulated considerable academic capital, and acquired fame as a prep school for future Nobel Prize economists, the Chicago School lent credibility to the new market ideology (Dezalay and Garth 2002, 73–74). The rigorous and advanced use of mathematical modelling enabled this new breed of economists to distinguish themselves from "'gentleman lawyers'", who, in the US and elsewhere, "dominated the field of state expertise—and thus indirectly that of economic knowledge" (Dezalay and Garth 2002, 74). The extension of market ideas and mathematical modelling to new empirical domains broadened the scope of applicability of the insurgent economic ideas and were skilfully popularized by the conservative counterrevolutionary think tanks and networks, positioning neoliberalism as a new language of both domestic and international statecraft (Dezalay and Garth 2002, 73–94).[25]

It is at this conjuncture, described in broad strokes over the preceding pages, that human rights began to appeal to some elite lawyers in the US. The latter would begin to undertake the juridical work necessary, which had largely been absent up to that point,[26] to provide human rights legitimacy as a form of emergent juridical capital in the legal field, and as a new path towards the American foreign policy establishment. The increased traction of the highly mediatized politics of Amnesty International and cognate organizations, the use of human rights in the American Congress to wrestle back some margin of influence over foreign policy, the Carter administration's championing of human rights as a foreign policy objective and as an unguent to soothe the trauma of the Vietnam War—reclaiming American virtue, the rise of conservative counterrevolutionaries and the "Chicago Boys" to power, displacing liberal elites from the foreign policy establishment,[27] are among the important factors, exogenous to the development of law itself, that made legal elites, in the US, look at human rights with lawyerly eyes.

Dezalay and Garth contend that human rights offered lawyers in the US a number of opportunities (2002, 127–40). As Amnesty International succeeded in drawing attention to dictatorships in Latin America, and leftists made the link between neoliberalism and Pinochet's coup, human rights became established as a weapon with which liberal elites could attack the conservative upstarts that had displaced them in the field of foreign policy. Equally, Helsinki and then Human Rights Watch's rise to prominence was significant because, unlike Amnesty International, which primarily focused on individuals, the former sought to exercise influence on American foreign policy by moving into more policy-oriented fields such as humanitarian law (2006, 249).[28] Human Rights Watch also linked the moral language of human rights more tightly to technical legal skills and the cutting edge of the law, drawing more strategically on legal instruments by opening up human rights to more established forms of international law, for example, the laws of war (Dezalay and Garth 2006, 249).[29]

As mentioned above, the Reagan administration had been critical of Carter's deployment of human rights as a foreign policy tool, and attempted initially to dismiss them, and then bend the arc of human rights towards anti-communism. The contest to define the meaning of human rights, argue Dezalay and Garth, contributed to the development and refinement of human rights arguments, underwritten by the introduction of new modes of legal reasoning in the area of international law. In particular, the authors draw attention to the highly mediatized debates between Reagan administration officials, Elliott Abrams in particular, and liberal human rights advocates such as Michael Posner and Aryeh Neier (2002, 135). As dictatorships multiplied, and human rights organizations engaged in more mediatized campaigns, the press pushed human rights organizations towards further professionalization as a way of bolstering their credibility, as Nash's cultural politics model would predict. While Amnesty had "paved the way for the new and more technical role of lawyers in foreign policy" in the 1970s (Dezalay and Garth 2002, 72), these later campaigns contributed enormously to the "legitimacy and importance of law and lawyers in foreign policy debates [as] [t]he expertise of a new generation of lawyers gained a more prominent place" (Dezalay and Garth 2002, 135).

Further impetus for the development of human rights came from Liberal Foundations, which financed courses on campuses and granted fellowships for graduates to apprentice in human rights NGOs. Because of the international orientation of most of the latter, graduates were able to make transnational connections, linking the local field of human rights with international networks (Dezalay and Garth 2006, 250; Keck and Sikkink 1998), enabling the circulation of people, social technologies, modes of political action and institutional organization, and providing the scaffolding for the formation of transnational ethico-political imaginary communities. The authors argue that as "the human rights movement gained in maturity and a level of respectability that garnered acceptance for it as law and not simply as a shield for political action, investment by US legal elites increased considerably" (2002, 164). A clear indicator of such respectability is the development of human rights programmes at elite and worldly campuses such as Columbia, Yale, Harvard, Princeton, and Berkeley (Dezalay and Garth 2002, 164).

Indeed, a number of law professors at elite universities, which had been actively engaged in civil rights in previous decades, moved towards human rights in the 1980s as a way of mitigating the decreasing prestige of the former (Dezalay and Garth 2002, 166). Dezalay and Garth, for instance, report that the launch of the human rights programme at Harvard, undertaken by Henry Steiner, appealed to him because it was "cosmopolitan, intellectual and political (but not so political that it was considered 'not law'), and it also possessed media appeal" (2002, 165). Students were attracted to human rights programmes because they understood human rights as supplying them with new legal weapons to combat injustice abroad, a reading that seemed credible because of the manner in which the liberal press linked the fall of dictatorial regimes to human rights activism (Dezalay and Garth 2002, 165).

As human rights organizations began to recruit from elite law schools (Dezalay and Garth 2006, 151), and the circulation of legal elites from prestigious law schools to human rights organizations and Liberal Foundations got underway, the conditions for the accumulation of human rights juridical capital and its use to re-establish a foothold in foreign policy were created (Dezalay and Garth 2006, 252). Dezalay and Garth conclude their analysis of elite legal investment in the field of human rights by arguing that "[t]he story of human rights [in the US] is one of the building of a relatively high prestige field of practice now connected strongly to the most elite law schools" (2002, 167).[30] Graduates who aspire to put their idealism into legal practice can do so by using human rights in an attempt to influence foreign policy (2002, 167). More broadly, while the investment in human rights has not enabled liberal elites to reclaim sole ownership of the foreign policy establishment, it has permitted them to strike a détente with their former adversaries. Using democracy promotion, good governance, and human rights, they have helped their erstwhile rivals put "a human face on market hegemony" (Dezalay and Garth 2002, 186–97).[31]

Madsen, whose work I discuss in the following section, has argued for the importance of undertaking an "analysis of the gradual emergence of a more structured fields of human rights on the basis of the practices of a series of agents and institutions, which during different historical stages have helped define this social space [the human rights field] and its overriding logics" (2011a, 265). An important logic that has structured the human rights political imaginary in the US, and elsewhere as a result of the US' role as a key contributor to the globalization of the law (Dezalay and Garth 1998, 2002, 2010),[32] has been its emergence and consolidation as a foreign policy tool. Consequently, one of the curious things about the US human rights political imaginary is its external orientation. This perhaps, in part, explains why in Nash's highly informative study, human rights have such little traction in domestic court systems and even amongst the mediated public in the US (2009b, 71–92).[33]

This, along with the US' reluctance to become party to international courts and tribunals or instruments that might boomerang back on to the homeland, is often taken as an instance of US hypocrisy, an instrumentalization of human rights for the narrow pursuit of US foreign policy interests. Though I would not discount hypocrisy in some cases, in the US and elsewhere, I think that perhaps a better explanation might reside in, to use Nash's term, the dynamics of the "cultural politics" that vernacularized the human rights political imaginary in the US. It is significant that human rights began to consolidate as a political imaginary in the US, as Keys (2014) has shown, precisely at a historical and social conjuncture when attention was being turned away from domestic issues such as civil rights and poverty to focus on injustice and oppression abroad. And, that this was to occur at a point where the failure of the grander projects of postwar development had chastised erstwhile liberal promoters, making the minimalist moral politics of the incipient human rights imaginary enticing (Keys 2014, 270). Likewise, the fact that legal elites invested in human rights as a way of recovering lost influence in the foreign policy establishment—rather than to litigate human rights cases in domestic courts, and were able to make links with liberal foundations, illustrious law schools, and leading human rights organizations—strengthened the outward focus of the American human rights political imaginary.

Finally, it is curious that the two main authors discussed above under the rubric of law naïveté, Michael Posner and Emilie M. Hafner-Burton, both American scholars, conclude their review and critique of myriad attempts to institutionalize international human rights legal instruments—that is to say, law naïveté—by arguing that a narrower foreign policy focus would better serve the promotion of human rights. In other words, against cosmopolitan idealism, they assert the need to recover the logic that grounded and, to a large extent, still continues to be the hard core of the US human rights political imaginary. This exclusive foreign policy focus, trained, for the most part, on the "postcolonial and developmentalist state" (Moyn 2014a, 155), though prominent today, is not the only manner in which law has become intertwined with human rights. This will become clear in my discussion, indebted to the work of Madsen, of the development of human rights in the European context in the next section. This provides another opportunity to explore how law and legality become entangled within a human rights political imaginary in a different social-relational and institutional context.

Human Rights in Europe

If, for all the reasons discussed in preceding sections, the US has been one of the key sites for the consolidation of contemporary international human rights, there can be little doubt about the equal significance of Europe. As seen in Chap. 5, many scholars of human rights, citizenship, and cosmopolitanism see Europe as having provided an intensely fertile soil for human rights (Soysal 1994, 2012), establishing a postnational universalism powered by the memory of past human rights abuses (Levy and Sznaider 2010, 122–41). Indeed as Christoffersen and Madsen have argued, "[i]n the broader picture of the build-up of international legal institutions over the twentieth and twenty-first centuries, the ECtHR [The European Court of Human Rights] in many ways is an unparalleled success, perhaps only equalled by the European Court of Justice (ECJ)" (2011, 3).[34] It is seen as a

> powerful international court able and willing to invalidate domestic legislation, constitutional provisions, and State action to fulfill its mandate of ensuring State compliance with the Convention [The European Convention on Human Rights, ECHR] – sometimes in the face of considerable national government opposition. (Cichowski 2011, 78)[35]

Given that the ECHR was created in 1950, by the Council of European States, and that the ECtHR, whose role was to enforce the convention, would follow by nine years (Greer 2006), it would seem that in Europe we have an instance of continuity of the postwar enthusiasm with human rights to the present. Moreover, unlike the US case, the existence of ECtHR would be conducive to the modes of legal reasoning that are the hallmark of the juridical field, contributing to developing human rights' transnational legal autonomy, providing European Human rights with some legal teeth.

At the level of abstract and decontextualized ideas, norms, and principles, it is indeed possible to sense a striking resonance between the UDHR and the ECHR. The latter does make reference to the former. Moreover, philosophical and legal analysis can, with relative ease, show that the same normative and moral lifeblood animates both.[36] However, as I have argued throughout this book, the choreography of philosophical and legal thought, while illuminating in some respects, has its limits. It does not shed light on the social-relational contexts through which normative and philosophical ideas become embedded, embodied, embrained, and inthinged, woven into a political imaginary. In other words, it cannot grasp the social practices that pattern modes of seeing and acting in the world: morality rarely "gets easily translated into laws and legal practice" (Madsen and Verschraegen 2016, 283).

Propounding an approach that dovetails with that proposed in this book, Madsen maintains that a conscious and reflexive effort is required to construct human rights as a "political sociological object of study". Especially so, if analysts intend to steer clear of the pull of the human rights normative riptide that flows into our contemporary moral sensibilities (2011a, 261).[37] Madsen, one of the most accomplished sociolegal scholars of the development of postwar human rights in Europe (Madsen 2007, 2010, 2011a; Christoffersen and Madsen 2011; Madsen and Verschraegen 2013b), argues for the need to understand "the structural transformations" initiated by the emergence of contemporary human rights. For him, "[t]his includes examining the simultaneous differentiation of human rights law and politics, nationally, as well as internationally, and the broad impact on society of these forms of differentiation, rationalization and integration" (2011a, 261).

Drawing on the Bourdieusian concept of the field, he asserts that rather than position one's analysis in terms of the explicit political, legal, or moral stakes delimited by contemporary human rights, sociological analysis must draw attention to the appropriation, circulation, and conversion of the different types of capital that make up human rights, to wit, moral, legal, and political capital (2011a, 263). The field of human rights, where, he notes, competition over the definition, accumulation, and the social power of these capitals take place, intersects with the fields of law, civil society organizations, and the state (2011a, 264), resonating with Nash's schema except for her emphasis on the mediated public. In addition, the human rights field is equally defined by the production and circulation of moral, political, and legal claims between the national, the European, the international, and the transnational spheres (Madsen 2011a, 264).

Madsen's detailed analysis of the development of the field of human rights against the background of its socio-relational and historical institutional context in France, Great Britain, and Scandinavian countries between 1945 and 1970 (2010) provides enormous insight with respect to the structural conditions that encouraged actors in the legal and state fields to (dis)invest in human rights. For instance, in France, juridical capital, hence jurists' ability to convert their capital into political power, was devalued as a result of collaboration with the Vichy Government, not least due to the widespread perception that conservative jurists had been all too willing to invoke "exceptional powers" when this was required by political elites (Madsen 2010, 57). Equally, post-liberation "law" had, in some instances, been politically expedient, legally deficient, if not entirely ad hoc, culminating in summary in situ executions, "justice au coin du bois", as it were (2010, 58).[38]

Human rights offered jurists, who had acquired moral capital as a result of their participation in the resistance, with a quasi-legal discourse with which to position themselves in the postwar, leading to the development of some organizations that took positions on the Cold War and on colonialism (2010, 69–93). However in the larger scale of things, human rights was the preserve of a relatively small group of jurists who drew upon it to facilitate particular political projects, rather than a broader professional strategy (Madsen 2010, 126). It remained marginal: in the words a Madsen, "a political hobby" (2010, 126).

In Great Britain, as in France, the centrality of the development of the postwar welfare state contributed to the decline of the value of juridical vis-à-vis economic and social science academic capital as a *science de l'état.* In response, juridical elites positioned themselves as the guardians of the hallowed public rights of the nation, namely, civil rights, underlining the significance of common law for social and political stability (Madsen 2010, 136). Amongst other things, this was a strategy to secure their bailiwick in the state, where their erstwhile influence was waning (2010, 146). However, because the postwar welfare state codified a consensus of a broader and richer conception of what the state owed its citizens, the citizenship rights described by T. H. Marshall (1950), civil rights paled in comparison.[39] This said, the emerging welfare state also provided ordinary citizens access, via legal aid, to legal services—the significance of which had been noted by T. H. Marshall (1950, 48–52). Legal services had hitherto been reserved to the well heeled. This, in combination with new tribunals where immigration, employment, and social service claims could be tested, opened up some space for more progressive lawyers in a profession that had been characterized by its conservatism (Madsen 2010, 146–49).

Interest in human rights, outside of the venerable civil rights tradition, remained fairly marginal in the early years of the postwar period in Great Britain. Insofar as human rights were mobilized, it was, not as we understand them today, as allegedly apolitical nation-transcending moral or legal principles, but as ideological markers on the terrain of the Cold War. Communists aligned themselves with the English section of the

International Association of Democratic Jurists (IADJ), originally founded by left-leaning French jurists, while anti-communists affiliated themselves with the International Commission of Jurists (ICJ) (Madsen 2010, 155–59).[40] It was the subsequent emergence of Amnesty International, and its ability, not without difficulty,[41] to frame a politically neutral, if not an apolitical, conception of human rights that, as indicated earlier in this book, became a game changer in the field of human rights.

Scandinavian countries reproduce patterns already encountered in the context of France and Great Britain. The considerable expansion of the welfare state and its concomitant citizenship rights, germinated in the postwar social-democratic hegemony, would make human rights virtually irrelevant at the national level (Madsen 2010, 295). The use of human rights as a quasi-legal marker of Cold War ideological allegiance, marginal as it was amongst jurists in France and Great Britain, was practically absent on the Scandinavian scene (Madsen 2010, 294). It is true, argues Madsen, Scandinavian countries invested heavily in the UN, committing themselves strongly to the ideals of peace and the institutionalization of mechanisms for dealing with global conflict. In fact, that first two Secretary Generals of the UN were of Scandinavian provenance, the Norwegian Trygve Halvdan Lie (1946–1952) and the Swede Dag Hammarskjöld (1953–1961) (2010, 225), leading some to talk about the "scandinavization of the UN" (Madsen 2010, 227). This said, many Scandinavian elites were deeply dismayed by the toothless nature of the UDHR (Madsen 2010, 233).

More generally, however, Scandinavian interest in the UN was not so much motivated by a desire to undermine national sovereignty through the internationalization of human rights. Rather, the UN's appeal was the prospect of deploying international tools to foster international cooperation and peace—in other words, to pre-empt wars that might put their own sovereignty at risk, as had occurred in Denmark and Norway during World War II (Madsen 2010, 221–47). To the extent that they were considered at all, and this was infrequent, human rights were subsumed under international public law, rarely being subject to legal refinement (Madsen 2010, 241). In Sweden, for instance, where the University of Uppsala became a pioneering centre for the study of international peace and its link to international development, or in Norway, at the Peace Research Institute in Oslo associated with the trailblazer in the field, Johan Galtung and the *Journal of Peace Research*, notes Madsen, human rights were "conspicuous by their absence" (Madsen 2010, 277, my translation). This leads him to conclude that in the period from 1945 to 1970, human rights were largely eclipsed by other political projects in Scandinavian countries, namely, international cooperation, development, and peace (2010, 296).

What about the ECHR? So closely does it resonate with contemporary human rights, showcasing an irrefutable anti-fascist pedigree, that the fact that it originated as a conservative, and, as seen in Chap. 2, a religious prophylaxis against democratically emerging national communist parties, and the fear of Soviet imperial expansionism, is frequently forgotten, if ever really known (Duranti 2016; Madsen 2007; Moyn 2015).[42] Its *raison d'être* was not to alter or unify the legal practices of the member states under the tutelage of a transnational legal instrument (Madsen 2007, 140), but rather to contain what was perceived as a civilizational threat (Duranti 2016; Moyn 2015). In this sense, key national players such as France and Great Britain understood the drafting of the ECHR as Europeanizing "their own national practices of respectively *libertés publiques* and civil rights" (Madsen 2007, 144), without imperilling their postwar imperial projects (Madsen 2007, 144–47). In other words, it was a reaffirmation of what already existed and was deemed threatened rather than a launching of a new progressive form of transnational legality. It was not an instance of out with the old and in with the new.

For example, despite its considerable contributions to the ECHR, France did not feel under any obligation to ratify the Convention; it did not do so until 1974 (Madsen 2007, 145)! Rather than seeing the ECHR as an international instrument with the capacity to constrain state action, Madsen argues, France folded the Convention into its extant understanding of international public law as "being an issue subject to diplomatic calculations" (2007, 145). This, in fact, mirrored the perception in Britain where human rights were garrisoned in the Foreign Office (Madsen 2007, 146) with the goal of "safeguarding national sovereignty and interests" (Madsen 2007, 147–48). Its emergence as a civilizational and ideological shield against the external and internal threats of communism—"a common conscience for all of (Western) Europe" (Madsen and Christoffersen 2011, 1)—and its instrumentalization as a negotiable diplomatic tool meant that the ECHR, and later the ECtHR, lacked the necessary autonomy to openly undertake the types of juridical modes of reasoning and decision-making associated with the functioning of a juridical field.[43] Another reason for the underdevelopment of ECHR jurisprudence is the ECtHR's virtual inexistent caseload: "[b]y 1964 the Court had decided only two individual cases – Lawless v. Ireland and De Becker v. Belgium – and, a decade later, fourteen years after it had been in operation, this figure had risen to only seventeen" (Greer 2006, 36). This has prompted the human rights legal scholar, Steven Greer, to characterize the mid-1950s to the mid-1980s as a period of "dormancy" for the ECHR system (Greer 2006, 34).

This, however, was to begin to change. Whereas in the immediate postwar period negotiations for the ECHR resonated little with the broader public (Moravcsik 2000, 236–37), by the 1970s, the human rights movement would begin to crystallize and develop as a political imaginary in a manner that it had theretofore not done. And, as was the case in the US, in Western Europe, human rights activism aimed its incipient and highly moralistic political imaginary outwards towards victimized distant and/or excluded others: the Greek colonels, Spain under Franco, Portugal under Salazar, Latin America, South Africa, and Eastern Europe (Madsen 2012, 272). Moreover, severed the highly politicized link between decolonization and the right to self-determination, the growth of the human rights movement, exemplified by Amnesty International, created in Europe, as in the US, a demand for human rights law as opposed to politics (Madsen 2007, 151).

The ECHR, writes Madsen, "began to step out of the cloudy smokescreen of postwar political strategies and jump on the bandwagon of this new legal practice of human rights", facilitated also by the arrival of a new cohort of judges and commissioners whose human rights sensibilities had not been incubated in the context of the subservience to diplomacy that had marked the early days of the ECHR (2007, 152).[44] By the late 1970s, the ECtHR concluded, in a landmark case, that "emergency interrogation measures used in Northern Ireland by the British security forces could not be justified by evoking emergency arguments in [...] Ireland v

United Kingdom", and Madsen notes, "it also reinterpreted the Warren Court's famous motion of 'evolving standards of decency in a maturing society' as the European Convention being a 'living instrument ... which must be interpreted in the light of present-day conditions ... standards in the ... member states'" (2012, 271).[45]

The subsequent trajectory of the European Convention and the Court has certainly taken many by surprise. Given the original wording and intention of the Convention, it would have been hard to predict that the ECHR system would concern itself with the laborious and politically sensitive task of attempting to harmonize human rights law across Europe (Madsen 2007, 138). If in the early years the court had been dormant, it now suffers from a severe "case-overload" (Greer 2006, 38), serving a population of over 800 million from over 40 member states. The ECHR system is not only concerned with securing human rights in Western Europe, it also has been involved in the "transition to democracy and rule of law in Eastern Europe" (Madsen and Christoffersen 2011, 3).

The centrality of contemporary human rights to the European project is not a product of the gradual unfolding of the normative and legal kernels buried in the UDHR or even the ECHR. Instead, it was the intersection of a quasi-legal diplomatic and Cold War dispositif—the ECHR and the ECtHR—with the eruption of the human rights political imaginary in the 1970s. This social-relational and historical juncture enabled Europe as it did the US, to see itself as "the cradle of human rights" with the mission of projecting them abroad (Madsen 2011b, 57). Unlike the US, however, in Europe, the human rights political imaginary not only points towards the outside, it equally points inwards. Indeed, it is frequently taken for granted that respect for human rights is a core value of the European social project (Manners 2006; Soysal 1994, 2012) and, not without difficulty, of its foreign policy (Balfour 2008).

This difference can perhaps be attributed to the fact that in the US the entanglement of law with the human rights political imaginary, and hence the emergence of human rights legal capital, coincided with the efforts of legal elites to recover their influence in the foreign policy establishment. In Europe, however, the ECtHR system became a site for the development of human rights law with the goal of both projecting human rights abroad and, crucially, also contributing to a process of

"Europeanization both in terms of integrating European society and building European law" (Madsen 2011b, 58).[46] In this sense, the Cold War ideological imperative of providing a broad European civilizational identity, embedded in the ECHR, was not lost as the human rights political imaginary took hold in Europe in the 1970s; it was successfully juridified.

Madsen, and Dezalay and Garth's analyses of the social-relational and historical contexts of how the juridical field became entangled with human rights contribute much to an understanding of human rights as political imaginary. In the next section, I more briefly discuss two more cases, Chile and Canada. However before doing so, there are two more aspects of Madsen's analysis that I would like to touch upon. Madsen, successfully to my mind, positions his work as contributing to the historical and sociolegal scholarship that draws attention to the 1970s as the period where human rights had their breakthrough (2012, 258). This said, Madsen has also been concerned to highlight some of the continuities between the postwar and the decade of the 1970s.

It is true that, in Europe, the ECHR was instrumentalized as an ideological and diplomatic tool in the context of the Cold War and the incipient movements of decolonization. However, he equally maintains that jurists-diplomats, precisely because they were jurist-diplomats, were, in fact, able to develop juridical mechanisms that would be activated in the 1970s as result of the aforementioned structural and geopolitical transformations (Madsen 2007, 2010, 2011b, 2012). On my reading, it is not clear whether he understands the intersection between the ECtHR and the rise of the human rights political imaginary as a contingent process for which he provides a genealogical survey—in the Foucauldian sense, or if the events of the 1970s liberated a potential contained in the ECHR and the ECtHR that had to await propitious conditions before being actualized. If it is the latter case, then his account could be read a socio-historically nuanced narrative of contemporary human rights whose roots are traced back to the UDHR. I would add that his apparent adhesion to a modernist/rationalist conceptions of human rights via Luhmannian theory (Madsen and Verschraegen 2013a, 7) makes such a reading plausible, though much of his empirical arguments, to my mind, point in the opposite direction.

Second, while Madsen's focus on the anti-communist ideological nature of the ECHR chimes with that of other scholars (Moravcsik 2000; Moyn 2015; Duranti 2016), the significance of the Christian conservative contribution to the ECHR is absent. As Moyn has shown, insofar as a critique of right-wing fascism was a component of the ECHR, it was in part an attempt to distance Christian conservative thought from the illiberalism with which, with disastrous ends, European conservatives had flirted earlier in the century (2015, 15; Duranti 2016, 9). Moreover this complicates the facile equation of the ECHR with anti-fascism. As Marco Duranti has argued, rather than a confrontation with the reality of Nazism in Germany, the ECHR was seen by many European conservatives as "a reconciliation with Germany, whose leaders were then seeking to distance the nation from its Nazi past through a return to the Christian ethos that they believed had once united it with the West" (2016, 193). What is more, the conservative adoption of the language of human rights facilitated reconciliation with and the amnesty of right-wing political prisoners, in effect putting an end to the processes of denazification. Duranti argues that while this might have contributed to the stabilization of democratic regimes in Europe, "it also strengthened the hand of apologists for collaborationist regimes and those refusing to acknowledge widespread complicity in the Holocaust" (2016, 403).

Duranti highlights, "[h]uman rights in the ECHR were not the rights of individuals abstracted from their socio-political context, past and present, as in the case of the Universal Declaration" (2016, 201). Instead, "[a]t the heart of postwar conservative Europeanism was the advance of *European* human rights, understood not as universal entitlements, but rather as the distinctive birthright of those living within the borders of what remained of Christendom" (2016, 209).[47] These issues are not merely historical curiosities. They raise the question of the extent to which this civilizational ethos remains embedded in the jurisprudence of the ECtHR and in the broader European political vision. Two recent scholarly contributions worryingly suggest they do (Moyn 2015, 137–67; Gündoğdu 2015, 109–16).[48]

Human Rights' Legal Entanglements in Chile and Canada

Having explored the entanglement of law with the human rights political imaginaries in the US and in Europe, I now more briefly discuss two more cases, Chile and Canada. This will enable me to point to the diversity of situations where law has met with and has become intertwined with the human rights political imaginary, and the different factors that influenced the braids that they plaited.

As I noted above, Dezalay and Garth argue that the legal field in the US is characterized by a schizophrenic quality. It is able to combine work on behalf of corporate interests with "investment in public service and law reform"; indeed, business lawyers who wish to pursue elite careers are "expected to invest in the promotion of legal services" (2002, 51). Human rights organizations and the field of human rights more generally have continued to be important recipients of such public service in the US. Not only does it exemplify the public commitments that the profession expects, it also enables legal capital to be trained on the "cutting edge of US foreign policy" (Dezalay and Garth 2002, 55). In their study of efforts to export "US-style law" to Latin America, in particular Argentina, Brazil, Chile, and Mexico, Dezalay and Garth find that US legal elites have been more successful in transplanting "US-style business law" than "US-style public interest law", such as human rights (Dezalay and Garth 2002, 56).

This is rather surprising not least in the context of Chile, which played an iconic role in the development and promotion of international human rights. As Keck and Sikkink argue,

> Chilean organizations that were formed to confront government repression, especially the Catholic church's human right office, the Vicaria de la Solidaridad, became models for human rights groups throughout Latin America and sources of information and inspiration for human rights activists in the United States and Europe. (1998, 90)

Chile's trailblazing role in the promotion of international human rights, however, did not arise from a long-established human rights tradition, or from the development of the possibilities inherent in the UDHR in the Latin American postwar era (Moyn 2010, 143–44). In fact, at the time of Pinochet's coup, whose brutal repression would be the catalyst for what was to become an internationally exemplary human rights movement, human rights as a discourse was largely absent in Chile. What is more, the Chilean legal profession had largely supported the deposing of the Allende government, so the question of the legality of the coup was not a key issue for the profession at large (Dezalay and Garth 2002, 145).

The human rights movement was seeded by an alliance of opposition politicians, Christian Democrats in particular, and the Chilean church, receiving strong international support via the World Council of Churches, the US National Council of Churches, as well as from several European sources (Dezalay and Garth 2002, 145–46). The formation of the Peace Committee, under the auspices of the church, initiatied the recruitment of opposition lawyers in an effort to use the discredited legal system, because nothing else was available, to introduce some restraint on the rampant and deadly impunity of the military regime. They attempted to do so by filing habeas corpus petitions for those detained, and by providing legal defence in military courts (Dezalay and Garth 2002, 146).

International interest in Chile had been triggered by Allende's socialist electoral success and did not abate after the military coup. Major international news organizations, the UN, and Amnesty International, amongst others, closely monitored the situation, attracting "visibility, funding and moral support to Chilean groups" (Keys 2014, 79). Peace Committee activists established links with Amnesty International and other human rights organizations at a time when some legal investment in human rights was underway in the US and elsewhere, and human rights as a political imaginary was taking institutional and social-relational shape, gaining international traction.[49] Although initially Chilean activists drew on the language of "the constitution" and "the rights of the defendant" in their opposition to the military regime, they would quickly adopt the emerging human rights vernacular (Dezalay and Garth 2002, 146). As Moyn argues, "Christian appeals to human rights were ideologically important at a time when the military dictatorship depended on its rhetorical association with Christianity" (2010, 145). Although the Peace Committee was disbanded in 1975 by the military regime, human rights activism and censure of the regime continued under the umbrella of the Vicaria de la Solidaridad (Dezalay and Garth 2002, 146). The religious and "the moral framing of this criticism [...] made it difficult simply to liquidate [the Vicaria de la Solidaridad] as a dangerous political threat" (Moyn 2010, 145). The representation of human rights as morally transcending partisan politics not only provided activists some measure of protection from the regime's violence, it also, and crucially, provided a moral and, protestations to the contrary, a minimalist political vocabulary that enabled a concatenation of diverse political positions to coalesce into a common front against the regime's impunity (Moyn 2010, 147).

Dezalay and Garth report that "legally oriented human rights organizations thrived" in both the US and Latin America in the late 1970s and 1980s (2002, 53), actively participating in the building of the political and moral scaffolding that would support the transitions to democracy (2002, 54). Lawyers, who had invested in human rights in Latin America, used their human rights equity as collateral to faciliate their entry into politics and to occupy positions of power in the post-dictatorship period. However, what is striking, note the authors, is that, unlike the US where elite legal investment continues to this day, and one might also add Europe, in Latin America, a second wave of significant legal investment in human rights did not take place (2002, 54). This is because human rights law did not become an important source of judicial capital in the fields of power of the respective countries. In their words,

> [t]he particular conjuncture that had united moral activism with law through the church and international actors did not continue. The newly created institutional structures that built the human rights NGOS unravelled, revealing the structures that had been in place prior to the 1970s. (2002, 54)[50]

If human rights frequently invokes, in people's minds, the struggles of Chilean groups battling the brutality and impunity of the Pinochet Regime in the 1970s, and other such struggles throughout Latin America, much less is known about a more peaceful, though certainly not conflict-free, contemporaneous transformation. It has been described as the *Canadian Human Rights Revolution* (Clément 2008), triggering the development of the "Canadian Human Rights State" (Clément 2008, 25), and, in the words of the sociologist Dominique Clément, one of the world's most sophisticated human rights legal regimes that incorporates

> professional human rights investigators, public education, promoting legal reform, representing complaints before formal inquiries, jurisdiction over public and private sectors, a focus on conciliation over litigation, independence from the government, and an adjudication process as an alternative to courts. (2013, 103)

Yet, as human rights scholar, former broadcaster, and politician, Michael Ignatieff notes, in his preface to an important contribution to the historiography of human rights (Heathorn and Goutor 2013), in Canada, all of this seems strangely disconnected from the processes that internationalized human rights,

> Canadian rights traditions did not provide a ready home for international human rights and to this day, when the United Nations human rights bodies dares criticize Canada's record, the hostile reactions tell you how strongly many Canadians believe that they have nothing to learn from international rights norms. The Canadian Charter of Rights and Freedoms incorporates [some of] these norms into the Canadian constitutional framework, and yet in doing so says to Canadians, in effect you need look no further than Canadian law for remedy. (2013, viii)

Indeed as scholars have shown, not only did Canada not welcome the UDHR; at times, it actually expressed open hostility towards it. The Canadian Government was extremely reluctant to vote in favour of the Declaration at the UN. It used the subterfuge that the UDHR represented an intrusion in provincial jurisdictions (Clément 2012; Schabas 1997), when, in reality, the concern was linked to some of the declaration's substantive norms, such as freedom of religion and association, not to mention cultural, social, and economic norms (Schabas 1997; MacLennan 2003, 69–82). In fact, the Canadian government only began participating in the covenant negotiations in earnest, when its early hopes that they would not come to pass was shattered, and even then only to make "the best of a bad job" (Tunnicliffe 2013, 184).

Many scholars writing about human rights in Canada generally accept that the term human rights is of recent provenance, but nonetheless insist on using it as a purported analytical category that can be projected backwards on to earlier civil liberty and anti-discrimination struggles. In other words, they transform it from a concrete crystallization of social-relational forces into an evaluative ethical, moral, or political category. For instance, the historian Christopher MacLennan provides an excellent account of the social and political trajectories that converged towards the first Canadian National Bill of Rights, introduced by the Diefenbaker Government in 1960. He draws on the human rights legal scholar and activist Philip Alston to define a bill of rights as "a formal commitment to the protection of those human rights which are considered at that moment in history, to be of particular importance" (Alston in MacLennan 2003, 11). MacLennan adds, "While Canadian bill of rights advocates seemed to have an intuitive grasp of what the concept meant, this definition captures the general meaning of the term as it would have been understood by the participants themselves", in effect framing earlier struggles as human rights struggles retroactively by philosophical fiat. Similarly, Evelyn Kallen, in her widely read *Ethnicity and Human Rights in Canada: A Human Rights Perspective on Race, Ethnicity, Racism and Systemic Inequality* (2003), draws on human rights as a normative category of analysis capable of subsuming all struggles against racial and ethnic discrimination, while the political scientist Brian Howe, who defines human rights as "universal moral rights" (1991, 784), uses the term to narrate the history of what is essentially anti-discrimination legislation in Ontario (1991) and in Canada (Howe and Johnson 2000). The historian Ross Lambertson equally excavates the origins of contemporary human rights in the activism in the 1930s (2005).[51]

Clément, who has contributed significantly to our understanding of the development of the politics of rights in Canada from the postwar to the 1970s and 1980s through a social movements lens (2008, 2009, 2012, 2013), differentiates between earlier forms of limited civil liberties campaigning and the more robust human rights activism. He links the latter to the human rights revolution in Canada (2008).[52] Following

Moyn, he locates the breakthrough period for human rights in Canada in the 1970s. He associates this phenomenon with the broader effervescence around human rights globally—as indicated by the ratifications of the two Covenants, the introduction of provincial and federal human rights legislation prohibiting discrimination in employment, housing, and accommodation and their concomitant human rights commissions, and the entry into force of the Canadian Charter of Rights and Freedoms (2012, 762). Much of the preceding, he argues, takes place against the background of the explosion of the new social movements, adopting the language of human rights and its associated defence of economic, social, and cultural rights to overcome the limits of civil liberties activism (2008).

Clément's exposition of key aspects of rights activism is extremely valuable; however, his account of the intersection, and interaction, between international and local "human rights", to my mind, is not altogether persuasive. In particular, his distinction between human rights and civil liberties is particularly troublesome. Not least because in the period of the 1970s and early 1980s, the focus in the international human rights movements, as the numerous historians cited throughout this book have underlined, was on civil and political rights. The international pivot towards economic, cultural, and social human rights came later, emerging in the late 1980s and early 1990s and, for the most part, in the global south (López 2015; Nelson and Dorsey 2008). It seems more plausible to see the social movements he describes as being primarily concerned with an intensification of citizenship rights claims, arising from anti-discrimination movements, and inspired more by the civil rights, and anti-poverty movements (Piven 1971; Piven and Cloward 1979), south of the border, than international human rights.

It has to be conceded, however, that when one conceptualizes human rights thinly as an idea or a principle of equality, there does, at first blush, seem to be some reason to entertain the notion that the UDHR had a role to play in the developments of the rights movements in Canada. There is throughout the postwar occasional mention of human rights or reference to the UDHR by civil libertarian and anti-discrimination activists. More rare still, but not entirely absent, are mentions of the UN instruments by jurists. For instance, Clément makes reference to a frequently quoted court decision made in 1945 by Ontario Justice MacKay where the justice cites the Charter of the United Nations in striking down a restrictive covenant. All the same, Justice MacKay equally cited "statements denouncing anti-Semitism from President Franklin D. Roosevelt, Prime Minister Winston Churchill, General Charles de Gaulle, the World Trade Union Congress, the Latin American–US Act of Chapultepec and the constitution of the Soviet Union" (Bruner 1979, 244). Said differently, the citation was strategic rather than authoritative.[53] What is undoubtedly true, though, is that in the postwar era, an important anti-discrimination movement did emerge; for social, demographic, and economic reasons, the province of Ontario provided one of its main stages on the Canadian scene. At times the term "human rights" was uttered from this stage. Even so, what is far from clear is the actual impact of the UDHR in plotting the course of this movement.

In Ontario, in the 1940s and 1950s, interest group movements were instrumental in pushing for an anti-discrimination agenda. Labour organizations, ethno-cultural groups—in particular Jewish associations—and civil liberty groups lobbied for anti-discrimination legislation, leading to the Racial Discrimination Act in 1944, which prohibited the public display of discriminatory signs and notices (Howe and Johnson 2000, 7; Bruner 1979; Patrias and Frager 2001). However, as Brian R. Howe and David Johnson argue, early efforts to criminalize discrimination were largely unsuccessful: victims were resistant to use the court system, police unlikely to investigate allegations, and "judges were reluctant to convict even if the evidence was substantial", not recognizing discrimination as a "real crime" (Howe and Johnson 2000, 7; Bruner 1979, 242). Subsequently, a "fair practices" approach focusing on employment and housing legislation, modelled on the legislation of New York State,[54] was introduced in the 1950s in Ontario, with a number of other provinces following suit (2000, 8). This process culminated in 1961 with the creation of Ontario Human Rights Commission, the first of its kind in Canada, to implement the 1962 Ontario Human Rights Code (Bruner 1979; Eberlee and Hill 1964; Howe 1991; Howe and Johnson 2000; Patrias and Frager 2001). Once again where Ontario led, the other provinces followed (Howe and Johnson 2000, 9–22).

Nonetheless, it must be born in mind that despite the fact that the term human rights appears in the abovementioned contexts, the real referent is more plausibly the anti-discrimination legislation south of the 49th parallel (Eberlee and Hill 1964, 448), which had little truck with the UDHR. For instance, the Jewish Labour Committee of Canada (JLC), an important pressure group in the movement to end discrimination, saw lobbying for US-style "fair practices" legislation as the most effective means of pursuing their agenda for social change (Bruner 1979, 237). More generally, if one can talk about transnational links in the anti-discrimination struggles of a variety of Jewish organizations, these were with US counterparts (Patrias and Frager 2001, 2013), rather than with the UDHR or international human rights jurisprudence. The latter, as I indicated above, was virtually non-existent until the late 1970s. Similarly, African-Canadian and Japanese-Canadian anti-discrimination activists paid close attention to and imitated their US analogues (Patrias and Frager 2001, 9). In fact, the 1958 Act, which led to the establishment of the Ontario Human Rights Commission, was formally called an Act to Establish the Ontario Anti-Discrimination Commission (Eberlee and Hill 1964, 448–49).[55]

In other words, it is only if we think of human rights as an "ideal" (Clément 2012, 754) of equality, abstracted from the social-relational context that would give it its international legs in the 1970s, that the peppering of anti-discrimination activism and legislation with the term "human rights" can be construed as deriving from the UDHR or international human rights. Thus, when strikingly, Frager and Patrias write, "[i] n fact, the organization and tactics of the Ontario campaigns for *human rights* legislation were remarkably similar to those of *campaigns against discrimination* in the United States" (2001, 16, my emphasis), they are displaying how their commitment to human rights as a normative category of analysis trumps their excellent historical scholarship that points to the significance of US anti-discrimination movements rather than to the international human rights political imaginary that would erupt on the scene in the 1970s.

Of course, subsequently, the international human rights political imaginary does intersect with domestic anti-discrimination and fair practices legislation. And, to be sure, National Human Rights Commissions (NHRC) have become part of the social technologies and organizational make-up of the contemporary human rights political imaginary (Hafner-Burton 2013, 164–75),[56] and Canada has attempted to exports its home-grown expertise in this field to exemplify its commitment to international human rights (Cardenas 2003). However, if the goal is to understand how Canadian anti-discrimination and equity legislation got entangled within the international human rights political imaginary, it behoves us to stop thinking of human rights as an idea or a principle and conceptualize it, instead, as the constellation of relatively stable, though certainly not unchanging, practices falling under the umbrella of the human rights political imaginary.

Another component of the Canadian human rights story, which Clément, as pointed out above, inserts into the chain reaction provoked by the "human rights revolution" is the coming into effect of the Canadian Charter of Rights of Freedoms in 1982, which today many Canadians effortlessly associate with human rights. All the same, it is important to be cognizant of the fact that though the Charter does echo the UDHR and other human rights instruments, its true inspiration is more likely the US Bill of Rights rather than the Universal Declaration or the related Covenants. As Canadian legal scholar Harry W. Arthurs has noted,

> beguiled by the civil rights jurisprudence of the Warren Court – Canada adopted its Charter of Rights and Freedoms in 1982, the predictable consequences of which include the increasingly frequent citation in Canadian courts of constitutional jurisprudence and secondary literature, and arguably, the slow transformation of Canada's legal and political culture. (2000, 390–91)[57]

It is certainly true that Canadian courts have drawn, along with US case law, on international case law, including jurisprudence from the European Court of Human Rights (Schabas 2000, 185). However, despite Canada recognizing the UDHR as "an authoritative interpretation of the human rights obligations contained in the U.N. charter", legal scholars have argued, "Canada does not view the Declaration itself as creating any legally binding obligation in international (or, presumably, domestic) law" (Hannum 1995, 331). Recourse to international case law and instruments can perhaps be understood, following John Claydon, as a fulfilment of the Charter's invitation to "consider comparative and international sources", or "the basic need to draw on the wisdom of other systems in giving meaning to the Charter, and a rule of construction which permits both customary and conventional international law to be used as aids for interpreting domestic law" (1986, 354). Thus, despite the resonance of international human rights instruments in the formulation of the Charter rights, which can perhaps more credibly be traced to the US Bill of Rights, Canadian courts have insisted, "the Charter is not implementing legislation for those international instruments" (Claydon 1986, 353).

As indicated above, my aim is not to deny that the Charter is now intertwined with the international human rights political imaginary. In fact, the globalization of law (Halliday and Osinsky 2006) is likely to continue ravelling the two in ever more complicated twists. This, however, does not obviate the fact that the international human rights political imaginary, which emerged in the late 1960s and 1970s, did not pave the road to the Charter. Two fundamental issues motivated the Charter's main architect, Prime Minister Pierre Elliott Trudeau (Russell 1983). First, fuelled by a lifetime commitment to civil libertarian principles, he aspired to entrench a bill of rights in the Canadian constitution (Behiels 2009, 201), *à l'américaine*. Second, by enshrining cherished Canadian political values in a constitution, he hoped that the Charter would strengthen Canadian identity and the sense of national unity, which Quebec separatism was putting to the test (Behiels 2009, 206).

That Canada, as was happening in the US and the EU, would define itself as having always already been a human rights nation in the late 1970s and 1980s is hardly surprising, not least because human rights was emerging as an international idiom for distinguishing between acceptable and unacceptable forms of political rule, of which more below. In addition, it is possible to concede that in the absence of a Canadian bill of rights entrenched in a constitution, civil libertarian and anti-discrimination activists would at times invoke human rights or the UDHR in the postwar (Bangarth 2013, 120). However, such appeals were for a constitutionally entrenched bill of rights or for anti-discrimination legislation and differed from the ethico-political claims on behalf of distant and/or excluded victimized others that, as I have argued, developed later around the emergence of the international human rights political imaginary. When the international human rights political imaginary intersected both with demands for a bill of rights and anti-discrimination activism and legislation, there is no doubt that the effect of legal resonance was produced. In other words, legal developments on the ground—anti-discrimination legislation, the human rights commission system, and political and legal arguments culminating in the Charter—appeared to respond to the ethico-political claims of the international human rights political imaginary. But the crucial question to which I return below is why. If one is to understand this resonance, there is no other option but to explore the intersections of international human rights, civil liberties, and anti-discrimination activism as constellations of practices, rather than assume their unity through recourse to a thin conception of human rights.

The entanglement of the human rights political imaginary with law in the US, the EU, Chile, and Canada has tied a variety of social-relational knots. The shape, thickness, and tightness of these knots have been a function of how a structured moral and political imaginary, initially devoid of the power of the law, intersected with differently structured legal fields, and the location of the latter in the broader fields of power in their corresponding polities. In the US, the foreign policy focus of a legally charged human rights political imaginary has to be understood as arising from the conjunction of legal elites' interest in recovering influence in the foreign policy establishment, and the broader social historical context that made the US receptive to a new morality for its foreign policy. This however precluded that the human rights political imaginary would be trained domestically, ensuring that the focus of human rights would be on the ethico-political claims of distant victimized others, shutting out the possibility that it might be directed domestically at those of excluded victimized others.

In the EU, a Cold War conservative proto-legal apparatus, which had been conceived principally as a vehicle to confront a civilizational threat through (Christian) continental unity—the ECHR and the ECtHR—had gained sufficient autonomy, via careful diplomatic manoeuvres, that it could credibly become a key site for the juridification of the emergent human rights political imaginary in the 1970s. To the initial outward focus on the ethico-political claims of distant victimized others, which had characterized the emergent human rights political imaginary, was added an inward-looking dimension. The legally entangled human rights political imaginary became a medium for imagining the shared transnational socio-political space of the EU. Unlike what happened in the US, then, in the EU a space was opened within the human rights political imaginary to receive and consider the ethico-political claims of excluded others.

In both the EU and the US, there was elite legal buy-in, assuring the legally entangled human rights imaginary a space in the broader field of state power, in the European transnational space and the individual member states in the former,[58] and in foreign policy in the case of the latter. In Chile, the human rights political imaginary met with the law via the ethico-political claims of victimized distant others that were directed at the international community and those of the victimized excluded others whose addressee was Chilean society. Despite playing an important role in framing transitional and post-transitional conceptions of justice and democracy, according to Dezalay and Garth, the broader legal field and the field of state power have been much less receptive to a legally entangled human rights political imaginary.[59]

In Canada, as far as I am aware, research has not been undertaken on elite legal reception of human rights, the status of the latter in legal education, or its value as a source of legal capital in the juridical field along the lines undertaken by Dezalay and Garth, and Madsen.[60] Anti-discrimination legislation had determined that the courts were not "the best mechanisms for addressing legally proscribed social behaviours" (Howe and Johnson 2000, 39). This eventuated in the agency/commission model, where "truth finding" administrative processes, eschewing an adversarial attitude, focused instead on conciliation and mediation (Howe and Johnson 2000, 44–45). When a conciliatory approach failed, there was provision for a semijudicial proceeding, adjudicated by notables who were, frequently, but not, always law professors (Howe and Johnson 2000, 46). The 1982 Charter of Rights and Freedoms was more significant for the legal profession and legal education, coming into effect in a context where increasing numbers of law school professors actively pursued "advocacy scholarship favouring liberal judicial interpretation of civil rights and liberties" (Epp 1996, 71).[61] It is these two sets of social-political processes—that is, anti-discrimination activism and legislation and a bill of rights, which have at times intersected—that have become the legal bearers of the international human rights political imaginary, and from which arises Canada's claim to being a human rights state both domestically and in its foreign policy (Clément 2012, 769).

However, as I argued above, these two institutional sites had evolved in relative isolation from the international human rights political imaginary. I think that it would not be controversial to say that both Canadian anti-discrimination legislation leading to the human rights commissions system and the Charter would have occurred absent the surge of the human rights political imaginary in the 1970s. This is not to deny that today both are entangled within the human rights political imaginary, but understanding these entanglements necessitates resisting the temptation to see them as having originally been cut from the same cloth.

The Canadian case is an excellent example of Posner's assertion that generally the international human rights systems have not required developed countries "to do anything different", *domestically* I would add, than they were already doing (2014, 31). This, in part, explains why when the human rights political imaginary matured internationally; these countries were able to credibly claim that they had always already been human rights nations. This is important because it has contributed to obscuring the origin of contemporary human rights, in the minimalist politics associated with the human rights political imaginary of the 1970s, and has been conducive towards presenting human and citizenship rights as endocentric compounds. This is a relationship that has subsequently been defended on normative, but not on sociological and historical grounds. In order to explore this further, in the next section, I return to the work of Anthony Woodiwiss, which I introduced in Chap. 4. Woodiwiss draws attention to the social-structural limits of the autonomy of the law and how the entanglement of the human rights political imaginary with international law at the UN has contributed to erasing the significance of social-structural variation within the contemporary human rights political imaginary.

Law's Autonomy in Embeddedness[62]

In Chap. 4, I presented Woodiwiss' conceptualization of human rights in the context of my discussion of the concept of a practice. It will be recalled that he argues that, viewed sociologically, "human rights are nothing special"; they are "simply a subset of the much larger set of social relations that produce and enforce behavioural expectations, a subset distinguished by their legal form and their focus on the limitations of abuses of power" (2012, 967). Not unlike the authors discussed above, he detects a degree of law naïveté in contemporary thinking about human rights. It is nested in the widely held assumption that once "certain rights have been proclaimed, they will either be self-enforcing or automatically enforced by *whatever sets of social relations,* or institutions already exist" (2003, 22, my emphasis). Whereas Hafner-Burton and Posner point to the weakness of the international human rights law system itself as an explanation for its contemporary lack of efficacy, Woodiwiss draws attention to the Achilles heel that threatens any legal enterprise: namely, a lack of embeddedness and congruence with the prevailing social relations. Let me explain.

In agreement with much contemporary sociolegal scholarship, Woodiwiss agrees that a *necessary* condition for the autonomy of the law is the use of modes of legal reasoning by jurists to produce consistency in the interpretation of the law (2003, 14). He adds, however, that

> "consistency" is never either a sufficient or a self-subsisting sign in legal, or in any other form of discourse. Legal consistency must, therefore, always be a means of ensuring that a substantive principle applies equally to all, to those that enunciate the law as well as to those to whom it is perhaps more directly addressed. (2003, 14)

What this means, contends Woodiwiss, is that the rule of law should not be understood as being intrinsically linked to any substantive political philosophy—such as liberalism—as is frequently the case. Instead, it must be grasped as "a social structural-effect, namely the reduction of arbitrariness" (2003, 15) in the exercise of social power. Moreover, and paradoxically, the autonomy of the law is ineradicably linked to its ability to mobilize a substantive principle—say liberty, equality, or familialism—

that is embedded within, and congruent with, "the wider discourses, structures and practices of society if it is to be enforceable" (2003, 15). As a consequence, the absence of any particular substantive philosophical ideal, for instance, "liberty", cannot be read as signalling the absence of the rule of law, as such. It is "judicial particularism/or inactivity" that indicates that the rule of law is at risk (Woodiwiss 2003, 15).

In formal terms, rights can be interpreted as

> discursively defined clusters of "liberties" to perform certain actions; "claims" or expectations vis-à-vis specified others; "powers" that allow legal subjects to assume certain specified roles and change certain social relations; and "immunities" against prosecution and/or civil suit when pursuing ends that are otherwise defined as illegal. (Woodiwiss 2003, 15)

The relative balance among these different components, as well as their content, cannot be abstracted from the social relations in which rights are inscribed, or the power relations that they are intended to curb, as suggested by Somers' felicitous expression "liberty in embeddedness" (1994a, 78), cited in Chap. 5. Rights, then, when seen sociologically, as a social mechanism for the reduction of arbitrariness in the exercise of power, cannot be defined in terms of concrete ends. They are better conceptualized as "practical means available to pursue a protective ethical end that can be very variously specified" (Woodiwiss 2003, 2). What is more, the ability to deliver the protection that they promise is, as just noted, contingent on the protective end, and its particular combination of components—that is, claims, powers, liberties, and immunities, resonating with the social discourses, practices, and structures of the social context in question.

A number of important conceptual and explanatory insights follow from Woodiwiss' iconoclastic, yet sociologically sound, conceptualization of rights. First, rights have to be understood not in opposition to power, but as a product of power (Woodiwiss 2005a, 15). Second, rights, and law more generally, "can only do what the remainder of social structure allows [them] to do, including contributing to social change, if there are supportive social-structural dynamics, and cannot change social relations on [their] own" (Woodiwiss 2003, 18). Third, rights should not be regarded as transcendent principles sketching the outline of the good society (Woodiwiss 2005a, 15). When they work effectively, and they do not always do so, they offer basic forms of protection such as freedom from certain types of state violence, hunger, and overwork and allow rights bearers to engage in certain forms of action such as speech, association, or collective bargaining (Woodiwiss 2003, 6), that is, Turner's "juridical shield" against vulnerability (Turner 2006, 29). Compared to more expansive, or even utopian, readings of rights, these minimal protections do not appear like much; yet we would be worse off, and many unfortunately are, in their absence.

Fourth, rights do not guarantee substantive equality and are therefore not equally beneficial for all right bearers (Woodiwiss 2005a, 136). T. H. Marshall, as noted in the preceding chapter, of course, discerned this in his account of citizenship rights through the recognition that the equality of citizenship status makes economic inequality and social stratification acceptable. Needless to say, there are other symptoms of such stratification such as the intractable incivility that can swell at the very core of civil society (Alexander 2006, 50). In fact, rights tend to sacralize the inequalities upon which they are founded. Thus, in capitalist society, the autonomy individuals enjoy rest on the inviolability of private property, and the inequities that are generated in consequence, not least because the legal force of autonomy is moored to the manner in which the legal concept of contract interfaces with both property and employment (Woodiwiss 2005a, 43).[63] And fifth, rights are generally conservative and contribute to reproducing the prevailing relations of power in society (Woodiwiss 2005a, 5). However, although rights generally accommodate and do not threaten dominant relations of power, they do enable right bearers to struggle to extend or entrench the protection rights offers. Such struggles though not capable of dislodging dominant relations of power, on their own, can contribute to curtailing the extremes of, and arbitrariness in, the exercise of social power (Woodiwiss 2003, 8), to my mind, a non-negligible social good.

What light, then, does this account of rights shed on our understanding of the entanglement of law with the human rights political imaginary? It suggests that, unlike more sanguine readings discussed in the preceding chapters, even in the best of situations, that is to say, when the legal field is receptive to the human rights political imaginary, and the resultant legal concepts are in alignment with the prevalent social relations, human rights, alone, are unlikely to become the vehicles with which current relations of domination are to be circumvented. In situations where there is little correspondence between the discourses and the social-structural arrangements around which social practices are organized, the lack of embeddedness of the law means that it will have limited autonomy, and more to the point, little social power. This perhaps might better account for, or at least significantly complement, the analyses focusing on the institutional weakness of the international human rights systems, and the proposed attempts to overcome them, described above. In addition, Woodiwiss' exploration of how "human rights" became entangled with law in the UN sheds light on how it is that we have come to think about human and citizenship rights as endocentric compounds, to which I now turn, before concluding this chapter.

For Woodiwiss, the UN is the cradle of "human rights". Limited to a cameo role in the founding Charter (2003, 24), they took centre stage in the UDHR in 1948, and the subsequent drafting of the covenants. Reflecting the geopolitical divisions of the time, "human rights" were torn between their political and legal personae. Scripted by diplomats, rather than lawyers, they enacted the geopolitical tension at the time between capitalist and socialist societies, played out in the distinction between civil and political rights, associated with Western liberal political and legal traditions, and the economic, social, and cultural rights that resonated with the socialist critique of capitalism. Woodiwiss notes that, ultimately, the starring role in the UDHR went to the former, as evidenced by the fact that of the 24 specific "human rights" articles, 18 refer to civil and political rights, with only the remaining six indexing economic and social rights (2005a, 89).

Economic, social, and cultural rights were cast in the role of a supporting, if not a minor, character. Overall, then, the rights enumerated in the UDHR conveyed a Western image of the "good society", to use Roosevelt's expression, in which private property was sacrosanct, and the rule of law was associated with well-entrenched civil and political rights and the broad range of social services that were emerging in the context of the welfare state (Woodiwiss 2005a, 89). In subsequent years, to the extent that "human rights" were invoked, it was as ideological political circumlocutions, rather than legal concepts or the site of a global consensus. In fact, human rights were used precisely to signify dissensus! This, however, would begin to change in the 1970s as the UN became more interested in "questions of enforcement and enforceability", and the two Covenants, having been approved by the General Assembly in 1966, travelled the road of ratifications, coming into force in 1976 (Woodiwiss 2003, 26). Perhaps most important of all, argues Woodiwiss, was the juridification of "human rights" as "legal concepts and ways of thinking gradually displac[ing] political ones in the UN's handling of 'human rights' issues" (2003, 29, scare quotes added).

One of the consequences of this transcription of "politically inspired texts into legal modes of reasoning" was that it erased from "human rights" discourse, at the UN, something that had been visible in the earlier period of political confrontation between political and civil, and social and economic rights, namely, that they were grounded in competing social-structural arrangements, capitalist and socialist, respectively (Woodiwiss 2003, 29). A second ramification of legal entanglement at the UN is that "human rights" became defined by the notion of justiciability, namely, "the requirement that for a right to be properly so called, judicial remedies must be available where violations occur" (2003, 29). This, naturally, led to the well-rehearsed distinction between the purported justiciable nature of civil and political rights and the programmatic and aspirational social, economic, and cultural "human rights". Significantly, developments since have moved "human rights" further in the direction of juridification, and their tight affiliation with justiciability. Indeed Woodiwiss concludes that

> legal and political discourses now co-exist under the terms established by the hegemony of the legal discourse, with the result that even the proponents of politically inspired arguments can only hope to make a difference if they use legal terms or, minimally, do not challenge legal norms or procedures – legal reasoning, then, is now virtually the only possible way of working within the conceptual field of "human rights". (2003, 32, scares quotes added)

In Chap. 5, I noted that one of the reasons why citizenship scholars have a tendency to think about human and citizenship rights as endocentric compounds is because the UDHR reads like a declaration of citizenship rights. Indeed, as Woodiwiss' analysis of the trajectory of "human rights" at the UN reveals, this is precisely what it was until it was made to be something else in the 1970s. This is my justification for putting scare quotes on human rights in my discussion of Woodiwiss' argument. On my reading of his research and the findings of the critical historiography cited throughout this book, the UDHR is not the announcement of an international legal and moral architecture seeking to curb national sovereignty, which is what we today associate with the human rights political imaginary. It is, in fact, an international effort to define the "good society", a hopeful coda to what had been a barbaric war.

Authors who trace contemporary human rights to the UDHR often highlight the optimism of the visionary figures such as Eleanor Roosevelt and René Cassin (Glendon 2002; Lauren 1998). To be sure, the hope for a better future was there. However, because this takes place in a context of the ideological confrontation of competing utopias, the consensus regarding the war is not translated onto the Declaration. The latter is dominated by the enunciation of liberal civil and political rights, deeply embedded and intertwined with capitalist property relationships and liberal democracy's social relations of power. However, because the citizenship rights associated with the welfare state were equally taking form, the Declaration was capacious enough to, at least symbolically, accommodate "socialist" socio-economic rights.[64]

Woodiwiss argues that the politicized opposition between civil and political, and social and economic rights prevented "human rights" from advancing further at the UN. It was only when this antithesis began to be overcome in the 1970s that the entanglement of "human rights" with the law could begin in earnest (2005a, 26). The particular factors that inaugurated this possibility, according to Woodiwiss, included the change in the balance of forces at the UN product of decolonization, which, amongst other things, provided allies for countries such as the USSR and China that had been isolated in the postwar era. He also draws attention to the adoption of corporatist policies in many Western European countries supportive of social and economic rights. Finally, he emphasizes the ratification of the two Covenants, the re-introduction of the notion of the indivisibility of the two sets of rights enunciated in them, as well as their conceptual distinction by making civil and political rights justiciable, and social and economic rights programmatic (2003, 26–27).

His account does not, though, acknowledge the influence of the emerging human rights political imaginary. However, given the significance of the broader impact of this imaginary in the US, the EU, Eastern Europe, and in Latin America, it is reasonable to assume it similarly reverberated throughout the UN. The imaginary sought to create an imagined community where the ethico-political claims made by, or on behalf of, distant and/or excluded victimized others became the moral basis for intervening in the world. Such a representation of the world and ways of acting in it were premised on what appeared like a moral or ethical reflex beyond politics. It was the recognition of the obviousness of the wrong, the violence or injustice that triggered the demand that something be done.

It is precisely the *crossing* of the human rights political imaginary with developments at the UN, and elsewhere, where it became entangled with the law that would *hybridize* the postwar liberal capitalist welfare citizenship rights, enunciated in the UDHR and specified in the Covenants, with the incipient human rights imaginary. The offspring of this cross are the juridified moral politics that we have come to know as human rights. To the extent that the human rights political imaginary could credibly stand for the moral and apparent transcendence of politics, UN lawyerly eyes could begin to undertake a principled rather than a political or ideological reading of the UDHR and the Covenants. These documents, which had crystallized the ideological struggle over the definition of the "good society", could be read as grounding and providing the resources for this new vision of, and for, the world. The timing could not have been more serendipitous, occurring precisely at a historical moment when, as Moyn (2010) has argued, the postwar utopias had lost much of their sheen stemming from their failure to deliver on their promises.

The actual texts of the UDHR and the Covenants, of course, were not changed by these hybridizations, but the social relations and institutional settings in which they were embedded had changed. Modes of reasoning and judicial practices injected into the human right political imaginary social technologies, representations, modes of advocacy and subjectivity, and organizational forms that brought to bear the "neutrality" and "autonomy" of the law on the claims of distant and/or excluded victimized others. Law reinforced the neutrality, which was and remains the lynchpin of the imaginary, adding a range of conceptual legal tools, and, seemingly, judicial power, hence the massive investment in what Hafner-Burton calls "global legalism" (2013).

Conclusion

In this chapter I have been concerned with exploring the entanglement of the human rights political imaginary with law. This has required interrogating the widely held assumption that human rights and law have always been intertwined and that human rights have always been legal rights. Drawing attention to some of the features that characterize law as a social practice, I have suggested that the absence of such practices in the context of the postwar period strongly indicates that human rights had no legal legs in this era. This of course raises the question of when and how the human rights political imaginary became entangled with law. In order to begin to sketch an answer to this question, I have reviewed the work of the pioneering scholars who set themselves this task, namely, Dezalay and Garth, Madsen, and Woodiwiss.

What their conceptual and empirical work shows is that the entanglement of the human rights political imaginary in the different countries they discuss cannot be grasped as the gradual acceptance, or the spread, of international legal principles born of a mythical international consensus. Instead, it was the intersection of the human rights political imaginary, understood as an ethico-political appeal by, or on behalf of, distant and/or excluded victimized others, with the historical and social-relational configurations of the legal fields of each of the polities that enabled the human rights imaginary to become intertwined with the law. Equally, it was the position of the legal fields in the broader field of political power that, in part, gave the different entanglements their form: a foreign policy focus in the US, a transnational project in the EU, an endogamous "human rights" tradition in Canada, and a minimalist politics in Chile at a critical moment when this was the only politics possible.

Human rights and citizenships rights, as many citizenship scholars claim, are indeed profoundly related. However, human rights are not an extension of citizenship rights or their universalization. They are the product of the social-relational and historical cross between a contested vision of the good society, the rights and legal framework of liberal capitalist society, and a moral practice, the human rights imaginary, premised on the transcendence of politics. This is clearest at the UN.

Law and human rights as social-relational species are characterized by their need to symbolically appear as separate from politics. It is this shared trait that made their hybridization possible. It is this cross that enables the normative resonance between human and citizenship rights, which many sociologist and citizenship scholars have detected. It is, also, why it is now possible to read the UDHR, and its subsequent development, retroactively as the sites of a postwar moral and legal consensus: a past occurrence that was activated by a future event yet to happen! Finally, it explains why human rights has become a sprawling global legalist machinery whose limited efficacy, generally, relies on moral persuasion rather than the force of the law.

As noted above, in my summary of Woodiwiss' analysis, this hybridization, as occurs in all crosses, rendered invisible traits that had been clearly expressed in the postwar. What was once intelligible, but is no longer, is the awareness that rights were attached to different social-structural arrangements and that the efficacy of the rights that dominated the UDHR and the Covenants depended on their being embedded in advanced liberal democratic capitalist social formations. Consequently the introduction of a set of legal means to constrain power, whose efficacy depends on their resonance with liberal capitalist social relations, into the human rights imaginary had the fateful consequence of making these legal means, as persuasively argued by Woodiwiss and shown by Hafner-Burton and Posner, generally powerless elsewhere where such social relations were absent. This is why despite the capillary spread of human rights law, human rights remained powered by moral persuasion. This, however, is easily missed because the moral persuasion takes on a juridified form.

Following Moyn, I have repeatedly emphasized that the human rights political imaginary represented a form of minimalist politics that eschewed grander visions of political, social, and economic transformations. It invoked a world where the worst forms of unjustifiable cruelty and barbarism could and should be curtailed. The ace for countries with advanced liberal capitalist welfare states is that this was something that citizenship rights had generally, if not consistently, secured for its citizens. Consequently, the human rights political imaginary was minimalist for these countries in the sense that it required little, practically nothing, from them. This is because they already had analogues for the new notion of human rights.

In the US the long-established nature of its analogue, the Bill of Rights, has meant that the language of human rights is superfluous in the domestic context. In Canada, because the analogues, namely, the statutory anti-discrimination system and the Charter, were so recent, they could be understood as an endogenous human rights tradition. In the EU, where there were so many individual analogues, human rights could be mobilized to harmonize the analogues, as it continues to do to this day. In all of these cases, the incorporation of human rights was relatively seamless. This, I believe, is why it was so easy for these countries to engage in the "invention" of their human rights "tradition" (Hobsbawm and Ranger 1983), encouraging historians, philosophers, and social scientist to seek out the deep roots of what turns out to be a recent development.

If the resonance of the juridified human rights political imaginary did little to alter the domestic situations of capitalist liberal democracy, it did more significantly impact their foreign policy, and the domestic situations of other countries. Insofar as the human rights political imaginary conveyed a vision of a (marginally) better future, it was a future at which Western liberal capitalist societies had already arrived, and to which laggards would need to aspire. However, the practical legal means, that is, citizenship rights, that produced modest but, important, constraints on social power in liberal democratic capitalist social formations are not likely to succeed elsewhere. Yet, this is precisely what global legalism and contemporary human rights law naïveté encourages. In a repeat of post-war international relations, it is likely that the current legal machinery has and continues to produce the "underdevelopment" of rights as protective means against the arbitrary use of social power in the global south. The human rights political imaginary has become developmentalism, or modernization, by legal rather than economic means. This, as I argue in the concluding chapter, has a strong bearing of where the human rights political imaginary might be able to take us in the struggle for global justice.

Notes

1. What is curious, as Deflem and Chicoine note, is that while human rights sociology scholars insist that human rights claims should be more broadly defined as "(social) claims for institutionalized protection" (2011, 105), they hold on to a reified and unsociological conception of law itself (2011, 112), in effect making it stand outside of the social.
2. Posner notes that strikingly, the only country that the UN Commission on Human Rights consistently criticized was Israel. While criticism of Israel may have been justified, it is remarkable that other nations should have escaped criticism as there are no shortage of states that have consistently violated human rights (2014, 44).
3. This has led some scholars to argue that individual human right complaints should be handled at a national level under the umbrella of the ECHR, and the ECtHR should move towards a constitutional role (Christoffersen 2011).
4. The Council of Europe should not be confused with the European Council or the Council of the EU. The latter body is the part of the administrative apparatus of the 28-nation EU, while the former is a component of the broader European human rights system.
5. Posner does note that international criminal courts, such as the International Criminal Court (ICC), are more akin to domestic courts insofar as the content of international law is more concretely specified and does enable courts to issue opinions and decide on punishment. However, he adds "the practicalities and limitations of enforcement in the context of mass atrocities entail that prosecutors be given immense discretion to choose who will be prosecuted. Because there is no 'neutral' way to exercise that discretion, states have been extremely reluctant to subject themselves to international criminal courts, and have gone at great lengths to limit their powers, just as they have done for human

rights bodies" (2014, 56–57). However, see Madsen and Christoffersen (2011) and Greer (2006) for more nuanced readings of the obstacles, but also the successes, of the European human rights system and ECtHR.

6. In many cases, Greer adds, this is because "systemic violations stem from problems which are simply too intractable to be dealt with by executive or legislative fiat, while in others the national and international legal and political costs of violation rank lower than those associated with making the necessary changes" (2006, 278).
7. For an interesting, though not an altogether, successful attempt (Munz 2000) to develop a sociology of philosophy, where philosophical ideas are conceptualized as sacred objects invested with emotional energy along the lines of Durkheim's collective effervescence, see Collins (1998). More effective in relating philosophical to social-structural change is the magnificent but insufficiently read, *Moral Codes and Social Structure in Ancient Greece*, by Joseph M. Bryant (1996).
8. Indeed as Susan S. Silbey argues, "[l]egality is much weaker and more vulnerable where it is more singularly conceived. If legality were ideologically consistent, it would be quite fragile" (2005, 350).
9. Harry W. Arthurs and Robert Kreklewich argue, "[i]t is a cultural artefact, a 'great code' which shapes the way we express ourselves, and imprints in our mind an image of social relations which is not easily dislodged, even when neither the state nor its law is present" (1996, 32). Counter-intuitively, the reason for this is probably not because the law is all powerful, but precisely because it is not. As I will describe in more detail below, in my discussion of the pioneering work of Anthony Woodiwiss, the law is "in a certain sense, a 'secondary force' in human affairs in that it can only really work when it mobilises pre-existing forces within social structures" (2003, 18).
10. Legality, following the pioneering work of Ewick and Silbey, is understood "as a structural component of society. That is, legality consists of cultural schemas and resources that operate to define and pattern social life. At the same time the schemas and resources shape social relations, they must also be continually produced and worked on – invoked and deployed – by individual and group actors. Legality is not inserted into situations; rather, through repeated invocations of the laws and legal concepts and terminology, as well as through imaginative and unusual associations between legality and other social structures, legality is constituted through everyday actions and practices" (1998, 43).

11. This is of course an analytical distinction, as I noted above in my discussion of law naïveté, despite an impressive human rights legal apparatus in the form of international texts and institutions; ultimately the ability to deliver remedy for human rights violations derives from moral suasion and political pressure. If the remedy is in most cases not the outcome of the law's self-execution, it is the product of the political pressure that convincingly and, in some instances, effectively draws attention to the responsibility that governments or agents have to enforce human rights law.
12. As I pointed out in a number of instances in the previous two chapters, bearing witness is an enormously complex and fragile mode of social recognition powered by specific forms of ethico-political labour.
13. Robert van Krieken (2004) however identifies some thought-provoking and productive intersections between these two very different approaches. Nonetheless, I am ultimately not convinced by the abstract rationalism and overreliance on the category of modernity in Luhmann's approach that attempts to account for much, too much one might say, by understanding modernity as a process of communicative and functional differentiation. As Anthony Woodiwiss has persuasively shown in a number of perceptive arguments, the category of "modernity" is rarely subject to critical sociological reflection, enabling it to account for much and explain little (Woodiwiss 1993, 1997, 2001, 2005b). For a treatment of human rights from an autopoetic perspective, see Verschraegen (2013). An interesting deployment of some aspects of Luhmann's framework is to be found in the work of Chris Thornhill's sociology of constitutions (Thornhill 2011, 2013). He presents an interesting critique of the generalized acceptance by political sociologist of the presupposition "that modern states are formed through a process in which, in a given society, prepotent or even dominant social agents deploy strategies of coercion and extraction in order to arrogate more or less exclusive power to themselves: this power is then concentrated in the institutions of the state" (2013, 26). One of the hitches to such an approach is that it understands law, rights, and constitutions as an apparatus of rule deployed instrumentally by state elites. Thornhill's historical overview of constitutions in modernity leads him to argue that "constitutions, and the rights that they contained, acted to confer a limited and differentiated organisation on states, and this organisation allowed states to utilize their power in a manner adequate to and sustainable in the pluralistic

reality of modern social order. In each of these instances, therefore, constitutions and constitutional rights can be seen as the externalized preconditions of society's emergent politics" (2013, 46). While I have qualms about the explanatory force of modernity, certainly such a cogent argument for the relative autonomy of constitutional norms and rights is certainly to be welcomed.

14. Of course the law has institutional conditions of possibility that can be grasped ethnographically (Wilson and Pence 2006) and relies on broadly distributed subjectivity or "legal consciousness" (Ewick and Silbey 1998; Silbey 2005).
15. This of course is not to discount other practices that contribute to the circulation of the law, such as the legal consciousness embedded in other spheres of social practice, even in the absence of the direct mention of the law (Ewick and Silbey 1998), or the concatenation of discourses, official and unofficial, that produce the effect of the law (Valverde 2003a, b). However, these practices, though not completely determined by, do, to a certain extent, depend on the effect of autonomy produced by jurists.
16. American legal realism explored how judicial decisions were underdetermined by the letter of the law and the formalism of legal reasoning, drawing attention to the political, economic, historical, and ideological context of legal decisions (Fisher et al. 1993), not a particularly fertile ground for the normative aspirations of the UDHR.
17. Even where some legal expertise was developed in "human rights" as in the case of the International Commission of Jurists (ICJ), the organization's inaugural concern was with the promotion of the rule of law, particularly to "mobilize the forces – in particular the juridical forces – of the free world for the defense of our fundamental legal principles and in doing so to organize the fight against all forms of systematic injustice of the Communist countries" (Tolley cited in Dezalay and Garth 2006, 234). The ICJ was created by establishment lawyers with strong links to the Council of Foreign Relations and with funds and administrative staff provided by the CIA (Dezalay and Garth 2006, 234) and should be understood, in its early years, as an ideological component of a Cold War strategy rather than a precursor to contemporary human rights organizations. This, however, does not prelude continuities in terms of personal relations between the ICJ and Amnesty. As Dezalay and Garth write, "The majority of the founders of Amnesty were leaders of Justice, the

British chapter of ICJ, which publicly supported the new organisation. Indeed, Sean McBride [who played a prominent role in ICJ] later became Amnesty's president" (Dezalay and Garth 2002, 71). What is more significant, to my mind, is the fact that Amnesty International defined itself in terms of its radical neutrality and its minimalism in opposition to the broader Cold War strategies espoused by the ICJ in its early days. Subsequently, in the late 1960s, as a result of the rising moral authority of human rights and in an attempt to recover from the sting of the public exposure of the role played by the CIA in its founding, the ICJ became a human rights organization in the contemporary sense. See Howard B. Tolley's (1994) extremely informative, yet, at times, insufficiently critical account of the ICJ.

18. Moreover, given the dominance of US law firms, law schools, and foundations in the export and internationalization of law, US legal interpretations of human rights would as a result travel widely (Dezalay and Garth 1998, 2002, 2010).
19. In the context of the US, as elsewhere, the structure of the national political field of power, as Barbara J. Keys' study persuasively shows, limited the impact of the initial forays of Amnesty International (2014, 91).
20. This is exemplified, at the level of the individual biography, by a key figure in both fields: Aryeh Neier went from being the director of the ACLU to becoming a founding member of Helsinki Watch and subsequently leader of the Human Rights Watch (Neier 2012). The ACLU experienced a strong decline in its membership: from 270,000 in 1974 to 185,000 in 1978 (Dezalay and Garth 2002, 279 n. 13).
21. This and cognate statements inevitably resonate with the "sense of heated exaggeration, suspiciousness, and conspiratorial fantasy" that historian Richard Hofstadter associated with *The Paranoid Style in American Politics*, the title of his widely read *Harper's Magazine* article in 1964 (1964a, 77), and leading essay in the book by the same title (1964b). However one need not resort to conspiracy theories in order to account for the shared worldview among liberal elites, which can sociologically be explained as a result of common career trajectories through prep schools, a passage through Harvard or Yale, and positions in Washington or Wall Street (Dezalay and Garth 2002, 66).
22. As Dezalay and Garth note, "In this ideological counteroffensive, these 'outsiders' skilfully managed to gain support through marketing and media promotions. The task was to produce messages that would be

simple, readily identifiable, and easy to diffuse: in other words, 'sound bites'. According to its director, the Heritage Foundation, established in 1973, specializes in 'marketing' and 'packaging' university ideas for mass consumption. The conservative policy entrepreneurs from the Heritage Foundation were put at the disposal of the press in order to organize ideological debates. These debates permitted them to put in question the image of neutrality and scholarly objectivity on which a good part of the authority of the eastern establishment rested. In addition, the emerging journalistic scene allowed them to place themselves on an equal footing with their opponents – despite the inequality of forces on the terrain of learned production" (2002, 80).

23. Many of the conservative counterrevolutionaries maintained that key establishment institutions such as the New York Times and the Ford Foundation had adopted an anti-business ethos (Dezalay and Garth 2002, 79; Silk and Silk 1980).
24. This was tremendously consequential: the Reagan presidency "brought to power a very conservative coalition that rejected social programs and political approaches that had long been the center of the federal government" (Dezalay and Garth 2006, 245).
25. It is worth keeping in mind that the mathematical techniques in economics preceded the pure economic theory of the Chicago School. The consecration of Keynesianism went hand in hand with the investment in mathematic techniques such as modelling and economic measurement, which were considered essential for the management of the economy (Dezalay and Garth 2002, 75).
26. This is not to say that there were not some "Academic idealists" (Dezalay and Garth 2006, 240) attempting to interpret the UDHR and other treaties as binding law; however, for the most part their arguments were largely marginal to the juridical fields where they were made (Moyn 2010, 176–211). It is worth pointing out that Dezalay and Garth distinguish between three moments in the development of human rights in the US: the first, spanning the 1950s and 1960s, coincides with International Commission of Jurists (ICJ) and corresponds to the deployment of the "rule of law" as a strategy to criticize the communist countries in the Cold War. The second, from the 1960s to the late 1970s, coincides with the emergence of Amnesty International and its highly moralistic and universalized conception of human rights. The last moment, taking off as the decade of 1970s was concluding, is represented

by the emergence of Helsinki, later to become Human Rights Watch; it is at this point that elite lawyers begin to invest in human rights and consequently the latter begin to become juridified (Dezalay and Garth 2006). To my mind, the inclusion of ICJ in its early days, when the ICJ was a Cold War tool, blurs the significance of the emergence of what are properly speaking, contemporary human rights. In the 1970s, the ICJ broke with its Cold War *modus operandi* and adopted the representations, social technologies, modes of subjectivity and of action, and the social organizational features associated with what we have come to identify as contemporary human rights.

27. A key indicator of their rise to prominence in foreign policy is the Neoliberal Washington Consensus.
28. Despite Amnesty International's ban on taking a position on foreign aid, and Amnesty International USA's charity status, in principle preventing it from lobbying the government, the reality is that behind the scenes, Amnesty International USA did contribute significantly to the legislative efforts in the 1970s, and "worked closely with the State Department's human rights officers" (Keys 2014, 208–9).
29. Dezalay and Garth report that Human Rights Watch relied on Theodor Meron, of NYU Law School, and Robert Goldman, at American University. According to one of their respondents, "They guided us through the complex set of commandments and got us comfortable in dealing with something [laws of war] that was really not considered a human rights issue" (2006, 249).
30. Today, the idea that human rights is tightly intertwined with law forms part of our everyday legality. However it is important to note that absent the right conditions, this might not have been so. In this respect, it is worth quoting one of Dezalay and Garth's respondents, a lawyer at Human Rights Watch, "If you have a functioning legal system [,] you can call on organizations that looks more like the ACLU where there is a prominent role for lawyers. But most of the countries where we work … have much more rudimentary if any legal systems [,] and so the challenge of the human rights movement is to create surrogate forms of protection pending the establishment of legally based rights [,] and the process of doing that doesn't require a law degree. I mean a law degree is very helpful but if you look at sort of our employees, maybe a third of them are lawyers but the rest are journalists, they are regional experts" (2006, 251–52).

31. Much has been written about the relationship between contemporary human rights and neoliberalism, with left critics arguing that human rights should be understood as an ideological tool in the neoliberal repetoire, while advocates argue that human rights may yet come to curb the worst excesses of neoliberalism (Moyn 2014a). Moyn argues, both neoliberalism and contemporary human rights emerged and developed at the same historical moment and were united in their shared suspicion of state power. However, he claims, rightly to my mind, that the most that can be said about their relationship is that they have travelled together, and have become intertwined, without one necessarily being the cause of the other (Moyn 2014a). Critics and advocates alike ascribe excessive power to human rights, whether this is by alleging that they secure the conditions of possibility of neoliberalism or that they have the power to clip the wings of global capitalism, respectively. Neither of these positions questions the social-relational conditions that have given rise to human rights in order to inform our understanding of the role human rights might (not) play in the struggle against the injustice and inequality produced by contemporary global capitalism. Were one to see human rights as political imaginary, perhaps more individuals would concur with Moyn, namely, that human rights has been a "powerless companion" in "the age of neoliberalism" (2014a).
32. Underpinning Dezalay and Garth's analyses of the globalization of law is the insight that "the force of law is constructed in elite contests, but also that law has little force until elite lawyers construct it" (Munger 2012, 477). Illuminating as this approach is, it nonetheless disregards another aspect of the efficacy of law that arises from, as we will see below in my discussion of Anthony Woodiwiss' work, the compatibility of law and the prevailing social-structural arrangements. Moreover, as Frank Munger convincingly argues, because of the focus of elite lawyers and their networks, "[w]e do not learn about what may have happened outside their networks, or when law is imported by other means, or in contexts where other beliefs about law or justice enter the field of state power [...] In sum, their exploration of the 'field of state power' leaves them with an incomplete map, with large gaps and patches of uncharted political terrain" (2012, 489).
33. Nash, drawing on the cultural politics approach I described in Chap. 5, analyses the "justifications which explain and attribute value to human rights in different ways according to different institutional settings"

(2009b, 62). She analyses the legal challenges to the status of prisoners in Guantanamo Bay and the corresponding debates that ensued in the mediated public sphere. She concludes, "International human rights have virtually no legal purchase in US courts, and nor have they proved effective in rousing public outrage or creating the political will to put pressure on the Bush Administration to act within international norms in granting prisoners a fair trial." Moreover, she adds, "Even where human rights are invoked in the mediated public sphere in the US they tend to be understood as 'special rights' for non-citizens, a set of second-class rights of last resort rather than the framework of universal principles of global justice within which the business of state should be conducted" (2009b, 92–93).

34. The ECJ is tasked with implementing EU rather than ECHR law. This said, as scholars have remarked both courts have begun to reference each other's jurisprudence, the consequences of which are yet to be determined (Douglas-Scott 2006).
35. As Duranti writes, "[n]o other international tribunal, including the various Hague courts and the Inter-American Court of Human Rights, possesses a similar capacity to act on an application from a private individual concerning a violation of his or her human rights. Nor has any UN body tasked with punishing human rights offenders handled more than a fraction of the Strasbourg court's caseload. The International Criminal Court of The Hague, for example, issued its first judgment in May 2012, nearly a decade after its creation. By comparison, the European Court of Human Rights issued 1,093 judgments in 2012 alone" (2016, 1).
36. For instance, the philosopher and legal scholar James W. Nickel refers to the ECHR as the "progeny" of the UDHR (1987, xi).
37. Drawing on the Bachelardian-inspired Bourdieusian conception of the "double rupture", Madsen understands sociological reflexivity as "the 'double historicisation' of both the object and the academic construction of the object. The booming contemporary engagement in human rights, both as activism and research, only highlights the need for such an approach. Due to the increase of human rights discourses and their normative aspirations, set against the proliferation of actors studying human rights, there is a growing need to 'step back' – or even 'out'– and critically examine these pre-constructions before attempting to approximate the object on more objective grounds" (2013, 84–85).

38. The creation of the École nationale d'administration (ENA) in 1946 as the institution for the training of high-level bureaucrats signalled the relative marginalization of juridical knowledge as *la science d'état* with respect to political science and economics in the context of the postwar welfare state (Madsen 2010, 57–58).
39. This is not to ignore that some of the cross-political consensus on the welfare state was linked to a political strategy to limit the rise of communist parties in France, England, and Scandinavian countries (Madsen 2010, 138).
40. See note 17 above.
41. In 1966–1967, it was revealed that Amnesty International had cooperated with the Foreign Office and British Intelligence in the context of two former colonies, Rhodesia and Aden, implicating Peter Benenson, the organization's founder, Robert Swann, its Secretary General, and Sean MacBride, the chair of International Executive Committee (IEC). Through some swift manoeuvres, the IEC was able to regain control of a spiralling situation. It "stressed that Amnesty would remain politically and financially independent, and would 'resist any attempt to influence Amnesty International … directly or indirectly whether by infiltration, financial grant, or any other means'" (Buchanan 2004, 286). This "relaunch of Amnesty International marked the rise of human rights as a broad social movement fighting for a relatively clearly defined objective" (Madsen 2012, 258–76).
42. As Duranti has noted, "[b]eginning in the 1950s, the role of conservative politics in launching the transformation of international law and organizations in Europe would be effaced through the construction of another set of invented traditions, ones that still retain their hold on official narratives of the birth of European institutions today" (2016, 212).
43. Ironically, however, notes Madsen, it was precisely the ability of jurists to adjust the Convention to diplomatic exigencies and national interest that carved up some autonomy for the ECHR and the ECtHR: "the ECHR system appeared to pose no significant threat to the specificities of the national ways of securing human rights and justice – as long as they were *justified*. Progressively, these early dynamics translated into the ECHR jurisprudence. Most notably, the (national) margin of appreciation, which provided a sophisticated legal response to the built-in conflict between the (European) universalism of human rights and the safeguarding of the national particularities of the protection of

human rights, was produced on the background of this initial approach" (2007, 151).

44. Having analysed a list of candidates for the first selections of judges for the ECtHR, Madsen deduces, "the preferred candidates were all jurists with top academic degrees – typically doctorates – as well as an acquaintance with international politics and diplomacy. In other words, the nominees who were selected were not one-dimensional actors in terms of pure judges, academics, practicing lawyers, etc. but, rather multi-dimensional in the sense of having knowledge of more fields of relevance. Jurists who appeared formally independent – typically academics or jurist with an academic career background – and could exhibit somewhat of a track record in international politics and law were in practice to be selected over other candidates" (2011b, 47).
45. Overall, Madsen draws attention to three important innovations in jurisprudence in the late 1970s that would set the ECtHR on a new course: (1) "a notion of fundamental rights", (2) "a dynamic approach to the understanding of the ECHR", and (3) "on obligation on the Member States to protect the rights of the Convention effectively and practically" (2011b, 54–55).
46. Of course, as Madsen notes, this was also driven by the national production of human rights and the contribution of pioneering human rights centres, contributing to the "'scientificization' and systematization of human rights" (2007, 154).
47. This of course raises important questions with respect to the progressive reading of postwar European human rights that underwrites Soysal's (1994) postnational thesis.
48. Moyn argues that there is evidence that the ECHR is now being used as a civilizational shield against Muslims in the same way that it was used in the past as a defence of Western civilization against communists, while Gündoğdu suggests that the ECtHR fails "to provide effective guarantees against [the condition] of rightlessness, especially in the case of migrants without a regular status, including rejected asylum seekers and undocumented migrants" (2015, 109).
49. Philanthropic foundations such as the Ford Foundation, as Dezalay and Garth report, were initially reluctant to invest in human rights activism as they perceived it as being too politically partisan (2002, 148). In response to the Cuban Revolution, the Ford Foundations had launched programmes in Latin America with the aim of building up "'friends of

America' while exporting US learning – especially but not only economics. These investments were directed toward building a new technocracy of development that was both competent and reformist and could be counted on to avoid polarizing the political field between an ultraconservative right and a radicalized left acting like revolutionaries" (Dezalay and Garth 2002, 65). Successes in Chile, and the desire to protect its earlier investment in social sciences, eventually encouraged the Ford Foundation to promote human rights strategies throughout Latin America (Dezalay and Garth 2002, 148).

50. This is not to say that human rights organizations have disappeared in Latin America, that lawyers are no longer involved in them, or that significant legal investments in human rights might not yet take place in the future. Rather, unlike in Europe and the US, law's entanglement within the human rights political imaginary did not get elite buy-in, deflating its value in the juridical and the broader field of political power.
51. See Tunnicliffe (2014) for an overview of the recent historiographical debates on the development of human rights in Canada. For more examples of human rights being telescoped backwards towards earlier anti-discrimination movements, see contributions to Janet Miron's edited volume (Miron 2009).
52. Yet, even in this case, his accounts of human rights in (2008, 2009) appear, to my mind, to be pushing back the origin of human rights to the 1950s. This is because he distinguishes between civil liberties and human rights by positing the latter as including both civil rights and advocacy of economic, social, and cultural rights, which the former did not embrace (2008, 7). This philosophical rather than sociological distinction when used in a historical context produces, perhaps unwittingly, a sense of continuity, that to my mind is unwarranted, between earlier civil liberties and the more recent international human rights movements that the political imaginary model tries to conceptually capture and empirically render.
53. Moreover, subsequent attempts to use Justice MacKay's judgement were generally unsuccessful (Bruner 1979, 245–46).
54. In the same year, fair practices legislation was also passed in New Jersey; subsequently similar legislation was adopted in Massachusetts in 1946, Connecticut in 1947, and New Mexico, Oregon, Rhode Island, and Washington in 1949 (Bruner 1979, 237, fn 4); see Bamberger and Lewin (1961) for an overview of early anti-discrimination efforts in the US.

55. “Anti-Discrimination” was replaced by “Human Rights” in 1961, the reason for which is not entirely clear. What is not in doubt however is that the Ontario Human Rights Code was an attempt to incorporate all the existing major fair practices statutes rather than an attempt to comply with international human rights legislation (Eberlee and Hill 1964, 448). T. M. Eberlee was Assistant Deputy Minister of Labour and D. G. Hill was the first Director of the Ontario Human Rights Commission, in their article providing an overview of the Ontario Human Rights Act; their referent is the anti-discrimination legislation in the US (1964, 450).
56. In 1993 the UN General Assembly approved the Paris Principles that provide guidelines and an international accreditation procedure for National Human Rights Institutions (NHRI), which includes NHRCs (Hafner-Burton 2013, 171).
57. Other authors understood the Charter as being rooted in the *Magna Carta* and the *English Bill of Rights* (La Forest 1983, 21–22) or saw the rights enshrined in the Charter as already “protected by statute or common law prior to 1982” (Morton 1987, 31), the Charter only adding a tier of judicial review by judges (Morton 1987, 51).
58. Human rights also informs EU foreign policy, but the latter is less coherent and unified (Balfour 2008). Needless to say there are important variations in the national vernacularization of the legally entangled EU human rights political imaginary (Hennette-Vauchez 2011).
59. More recently the political scientist Elin Skaar (2011) has argued in her analysis of Chile, Argentina, and Uruguay that the potential of human rights-inspired post-transitional justice processes in the countries under study have been limited by the lack of independence of the judiciary. Despite the mobilizations of human rights organizations, and some activist judges, prosecution for human rights violations has only taken place when the political executive has been favourably predisposed. Absent a structural transformation in the legal field of each of the countries, in other words, a real rather than a mere formal independence of human rights from the executives, it is unlikely that a legally entangled human rights will thrive. Equally, in an analysis of ethico-political claims of victimized excluded others in contemporary Argentinian politics, Humphrey and Valverde have argued that rather than activating state enabled rights, such claims are producing a moral economy where the state's response has been to “produce a hierarchy of victims ranked

according to innocence and correlated with rights. The more innocent, the more rights; the less innocent, less rights" (2007, 194). This said, the human rights political imaginary, in Latin America, appears to have been more securely entangled with the politics of memory as attested by Lessa and Druliolle (2011), Ros (2012), and Van Drunen (2010).

60. Recent doctoral research by Andrea Chisholm suggests that human rights remains marginal in Canadian law faculties, "Other courses such as human rights, poverty law, aboriginal law, social justice issues and ethics are offered as electives or injected peripherally into the core curricula" (2008, 67).
61. The political scientist Charles Epp notes that interest group activism, governmental financial support for litigation, and transformations in the legal profession and education occurred before the Charter came into effect, and better explains the transformation of the Canadian Supreme Court into a "major constitutional policymaker, focus[ing] much of its attention on civil rights and liberties" (1996, 775).
62. Here I am referencing Somers' characterization, introduced in Chap. 5, of English citizenship as "autonomy in membership" and "liberty in embeddedness" (1994a, 78–79).
63. In actual fact, Woodiwiss draws on the metaphor of human sacrifice to convey the entanglement of property and individual rights under the halo of natural rights in capitalism, writing, "in the case of 'natural' rights, what was made sacred was not the whole person but rather certain aspects of their lives – the freedoms to own property, to work and make contracts, for example – as well as, of course, capitalist production relations in general. And the major sacrifice was, again, not of whole human beings but of other aspects of their lives such as their labour power and therefore any expectation of economic security. Thus 'natural' rights, like the rites associated with human sacrifice, represent an assertion of state power rather than an antidote to it with the result that the protections and/or support they promise come at a price" (2005a, 9).
64. Woodiwiss (2005a) convincingly illustrates that though the Western rights tradition is monomanically associated with autonomy, there is also minor tradition of reciprocity capable of accommodating "socialist" social and economic rights.

Bibliography

Alexander, Jeffrey C. 2006. *The Civil Sphere*. Oxford and New York: Oxford University Press.

Arthurs, Harry W. 2000. "Poor Canadian Legal Education: So Near to Wall Street, So Far from God." *Osgoode Hall Law Journal* 38:381–408.

Arthurs, Harry W., and Robert Kreklewich. 1996. "Law, Legal Institutions, and the Legal Profession in the New Economy." *Osgoode Hall Law Journal* 34:1.

Balfour, Rosa. 2008. "Human Rights Promotion." In *The Search for a European Identity: Values, Policies and Legitimacy of the European Union*, edited by Furio Cerutti and Sonia Lucarelli, 159–175. London: Routledge.

Bamberger, Michael A., and Nathan Lewin. 1961. "The Right to Equal Treatment: Administrative Enforcement of Anti-Discrimination Legislation." *Harvard Law Review* 526 (74):526–589.

Bangarth, Stephanie. 2013. "'Their Equality Is My Equality': F. Andrew Brewisn and Human Rights Activism, 1940s–1970s." In *Taking Liberties: A History of Human Rights in Canada*, edited by Stephen J. Heathorn and David Goutor, 114–138. Don Mills, ON: Oxford University Press.

Behiels, Michael D. 2009. "Pierre Elliot Trudeau's Legacy: The Canadian Charter of Rights and Freedoms." In *A History of Human Rights in Canada: Essential Issues*, edited by Janet Miron, 201–217. Toronto: Canadian Scholars' Press.

Blumenthal, Sidney. 2008. *The Rise of the Counter-Establishment: The Conservative Ascent to Political Power*. New York: Union Square Press.

Bourdieu, Pierre. 1986. "Force of Law: Toward a Sociology of the Juridical Field." *The Hastings Law Journal* 38:814–853.

Bourdieu, Pierre. 1998b. *The State Nobility: Elite Schools in the Field of Power*. Cambridge and New York: Polity Press.

Bruner, Arnold. 1979. "The Genesis of Ontario's Human Rights Legislation: A Study in Law Reform." *University of Toronto Faculty of Law Review* 37:236–253.

Bryant, Joseph M. 1996. *Moral Codes and Social Structure in Ancient Greece: A Sociology of Greek Ethics from Homer to the Epicureans and Stoics*. Albany, NY: SUNY Press.

Buchanan, Tom. 2004. "Amnesty International in Crisis, 1966–7." *Twentieth Century British History* 15 (3):267–289.

Cardenas, Sonia. 2003. "Transgovernmental Activism: Canada's Role in Promoting National Human Rights Commissions." *Human Rights Quarterly* 25 (3):775–790.

Chisholm, Andrea. 2008. *Legal Education in Crisis: Healing and Humanizing Canadian Law Schools*. Peterborough: Brock University. http://www.dr.library.brocku.ca/handle/10464/1543.

Christoffersen, Jonas. 2011. "Individual and Constitutional Justice: Can the Power Balance of Adjudication Be Reversed." In *The European Court of Human Rights Between Law and Politics*, edited by Jonas Christoffersen and Mikael Rask Madsen, 181–203. Oxford and New York: Oxford University Press.

Christoffersen, Jonas, and Mikael Rask Madsen, eds. 2011. *The European Court of Human Rights Between Law and Politics*. Oxford and New York: Oxford University Press.

Cichowski, Rachel A. 2011. "Civil Society and the European Court of Human Rights." In *The European Court of Human Rights Between Law and Politics*, edited by Jonas Christoffersen and Mikael Rask Madsen, 77–97. Oxford and New York: Oxford University Press.

Claydon, John. 1986. "The Use of International Human Rights Law to Interpret Canada's Charter of Rights and Freedoms." *Connecticut Journal of International Law* 2:349–359.

Clément, Dominique. 2008. *Canada's Rights Revolution: Social Movements and Social Change, 1937–82*. Vancouver: UBC Press.

Clément, Dominique. 2009. "Rights Without the Sword Are but Mere Words." In *A History of Human Rights in Canada: Essential Issues*, edited by Janet Miron, 43–60. Toronto: Canadian Scholars' Press.

Clément, Dominique. 2012. "Human Rights in Canadian Domestic and Foreign Politics: From 'Niggardly Acceptance' to Enthusiastic Embrace." *Human Rights Quarterly* 34 (3):751–778.

Clément, Dominique. 2013. "The Rights Revolution in Canada and Australia." In *Taking Liberties: A History of Human Rights in Canada*, edited by Stephen J. Heathorn and David Goutor, 88–113. Don Mills, ON: Oxford University Press.

Collins, Hugh. 1982. *Marxism and Law*. Oxford: Oxford University Press.

Collins, Randall. 1998. *The Sociology of Philosophies: A Global Theory of Intellectual Change*. Cambridge, MA: Belknap Press of Harvard University Press.

Crenshaw, Kimberlé. 1995. *Critical Race Theory: The Key Writings That Formed the Movement*. New York: The New Press.

Deflem, Mathieu, and Stephen Chicoine. 2011. "The Sociological Discourse on Human Rights: Lessons from the Sociology of Law." *Development and Society* 40 (1):101–115.

Delgado, Richard, and Jean Stefancic. 2017. *Critical Race Theory: An Introduction*. New York: NYU Press.

Dezalay, Yves, and Bryant G. Garth. 1998. *Dealing in Virtue: International Commercial Arbitration and the Construction of a Transnational Legal Order*. Chicago and London: University of Chicago Press.

Dezalay, Yves, and Bryant G. Garth. 2002. *The Internationalization of Palace Wars: Lawyers, Economists, and the Contest to Transform Latin American States*. Chicago and London: University of Chicago Press.

Dezalay, Yves, and Bryant G. Garth. 2006. "From the Cold War to Kosovo: The Rise and Renewal of the Field of International Human Rights." *Annual Review of Law and Social Science* 2:231–255.

Dezalay, Yves, and Bryant G. Garth. 2010. *Asian Legal Revivals: Lawyers in the Shadow of Empire*. Chicago and London: University of Chicago Press.

Dezalay, Yves, and Bryant G. Garth. 2012a. "Introduction: Constructing Transnational Justice." In *Lawyers and the Construction of Transnational Justice*, edited by Yves Dezalay and Bryant Garth, 3–12. Milton Park and New York: Routledge.

Dezalay, Yves, and Bryant G. Garth, eds. 2012b. *Lawyers and the Construction of Transnational Justice*. Milton Park and New York: Routledge.

Douglas-Scott, S. 2006. "A Tale of Two Courts: Luxembourg, Strasbourg and the Growing European Human Rights *Acquis*." *Common Market Law Review* 43 (3):629–665.

Duranti, Marco. 2016. *The Conservative Human Rights Revolution: European Identity, Transnational Politics, and the Origins of the European Convention*. Oxford: Oxford University Press.

Eberlee, T. M., and D. G. Hill. 1964. "The Ontario Human Rights Code." *The University of Toronto Law Journal* 15 (2):448–455.

Ehrman, John. 1996. *The Rise of Neoconservatism: Intellectuals and Foreign Affairs, 1945–1994*. Yale, NH: Yale University Press.

Epp, Charles R. 1996. "Do Bills of Rights Matter? The Canadian Charter of Rights and Freedoms." *American Political Science Review* 90 (4):765–779.

Ewick, Patricia, and Susan S. Silbey. 1998. *The Common Place of Law: Stories from Everyday Life*. Chicago and London: University of Chicago Press.

Fine, Robert. 2002. "Marxism and the Social Theory of Law." In *An Introduction to Law and Social Theory*, edited by Reza Banakar and Max Travers, 101–118. Oxford and Portland, OR: Hart Publishing.

Fineman, Martha Albertson, and Nancy Sweet Thomadsen. 2013. *At the Boundaries of Law (RLE Feminist Theory): Feminism and Legal Theory*. London and New York: Routledge.

Finley, Lucinda M. 1989. "Breaking Women's Silence in Law: The Dilemma of the Gendered Nature of Legal Reasoning." *Notre Dame Law Review* 64:886–910.

Fisher, William W., Morton J. Horwitz, and Thomas Reed, eds. 1993. *American Legal Realism*. Oxford: Oxford University Press.

Frager, Ruth A., and Carmela Patrias. 2013. "Transnational Links and Citizens' Rights: Canadian Jewish Human Rights Activists and Their American Allies in the 1940s and 1950s." In *Taking Liberties: A History of Human Rights in Canada*, edited by Stephen J. Heathorn and David Goutor, 139–165. Don Mills, ON: Oxford University Press.

Glendon, Mary Ann. 2002. *A World Made New: Eleanor Roosevelt and the Universal Declaration of Human Rights*. New York: Random House.

Greer, Steven. 2006. *The European Convention on Human Rights: Achievements, Problems and Prospects*. Cambridge and New York: Cambridge University Press.

Grimes, William. 2010. "Louis Henkin, Leader in Field of Human Rights Law, Dies at 92." *The New York Times*, October 16, 2010, sec. US https://www.nytimes.com/2010/10/17/us/17henkin.html.

Gündoğdu, Ayten. 2015. *Rightlessness in an Agee of Rights: Hannah Arendt and the Contemporary Struggles of Migrants*. Oxford and New York: Oxford University Press.

Hafner-Burton, Emilie M. 2013. *Making Human Rights a Reality*. Princeton, NJ: Princeton University Press.

Halliday, Terence C., and Pavel Osinsky. 2006. "Globalization of Law." *Annual Review of Sociology* 32:447–470.

Hannum, Hurst. 1995. "The Status of the Universal Declaration of Human Rights in National and International Law." *Georgia Journal of International and Comparative Law* 25:287–398.

Heathorn, Stephen J., and David Goutor, eds. 2013. *Taking Liberties: A History of Human Rights in Canada*. Don Mills, ON: Oxford University Press.

Hennette-Vauchez, Stéphanie. 2011. "Constitutional v International? When Unified Reformaory Rationales Mismatch the Plural Paths of Legitimacy of

ECHR Law." In *The European Court of Human Rights Between Law and Politics*, edited by Jonas Christoffersen and Mikael Rask Madsen, 146–164. Oxford and New York: Oxford University Press.

Hobsbawm, Eric, and Terence Ranger. 1983. *The Invention of Tradition*. Cambridge: Cambridge University Press.

Hofstadter, Richard. 1964a. "The Paranoid Style in American Politics." *Harper's Magazine* 229 (1374):77–86.

Hofstadter, Richard. 1964b. *The Paranoid Style in American Politics*. New York: Vintage.

Howe, R. Brian. 1991. "The Evolution of Human Rights Policy in Ontario." *Canadian Journal of Political Science/Revue Canadienne de Science Politique* 24 (4):783–802.

Howe, R. Brian, and David Johnson. 2000. *Restraining Equality: Human Rights Commissions in Canada*. Toronto: University of Toronto Press.

Humphrey, Michael, and Estela Valverde. 2007. "Human Rights, Victimhood, and Impunity: An Anthropology of Democracy in Argentina." *Social Analysis* 51 (1):179–197.

Hunt, Alan. 1985. "The Ideology of Law: Advances and Problems in Recent Applications of the Concept of Ideology to the Analysis of Law." *Law and Society Review*, 11–37.

Hunt, Alan. 1993. *Explorations in Law and Society: Towards a Constitutive Theory of Law*. London: Routledge.

Ishay, Micheline R. 2004. *The History of Human Rights*. Berkeley and London: University of California Press.

Kallen, Evelyn. 2003. *Ethnicity and Human Rights in Canada a Human Rights Perspective on Ethnicity, Racism and Systemic Inequality*. 3rd ed. desLibris. Don Mills, ON and New York: Oxford University Press.

Kalman, Laura. 1986. *Legal Realism at Yale, 1927–1960*. Chapel Hill, NC: UNC Press Books.

Keck, Margaret E., and Kathryn Sikkink. 1998. *Activists Beyond Borders: Advocacy Networks in International Politics*. Ithaca, NY and London: Cornell University Press.

Keys, Barbara J. 2014. *Reclaiming American Virtue*. Cambridge, MA: Harvard University Press.

La Forest, Gerard V. 1983. "The Canadian Charter of Rights and Freedoms: An Overview." *Canadian Bar Review* 61:19.

Lambertson, Ross. 2005. *Repression and Resistance Canadian Human Rights Activists, 1930–1960*. Toronto: University of Toronto Press.

Lauren, Paul Gordon. 1998. *The Evolution of International Human Rights: Visions Seen*. Philadelphia: University of Pennsylvania Press.

Lessa, Francesca, and Vincent Druliolle. 2011. *The Memory of State Terrorism in the Southern Cone: Argentina, Chile, and Uruguay*. New York: Palgrave Macmillan.

Levy, Daniel, and Natan Sznaider. 2010. *Human Rights and Memory*. Philadelphia: Penn State Press.

López, José Julián. 2015. "The Human Right to Food as Political Imaginary." *Journal of Historical Sociology* 30 (2): 239–261.

López, José Julián, and Janet Lunau. 2012. "ELSIfication in Canada: Legal Modes of Reasoning." *Science as Culture* 21 (1):77–99.

Luhmann, Niklas. 1991. "Operational Closure and Structural Coupling: The Differentiation of the Legal System." *Cardozo Law Review* 13:1419.

Luhmann, Niklas. 2004. *Law as a Social System*. Oxford and New York: Oxford University Press.

MacLennan, Christopher. 2003. *Toward the Charter: Canadians and the Demand for a National Bill of Rights, 1929–1960*. Montreal and Kingston: McGill-Queen's Press-MQUP.

Madsen, Mikael Rask. 2007. "From Cold War Instrument to Supreme European Court: The European Court of Human Rights at the Crossroads of International and National Law and Politics." *Law & Social Inquiry* 32 (1):137–159.

Madsen, Mikael Rask. 2010. *La Genèse de l'Europe Des Droits de L'homme: Enjeux Juridiques et Stratégies d'Etat (1945–1970)*. Strasbourg: Presses Universitaires de Strasbourg.

Madsen, Mikael Rask. 2011a. "Reflexivity and the Construction of the International Object: The Case of Human Rights." *International Political Sociology* 5 (3):259–275.

Madsen, Mikael Rask. 2011b. "The Protracted Institutionalization of the Strasbourg Court: From Legal Diplomacy to Integrationist Jurisprudence." In *The European Court of Human Rights Between Law and Politics*, edited by Jonas Christoffersen and Mikael Rask Madsen, 43–59. Oxford and New York: Oxford University Press.

Madsen, Mikael Rask. 2012. "Human Rights and the Hegemony of Ideology: European Lawyers and the Cold War Battle over International Human Rights." In *Lawyers and the Construction of Transnational Justice*, edited by Yves Dezalay and Bryant Garth, 258–276. Milton Park and New York: Routledge.

Madsen, Mikael Rask. 2013. "Towards a Reflexive Sociology of Human Rights." In *Making Human Rights Intelligible: Towards a Sociology of Human Rights*, edited by Mikael Rask Madsen and Gert Verschraegen, 81–103. Oxford and Portland, Oregon: Hart Publishing.

Madsen, Mikael Rask, and Jonas Christoffersen. 2011. "Introduction." In *The European Court of Human Rights Between Law and Politics*, edited by Jonas Christoffersen and Mikael Rask Madsen, 1–13. Oxford and New York: Oxford University Press.

Madsen, Mikael Rask, and Yves Dezalay. 2002. "The Power of the Legal Field." In *An Introduction to Law and Social Theory*, edited by Max Travers and Reza Banakar, 189–204. Oxford and Portland, Oregon: Hart Publishing.

Madsen, Mikael Rask, and Gert Verschraegen. 2013a. "An Introduction to a Sociology of Human Rights." In *Making Human Rights Intelligible: Towards a Sociology of Human Rights*, edited by Mikael Rask Madsen and Gert Verschraegen, 1–24. Oxford and Portland, Oregon: Hart Publishing.

Madsen, Mikael Rask, and Gert Verschraegen, eds. 2013b. *Making Human Rights Intelligible: Towards a Sociology of Human Rights*. Book, Whole. Oxford and Portland Oregon: Hart Publishing.

Madsen, Mikael Rask, and Gert Verschraegen. 2016. "Toward a New Sociology of Human Rights?" *Humanity: An International Journal of Human Rights, Humanitarianism* 7 (2):273–293.

Manners, Ian. 2006. "The Constitutive Nature of Values, Images and Principles in the European Union." In *Values and Principles in European Union Foreign Policy*, edited by Sonia Lucarelli and Ian Manners, 19–41. London: Routledge.

Marshall, Thomas H. 1950. *Citizenship and Social Class*. Cambridge: Cambridge University Press.

Mazower, Mark. 2009. *No Enchanted Palace: The End of Empire and the Ideological Origins of the United Nations*. Princeton, NJ: Princeton University Press.

Miron, Janet, ed. 2009. *A History of Human Rights in Canada: Essential Issues*. Toronto: Canadian Scholars' Press.

Moravcsik, Andrew. 2000. "The Origins of Human Rights Regimes: Democratic Delegation in Postwar Europe." *International Organization* 54 (2):217–252.

Morton, F. L. 1987. "The Political Impact of the Canadian Charter of Rights and Freedoms." *Canadian Journal of Political Science/Revue Canadienne de Science Politique* 20 (1):31–55.

Moyn, Samuel. 2010. *The Last Utopia*. Harvard University Press.

Moyn, Samuel. 2014a. "A Powerless Companion: Human Rights in the Age of Neoliberalism." *Law and Contemporary Problems* 77:147.

Moyn, Samuel. 2014b. *Human Rights and the Uses of History*. London: Verso.
Moyn, Samuel. 2015. *Christian Human Rights*. Philadelphia: University of Pennsylvania Press: Philadelphia.
Munger, Frank. 2012. "Globalization Through the Lens of Palace Wars: What Elite Lawyers' Careers Can and Cannot Tell Us About Globalization of Law." *Law & Social Inquiry* 37 (2):476–499.
Munz, Peter. 2000. "The Poverty of Randall Collins's Formal Sociology of Philosophy." *Philosophy of the Social Sciences* 30 (2):207–226.
Nash, Kate. 2009b. *The Cultural Politics of Human Rights*. Cambridge and New York: Cambridge University Press.
Neier, Aryeh. 2012. *The International Human Rights Movement: A History*. Princeton, NJ and Oxford: Princeton University Press.
Nelson, Paul J., and Ellen Dorsey. 2008. *New Rights Advocacy: Changing Strategies of Development and Human Rights NGOs*. Washington, DC: Georgetown University Press.
Nickel, James W. 1987. *Making Sense of Human Rights: Philosophical Reflections on the Universal Declaration of Human Rights*. Berkeley and London: University of California Press.
Oberleitner, Gerd. 2012. "Does Enforcement Matter?" In *Human Rights Law*, edited by Costas Douzinas and Conor Gearty, 249–268. Cambridge and New York: Cambridge University Press.
Pashukanis, Eugenio Bronislavovich. 1980. *Selected Writings on Marxism and the Law*. Edited by Piers Beirne and Robert Sharlet S. London: Academic Press.
Pashukanis, Eugenio Bronislavovich. 1983. *Law and Marxism*. Edited by C. Arthur. London: Pluto Press.
Patrias, Carmela, and Ruth A. Frager. 2001. "'This Is Our Country, These Are Our Rights': Minorities and the Origins of Ontario's Human Rights Campaigns." *The Canadian Historical Review* 82 (1):1–35.
Piven, Frances Fox. 1971. *Regulating the Poor; the Functions of Public Welfare*. Vol. [1st ed.]. Book, Whole. New York: Pantheon Books.
Piven, Frances Fox, and Richard A. Cloward. 1979. *Poor People's Movements: Why They Succeed, How They Fail*. Vol. 697. New York: Vintage.
Posner, Eric A. 2014. *The Twilight of Human Rights Law*. Oxford and New York: Oxford University Press.
Ros, Ana. 2012. *The Post-Dictatorship Generation in Argentina, Chile, and Uruguay: Collective Memory and Cultural Production*. Basingstoke and New York: Palgrave Macmillan.
Russell, Peter H. 1983. "The Political Purposes of the Canadian Charter of Rights and Freedoms." *Canadian Bar Review* 61:30–54.

Saunders, Frances Stonor. 1999. *The Cultural Cold War*. New York: The Free Press.
Schabas, William A. 1997. "Canada and the Adoption of the Universal Declaration of Human Rights." *McGill Law Journal* 43:403–444.
Schabas, William A. 2000. "Twenty-Five Years of Public International Law at the Supreme Court of Canada." *Canadian Bar Review* 79:174–195.
Scheingold, Stuart A. 2004. *The Politics of Rights: Lawyers, Public Policy, and Political Change*. Ann Arbor: University of Michigan Press.
Silbey, Susan S. 2005. "After Legal Consciousness." *Annual Review of Law and Social Science* 1:323–368.
Silk, Leonard, and Mark Silk. 1980. *The American Establishment*. New York: Basic Books.
Skaar, Elin. 2011. *Judicial Independence and Human Rights in Latin America: Violations, Politics, and Prosecution*. New York: Palgrave Macmillan.
Smith, James A. 1993. *Idea Brokers: Think Tanks and the Rise of the New Policy Elite*. New York: Simon and Schuster.
Snyder, Emily. 2014. "Indigenous Feminist Legal Theory." *Canadian Journal of Women and the Law* 26 (2):365–401.
Somers, Margaret R. 1994a. "Rights, Relationality, and Membership: Rethinking the Making and Meaning of Citizenship." *Law & Social Inquiry* 19 (1):63–114.
Somers, Margaret R. 1994b. "The Narrative Constitution of Identity: A Relational and Network Approach." *Theory and Society* 23 (5):605–649.
Soysal, Yasemin Nuhoğlu. 1994. *Limits of Citizenship: Migrants and Postnational Membership in Europe*. Chicago and London: University of Chicago Press.
Soysal, Yasemin Nuhoğlu. 2012. "Citizenship, Immigration, and the European Social Project: Rights and Obligations of Individuality." *The British Journal of Sociology* 63 (1):1–21.
Stammers, Neil. 2009. *Human Rights and Social Movements*. London: Pluto Press.
Thornhill, Chris. 2011. *A Sociology of Constitutions: Constitutions and State Legitimacy in Historical-Sociological Perspective*. Cambridge and New York: Cambridge University Press.
Thornhill, Chris. 2013. "State Building, Constitutional Rights and the Social Construction of Norms: Outline for a Sociology of Constitutions." In *Making Human Rights Intelligible: Towards a Sociology of Human Rights*, edited by Mikael Rask Madsen and Gert Verschraegen, 25–59. Oxford and Portland Oregon: Hart Publishing.

Tolley Jr, Howard B. 1994. *The International Commission of Jurists: Global Advocates for Human Rights*. Philadelphia: University of Pennsylvania Press.
Tunnicliffe, Jennifer. 2013. "A Limited Vision: Canadian Participation in the Adoption of the International Covenants on Human Rights." In *Taking Liberties: A History of Human Rights in Canada*, edited by Stephen J. Heathorn and David Goutor, 166–187. Don Mills, ON: Oxford University Press.
Tunnicliffe, Jennifer. 2014. "Canada and the Human Rights Framework: Historiographical Trends." *History Compass* 12 (10):807–817.
Turner, Bryan S. 2006. *Vulnerability and Human Rights*. Philadelphia: Penn State Press.
Unger, Roberto Mangabeira. 1983. *The Critical Legal Studies Movement: Another Time, a Greater Task*. Boston, MA: Harvard University Press.
Valverde, Mariana. 2003a. "'Which Side Are You On?' Uses of the Everyday in Sociolegal Scholarship." *PoLAR: Political and Legal Anthropology Review* 26 (1):86–98.
Valverde, Mariana. 2003b. *Law's Dream of a Common Knowledge*. Princeton and Oxford: Princeton University Press.
Van Drunen, Saskia Paula Caecilia. 2010. *Struggling with the Past: The Human Rights Movement and the Politics of Memory in Post-Dictatorship Argentina, 1983–2006*. Amsterdam: Rozenberg.
Van Krieken, Robert. 2004. "Legal Reasoning as a Field of Knowledge Production: Luhmann, Bourdieu and Law's Autonomy." Conference paper, Law and Society Association Conference, Chicago, 27–20, May.
Verschraegen, Gert. 2013. "Differentiation and Inclusion: A Neglected Sociological Approach to Fundamental Rights." In *Making Human Rights Intelligible: Towards a Sociology of Human Rights/Madsen, M.[edit.]; Ea*, edited by Gert Verschraegen and Mikael Rask Madsen, 61–80. Oxford and Portland Oregon.
Weinreb, Lloyld L. 2005. *Legal Reason: The Use of Analogy in Legal Argument*. Cambridge and Malden, MA: Cambridge University Press.
Weisberg, Kelly, ed. 1993. *Feminist Legal Theory: Foundations*. Philadelphia: Temple University Press.
Wilson, Alex, and Ellen Pence. 2006. "In the Lives of Battered Women: An Indigenous Assessment." In *Institutional Ethnography as Practice*, edited by Dorothy E. Smith, 199–225. New York: Rowman & Littlefield.
Woodiwiss, Anthony. 1993. *Postmodernity USA: The Crisis of Social Modernism in Postwar America*. London and New York: SAGE Publications Limited.

Woodiwiss, Anthony. 1997. "Against 'Modernity': A Dissident Rant." *Economy and Society* 26 (1):1–21.

Woodiwiss, Anthony. 2001. *The Visual in Social Theory*. London: The Athlone Press.

Woodiwiss, Anthony. 2003. *Making Human Rights Work Globally*. London: The Glass House Press.

Woodiwiss, Anthony. 2005a. *Human Rights*. London and New York: Routledge.

Woodiwiss, Anthony. 2005b. *Scoping the Social*. London and New York: McGraw-Hill Education.

Woodiwiss, Anthony. 2012. "Asia, Enforceable Benevolence and the Future of Human Rights." *Sociology* 46 (5):966–981.

7

Conclusion

Introduction

In this conclusion, I do not rehearse the arguments developed at length throughout the book. I do, nonetheless, want to make an overall assessment of what the human rights political imaginary can help us see about the field of the sociology of human rights, as well as human rights. I begin by taking up the metaphor to which I made reference in the introduction, namely, the archipelago. The latter draws attention to the fact that there has not yet been a critical overview of the sociology of human rights. When one views the field, one sees islands in close proximity to one another, without actually being able to distinguish their differences or commonalities. I begin by highlighting some of their shared assumptions. Following this, I develop a stylized account that presents the insights gleaned from my critical, yet sympathetic, discussion of the different sociological approaches surveyed in the book. Finally, I finish by exploring some real-world consequences arising from the political imaginary model.

J. Julián López, *Human Rights as Political Imaginary*,
https://doi.org/10.1007/978-3-319-74274-8_7

The Sociology of the Human Rights Archipelago

In the introduction to the book, I suggest that the metaphor of the archipelago is a useful heuristic for grasping something crucial about the contemporary situation in the field of the sociology of human rights. Although it is possible to discern a shared and nascent conceptual and empirical space, it is largely constituted by a cluster of approaches that are predominantly insular in nature. The different approaches, to be sure, acknowledge each other, through the courtesy of academic citation, but rarely reveal what they share. The suggestion that they are embarked on a common project lingers, but the commonality is not easily detected. One of the objectives of this book has been to use the political imaginary model as a conceptual space from which to speak simultaneously about human rights as a social phenomenon and its manifestations as an object of sociological analysis.

Geologists distinguish amongst a number of archipelago formations; one variant, the continental archipelago, is particularly apropos for the sociology of human rights. It refers to an island chain that is the product of exposed sections on a continuous continental shelf. This means that the apparent disconnectedness of the constituent islands is belied by the fact that they are protrusions of the same land mass. Similarly, despite visible and consequential differences amongst the various approaches in the sociology of human rights, which I have reviewed throughout this book, it is possible to detect unnoticed, because submerged, commonalities.

First, sunken amidst the waves of empirical and conceptual thought, is, to my mind, a surprisingly thin reading of human rights. With the exception of the sociolegal scholars discussed in Chap. 6, the practical totality of the scholars, whose work I have discussed, think about human rights as an idea, ideal, or legal principle. As a consequence, the thin historical narrative of the emergence and development of human rights is rarely subject to sustained critical scrutiny. What is more, as I highlighted in Chap. 4, even those scholars who have recourse to the considerable conceptual possibilities associated with the concept of social practice tend to oppose the idea, or ideal, of human rights to the actuality of its implementation in practice. They draw attention to the empirical reality of the structured forms of injustice and suffering that the idea of human rights fails to capture, or the social-structural obstacles that thwart the implementation of the human rights ideal.

Second, sociologists who anchor their analyses of human rights in another tried and tested sociological concept, namely, citizenship, for the most part fare no better. Despite a rich tradition gifting a wealth of empirical and theoretical tools geared towards conceptualizing institutional, political, social, cultural, economic, and historical contexts that animate and embed the idea of citizenship, scholars tend to equate citizenship to human rights via extension or succession. Thus, they obviate the need to determine the specificity of the contextual factors that gave rise to human rights. Tellingly, it is sociolegal scholars who are more adept at identifying the historical, institutional, and social-relational assemblages in which human rights emerged and have subsequently developed. This is, no doubt, because their focus is on the legal nature of human rights, and, as sociolegal scholars, they are well habituated to examining the practices and the structured relations in and through which the effects of law and legality are produced in society. As a point of epistemological departure, they do not accept law's self-presentation as an adequate account of the law. Said differently, they are inoculated against the law naiveté that many social science scholars researching human rights have difficulty resisting. The latter, discussed at length in Chap. 6, is, of course, the third feature of the submerged and shared commonality.

Fourth is a tendency to take the normative claims of human rights, more or less, at face value. This is hardly surprising given that human rights is at its most persuasive when experienced as an ineluctable normative demand for redress or remedy, be this via ethical or political action, or by activating the force of the law. In some instances, the normative self-evidence is so tenacious that scholars insist, as discussed in Chap. 3, that sociology itself become a normative undertaking by making the goals of human rights the discipline's own—an approach that, as I strongly suggested, prevents a fuller sociological understanding of what human rights might (not) be able to do.

Even scholars not committed to this normative path still have difficulty releasing themselves from human rights' normative clasp. As indicated in Chap. 4, they make human rights stand in as the normative ideal of justice and equality against which contemporary forms of systemic violence and inequality can, and must, be judged. However, why the ideal of human rights is chosen over others, or, even, if human rights is up to the task, is papered over by human rights' normative self-evidence. Equally, those who argue that human rights, or human rights-fuelled postnational citizenship, provide the indispensable moral grammar for enunciating the legitimate claims to which individuals are entitled in virtue of their humanity ground their argument in the incontestable superiority of human rights, asserted rather than demonstrated.

To my mind, and for reasons that I have developed at great length in this book, these four features are liabilities from which social scientists researching human rights and activist struggling for human rights and global justice would do well to release themselves. The motivation for proposing the political imaginary model is not merely to draw attention to some of the limitations of the existing scholarship. It is, instead, to take advantage of the significant contributions that already exist in the field. Conceptual and empirical work in the social sciences, knowingly or not, always takes existing work as the raw materials on and through which it labours. Indeed, the political imaginary model preserves, and this book has been organized around some of the field's key insights: the normative charge and pull of human rights' claims, the centrality of the notion of practice as a way of thinking about human rights, the latter's fateful intersection with citizenship rights, and human rights' highly juridified nature. A second motivation for developing the model is to reconnoitre the origin of the field's limitations, with an eye to seeing how they might be overcome. And, this is not out of intellectual conceit or mere curiosity, but as a way of determining what human rights can(not) do and, in consequence, how political and ethical energy might best be channelled.

The arguments explored in this book lead me to propose that the most significant challenge that needs to be met head on is the prevalence of thin historical and sociological accounts. As I have attempted to highlight in numerous instances in the preceding pages, the persistence of thin accounts arises from human rights' own self-representation. Put succinctly, it takes the following form: human rights refers to normative ideals or legal principles product of a postwar consensus, with which any ethical person, institution, or nation would agree or would be legally bound to enforce. The political imaginary model does not represent an attempt to efface the "idea" of human rights; instead, drawing on the emerging critical historiography introduced in Chap. 2, it tries to understand the historical and social-relational context in which contemporary human rights emerged. This is not to say that ideas are not important, or even decisive in some circumstances. They are. But ideas only have social force when they resonate with, or mobilize, existing social-structural arrangements and dynamics. This (pace Alexander and Smith 2003) is not the same as saying that they are reducible to, or are the product of, social-structural configurations or group interests.

In other words, the model is also concerned with addressing which features of its historical social-relational context enabled the idea of human rights to have traction in, and move through, social space as assemblages of modular practices. The model proposes that a political imaginary is a way of representing and acting in the world, with a view to improving it. These representations are linked to the existence of social technologies that pattern behaviour and rest on modes of subjectivity and action, individual and collective, that embody and embrain the idea of human rights. These configurations of ideas, forms of being and acting, are often, but not always, inthinged in particular artefacts or organizational clusters. Thus, an appeal on behalf of an individual imprisoned unjustly, made by a human rights organization, invokes a representation of a world in which such an act is deemed unjustifiable, documents, and disseminates this idea using particular social technologies, such as factual genres of recording, modes of legal reasoning, and well-honed media strategies. Individuals who understand themselves as human rights subjects are interpellated to act, to discuss, write letters, protest, participate in lobbying measures, or, at the very least, to express their moral outrage.

The human rights political imaginary, as sketched here, is a social dispositif for making claims and patterning behaviour to elicit certain types of responses, ways of acting and being in the world. It generates particular types of embodied, embrained, inthinged, and embedded claims and responses. More specifically, it is premised on a minimalist politics, if not an anti-politics, which gave the human rights of the 1970s the traction of which the "human rights" of the 1940s was bereft. What is more, the human rights political imaginary, initially, in part, as a way of securing the neutrality that to this day remains its moral surety, is concerned with making visible the claims made by, or on behalf of, distant and/or excluded others subject to injustice and violence. The claiming, or the amplification of claims made by others, is best understood, following Kurasawa's extremely felicitous phrase, as an ongoing ethico-political labour.

This, crucially, draws attention to the fact that the community of individuals who might receive the human rights claim is an imaginary community, always fragile, always being made, unmade, and remade. Aspiring to be heard transnationally, making themselves a "matter of international concern", to use Beitz's pithy phrase, claims can, nonetheless, be dampened by local circumstances or deadened by transnational misunderstanding, disinterest, and now, more frequently, exhaustion. In addition, even when claims are successfully heard, understood, and trigger the desire for an ethical, political, and/or legal response, which presuppose considerable ethico-political labour, the actor(s) might not be able to activate the necessary levers. Alternatively, the levers might fail to engage the corresponding mechanisms, or the mechanisms might fail to produce the desired effects.

Because the contemporary human rights political imaginary had its origin in a morality of anti-politics, it became consecrated around the figure of the innocent victim. It was the dual status of innocence and victimhood that made it possible to, seemingly, eschew politics. The neutral representation of innocence and victimhood, a *cinéma vérité* in moral register, became the ethical Archimedean point that engendered new forms of patterned ethico-political labour geared, modestly, towards limiting the abuse, violence, and injustice visited upon the guiltless in faraway places. Moreover, just as the injustice was not abstract—prisoners of conscious were named, their situation described—the response was not either. It was pragmatic. It could be undertaken immediately, epitomized by the centrality of letter writing, an old political tool repurposed for new means within the incipient imaginary.

Subsequently, as discussed in Chap. 5, the moral economy of victimhood has mushroomed, not, of course, only as a result of the efflorescence of the human rights political imaginary. Nonetheless, it is arguably the case that the broader contemporary ecology of victimhood, whatever its origins and its mode of reproduction, makes human rights claims that foreground innocence and victimhood, ring ethically and politically true. The centrality of innocence and victimhood within the human rights political imaginary speaks, to my mind, against the wisdom of politically or ethically defending human rights as a supersession of citizenship rights. The latter, I would argue, is a clear instance of one step forward and five backwards. This however does not mean that the category of the victim needs to be abandoned. Whether it pleases us or not, victimhood does have the potential to index the untenable situation of suffering and powerlessness of some individuals. It therefore has political and ethical value. I do think, however, that it would be best to be wary of its overextension, of contributing to its further normalization as the natural, to the exclusion of all others, ground for the formation of ethical and political claims.

Finally law, which is so effortlessly associated with human rights, fuelling a law naïveté for which contemporary global legalism and everyday human rights legality are testaments, did not so much engender the human rights political imaginary, but intersect with it. Though rarely considered, it is possible to entertain the counterfactual scenario where the human rights political imaginary might have developed otherwise. It need not have been juridified, or perhaps juridified differently. It could have continued functioning as a secular morality, making, and remaking transnational ethico-political communities where the claims of distant and/or excluded victimized others were receivable, and upon which ethical or political action could be taken. It could have become one of the many practices that make up the contemporary flows of cosmopolitan affect, and ethical responsibility for the other, which faintly hint at the prospect of a human community.

However, fatefully, and unfortunately to my mind, the human rights political imaginary was linked to the UDHR, and the Covenants. Because these texts crystallized the balance of global forces in the postwar, where Western liberal democracy, welfare citizenship, and capitalist social relations had gotten the upper hand, human rights began to resonate with societies, thus organized. More consequentially, the human rights political imaginary originated as a means to achieve the modest, though far from easy, goal of alleviating the more extreme, and socially blatant, forms of violence and oppression. Because this had been largely, though unevenly, achieved in countries with liberal democratic and capitalist social relations, these countries were instantly transformed into human rights nations. Via processes specific to each of the polities, and described in Chap. 6, the US reclaimed its lost virtue in foreign policy; Canada, overnight, engendered an endogamous (international) human rights tradition; and Europe began to speak a European political Esperanto, seamlessly translatable into the ethical and political language of its constituent countries.

The newly ordained human rights nations correctly determined that it was their tradition of civil and political rights that enabled them, apparently effortlessly, to protect their citizens against the types of violence around which the human rights political imaginary had mobilized. Forgotten here was the fact that these rights were the product of long historical struggle and complex social-relational contingencies. Consequently, the new vision of a minimally better world, but decisively so for the many who aspired at least to this, required little domestically from the newly minted human rights nations. Internationally, they shared and promoted what they understood to be the secrets of their success, namely, the rule of law via justiciable civil and political rights, and the more diffuse aspiration of socio-economic rights, only if affordable. At this point, human rights inevitably became associated with citizenship rights in liberal democratic capitalist societies, where legal claims could circulate in a social-structural ecology where they had, and have, persuasive force. Ignoring the pithy phrase that all social science students learn—correlation is not causation—the simultaneous generalized absence of the types of violence that human rights emerged to combat and the presence of civil and political rights suggested, but did not demonstrate, that these rights might achieve the same in other places.

Elsewhere, human rights activists courageously and tirelessly continue with the, frequently hazardous, ethico-political labour of building communities where the claims of distant and/or excluded victimized others can be received and acted upon. They bear witness. They document. They disseminate. They invoke the law. They mobilize. They lobby. They protest. They name. And, they shame. When successful, they make an impact on the lives of individuals and in their communities. Seen from the perspective of those who labour tenaciously and tediously for human rights, one could understand the desire for an ethico-political labour-saving machine. The rule of law: a legal machine that would obviate the need to undertake the demanding ethico-political labour of the human right political imaginary every time a human rights violation takes place. If this ethico-political work could be congealed in a self-executing and self-enforcing legal apparatus, attention could, perhaps, be directed elsewhere. Alas, as discussed in Chap. 6, these legal machines exist in the form of global legalism. Their fatal design flaw is their legal naïveté. They fail, as seen in Chap. 6, for reasons that Tony Woodiwiss has explained better than no other.

This, then, is a summary of the book's arguments and conclusions in a highly stylized form. There is, I hope to have shown, much work to be done in the sociology of human rights. For too long, thin conceptions and histories of human rights have prevented scholars from tracing the actual social-relational and historical trajectories that have made human rights the types of social assemblages of ideas, actions, and institutions that they are today. Understood as a political imaginary, questions that focus on the interaction of the different components of the political imaginary—representations, social technologies, modes of subjectivity and action, and organizational forms—or, indeed, that lead to the uncovering of new components will contribute to thickening our understanding of human rights. Equally, asking what it means to vernacularize a political imaginary rather than an idea or ideal will no doubt prove fruitful. New insights are, also, to be secured by attempts to understand the contradictory dynamics and tensions that are reproduced within the imaginary as it travels, becomes embedded in new social-structural arrangements, encounters different modes of cultural politics, and/or interfaces with other political imaginaries. Finally, I am convinced that the political imaginary offers explanatory avenues through which to gauge the likelihood of success or failures of the human rights imaginary in specific contexts.

I noted that one of the fundamental tasks with which sociologists are continuously confronted is that of *understanding anew something that one understands*. If we understand human rights as normatively self-evident, or as ideas or ideals to be implemented, I do not believe that we understand them sociologically. Neither can we really understand them, if we think of them as some neo-colonial-western-ethno-centric ruse. Human rights are historically and socially relationally complex phenomena. The human rights political imaginary model, though certainly incomplete and imperfect, is an attempt to seize some of that complexity with an eye towards developing empirical questions that can be researched sociologically and provide clues for action. My hope in sharing the model is that I will in turn be prompted *to understand anew what I understand* about human rights as a political imaginary.

Bearing Sociological Witness to Human Rights

Drawing on the invaluable work of Fuyiko Kurasawa, I have emphasized the complexity and fragility of bearing witness to the suffering of distant and/or excluded victimized others. Such witnessing brings together our human capacity for empathy and affect with the ethico-political labour that tutors our ethical capacities and educates our political sensibilities. Bearing witness is not just seeing. It is above all a mode of contextualized understanding, of understanding ourselves through the situation of the other, and of understanding the other through our own situated self-understanding. In Chap. 4, I discussed a mode of sociological witnessing that took the form of sociologically documenting the situations of systemic violence and injustice. While sociologists frequently record these ongoing forms of social inequity, and this constitutes a valuable contribution to society's self-understanding, I suggested that it was far from clear that this sociological witnessing would necessarily contribute to the human rights political imaginary. This is so, in part, because the figure of the victim and the perpetrator are partly effaced by the operation of social-structural mechanisms. How then might sociologists use the tools of our trade to bear witness?

Paradoxically, for sociologists, bearing witness involves interrupting the flow of everyday conceptions and common sense. It requires us to be irreverent, not to individuals, but to many of the ideas, practices, and social relations through which we all make sense of the world. Not because sociologists know better, but because there is reason to believe that there might be a gap between our everyday conceptions and what powers the ongoing unfolding of the social relations that make up our experience of the social world. Sociologists approach the social world not with the hubris that they already know, but with the humility that they do not know, and the modesty that it is possible to know. It is from this position that I offer some of the insights that I have gleaned from studying human rights through the prism of the human rights political imaginary model. It is not much, but I hope that it might be of some use to individuals engaged in the struggle for human rights and global justice.

Human rights arose out of political minimalism. It was not at its inception a grand plan to transform the world, but rather a hope that some minor concessions might be secured. It was precisely this, Samuel Moyn argues, that allowed human rights to gain traction. Exhausted by the empty promises of the grand utopias of the postwar, the minimalist and pragmatic politics of human rights offered the prospect of limited progress, to be sure, but of success all the same. How it is that the human rights political imaginary was transformed into a maximalist project is one of the many things associated with human rights that yet remains to be fully understood. As I suggested in Chap. 6, it might, in part, be the product of the intersection of human rights with the law and citizenship rights. However, what is clear is that human rights as a maximalist project has not thus far succeeded and, to my mind, is not likely to succeed. Indeed the clearest attempt to operationalize the human rights political imaginary as a maximalist project in the form of global legalism has helped least those that need it the most.

Understood in terms of its original minimalism, human rights remain as valuable today as they were in the 1970s. The notion that a transnational ethical disposition might be cultivated, and not asserted, founded on the rejection of extreme forms of violence and injustice remains a hopeful and worthy one. Today, the ongoing explosion and decentralization of communications media and the increased mobility of people and things, while not a guarantee, provide scaffolding for the continued cultivation and extension of such an ethical disposition. The contemporary networked world not only enables the formation of ethical-political communities to bear witness, it also reduces the cost of responding. As discussed in Chap. 5, there are numerous instances when and sites where transnational solidarity and politics are practised. The denunciation of abuse and the mobilization of ethical and political energy to curb violence remain crucial elements in the development of a better world. These practices in themselves will not radically change the world for the better, but their absence would likely change individuals for the worst. There is also a fundamental ethical and political lesson inscribed in the modesty of the incipient human rights imaginary, the notion that every person counts. The ability to make this notion resonate transnationally is certainly one of human rights' most significant achievements.

The figure of the innocent victim was and continues to be a key aspect of the functioning of the human rights political imaginary. I would suggest that insofar as it is possible, we must try to develop ethico-political practices that might engender new figures capable of generating new modalities of effective ethico-political responsibility for the other, or just for others. Whether this is possible or not, I cannot say. However in the meantime we can lean on Woodiwiss' sociological and social-structural cosmopolitanism as a way of attempting to improve the efficacy of existing human rights practice. In Chap. 4, in my discussion of bearing witness, I put the emphasis on the reception of the claim of the distant and/or excluded victimized other and its ability to trigger an ethico-political response. I emphasized that the victimized other had to be legible as a genuine "victim" if the claim was to trigger a response.

However, if Woodiwiss is right in arguing that rights are only enforceable insofar as they resonate with or mobilize prevailing values and social relations of power, and I am persuaded that he is, we can reason that this is likely to be true with respect to representations of victimhood. Whatever pressure a transnational ethico-political community can apply on states, individuals, or entities engaged in unconscionable acts of violence is likely to be enhanced if it is founded on representations of innocent victimhood that correspond with the prevailing social relations and cultural politics of the society where the violence originates. I suspect that this is something that frontline human rights activists know only too well. It is stunningly ethnocentric to think that only our own social-structural arrangements are capable of engendering ethical means to curtail the ruthless exercise of social power. Understanding what potential there is implicit in forms of social organization that are very different from those associated with juridified human rights is a mode of human rights activism where sociologist can potentially make significant contributions, as Woodiwiss has demonstrated with his work on labour rights in the Pacific Rim.

If a human rights-inspired global legalism, as currently conceived, is not likely to deliver what it promises, this is not, itself, a reason for abandoning attempts to generate ethico-political labour-saving legal mechanisms, namely, in the form of codified rights. There are as many good reasons for legally codifying immunities, liberties, powers, and claims into rights as there are possible beneficent combinations of these components. The focus should be, as Woodiwiss persuasively argues, on struggling to codify rights that constrain the exercise and abuse of social power and that take advantage of the protective possibilities inherent in the prevailing relations of social power. If these rights can be made to resonate with the broader values and discourses in particular social formations, and they can be applied in a consistent and non-arbitrary manner, by a species of legal machinery best suited to the social-structural context, they can be the source of minimal, to be sure, but valuable forms of social protection.

In turn, these can provide the analogues, and not the clones, for the civil, political, social, cultural, and economic rights that enable political actors in liberal democratic capitalist societies to fight against the retrenchment and for the extension of these rights. I take this to be at the very core of what I have called, in reference to the work of Woodiwiss, social-structural cosmopolitanism. This social-structural cosmopolitanism, my term and not his as far as I am aware, is a noteworthy, yet not sufficiently appreciated, contribution to the field of cosmopolitanism. Much cosmopolitan writing, for reasons that cannot be explored here, tends to be almost exclusively focused on culture. It is true that authors such as David Held will talk about legal, political, economic, and cultural cosmopolitanism, but on my reading the concern is with the development of cosmopolitan legal, political, and economic cultures, rather than social-structural variations.

The key trope in the field of cosmopolitanism is the metaphor of the dialogue. Though valuable, it nonetheless tends to privilege culture understood as ideas, identities, and worldviews by focusing on the exchange between two individuals, or communities, which under the right conditions can arrive at some type of mutual understanding under the best of circumstances, or tolerance under the least. It is the shift in ideas, perceptions, and understanding that makes cultural cosmopolitan possible, and it is relatively straightforward to conceptualize and model this process. The metaphor of dialogue has less to say about social-structural arrangements. Social-structural cosmopolitanism, then, shifts the focus to trying to understand how the protective potential or practical means for individual flourishing can be discovered within social-structural arrangements rather than by philosophical deductions or legal reasoning.

In a final reference to Woodiwiss, which reveals the extent of my intellectual indebtedness to his work, I think it is important to take seriously the idea that rights, evenly rigorously and consistently applied, will always confront *the glass-ceiling of the prevailing social relations of power*. This is why I think it is important to retreat from a maximalist understanding of human rights. By this, I mean the current trend in which all worthy political or ethical objectives must be grounded in the human rights political imaginary. Doing so limits the range of projects of social transformation that might be imagined and undertaken. In a well-known essay, the political theorist Wendy Brown has, eloquently, raised the question of whether the human rights politics of fatalism is "the best we can hope for" (2004). I would respond that human rights is not the best we can hope for, but it is nonetheless worth hoping for, in a minimalist form.

Having a better understanding of what human rights might (not) achieve releases us from the obligation of refracting our future political fortunes through them. If, following Gerard Delanty, we think about cosmopolitanism as "moments of world openness created out of the encounter of the local with the global" (2006, 27), there are certainly other modalities of ethico-political labour taking place that might engender the responsibility to struggle against ongoing forms of oppression and domination, once the long contemporary shadow cast by human right is trimmed. Perhaps new modalities of ethico-political labour that will interpellate us beyond what we owe other humans, and include what we might owe other non-human entities as well, exist or are to develop. As we proceed in the articulations of new political imaginaries, and as they constitute us as political subjects, we will need to remember the responsibility *to understand anew what we already understand.*

Bibliography

Alexander, Jeffrey C., and Pjillip Smith. 2003. "The Strong Program in Cultural Sociology: Elements of a Structural Hermeneutics." In *The Meanings of Social Life: A Cultural Sociology*, edited by Jeffrey C. Alexander, 11–26. New York and Oxford: Oxford University Press.

Brown, Wendy. 2004. "'The Most We Can Hope For…': Human Rights and the Politics of Fatalism." *The South Atlantic Quarterly* 103 (2):451–463.

Delanty, Gerard. 2006. "The Cosmopolitan Imagination: Critical Cosmopolitanism and Social Theory." *The British Journal of Sociology* 57 (1):25–47.

Bibliography

Abbott, Andrew. 2004. *Methods of Discovery: Heuristics for the Social Sciences*. New York: W. W. Norton & Company.

Abizadeh, Arash. 2005. "Does Collective Identity Presuppose an Other? On the Alleged Incoherence of Global Solidarity." *American Political Science Review* 99 (1):45–60.

Adler, Emanuel. 2013. "Constructivism in International Relations: Sources, Contributions, and Debates." In *Handbook of International Relations*, edited by Walter Carlsnaes, Tomas Risse and Beth A. Simmons, 122–144. London: SAGE.

Afshari, Reza. 2007. "On Historiography of Human Rights Reflections on Paul Gordon Lauren's The Evolution of International Human Rights: Visions Seen." *Human Rights Quarterly* 29 (1):1–67.

Agger, Ben. 2007. *Public Sociology: From Social Facts to Literary Acts*. Lanham and New York: Rowman & Littlefield.

Ake, Claude. 1987. "The African Context of Human Rights." *Africa Today* 34 (1/2):5–12.

Alba, Richard D. 1995. "Review of Limits of Citizenship: Migrants and Postnational Membership in Europe." *Contemporary Sociology* 24 (4):326–329.

Aldunate, Jose. 1994. "Human Rights as the Rights of the Poor: The Perspective from Liberation Theology." *Journal of Moral Education* 23 (3):297–303.

J. Julián López, *Human Rights as Political Imaginary*,
https://doi.org/10.1007/978-3-319-74274-8

Alexander, Jeffrey C. 2003. *The Meanings of Social Life: A Cultural Sociology*. Oxford and New York: Oxford University Press.

Alexander, Jeffrey C. 2006. *The Civil Sphere*. Oxford and New York: Oxford University Press.

Alexander, Jeffrey C. 2011. *Performance and Power*. Cambridge and Malden, MA: Polity.

Alexander, Jeffrey C. 2013. "Struggling over the Mode of Incorporation: Backlash Against Multiculturalism in Europe." *Ethnic and Racial Studies* 36 (4):531–556.

Alexander, Jeffrey C., and Pjillip Smith. 2003. "The Strong Program in Cultural Sociology: Elements of a Structural Hermeneutics." In *The Meanings of Social Life: A Cultural Sociology*, edited by Jeffrey C. Alexander, 11–26. New York and Oxford: Oxford University Press.

Althusser, Louis. 1971. *Lenin and Philosophy*, Trans. Ben Brewster. New York: Monthly Review Press.

Althusser, Louis, and Etienne Balibar. 1970. *Reading Capital*, Trans. Ben Brewster. London: NLB.

Anderson, Benedict. 2004. *Imagined Communities: Reflections on the Origin and Spread of Nationalism*. London: Verso.

Anderson, Carol Elaine. 2003. *Eyes off the Prize: The United Nations and the African American Struggle for Human Rights, 1944–1955*. Cambridge and New York: Cambridge University Press.

Anleu, Sharyn Roach. 1999. "Sociologists Confront Human Rights: The Problem of Universalism." *Journal of Sociology* 35 (2):198–212.

An-Na'im, Abdullahi Ahmed, ed. 2010. *Human Rights in Cross-Cultural Perspectives: A Quest for Consensus*. Philadelphia: University of Pennsy lvania Press.

Apodaca, Clair, and Michael Stohl. 1999. "United States Human Rights Policy and Foreign Assistance." *International Studies Quarterly* 43 (1):185–198.

Archibugi, Daniele. 2008. *The Global Commonwealth of Citizens: Toward Cosmopolitan Democracy*. Princeton, NJ: Princeton University Press.

Archibugi, Daniele. 2012. "Cosmopolitan Democracy: A Restatement." *Cambridge Journal of Education* 42 (1):9–20.

Armaline, William T., Davita S. Glasberg, and Bandana Purkayastha. 2015. *The Human Rights Enterprise: Political Sociology, State Power, and Social Movements*. Cambridge and Malden, MA: Polity.

Arthurs, Harry W. 2000. "Poor Canadian Legal Education: So Near to Wall Street, So Far from God." *Osgoode Hall Law Journal* 38:381–408.

Arthurs, Harry W., and Robert Kreklewich. 1996. "Law, Legal Institutions, and the Legal Profession in the New Economy." *Osgoode Hall Law Journal* 34:1.

Austin, John. 1962. *How to Do Things with Words*. Oxford and New York: Oxford University Press.

Badiou, Alain. 2001. *Ethics: An Essay on the Understanding of Evil*. London: Verso.

Baer, Douglas Edward. 2005. "On the Crisis in Canadian Sociology: Comment on McLaughlin." *The Canadian Journal of Sociology* 30 (4):491–502.

Baghai, Katayoun. 2012. "Privacy as a Human Right: A Sociological Theory." *Sociology* 46 (5):951–965.

Baldi, Gregory, and Sara Wallace Goodman. 2015. "Migrants into Members: Social Rights, Civic Requirements, and Citizenship in Western Europe." *West European Politics* 38 (6):1152–1173.

Balfour, Rosa. 2008. "Human Rights Promotion." In *The Search for a European Identity: Values, Policies and Legitimacy of the European Union*, edited by Furio Cerutti and Sonia Lucarelli, 159–175. London: Routledge.

Bamberger, Michael A., and Nathan Lewin. 1961. "The Right to Equal Treatment: Administrative Enforcement of Anti-Discrimination Legislation." *Harvard Law Review* 526 (74):526–589.

Banerjee, Kiran. 2014. "Toward Post-National Membership-Tensions and Transformation in German and EU Citizenship." *Journal of International Law and International Relations* 10:4–30.

Bangarth, Stephanie. 2013. "'Their Equality Is My Equality': F. Andrew Brewisn and Human Rights Activism, 1940s–1970s." In *Taking Liberties: A History of Human Rights in Canada*, edited by Stephen J. Heathorn and David Goutor, 114–138. Don Mills, ON: Oxford University Press.

Bannister, Robert C. 1987. *Sociology and Scientism*. Chapel Hill: University of North Carolina.

Barbalet, Jack M. 1988. *Citizenship: Rights, Struggle, and Class Inequality*. Maidenhead and Philadelphia: Open University Press.

Barber, Tony. 2017. "Europe's New Political Divisions." *Financial Times*. May 14, 2017. https://www.ft.com/content/21138f54-35ab-11e7-bce4-9023f8c0fd2e.

Barnett, Michael N. 2011. *Empire of Humanity: A History of Humanitarianism*. Ithaca, NY: Cornell University Press.

Bauer, Laurie. 2008. "Exocentric Compounds." *Morphology* 18 (1):51–74.

Bauman, Richard, and Charles L. Briggs. 1990. "Poetics and Performance as Critical Perspectives on Language and Social Life." *Annual Review of Anthropology* 19:59–88.

Baxi, Upendra. 1998. "Voices of Suffering and the Future of Human Rights." *Transnational Law and Contemporary Problems* 8:125–169.

Baxi, Upendra. 2002. *The Future of Human Rights*. Oxford: Oxford University Press.

Beck, Ulrich. 1992. *Risk Society: Towards a New Modernity*. London: Sage.

Beck, Ulrich. 2000a. "The Cosmopolitan Perspective: Sociology of the Second Age of Modernity." *The British Journal of Sociology* 51 (1):79–105.

Beck, Ulrich. 2000b. *What Is Globalization?* Cambridge and Malden, MA: Polity Press.

Beck, Ulrich. 2006. *Cosmopolitan Vision*. Cambridge and Malden, MA: Polity.

Becker, Howard S. 1967. "Whose Side Are We on." *Social Problems* 14 (3):239–247.

Behiels, Michael D. 2009. "Pierre Elliot Trudeau's Legacy: The Canadian Charter of Rights and Freedoms." In *A History of Human Rights in Canada: Essential Issues*, edited by Janet Miron, 201–217. Toronto: Canadian Scholars' Press.

Beitz, Charles R. 2011. *The Idea of Human Rights*. Oxford and New York: Oxford University Press.

Beitz, Charles R., and Robert E. Goodin. 2009. *Global Basic Rights*. Oxford and New York: Oxford University Press.

Bell, Daniel A. 2000. *East Meets West: Human Rights and Democracy in East Asia*. Princeton, NJ: Princeton University Press.

Benczes, Réka. 2006. *Creative Compounding in English*. Amsterdam and Philadelphia: John Benjamins Publishing Company.

Bengtsson, Jan Olof. 2006. *The Worldview of Personalism: Origins and Early Development*. Oxford and New York: Oxford University Press.

Benhabib, Seyla (1986) Critique, Norm and Utopia: A Study of the Foundations of Critical Theory. New York: Columbia University Press.

Benhabib, Seyla. 1992. *Situating the Self: Gender, Community and Postmodernism in Contemporary Ethics*. Cambridge and Malden, MA: Polity Press.

Benhabib, Seyla. 1994. "Deliberative Rationality and Models of Democratic Legitimacy." *Constellations* 1 (1):26–52.

Benhabib, Seyla. 2004. *The Rights of Others: Aliens, Residents, and Citizens*. Cambridge and New York: Cambridge University Press.

Benhabib, Seyla. 2013a. *Dignity in Adversity: Human Rights in Troubled Times*. Cambridge and New York: Polity.

Benhabib, Seyla. 2013b. "Moving Beyond False Binarisms: On Samuel Moyn's The Last Utopia." *Qui Parle: Critical Humanities and Social Sciences* 22 (1):81–93.

Berger, Peter L. 1969. *The Sacred Canopy: Elements of a Sociological Theory of Religion*. New York: Anchor Books.

Bhaskar, Roy. 1978. *A Realist Theory of Science, Brighton*. Brighton: Harvester Press.

Bhatt, Chetan. 2012. "Human Rights and the Transformations of War." *Sociology* 46 (5):813–828.

Blackburn, Robin. 2013. *The American Crucible: Slavery, Emancipation and Human Rights*. London: Verso.

Blau, Judith R. 2012. "Comparing Constitutions." In *Sociology and Human Rights: A Bill of Rights for the Twenty-First Century*, edited by Judith Blau and Mark Frezzo, 129–152. London and Los Angeles: Sage.

Blau, Judith R., and Alberto Moncada. 2005. *Human Rights: Beyond the Liberal Vision*. Lanham, MD and New York: Rowman & Littlefield.

Blau, Judith R., and Alberto Moncada. 2007. "It Ought to Be a Crime: Criminalizing Human Rights Violations." *Sociological Forum* 22:364–371.

Blau, Judith R., and Alberto Moncada. 2008. "Freedom and Security." In *The Leading Rogue State: The United States and Human Rights*, edited by Judith R. Blau, David L. Brunsma, Alberto Moncada, and Catherine Zimmer, 233–237. Boulder and London: Paradigm Publishers.

Blau, Judith R., and Alberto Moncada. 2009a. "Sociological Theory and Human Rights: Two Logics, One World." In *The Blackwell Companion to Social Theory*, edited by Bryan S. Turner, 496–512. Oxford: Wiley-Blackwell.

Blau, Judith R., and Alberto Moncada. 2009b. "The New Humanism: Beyond Modernity and Postmodernism." In *Human Rights: Social Science Perspectives*, edited by Rhiannon Morgan and Bryan S. Turner, 147–156. London and New York: Routledge.

Blau, Judith R., and Alberto Moncada. 2016. *Human Rights: A Primer*. New York: Routledge.

Blau, Judith R., and Keri E. Iyall Smith. 2006. *Public Sociologies Reader*. Lanham, MD: Rowman & Littlefield.

Blau, Judith R., and Mark Frezzo, eds. 2012a. "Going Forward." In *Sociology and Human Rights*, 271–280. Los Angeles and London: Sage.

Blau, Judith R., and Mark Frezzo, eds. 2012b. *Sociology and Human Rights: A Bill of Rights for the Twenty-First Century*. Los Angeles and London: Sage.

Blau, Judith R., David L. Brunsma, Alberto Moncada, and Catherine Zimmer, eds. 2008. *The Leading Rogue State: The United States and Human Rights*. Boulder and London: Paradigm Books.

Block, Fred. 2007. "Understanding the Diverging Trajectories of the United States and Western Europe: A Neo-Polanyian Analysis." *Politics & Society* 35 (1):3–33.

Blumenthal, Sidney. 2008. *The Rise of the Counter-Establishment: The Conservative Ascent to Political Power*. New York: Union Square Press.

Boli, John, and George M. Thomas. 1999. *Constructing World Culture: International Nongovernmental Organizations Since 1875*. Stanford: Stanford University Press.

Boltanski, Luc. 1999. *Distant Suffering: Morality, Media and Politics*. Cambridge and New York: Cambridge University Press.

Boltanski, Luc, and Laurent Thévenot. 2006. *On Justification: Economies of Worth*. Princeton, NJ: Princeton University Press.

Bond, Niall. 2009. "Ferdinand Tönnies and Western European Positivism." *Intellectual History Review* 19 (3):353–370.

Boot, Max. 2004. "Neocons." *Foreign Policy* 140:20–28.

Borgwardt, Elizabeth. 2007. *A New Deal for the World*. Cambridge, MA: Harvard University Press.

Bosniak, Linda. 2000. "Citizenship Denationalized." *Indiana Journal of Global Legal Studies* 7 (2):447–509.

Bosniak, Linda. 2006. *The Citizen and the Alien: Dilemmas of Contemporary Membership*. Princeton, NJ: Princeton University Press.

Bourdieu, Pierre. 1977. *Outline of a Theory of Practice*. Cambridge and New York: Cambridge University Press.

Bourdieu, Pierre. 1986. "Force of Law: Toward a Sociology of the Juridical Field." *The Hastings Law Journal* 38:814–853.

Bourdieu, Pierre. 1998a. *Practical Reason: On the Theory of Action*. Stanford: Stanford University Press.

Bourdieu, Pierre. 1998b. *The State Nobility: Elite Schools in the Field of Power*. Cambridge and New York: Polity Press.

Bourdieu, Pierre. 1992. "The Paris Workshop" in Pierre Bourdieu and Loïc JD Wacquant, An Invitation to Reflexive Sociology. Chicago: University of Chicago press, pp. 218–260.

Bourdieu, Pierre, and Loïc J.D. Wacquant. 1992. *An Invitation to Reflexive Sociology*. Chicago and London: University of Chicago press.

Bradley, Mark Philip. 2012. "Approaching the Universal Declaration of Human Rights." In *The Human Rights Revolution: An International History*, edited by Akara Iriye, Petra Goedde, and William I. Hitchcock, 327–344. Oxford: Oxford University Press.

Brady, David. 2004. "Why Public Sociology May Fail." *Social Forces* 82 (4):1629–1638.

Brenner, Neil, Bob Jessop, Martin Jones, and Gordon Macleod, eds. 2008. *State/Space: A Reader*. Oxford and Malden, MA: Blackwell.

Bricmont, Jean. 2006. *Humanitarian Imperialism: Using Human Rights to Sell War*. New York: NYU Press.

Broeders, Dennis. 2007. "The New Digital Borders of Europe: EU Databases and the Surveillance of Irregular Migrants." *International Sociology* 22 (1):71–92.

Brown, Garrett W., and David Held. 2010. "Editor's Introduction." In *The Cosmopolitanism Reader*, edited by Garrett W. Brown and David Held, 1–14. Cambridge and Malden, MA: Polity Press.

Brown, Garrett W., and David Held, eds. 2010. *The Cosmopolitanism Reader*. Cambridge and Malden, MA: Polity Press.

Brown, Wendy. 1995. *States of Injury*. Princeton, NJ: Princeton University Press.

Brown, Wendy. 2004. "'The Most We Can Hope For...': Human Rights and the Politics of Fatalism." *The South Atlantic Quarterly* 103 (2):451–463.

Brubaker, William Rogers. 1989a. "Introduction." In *Immigration and the Politics of Citizenship in Europe and North America*, edited by William Rogers Brubaker. Lanham, MD: University Press of America, 1–27.

Brubaker, William Rogers. 1989b. "Membership Without Citizenship: The Economic and Social Rights of Noncitizens." In *Immigration and the Politics of Citizenship in Europe and North America*, edited by William Rogers Brubaker. Lanham, MD: University Press of America, 145–181.

Brubaker, Williams Rogers, and Frederick Cooper. 2000. "Beyond 'Identity.'" *Theory and Society* 29 (1):1–47.

Bruner, Arnold. 1979. "The Genesis of Ontario's Human Rights Legislation: A Study in Law Reform." *University of Toronto Faculty of Law Review* 37:236–253.

Bryant, Christopher G. A. 1985. *Positivism in Social Theory and Research*. London: Macmillan.

Bryant, Joseph M. 1996. *Moral Codes and Social Structure in Ancient Greece: A Sociology of Greek Ethics from Homer to the Epicureans and Stoics*. Albany, NY: SUNY Press.

Brym, Robert, and Celine Saint-Pierre. 1997. "Canadian Sociology." *Contemporary Sociology* 26 (5):543–546.

Brysk, Alison. 2002. *Globalization and Human Rights*. Berkeley, CA. University of California Press.

Brysk, Alison. 2013. *Speaking Rights to Power: Constructing Political Will*. Oxford and New York: Oxford University Press.

Brysk, Alison, and Gershon Shafir. 2004. *People Out of Place: Globalization, Human Rights and the Citizenship Gap*. London: Routledge.

Buchanan, Tom. 2004. "Amnesty International in Crisis, 1966–7." *Twentieth Century British History* 15 (3):267–289.

Burawoy, Michael. 2003. "For a Sociological Marxism: The Complementary Convergence of Antonio Gramsci and Karl Polanyi." *Politics & Society* 31 (2):193–261.

Burawoy, Michael. 2005. "For Public Sociology." *American Sociological Review* 70 (1):4–28.

Burawoy, Michael. 2006. "Introduction: A Public Sociology for Human Rights." In *Public Sociologies Reader*, edited by Judith Blau and Keri E. Iyall-Smith, 1–18. Boulder: Rowan and Littlefield.

Burggraeve, Roger. 1999. "Violence and the Vulnerable Face of the Other: The Vision of Emmanuel Levinas on Moral Evil and Our Responsibility." *Journal of Social Philosophy* 30 (1):29–45.

Burke, Roland. 2011. *Decolonization and the Evolution of International Human Rights*. Philadelphia: University of Pennsylvania Press.

Burke, Roland. 2015. "Human Rights Day After the 'Breakthrough': Celebrating the Universal Declaration of Human Rights at the United Nations in 1978 and 1988." *Journal of Global History* 10 (1):147–170.

Butler, Judith. 1988. "Performative Acts and Gender Constitution: An Essay in Phenomenology and Feminist Theory." *Theatre Journal* 40 (4):519–531.

Butler, Judith. 1995. "Conscience Doth Make Subjects of Us All." *Yale French Studies* 88:6–26.

Butler, Judith. 2011. *Bodies That Matter: On the Discursive Limits of Sex*. London and New York: Routledge.

Buzan, Barry, and Richard Little. 2001. "Why International Relations Has Failed as an Intellectual Project and What to Do About It." *Millennium* 30 (1):19–39.

Canning, Victoria. 2010. "Who's Human? Developing Sociological Understandings of the Rights of Women Raped in Conflict." *The International Journal of Human Rights* 14 (6):849–864.

Cardenas, Sonia. 2003. "Transgovernmental Activism: Canada's Role in Promoting National Human Rights Commissions." *Human Rights Quarterly* 25 (3):775–790.

Carleton, David, and Michael Stohl. 1985. "The Foreign Policy of Human Rights: Rhetoric and Reality from Jimmy Carter to Ronald Reagan." *Human Rights Quarterly*, 205–229.

Carlson, Marvin. 2013. *Performance: A Critical Introduction*. London and New York: Routledge.

Castoriadis, Cornelius. 1998. *The Imaginary Institution of Society*. Cambridge, MA: MIT Press.

Cetina, Karin Knorr, Theodore R. Schatzki, and Eike von Savigny, eds. 2005. *The Practice Turn in Contemporary Theory*. London and New York: Routledge.

Checkel, Jeffrey T. 1998. "The Constructive Turn in International Relations Theory." *World Politics* 50 (2):324–348.

Checkel, Jeffrey T. 2013. "Theoretical Pluralisms in IR: Possibilities and Limits." In *Handbook of International Relations*, edited by Walter Carlsnaes, Tomas Risse, and Beth A. Simmons, 220–242. London: Sage.

Chimienti, Milena, and John Solomos. 2011. "Social Movements of Irregular Migrants, Recognition, and Citizenship." *Globalizations* 8 (3):343–360.

Chisholm, Andrea. 2008. *Legal Education in Crisis: Healing and Humanizing Canadian Law Schools*. Peterborough: Brock University. http://www.dr.library.brocku.ca/handle/10464/1543.

Christie, Nancy. 2000. *Engendering the State: Family, Work, and Welfare in Canada*. Toronto: University of Toronto Press.

Christoffersen, Jonas. 2011. "Individual and Constitutional Justice: Can the Power Balance of Adjudication Be Reversed." In *The European Court of Human Rights Between Law and Politics*, edited by Jonas Christoffersen and Mikael Rask Madsen, 181–203. Oxford and New York: Oxford University Press.

Christoffersen, Jonas, and Mikael Rask Madsen, eds. 2011. *The European Court of Human Rights Between Law and Politics*. Oxford and New York: Oxford University Press.

Cichowski, Rachel A. 2011. "Civil Society and the European Court of Human Rights." In *The European Court of Human Rights Between Law and Politics*, edited by Jonas Christoffersen and Mikael Rask Madsen, 77–97. Oxford and New York: Oxford University Press.

Claeys, Priscilla. 2012. "The Creation of New Rights by the Food Sovereignty Movement: The Challenge of Institutionalizing Subversion." *Sociology* 46 (5):844–860.

Claydon, John. 1986. "The Use of International Human Rights Law to Interpret Canada's Charter of Rights and Freedoms." *Connecticut Journal of International Law* 2:349–359.

Clément, Dominique. 2008. *Canada's Rights Revolution: Social Movements and Social Change, 1937–82*. Vancouver: UBC Press.

Clément, Dominique. 2009. "Rights Without the Sword Are but Mere Words." In *A History of Human Rights in Canada: Essential Issues*, edited by Janet Miron, 43–60. Toronto: Canadian Scholars' Press.

Clément, Dominique. 2012. "Human Rights in Canadian Domestic and Foreign Politics: From 'Niggardly Acceptance' to Enthusiastic Embrace." *Human Rights Quarterly* 34 (3):751–778.

Clément, Dominique. 2013. "The Rights Revolution in Canada and Australia." In *Taking Liberties: A History of Human Rights in Canada*,

edited by Stephen J. Heathorn and David Goutor, 88–113. Don Mills, ON: Oxford University Press.
Clifford, James. 1988. *The Predicament of Culture: Twentieth-Century Ethnography, Literature and Art*. Cambridge, MA: Harvard University Press.
Cmiel, Kenneth. 2004. "The Recent History of Human Rights." *The American Historical Review* 109 (1):117–135.
Cobbah, Josiah A.M. 1987. "African Values and the Human Rights Debate: An African Perspective." *Human Rights Quarterly* 9 (3):309–331.
Cohen, G. Daniel. 2012. "The Holocaust and the 'Human Rights Revolution': A Reassessment." In *The Human Rights Revolution: An International History*, edited by Akara Iriye, Petra Goedde, and William I. Hitchcock, 53–72. Oxford: Oxford University Press.
Cohen, Jean L. 1995. "Critical Social Theory and Feminist Critiques: The Debate with Jurgen Habermas." In *Feminists Read Habermas (RLE Feminist Theory): Gendering the Subject of Discourse*, edited by Johanna Meehan, 57–90. London and New York: Routledge.
Cohen, Stan. 2001. *States of Denial: Knowing About Atrocities and Suffering*. Cambridge and New York: Polity Press.
Cole, Alyson M. 2007. *The Cult of True Victimhood: From the War on Welfare to the War on Terror*. Stanford, CA: Stanford University Press.
Cole, Wade M. 2012. "Human Rights as Myth and Ceremony? Reevaluating the Effectiveness of Human Rights Treaties, 1981–2007 1." *American Journal of Sociology* 117 (4):1131–1171.
Collins, Hugh. 1982. *Marxism and Law*. Oxford: Oxford University Press.
Collins, Randall. 1998. *The Sociology of Philosophies: A Global Theory of Intellectual Change*. Cambridge, MA: Belknap Press of Harvard University Press.
Connolly, Nicholas. 2012. "Corporate Social Responsibility: A Duplicitous Distraction?" *The International Journal of Human Rights* 16 (8):1228–1249.
Cowan, Jane K., Marie-Bénédicte Dembour, and Richard A. Wilson, eds. 2001. *Culture and Rights: Anthropological Perspectives*. Cambridge and New York: Cambridge University Press.
Crenshaw, Kimberlé. 1995. *Critical Race Theory: The Key Writings That Formed the Movement*. New York: The New Press.
Crouch, Colin, Klau Eder, and Damian Tambini. 2000. *Citizenship, Markets, and the State*. Oxford: Oxford University Press.
Dale, Gareth. 2010a. *Karl Polanyi: The Limits of the Market*. Cambridge and Malden, MA: Polity.

Dale, Gareth. 2010b. "Social Democracy, Embeddedness and Decommodification: On the Conceptual Innovations and Intellectual Affiliations of Karl Polanyi." *New Political Economy* 15 (3):369–393.
Dale, Gareth. 2011. "Lineages of Embeddedness: On the Antecedents and Successors of a Polanyian Concept." *American Journal of Economics and Sociology* 70 (2):306–339.
Dale, Gareth. 2012. "Double Movements and Pendular Forces: Polanyian Perspectives on the Neoliberal Age." *Current Sociology* 60 (1):3–27.
Davis, Kathy. 2008. "Intersectionality as Buzzword: A Sociology of Science Perspective on What Makes a Feminist Theory Successful." *Feminist Theory* 9 (1):67–85.
Dawes, James. 2009. *That the World May Know: Bearing Witness to Atrocity*. Cambridge, MA: Harvard University Press.
De Sousa Santos, Boaventure. 2008. "Human Rights as an Emancipatory Script: Cultural and Political Conditions." In *Another Knowledge Is Possible*, edited by Boaventura De Sousa Santos, 3–40. London: Verso.
Deflem, Mathieu, and Stephen Chicoine. 2011. "The Sociological Discourse on Human Rights: Lessons from the Sociology of Law." *Development and Society* 40 (1):101–115.
DeLanda, Manuel. 2002. *Intensive Science and Virtual Philosophy*. London: Athlone Press.
Delanty, Gerard. 2006. "The Cosmopolitan Imagination: Critical Cosmopolitanism and Social Theory." *The British Journal of Sociology* 57 (1):25–47.
Delanty, Gerard, ed. 2012. *Routledge Handbook of Cosmopolitanism Studies*. London and New York: Routledge.
Deleuze, Gilles. 1994. *Difference and Repetition*. New York: Columbia University Press.
Delgado, Richard, and Jean Stefancic. 2017. *Critical Race Theory: An Introduction*. New York: NYU Press.
Dezalay, Yves, and Bryant G. Garth. 1998. *Dealing in Virtue: International Commercial Arbitration and the Construction of a Transnational Legal Order*. Chicago and London: University of Chicago Press.
Dezalay, Yves, and Bryant G. Garth. 2002. *The Internationalization of Palace Wars: Lawyers, Economists, and the Contest to Transform Latin American States*. Chicago and London: University of Chicago Press.
Dezalay, Yves, and Bryant G. Garth. 2006. "From the Cold War to Kosovo: The Rise and Renewal of the Field of International Human Rights." *Annual Review of Law and Social Science* 2:231–255.

Dezalay, Yves, and Bryant G. Garth. 2010. *Asian Legal Revivals: Lawyers in the Shadow of Empire*. Chicago and London: University of Chicago Press.

Dezalay, Yves, and Bryant G. Garth. 2012a. "Introduction: Constructing Transnational Justice." In *Lawyers and the Construction of Transnational Justice*, edited by Yves Dezalay and Bryant Garth, 3–12. Milton Park and New York: Routledge.

Dezalay, Yves, and Bryant G. Garth, eds. 2012b. *Lawyers and the Construction of Transnational Justice*. Milton Park and New York: Routledge.

Diner, Dan. 1997. "On Guilt Discourse and Other Narratives: Epistemological Observations Regarding the Holocaust." *History and Memory* 9 (1/2):301–320.

Diner, Dan. 2003. "Restitution and Memory: The Holocaust in European Political Cultures." *New German Critique* 90:36–44.

Diner, Hasia. 2010. *We Remember with Reverence and Love: American Jews and the Myth of Silence After the Holocaust, 1945–1962*. New York: NYU Press.

Domínguez, Edmé, Rosalba Icaza, Cirila Quintero, Silvia López, and Åsa Stenman. 2010. "Women Workers in the Maquiladoras and the Debate on Global Labor Standards." *Feminist Economics* 16 (4):185–209.

Donnelly, Jack. 1984. "Cultural Relativism and Universal Human Rights." *Human Rights Quarterly* 6:400–419.

Donnelly, Jack. 1986. "International Human Rights: A Regime Analysis." *International Organization* 40 (3):599–642.

Douglas-Scott, S. 2006. "A Tale of Two Courts: Luxembourg, Strasbourg and the Growing European Human Rights *Acquis*." *Common Market Law Review* 43 (3):629–665.

Douzinas, Costas. 2000. *The End of Human Rights: Critical Thought at the Turn of the Century*. Oxford and Portland, OR: Hart Publishing

Douzinas, Costas. 2007. *Human Rights and Empire: The Political Philosophy of Cosmopolitanism*. London and New York: Routledge.

Drori, Gili S., John W. Meyer, Francisco O. Ramirez, and Evan Schofer. 2003. "World Society and the Authority and Empowerment of Science." In *Science in the Modern World Polity: Institutionalization and Globalization*, edited by Gili S. Drori, 23–42. Stanford, CA: Stanford University Press.

Dubiel, Helmut. 2003. "The Remembrance of the Holocaust as a Catalyst for a Transnational Ethic?" *New German Critique* 90:59–70.

Dubois, Michel. 2007. "La Construction Métaphorique Du Collectif: Dimensions Implicites Du Prêt-À-Penser Constructiviste et Théorie de L'acteur-Réseau." *L'Année Sociologique* 57 (1):127–150.

Dudziak, Mary L. 2011. *Cold War Civil Rights: Race and the Image of American Democracy*. Princeton, NJ: Princeton University Press.
Dunne, Tim, and Matt McDonald. 2013. "The Politics of Liberal Internationalism." *International Politics* 50 (1):1–17.
Duranti, Marco. 2012. "The Holocaust, the Legacy of 1789 and the Birth of International Human Rights Law: Revisiting the Foundation Myth." *Journal of Genocide Research* 14 (2):159–186.
Duranti, Marco. 2016. *The Conservative Human Rights Revolution: European Identity, Transnational Politics, and the Origins of the European Convention*. Oxford: Oxford University Press.
Durkheim, Emile. 1974. *Sociology and Philosophy*. Book, Whole. Simon and Schuster.
Eberhard, Christoph. 2001. "Towards an Intercultural Legal Theory: The Dialogical Challenge." *Social & Legal Studies* 10 (2):171–201.
Eberlee, T. M., and D. G. Hill. 1964. "The Ontario Human Rights Code." *The University of Toronto Law Journal* 15 (2):448–455. .
Eckel, Jan. 2014. "The Rebirth of Politics from the Spirit of Morality: Explaining the Human Rights Revolution of the 1970s." In *The Breakthrough: Human Rights in the 1970s*, edited by Jan Eckel and Samuel Moyn, 226–260. Philadelphia: University of Pennsylvania Press.
Eckel, Jan, and Samuel Moyn. 2014. *The Breakthrough: Human Rights in the 1970s*. Philadelphia: University of Pennsylvania Press.
Edmunds, June. 2012. "The Limits of Post-National Citizenship: European Muslims, Human Rights and the Hijab." *Ethnic and Racial Studies* 35 (7):1181–1199.
Ehrman, John. 1996. *The Rise of Neoconservatism: Intellectuals and Foreign Affairs, 1945–1994*. Yale, NH: Yale University Press.
Emirbayer, Mustafa. 2004. "The Alexander School of Cultural Sociology." *Thesis Eleven* 79 (1):5–15.
Engel, David M., and Frank W. Munger. 2003. *Rights of Inclusion: Law and Identity in the Life Stories of Americans with Disabilities*. Chicago and London: University of Chicago Press.
Engler, Mark. 2000. "Toward the 'Rights of the Poor' Human Rights in Liberation Theology." *Journal of Religious Ethics* 28 (3):339–365.
Englund, Harri. 2006. *Prisoners of Freedom: Human Rights and the African Poor*. Cambridge: Cambridge University Press.
Epp, Charles R. 1996. "Do Bills of Rights Matter? The Canadian Charter of Rights and Freedoms." *American Political Science Review* 90 (4):765–779.

Esping-Andersen, Gosta. 1998. *The Three Worlds of Welfare Capitalism*. Cambridge: Polity Press.

Ewick, Patricia, and Susan S. Silbey. 1998. *The Common Place of Law: Stories from Everyday Life*. Chicago and London: University of Chicago Press.

Fairclough, Norman. 2003. *Analysing Discourse: Textual Analysis for Social Research*. London: Routledge.

Fairclough, Norman, Bob Jessop, and Andrew Sayer. 2002. "Critical Realism and Semiosis." *Alethia* 5 (1):2–10.

Fassin, Didier. 2012. *Humanitarian Reason: A Moral History of the Present*. Berkeley, CA: University of California Press.

Fassin, Didier, and Richard Rechtman. 2009. *The Empire of Trauma: An Inquiry into the Condition of Victimhood*. Princeton, NJ: Princeton University Press.

Ferrie, Joanna. 2010. "Sociology and Human Rights: What Have They Got to Say About Care and Dignity?" *The International Journal of Human Rights* 14 (6):865–879.

Fine, Robert. 2002. "Marxism and the Social Theory of Law." In *An Introduction to Law and Social Theory*, edited by Reza Banakar and Max Travers, 101–118. Oxford and Portland, OR: Hart Publishing.

Fine, Robert. 2009. "Cosmopolitanism and Human Rights: Radicalism in a Global Age." *Metaphilosophy* 40 (1):8–23.

Fineman, Martha Albertson, and Nancy Sweet Thomadsen. 2013. *At the Boundaries of Law (RLE Feminist Theory): Feminism and Legal Theory*. London and New York: Routledge.

Finley, Lucinda M. 1989. "Breaking Women's Silence in Law: The Dilemma of the Gendered Nature of Legal Reasoning." *Notre Dame Law Review* 64:886–910.

Finnemore, Martha, and Kathryn Sikkink. 2001. "TAKING STOCK: The Constructivist Research Program in International Relations and Comparative Politics." *Annual Review of Political Science* 4:391–416.

Fisher, William W., Morton J. Horwitz, and Thomas Reed, eds. 1993. *American Legal Realism*. Oxford: Oxford University Press.

Fleischer, Doris Zames, Fleischer Doris Zames, and Frieda Zames. 2012. *The Disability Rights Movement: From Charity to Confrontation*. Philadelphia: Temple University Press.

Foroohar, Manzar. 1986. "Liberation Theology: The Response of Latin American Catholics to Socioeconomic Problems." *Latin American Perspectives* 13 (3):37–58.

Foucault, Michel. 1972. *The Archaeology of Knowledge*. New York: Pantheon Books.

Foucault, Michel. 1995. *Discipline and Punish*. New York: Vintage Books.

Frager, Ruth A., and Carmela Patrias. 2013. "Transnational Links and Citizens' Rights: Canadian Jewish Human Rights Activists and Their American Allies in the 1940s and 1950s." In *Taking Liberties: A History of Human Rights in Canada*, edited by Stephen J. Heathorn and David Goutor, 139–165. Don Mills, ON: Oxford University Press.

Fraser, Nancy, and Linda Gordon. 1992. "Contract Versus Charity." *Socialist Review* 22 (3):45–67.

Freeman, Michael. 1994. "The Philosophical Foundations of Human Rights." *Human Rights Quarterly* 16:491–514.

Frezzo, Mark. 2011. "Sociology and Human Rights in the Post-Development Era." *Sociology Compass* 5 (3):203–214.

Frezzo, Mark. 2012. "Introduction." In *Sociology and Human Rights: A Bill of Rights for the Twenty-First Century*, edited by Judith Blau and Mark Frezzo, 3–14. London and New York: Sage Publications.

Gandsman, Ari. 2013. "Narrative, Human Rights and the Ethnographic Reproduction of Conventional Knowledge." *Anthropologica*, 127–140.

Gaonkar, Dilip Parameshwar. 2002. "Toward New Imaginaries: An Introduction." *Public Culture* 14 (1):1–19.

Giddens, Anthony. 1999. *Runaway World: How Globalization Is Reshaping Our Lives*. London: Profile Books.

Glendon, Mary Ann. 2002. *A World Made New: Eleanor Roosevelt and the Universal Declaration of Human Rights*. New York: Random House.

Golash-Boza, Tanya, and Cecilia Menjívar. 2012. "Causes and Consequences of International Migration: Sociological Evidence for the Right to Mobility." *The International Journal of Human Rights* 16 (8):1213–1227.

Gonquergood, Dwight. 1989. "Poetics, Play, Process, and Power: The Performative Turn in Anthropology." *Text and Performance Quarterly* 9 (1):82–88.

Goodale, Mark. 2002. "The Globalization of Sympathetic Law and Its Consequences." *Law & Social Inquiry* 27 (3):595–608.

Goodale, Mark. 2009. *Surrendering to Utopia: An Anthropology of Human Rights*. Stanford, CA: Stanford University Press.

Goodman, Sara Wallace. 2012. "Fortifying Citizenship: Policy Strategies for Civic Integration in Western Europe." *World Politics* 64 (4):659–698.

Gough, Ian. 1975. "State Expenditure in Advanced Capitalism." *New Left Review* 92:53–92.

Gouldner, Alvin W. 1962. "Anti-Minotaur: The Myth of a Value-Free Sociology." *Social Problems* 9 (3):199–213.

Gramsci, Antonio. 1971. *Selections Form the Prison Notebooks. Edited and Translated by Q.Hoare & GN Smith*. New York: International Publishers.

Greer, Steven. 2006. *The European Convention on Human Rights: Achievements, Problems and Prospects*. Cambridge and New York: Cambridge University Press.

Gregg, Benjamin. 2011. *Human Rights as Social Construction*. Cambridge and New York: Cambridge University Press.

Grigolo, Michele. 2010. "Human Rights and Cities: The Barcelona Office for Non-Discrimination and Its Work for Migrants." *The International Journal of Human Rights* 14 (6):896–914.

Grimes, William. 2010. "Louis Henkin, Leader in Field of Human Rights Law, Dies at 92." *The New York Times*, October 16, 2010, sec. US https://www.nytimes.com/2010/10/17/us/17henkin.html.

Gündoğdu, Ayten. 2015. *Rightlessness in an Agee of Rights: Hannah Arendt and the Contemporary Struggles of Migrants*. Oxford and New York: Oxford University Press.

Habermas, Jürgen. 1992. "Further Reflections on the Public Sphere." In *Habermas and the Public Sphere*, edited by Craig J. Calhoun, 421–461. Cambridge, MA: MIT Press.

Habermas, Jürgen. 2004. "Why Europe Needs a Constitution." In *Developing a Constitution for Europe*, edited by Erik O. Eriksen, John E. Fossum, and Augustin J. Menendez, 1:17–33. London and New York: Routledge.

Habermas, Jürgen. 2012. "The Concept of Human Dignity and the Realistic Utopia of Human Rights." *Metaphilosophy* 41 (4):464–480.

Hafner-Burton, Emilie M. 2013. *Making Human Rights a Reality*. Princeton, NJ: Princeton University Press.

Hafner-Burton, Emilie M., and Kiyoteru Tsutsui. 2005. "Human Rights in a Globalizing World: The Paradox of Empty Promises1." *American Journal of Sociology* 110 (5):1373–1411.

Hafner-Burton, Emilie M., and Kiyoteru Tsutsui. 2007. "Justice Lost! The Failure of International Human Rights Law to Matter Where Needed Most." *Journal of Peace Research* 44 (4):407–425.

Hall, John A. 1996. "How Homogenous Need We Be? Reflections on Nationalism and Liberty." *Sociology* 30 (1):163–171.

Hall, Kita. 1999. "Performativity." *Journal of Linguistic Anthropology* 9 (1/2):184–187.

Halliday, Terence C., and Pavel Osinsky. 2006. "Globalization of Law." *Annual Review of Sociology* 32:447–470.

Halsey, A. H. 1984. "TH Marshall: Past and Present 1893–1981: President of the British Sociological Association 1964–1969." *Sociology* 18 (1):1–18.

Hammar, Tomas. 1986. "Citizenship: Membership of a Nation and of a State." *International Migration* 24 (4):735–748.
Hammar, Tomas. 1990. *International Migration, Citizenship and Democracy*. Aldershot: Gower.
Hannum, Hurst. 1995. "The Status of the Universal Declaration of Human Rights in National and International Law." *Georgia Journal of International and Comparative Law* 25:287–398.
Hansen, Randall. 2003. "Citizenship and Integration in Europe." In *Toward Assimilation and Citizenship: Immigrants in Liberal Nation-States*, edited by Christian Joppke and Ewa Morawska, 87–109. New York and London: Palgrave Macmillan.
Hansen, Randall. 2009. "The Poverty of Postnationalism: Citizenship, Immigration, and the New Europe." *Theory and Society* 38 (1):1–24.
Harding, Sandra. 1992. "Rethinking Standpoint Epistemology: What Is 'Strong Objectivity?'" *The Centennial Review* 36 (3):437–470.
Harris, Jose. 1992. "Political Thought and the Welfare State 1870–1940: An Intellectual Framework for British Social Policy." *Past & Present* 135:116–141.
Hasenclever, Andreas, Peter Mayer, and Volker Rittberger. 1996. "Interests, Power, Knowledge: The Study of International Regimes." *Mershon International Studies Review* 40 (2):177–228.
Heathorn, Stephen J., and David Goutor, eds. 2013. *Taking Liberties: A History of Human Rights in Canada*. Don Mills, ON: Oxford University Press.
Heisler, Martin O., and Barbara Schmitter Heisler. 1991. "Citizenship—Old, New and Changing: Inclusion, Exclusion and Limbo for Ethnic Groups and Migrants in the Modern Democratic State." In *Dominant National Cultures and Ethnic Identities*, edited by J. Fijalkowski, H. Merkens and F. Schmidt, 91–128. Berlin: Free University.
Held, David. 1987. *Models of Democracy*. Stanford, CA: Stanford University Press.
Held, David. 2002. "Law of States, Law of Peoples." *Legal Theory* 8 (1):1–44.
Held, David. 2004. *Global Covenant: The Social Democratic Alternative to the Washington Consensus*. Cambridge and Malden, MA: Polity Press.
Held, David. 2009. "Restructuring Global Governance: Cosmopolitanism, Democracy and the Global Order." *Millennium: Journal of International Studies* 37 (3):535–547.
Held, David. 2010. *Cosmopolitanism: Ideals and Realities*. Cambridge and Malden, MA: Polity.
Hennette-Vauchez, Stéphanie. 2011. "Constitutional v International? When Unified Reformaory Rationales Mismatch the Plural Paths of Legitimacy of ECHR Law." In *The European Court of Human Rights Between Law and*

Politics, edited by Jonas Christoffersen and Mikael Rask Madsen, 146–164. Oxford and New York: Oxford University Press.

Hesford, Wendy S. 2004. "Documenting Violations: Rhetorical Witnessing and the Spectacle of Distant Suffering." *Biography* 27 (1):104–144.

Hesford, Wendy S. 2011. *Spectacular Rhetorics: Human Rights Visions, Recognitions, Feminisms*. Durham, NC: Duke University Press.

Hilhorst, Dorothea, and Bram J. Jansen. 2012. "Constructing Rights and Wrongs in Humanitarian Action: Contributions from a Sociology of Praxis." *Sociology* 46 (5):891–905.

Hintjens, Helen M. 1995. Review of *Review of Limits of Citizenship: Migrants and Postnational Membership in Europe*, by Yasemin Nuhoglu Soysal. *International Affairs (Royal Institute of International Affairs 1944–)* 71 (4):887–888.

Hirst, Paul. 1976. "Althusser and the Theory of Ideology." *Economy and Society* 4 (5):385–412.

Hobsbawm, Eric, and Terence Ranger. 1983. *The Invention of Tradition*. Cambridge: Cambridge University Press.

Hofstadter, Richard. 1964a. "The Paranoid Style in American Politics." *Harper's Magazine* 229 (1374):77–86.

Hofstadter, Richard. 1964b. *The Paranoid Style in American Politics*. New York: Vintage.

Holmwood, John. 2007. "Sociology as Public Discourse and Professional Practice: A Critique of Michael Burawoy." *Sociological Theory* 25 (1):46–66.

Hopgood, Stephen. 2006. *Keepers of the Flame. Understanding Amnesty International*. Ithaca, NY: Cornell University Press.

Hopgood, Stephen. 2013. *The Endtimes of Human Rights*. Ithaca, NY: Cornell University Press.

Howard, Rhoda E. 1986. *Human Rights in Commonwealth Africa*. Totowa, NJ: Rowan and Littlefield.

Howard, Rhoda E. 1995a. "Human Rights and the Search for Community." *Journal of Peace Research* 32 (1):1–8.

Howard, Rhoda E. 1995b. *Human Rights and the Search for Community*. Boulder, CO: Westview.

Howard, Rhoda E., and Jack Donnelly. 1986. "Human Dignity, Human Rights and Political Regimes." *American Political Science Review* 80 (3):801–817.

Howard-Hassmann, Rhoda E. 2005. "The Second Great Transformation: Human Rights Leapfrogging in the Era of Globalization." *Human Rights Quarterly* 27 (1):1–40.

Howe, R. Brian. 1991. "The Evolution of Human Rights Policy in Ontario." *Canadian Journal of Political Science/Revue Canadienne de Science Politique* 24 (4):783–802.

Howe, R. Brian, and David Johnson. 2000. *Restraining Equality: Human Rights Commissions in Canada.* Toronto: University of Toronto Press.

Humphrey, Michael, and Estela Valverde. 2007. "Human Rights, Victimhood, and Impunity: An Anthropology of Democracy in Argentina." *Social Analysis* 51 (1):179–197.

Hunt, Alan. 1985. "The Ideology of Law: Advances and Problems in Recent Applications of the Concept of Ideology to the Analysis of Law." *Law and Society Review*, 11–37.

Hunt, Alan. 1993. *Explorations in Law and Society: Towards a Constitutive Theory of Law.* London: Routledge.

Hunt, Lynn Avery. 2007. *Inventing Human Rights: A History*. W. W. Norton & Company. New York and London.

Hynes, Patricia. 2010. "Global Points of 'Vulnerability': Understanding Processes of the Trafficking of Children and Young People Into, Within and Out of the UK." *The International Journal of Human Rights* 14 (6):952–970.

Hynes, Patricia, Michele Lamb, Damien Short, and Matthew Waites. 2010. "Sociology and Human Rights: Confrontations, Evasions and New Engagements." *The International Journal of Human Rights* 14 (6):811–32.

Hynes, Patricia, Michele Lamb, Damien Short, and Matthew Waites. 2012a. "New Directions in the Sociology of Human Rights: Foreword." *The International Journal of Human Rights* 16 (8):1123–1126.

Hynes, Patricia, Michele Lamb, Damien Short, and Matthew Waites. 2012b. "The Sociology of Human Rights: Editorial Foreword." *Sociology* 46 (5):787–796.

Ignatieff, Michael. 2001. *Human Rights as Politics and Human Rights as Idolatry.* Princeton, NJ: Princeton University Press.

Ignatieff, Michael. 2013. "Preface." In *Taking Liberties: A History of Human Rights in Canada*, edited by Stephen J. Heathorn and David Goutor, v–ix. Don Mills, ON: Oxford University Press.

Iriye, Akira. 2002. *Global Community: The Role of International Organizations in the Making of the Contemporary World.* Berkeley: University of California Press.

Ishay, Micheline R. 2004. *The History of Human Rights.* Berkeley and London: University of California Press.

Isin, Engin F., and Bryan S. Turner. 2007. "Investigating Citizenship: An Agenda for Citizenship Studies." *Citizenship Studies* 11 (1):5–17.

Jacobson, David. 1996. *Rights Across Borders: Immigration and the Decline of Citizenship*. Baltimore and London: The John Hopkins University Press.

Jeffery, Laura, and Matei Candea. 2006. "The Politics of Victimhood." *History and Anthropology* 17 (4):287–296.

Jensen, Steffen, and Henrik Ronsbo. 2014. "Introduction. Histories of Victimhood: Assemblages, Transactions, and Figures." In *Histories of Victimhood*, edited by Steffen Jensen and Henrik Ronsbo. Philadelphia: University of Pennsylvania Press, 1–22.

Jessop, Bob. 1999. "The Changing Governance of Welfare: Recent Trends in Its Primary Functions, Scale, and Modes of Coordination." *Social Policy & Administration* 33 (4):348–359.

Jessop, Bob. 2004. "Critical Semiotic Analysis and Cultural Political Economy." *Critical Discourse Studies* 1 (2):159–174.

Jessop, Bob. 2010. "Cultural Political Economy and Critical Policy Studies." *Critical Policy Studies* 3 (3–4):336–356.

Jessop, Bob. 2013. "Recovered Imaginaries, Imagined Recoveries: A Cultural Political Economy of Crisis Construals and Crisis Management in the North Atlantic Financial Crisis." In *Before and Beyond the Global Economics Crisis: Economics, Politics and Settlement*, edited by Mats Brenner, 234–254. Cheltenham: Edward Elgar Publishing.

Jessop, Bob, and Stijn Oosterlynck. 2008. "Cultural Political Economy: On Making the Cultural Turn Without Falling into Soft Economic Sociology." *Geoforum* 39 (3):1155–1169.

Jessop, Bob, and Ngai-Ling Sum. 2006. "Towards a Cultural International Political Economy: Poststructuralism and the Italian School." In *International Political Economy and Poststructural Politics*, 157–176. Springer.

Jo, Hyeran, and Beth A. Simmons. 2016. "Can the International Criminal Court Deter Atrocity?" *International Organization* 70 (3):443–475.

Johnson, Pauline. 2001. "Distorted Communications Feminism's Dispute with Habermas." *Philosophy & Social Criticism* 27 (1):39–62.

Joppke, Christian. 2010a. *Citizenship and Immigration*. Cambridge and Malden, MA: Polity Press.

Joppke, Christian. 2010b. "The Inevitable Lightening of Citizenship." *European Journal of Sociology* 51 (1):9–32.

Joppke, Christian, and Ewa Morawska. 2003. "Integrating Immigrants in Liberal Nation-States: Policies and Practices." In *Toward Assimilation and Citizenship: Immigrants in Liberal Nation-States*, edited by Christian Joppke and Ewa Morawska, 1–36. London and New York: Palgrave Macmillan.

Kaiser, Wolfram. 2007. *Christian Democracy and the Origins of European Union*. Cambridge and New York: Cambridge University Press.
Kaldor, Mary. 2013. *Global Civil Society: An Answer to War*. Cambridge and Malden, MA: Polity.
Kallen, Evelyn. 2003. *Ethnicity and Human Rights in Canada a Human Rights Perspective on Ethnicity, Racism and Systemic Inequality*. 3rd ed. desLibris. Don Mills, ON and New York: Oxford University Press.
Kalman, Laura. 1986. *Legal Realism at Yale, 1927–1960*. Chapel Hill, NC: UNC Press Books.
Kausikan, Bilahari. 1993. "Asia's Different Standard." *Foreign Policy* 92:24–41.
Keck, Margaret E., and Kathryn Sikkink. 1998. *Activists Beyond Borders: Advocacy Networks in International Politics*. Ithaca, NY and London: Cornell University Press.
Kelly, Patrick William. 2014a. "'Magic Words': The Advent of Transnational Human Rights Activism in Latin America's Southern Cone in the Long 1970s." In *The Breakthrough: Human Rights in the 1970s*, edited by Jan Eckel and Samuel Moyn, 88–106. Philadelphia: University of Pennsylvania Press.
Kelly, Tobias. 2014b. "Recognizing Torture: Credibility and the Unstable Codification of Victimhood." In *Histories of Victimhood*, edited by Steffen Jensen and Henrik Ronsbo, 144–160. Philadelphia: University of Pennsylvania Press.
Kendall, Gavin, Ian Woodward, and Zlatko Skrbis. 2009. *The Sociology of Cosmopolitanism: Globalization, Identity, Culture and Government*. New York: Palgrave Macmillan.
Kennedy, David. 2005. *The Dark Sides of Virtue: Reassessing International Humanitarianism*. Princeton, NJ: Princeton University Press.
Kersbergen, Kees van, and Bertjan Verbeek. 1994. "The Politics of Subsidiarity in the European Union." *JCMS: Journal of Common Market Studies* 32 (2):215–236.
Keys, Barbara J. 2012. "Anti-Torture Politics: Amnesty International, the Greek Junta, and the Origins of the Human Rights Boom in the United States." In *The Human Rights Revolution: An International History*, edited by Akara Iriye, Petra Goedde, and William I. Hitchcock, 201–222. Oxford and New York: Oxford University Press.
Keys, Barbara J. 2014. *Reclaiming American Virtue*. Cambridge, MA: Harvard University Press.
"Kim Dae-Jung – Facts." n.d. Accessed December 21, 2016. https://www.nobelprize.org/nobel_prizes/peace/laureates/2000/dae-jung-facts.html.

Klopp, Brett. 1995. Review of *Limits of Citizenship: Migrants and Postnational Membership in Europe*, by Yasemin Nuhoglu Soysal. *American Journal of Sociology* 101 (3):779–781.

Kofman, Eleonore. 2005. "Citizenship, Migration and the Reassertion of National Identity." *Citizenship Studies* 9 (5):453–467.

Koopmans, Ruud. 2012. "The Post-Nationalization of Immigrant Rights: A Theory in Search of Evidence1." *The British Journal of Sociology* 63 (1):22–30.

Koopmans, Ruud, Ines Michalowski, and Stine Waibel. 2012. "Citizenship Rights for Immigrants: National Political Processes and Cross-National Convergence in Western Europe, 1980–2008." *American Journal of Sociology* 117 (4):1202–1245.

Kumar, Krishan. 2007. "Global Civil Society." *European Journal of Sociology / Archives Européennes de Sociologie* 48 (3):413–434.

Kurasawa, Fuyuki. 2007. *The Work of Global Justice: Human Rights as Practices.* Cambridge and New York: Cambridge University Press.

La Forest, Gerard V. 1983. "The Canadian Charter of Rights and Freedoms: An Overview." *Canadian Bar Review* 61:19.

Lacan, Jacques. 1977. *Ecrits: A Selection.* New York: W. W. Norton & Company.

Laclau, Ernesto, and Chantal Mouffe. 1985. *Hegemony and Socialist Strategy: Towards a Radical Democratic Politics.* London: Verso.

Lamb, Michele. 2010. "Loyalty and Human Rights: Liminality and Social Action in a Divided Society." *The International Journal of Human Rights* 14 (6):994–1012.

Lambertson, Ross. 2005. *Repression and Resistance Canadian Human Rights Activists, 1930–1960.* Toronto: University of Toronto Press.

Landman, Todd, and Edzia Carvahlho. 2010. *Measuring Human Rights.* London and New York: Routledge.

Latour, Bruno. 1987. *Science in Action: How to Follow Scientists and Engineers Through Society.* Cambridge, MA: Harvard University Press.

Lauren, Paul Gordon. 1998. *The Evolution of International Human Rights: Visions Seen.* Philadelphia: University of Pennsylvania Press.

Laxer, Gordon, and Sandra Halperin. 2003. *Global Civil Society and Its Limits.* New York: Palgrave Macmillan

Lazaridis, Gabriella. 1995. "Reviews – From Aliens to Citizens: Redefining the Status of Immigrants in Europe Edited by Rainer Baubock / Limits of Citizenship: Migrants and Postnational Membership in Europe by Yasemin Nuhoglu Soysal." *Journal of Social Policy* 24:573.

Lee-Gong, Eunna. 2010. "Contestations over Rights: From Establishment to Implementation of the National Basic Livelihood Security System in South Korea." *The International Journal of Human Rights* 14 (6):880–895.

Lemert, Charles. 1995. *Sociology After the Crisis*. Boulder: Westview Press.

Lessa, Francesca, and Vincent Druliolle. 2011. *The Memory of State Terrorism in the Southern Cone: Argentina, Chile, and Uruguay*. New York: Palgrave Macmillan.

Levine, Daniel H. 1988. "Assessing the Impacts of Liberation Theology in Latin America." *The Review of Politics* 50 (2):241–263.

Levine, Donald N. 1995. *Visions of the Sociological Tradition*. Chicago and London: University of Chicago Press.

Levy, Daniel, and Natan Sznaider. 2006. "Sovereignty Transformed: A Sociology of Human rights1." *The British Journal of Sociology* 57 (4):657–676.

Levy, Daniel, and Natan Sznaider. 2010. *Human Rights and Memory*. Philadelphia: Penn State Press.

Lister, Ruth, ed. 2003. *Citizenship: Feminist Perspectives*. New York: NYU Press.

Lockwood, David. 1996. "Civic Integration and Class Formation." *British Journal of Sociology*, 531–550.

López, José Julián. 2003. *Society and Its Metaphors: Language, Social Theory and Social Structure*. London: Continuum Books.

López, José Julián. 2009. "Par-Delà L'éthique: Vers Une Sociologie Des Pratiques Éthiques Contemporaines." *Cahiers de Recherche Sociologique* 48:27–44.

López, José Julián. 2015. "The Human Right to Food as Political Imaginary." *Journal of Historical Sociology* 30 (2): 239–261.

López, José Julián. 2016. "Disembedding the Embedded/Disembedded Opposition." In *Markets, Communities and Nostalgia*, edited by Christian Karner and Bernhard Weicht. London and New York: Palgrave Macmillan, 223–247.

López, José Julián, and Janet Lunau. 2012. "ELSIfication in Canada: Legal Modes of Reasoning." *Science as Culture* 21 (1):77–99.

López, José, and Garry Potter, eds. 2001. *After Postmodernism: An Introduction to Critical Realism*. London: Athlone Press.

Löwy, Michael. 1996. *The War of Gods: Religion and Politics in Latin America*. London: Verso.

Luhmann, Niklas. 1991. "Operational Closure and Structural Coupling: The Differentiation of the Legal System." *Cardozo Law Review* 13:1419.

Luhmann, Niklas. 1995. *Social Systems*. Stanford, CA: Stanford University Press.

Luhmann, Niklas. 2004. *Law as a Social System*. Oxford and New York: Oxford University Press.

Lyotard, Jean-François. 1984. *The Postmodern Condition: A Report on Knowledge*. Minnesota: University of Minnesota Press.

MacLennan, Christopher. 2003. *Toward the Charter: Canadians and the Demand for a National Bill of Rights, 1929–1960*. Montreal and Kingston: McGill-Queen's Press-MQUP.

Madison, D. Soyini. 2010. *Acts of Activism: Human Rights as Radical Performance*. Cambridge and New York: Cambridge University Press.

Madsen, Mikael Rask. 2007. "From Cold War Instrument to Supreme European Court: The European Court of Human Rights at the Crossroads of International and National Law and Politics." *Law & Social Inquiry* 32 (1):137–159.

Madsen, Mikael Rask. 2010. *La Genèse de l'Europe Des Droits de L'homme: Enjeux Juridiques et Stratégies d'Etat (1945–1970)*. Strasbourg: Presses Universitaires de Strasbourg.

Madsen, Mikael Rask. 2011a. "Reflexivity and the Construction of the International Object: The Case of Human Rights." *International Political Sociology* 5 (3):259–275.

Madsen, Mikael Rask. 2011b. "The Protracted Institutionalization of the Strasbourg Court: From Legal Diplomacy to Integrationist Jurisprudence." In *The European Court of Human Rights Between Law and Politics*, edited by Jonas Christoffersen and Mikael Rask Madsen, 43–59. Oxford and New York: Oxford University Press.

Madsen, Mikael Rask. 2012. "Human Rights and the Hegemony of Ideology: European Lawyers and the Cold War Battle over International Human Rights." In *Lawyers and the Construction of Transnational Justice*, edited by Yves Dezalay and Bryant Garth, 258–276. Milton Park and New York: Routledge.

Madsen, Mikael Rask. 2013. "Towards a Reflexive Sociology of Human Rights." In *Making Human Rights Intelligible: Towards a Sociology of Human Rights*, edited by Mikael Rask Madsen and Gert Verschraegen, 81–103. Oxford and Portland, Oregon: Hart Publishing.

Madsen, Mikael Rask, and Jonas Christoffersen. 2011. "Introduction." In *The European Court of Human Rights Between Law and Politics*, edited by Jonas Christoffersen and Mikael Rask Madsen, 1–13. Oxford and New York: Oxford University Press.

Madsen, Mikael Rask, and Yves Dezalay. 2002. "The Power of the Legal Field." In *An Introduction to Law and Social Theory*, edited by Max Travers and Reza Banakar, 189–204. Oxford and Portland, Oregon: Hart Publishing.

Madsen, Mikael Rask, and Gert Verschraegen. 2013a. "An Introduction to a Sociology of Human Rights." In *Making Human Rights Intelligible: Towards a Sociology of Human Rights*, edited by Mikael Rask Madsen and Gert Verschraegen, 1–24. Oxford and Portland, Oregon: Hart Publishing.

Madsen, Mikael Rask, and Gert Verschraegen, eds. 2013b. *Making Human Rights Intelligible: Towards a Sociology of Human Rights*. Book, Whole. Oxford and Portland Oregon: Hart Publishing.

Madsen, Mikael Rask, and Gert Verschraegen. 2016. "Toward a New Sociology of Human Rights?" *Humanity: An International Journal of Human Rights, Humanitarianism*, 1–24.

Mann, Michael. 1987. "Ruling Class Strategies and Citizenship." *Sociology* 21 (3):339–354.

Manners, Ian. 2006. "The Constitutive Nature of Values, Images and Principles in the European Union." In *Values and Principles in European Union Foreign Policy*, edited by Sonia Lucarelli and Ian Manners, 19–41. London: Routledge.

Manzo, Kate. 2008. "Imaging Humanitarianism: NGO Identity and the Iconography of Childhood." *Antipode* 40 (4):632–657.

Marchetti, Raffaele. 2006. "Global Governance or World Federalism? A Cosmopolitan Dispute on Institutional Models." *Global Society* 20 (3):287–305.

Marshall, Thomas H. 1950. *Citizenship and Social Class*. Cambridge: Cambridge University Press.

Martiniello, Marco. 1997. "Citizenship, Ethnicity and Multiculturalism: Post-national Membership Between Utopia and Reality." *Ethnic and Racial Studies* 20 (3):635–641.

Mauzy, Diane K. 1997. "The Human Rights and 'Asian Values' Debate in Southeast Asia: Trying to Clarify the Key Issues." *The Pacific Review* 10 (2):210–236.

Mazower, Mark. 2004. "The Strange Triumph of Human Rights, 1933–1950." *The Historical Journal* 47 (2):379–398.

Mazower, Mark. 2009. *No Enchanted Palace: The End of Empire and the Ideological Origins of the United Nations*. Princeton, NJ: Princeton University Press.

McGarry, Ross, Gabe Mythen, and Sandra Walklate. 2012. "The Soldier, Human Rights and the Military Covenant: A Permissible State of Exception?" *The International Journal of Human Rights* 16 (8):1183–1195.

McLagan, Meg. 2006. "Introduction: Making Human Rights Claims Public." *American Anthropologist* 108 (1):191–195.

Meehan, Johanna. 2013. *Feminists Read Habermas (RLE Feminist Theory): Gendering the Subject of Discourse*. London and New York: Routledge.

Melvin, Jennifer. 2010. "Reconstructing Rwanda: Balancing Human Rights and the Promotion of National Reconciliation." *The International Journal of Human Rights* 14 (6):932–951.

Merry, Sally Engle. 2006. "Transnational Human Rights and Local Activism: Mapping the Middle." *American Anthropologist* 108 (1):38–51.
Merry, Sally Engle. 2007. "Introduction: Conditions of Vulnerability." In *The Practice of Human Rights: Tracking Law Between the Global and the Local*, edited by Mark Goodale and Sally Engle Merry, 195–203. Cambridge: Cambridge University Press.
Merry, Sally Engle. 2009. *Human Rights and Gender Violence: Translating International Law into Local Justice*. Cambridge and New York: University of Chicago Press.
Merton, Robert King. 1967. *On Theoretical Sociology: Five Essays, Old and New*. New York: Free Press.
Messina, Anthony M. 1996. "The Not So Silent Revolution: Postwar Migration to Western Europe." *World Politics* 49 (1):130–154.
Messina, Anthony M. 2007. *The Logics and Politics of Post-WWII Migration to Western Europe*. New York: Cambridge University Press.
Meunier, E-Martin. 2007. *Le Pari Personnaliste: Modernité et Catholicisme Au XXe Siècle: Essai*. Montreal: Les Editions Fides.
Meyer, John W. 1977. "The Effects of Education as an Institution." *American Journal of Sociology*, Journal Article:55–77.
Meyer, John W. 2009. "World Society, the Welfare State, and the Life Course: An Institutionalist Perspective." In *World Society: The Writings of John W. Meyer*, edited by Georg Krücken and Gili S. Drori, 280–295. Oxford and New York: OUP.
Meyer, John W., John Boli, George M. Thomas, and Francisco O. Ramirez. 1997. "World Society and the Nation-State." *American Journal of Sociology* 103 (1):144–181.
Meyer, John W., and Ronald L. Jepperson. 2000. "The 'Actors' of Modern Society: The Cultural Construction of Social Agency." *Sociological Theory* 18 (1):100–120.
Meyer, John W., and Brian Rowan. 1977. "Institutionalized Organizations: Formal Structure as Myth and Ceremony." *American Journal of Sociology* 83 (2):340–363.
Meyers, Diana Tietjens. 2011. "Two Victim Paradigms and the Problem of 'Impure' Victims." *Humanity: An International Journal of Human Rights, Humanitarianism, and Development* 2 (2):255–275.
Miller, Hannah. 2010. "From 'Rights-Based' to 'Rights-Framed' Approaches: A Social Constructionist View of Human Rights Practice." *The International Journal of Human Rights* 14 (6):915–931.

Miron, Janet, ed. 2009. *A History of Human Rights in Canada: Essential Issues.* Toronto: Canadian Scholars' Press.

Mirowski, Philip. 2013. *Never Let a Serious Crisis Go to Waste: How Neoliberalism Survived the Financial Meltdown.* London: Verso Books.

Mishra, Ramesh. 2014. *Welfare State Capitalist Society.* London and New York: Routledge.

Mollenkopf, John, and Jennifer Hochschild. 2010. "Immigrant Political Incorporation: Comparing Success in the United States and Western Europe." *Ethnic and Racial Studies* 33 (1):19–38.

Moon, Claire. 2008. *Narrating Political Reconciliation: South Africa's Truth and Reconciliation Commission.* Plymouth, UK: Lexington Books.

Moon, Claire. 2012. "What One Sees and How One Files Seeing: Human Rights Reporting, Representation and Action." *Sociology* 46 (5):876–890.

Moravcsik, Andrew. 2000. "The Origins of Human Rights Regimes: Democratic Delegation in Postwar Europe." *International Organization* 54 (2):217–252.

Morris, Lydia. 2012. "Understanding Torture: The Strengths and the Limits of Social Theory." *The International Journal of Human Rights* 16 (8):1127–1141.

Morris, Lydia. 2013. *Human Rights and Social Theory.* New York: Palgrave Macmillan.

Morrow, Virginia, and Kirrily Pells. 2012. "Integrating Children's Human Rights and Child Poverty Debates: Examples from Young Lives in Ethiopia and India." *Sociology* 46 (5):906–920.

Morsink, Johannes. 1999. *The Universal Declaration of Human Rights: Origins, Drafting, and Intent.* Philadelphia: University of Pennsylvania Press.

Morton, F. L. 1987. "The Political Impact of the Canadian Charter of Rights and Freedoms." *Canadian Journal of Political Science/Revue Canadienne de Science Politique* 20 (1):31–55.

Mouritsen, Per. 2011. "Beyond Post-National Citizenship. Access, Consequence, Conditionality." In *European Multiculturalisms: Cultural, Religious and Ethnic Challenges*, edited by Anna Triandafyllidou, Tariq Modood, and Nasar Meer, 88–115. Edinburgh: Edinburgh University Press.

Moyn, Samuel. 2010. *The Last Utopia.* Harvard University Press. Cambridge: MA.

Moyn, Samuel. 2012a. "Do Human Rights Treaties Make Enough of a Difference?" In *Cambridge Companion to Human Rights Law*, edited by Conor Gearty and Costas Douzinas, 329–347. Cambridge and New York: Cambridge University Press.

Moyn, Samuel. 2012b. "Imperialism, Self-Determination, and the Rise of Human Rights." In *The Human Rights Revolution: An International History*, edited by Akara Iriye, Petra Goedde, and William I. Hitchcock, 159–178. Oxford and New York: Oxford University Press.

Moyn, Samuel. 2013a. "On the Nonglobalization of Ideas." In *Global Intellectual History*, 187–204. New York: Columbia University Press.

Moyn, Samuel. 2013b. "The Continuing Perplexities of Human Rights." *Qui Parle: Critical Humanities and Social Sciences* 22 (1):95–115.

Moyn, Samuel. 2014a. "A Powerless Companion: Human Rights in the Age of Neoliberalism." *Law and Contemporary Problems* 77:147.

Moyn, Samuel. 2014b. *Human Rights and the Uses of History.* London: Verso.

Moyn, Samuel. 2015. *Christian Human Rights*. Philadelphia: University of Pennsylvania Press: Philadelphia.

Mueller, Susanne D. 2014. "Kenya and the International Criminal Court (ICC): Politics, the Election and the Law." *Journal of Eastern African Studies* 8 (1):25–42.

Munger, Frank. 2012. "Globalization Through the Lens of Palace Wars: What Elite Lawyers' Careers Can and Cannot Tell Us About Globalization of Law." *Law & Social Inquiry* 37 (2):476–499.

Munz, Peter. 2000. "The Poverty of Randall Collins's Formal Sociology of Philosophy." *Philosophy of the Social Sciences* 30 (2):207–226.

Mutua, Makau W. 2001. "Savages, Victims, and Saviors: The Metaphor of Human Rights." *Harvard International Law Journal* 42 (1):201–245.

Nash, Kate. 2009a. *Contemporary Political Sociology: Globalization, Politics and Power*. Chichester and Malden, MA: John Wiley & Sons.

Nash, Kate. 2009b. *The Cultural Politics of Human Rights*. Cambridge and New York: Cambridge University Press.

Nash, Kate. 2012. "Towards a Political Sociology of Human Rights." In *The Wiley-Blackwell Companion to Political Sociology*, edited by Kate Nash, Edwin Amenta Scott, and Alan Edwin, 444–454. Malden: Wiley Blackwell.

Neier, Aryeh. 2012. *The International Human Rights Movement: A History*. Princeton, NJ and Oxford: Princeton University Press.

Nelson, Paul J., and Ellen Dorsey. 2008. *New Rights Advocacy: Changing Strategies of Development and Human Rights NGOs*. Washington, DC: Georgetown University Press.

Neocleous, Mark. 2003. *Imagining the State*. Maidenhead and Philadelphia: Open University Press.

Neocleous, Mark. 2008. *Critique of Security*. Edinburgh: Edinburgh University Press.

Nickel, James W. 1987. *Making Sense of Human Rights: Philosophical Reflections on the Universal Declaration of Human Rights*. Berkeley and London: University of California Press.

Nielsen, François. 2004. "The Vacant 'We': Remarks on Public Sociology." *Social Forces* 82 (4):1619–1627.

Nora, Pierre. 1989. "Between Memory and History: Les Lieux de Mémoire." *Representations* 26:7–24.

Normand, Roger, and Sarah Zaidi. 2008. *Human Rights at the UN: The Political History of Universal Justice*. Bloomington and Indianapolis: Indiana University Press.

Novick, Peter. 2000. *The Holocaust in American Life*. Boston and New York: Houghton Mifflin Harcourt.

Nussbaum, Martha C. 1997. "Capabilities and Human Rights." *Fordham Law Review* 66:273–300.

Nussbaum, Martha C. 1996. "Patriotism and Cosmopolitanism." In *For Love of Country?* edited by Joshua Cohen, 2–20. Boston, MA: Beacon Press.

Nussbaum, Martha C. 1998. *Cultivating Humanity*. Cambridge, MA: Harvard University Press.

Oberleitner, Gerd. 2012. "Does Enforcement Matter?" In *Human Rights Law*, edited by Costas Douzinas and Conor Gearty, 249–268. Cambridge and New York: Cambridge University Press.

Oberschall, Anthony. 1978. "Theories of Social Conflict." *Annual Review of Sociology*, Journal Article:291–315.

O'Connell, Paul. 2009. "Not Seeing the Forest for the Trees: A Reply to Rhoda Howard-Hassmann." *Human Rights Law Review* 9 (1):135–141.

Offe, Claus. 1972. "Advanced Capitalism and the Welfare State." *Politics & Society* 2 (4):479–488.

Olick, Jeffrey K., and Joyce Robbins. 1998. "Social Memory Studies: From 'Collective Memory' to the Historical Sociology of Mnemonic Practices." *Annual Review of Sociology* 24 (1):105–140.

Ong, Aihwa. 1999. *Flexible Citizenship: The Cultural Logics of Transnationality*. Durham, NC: Duke University Press.

Ortner, Sherry B. 1984. "Theory in Anthropology Since the Sixties." *Comparative Studies in Society and History* 26 (1):126–166.

Oxford University Press. 2003. *Oxford English Dictionary*. Oxford University Press.

Pakulski, Jan. 1997. "Cultural Citizenship." *Citizenship Studies* 1 (1):73–86.

Panitch, Leo, and Sam Gindin. 2012. *The Making of Global Capitalism*. London: Verso Books.

Parsons, Talcott, 1902–1967. *Sociological Theory and Modern Society*. New York: New York Free Press.

Pashukanis, Eugenio Bronislavovich. 1980. *Selected Writings on Marxism and the Law*. Edited by Piers Beirne and Robert Sharlet S. London: Academic Press.

Pashukanis, Eugenio Bronislavovich. 1983. *Law and Marxism*. Edited by C. Arthur. London: Pluto Press.

Patrias, Carmela, and Ruth A. Frager. 2001. "'This Is Our Country, These Are Our Rights': Minorities and the Origins of Ontario's Human Rights Campaigns." *The Canadian Historical Review* 82 (1):1–35.

Payne, Geoff, Malcolm Williams, and Suzanne Chamberlain. 2004. "Methodological Pluralism in British Sociology." *Sociology* 38 (1):153–163.

Pearce, Andy. 2008. "The Development of Holocaust Consciousness in Contemporary Britain, 1979–2001." *Holocaust Studies* 14 (2):71–94.

Peck, James. 2011. *Ideal Illusions: How the US Government Co-opted Human Rights*. New York: Macmillan.

Peretz, Pauline. 2017. *Let My People Go: The Transnational Politics of Soviet Jewish Emigration During the Cold War*. London and New York: Routledge.

Piven, Frances Fox. 1971. *Regulating the Poor; the Functions of Public Welfare*. Vol. [1st ed.]. New York: Pantheon Books.

Piven, Frances Fox, and Richard A. Cloward. 1979. *Poor People's Movements: Why They Succeed, How They Fail*. Vol. 697. New York: Vintage.

Pogge, Thomas W. 2008. *World Poverty and Human Rights*. Cambridge and Malden, MA: Polity.

Polanyi, Karl. 1957. Book, Whole. Beacon Hill, Boston: Beacon Hill.

Porat, Dan A. 2004. "From the Scandal to the Holocaust in Israeli Education." *Journal of Contemporary History* 39 (4):619–636.

Posner, Eric A. 2014. *The Twilight of Human Rights Law*. Oxford and New York: Oxford University Press.

Postone, Moishe. 1980. "Anti-Semitism and National Socialism: Notes on the German Reaction to 'Holocaust.'" *New German Critique* 19:97–115.

Poulantzas, Nicos Ar. 1978. *State, Power, Socialism*. London: NLB.

Probst, Lothar. 2003. "Founding Myths in Europe and the Role of the Holocaust." *New German Critique* 90:45–58.

Purvis, Trevor, and Alan Hunt. 1993. "Discourse, Ideology, Discourse, Ideology, Discourse, Ideology…" *British Journal of Sociology*:473–499.

Rae, Paul. 2009. *Theatre and Human Rights*. London and New York: Palgrave Macmillan.

Ramos, Howard, James Ron, and Oskar N.T. Thoms. 2007. "Shaping the Northern Media's Human Rights Coverage, 1986–2000." *Journal of Peace Research* 44.

Rashed, Haifa, and Damien Short. 2012. "Genocide and Settler Colonialism: Can a Lemkin-Inspired Genocide Perspective Aid Our Understanding of the Palestinian Situation?" *The International Journal of Human Rights* 16 (8):1142–1169.

Reckwitz, Andreas. 2002a. "The Status of the 'Material' in Theories of Culture: From 'Social Structure' to 'Artefacts.'" *Journal for the Theory of Social Behaviour* 32 (2):195–217.

Reckwitz, Andreas. 2002b. "Toward a Theory of Social Practices a Development in Culturalist Theorizing." *European Journal of Social Theory* 5 (2):243–263.

Redhead, Robin, and Nick Turnbull. 2011. "Towards a Study of Human Rights Practitioners." *Human Rights Review* 12 (2):173–189.

Richey, Lisa Ann, and Stefano Ponte. 2011. *Brand Aid: Shopping Well to Save the World.* Minnesota: University of Minnesota Press.

Riga, Liliana, and James Kennedy. 2012. "'Putting Cruelty First': Interpreting War Crimes as Human Rights Atrocities in US Policy in Bosnia and Herzegovina." *Sociology* 46 (5):861–875.

Risse, Thomas, C. Ropp Stephen, and Kathryn Sikkink. 1999. *The Power of Human Rights: International Norms and Domestic Change.* Cambridge and New York: Cambridge University Press.

Risse, Thomas, C. Ropp Stephen, and Kathryn Sikkink. 2013. *The Persistent Power of Human Rights: From Commitment to Compliance.* Cambridge and New York: Cambridge University Press.

Ron, James, Howard Ramos, and Kathleen Rodgers. 2005. "Transnational Information Politics: NGO Human Rights Reporting, 1986–2000." *International Studies Quarterly* 49 (3):557–588.

Ron, James, Howard Ramos, and Kathleen Rodgers. 2006. "What Shapes the West's Human Rights Focus?" *Contexts* 5 (3):23–28.

Ros, Ana. 2012. *The Post-Dictatorship Generation in Argentina, Chile, and Uruguay: Collective Memory and Cultural Production.* Basingstoke and New York: Palgrave Macmillan.

Rose, Nikolas, and Peter Miller. 1992. "Political Power Beyond the State: Problematics of Government." *British Journal of Sociology*:173–205.

Rouse, Joseph. 2007. "Practice Theory" Division I Faculty Publications. Paper 43. http://wescholar.wesleyan.edu/div1facpubs/43.

Rule, James B. 1997. *Theory and Progress in Social Science.* Cambridge and New York: Cambridge University Press.

Russell, Peter H. 1983. "The Political Purposes of the Canadian Charter of Rights and Freedoms." *Canadian Bar Review* 61:30–54.

Sainsbury, Diane. 2006. "Immigrants' Social Rights in Comparative Perspective: Welfare Regimes, Forms in Immigration and Immigration Policy Regimes." *Journal of European Social Policy* 16 (3):229–244.

Sarat, Austin, and Thomas R. Kearns. 2009. eds. *Law in Everyday Life*. Ann Arbor: University of Michigan Press.

Sargent, Daniel. 2014. "Oasis in the Desert? America's Human Rights Rediscovery." In *The Breakthrough: Human Rights in the 1970s*. Philadelphia, PA: University of Pennsylvania Press, 125–145.

Sassen, Saskia. 1996. *Losing Control?: Sovereignty in the Age of Globalization*. New York: Columbia University Press.

Sassen, Saskia. 2002. "Towards Post-National and Denationalized Citizenship." *Handbook of Citizenship Studies*, 277–292.

Sassen, Saskia. 2006. *Territory, Authority, Rights: From Medieval to Global Assemblages*. Cambridge and New York: Cambridge University Press.

Sassen, Saskia. 2009. "Incompleteness and the Possibility of Making: Towards Denationalized Citizenship?" In *Political Power and Social Theory*, 229–258. Emerald Group Publishing Limited.

Sassen, Saskia. 2015. "From National Borders to Embedded Borderings: One Angle into the Question of Territory and Space in a Global Age." In *Crossroads in New Media, Identity and Law: The Shape of Diversity to Come*, edited by Wouter De Been, Arora Payal, and Mireille Hildebrandt, 17–42. London and New York: Palgrave Macmillan.

Saunders, Frances Stonor. 1999. *The Cultural Cold War*. New York: The Free Press.

Sayer, Andrew. 2005. *The Moral Significance of Class*. Book, Whole. Cambridge University Press.

Schabas, William A. 1997. "Canada and the Adoption of the Universal Declaration of Human Rights." *McGill Law Journal* 43:403–444.

Schabas, William A. 2000. "Twenty-Five Years of Public International Law at the Supreme Court of Canada." *Canadian Bar Review* 79:174–195.

Schaffer, Kay, and Sidonie Smith. 2004. *Human Rights and Narrated Lives: The Ethics of Recognition*. New York: Palgrave Macmillan.

Schain, Martin A. 2009. "The State Strikes Back: Immigration Policy in the European Union." *European Journal of International Law* 20 (1):93–109.

Schatzki, Theodore R. 1996. *Social Practices: A Wittgensteinian Approach to Human Activity and the Social*. Cambridge and New York: Cambridge University Press.

Schechner, Richard. 2004. *Performance Theory*. London and New York: Routledge.

Scheingold, Stuart A. 2004. *The Politics of Rights: Lawyers, Public Policy, and Political Change*. Ann Arbor: University of Michigan Press.

Scheppele, Kim Lane. 1994. "Legal Theory and Social Theory." *Annual Review of Sociology* 20:383–406.

Scheppele, Kim Lane. 2004. "Constitutional Ethnography: An Introduction." *Law & Society Review* 38 (3):389–406.

Schmidtke, Oliver. 2012. "Commodifying Migration: Excluding Migrants in Europe's Emerging Social Model." *The British Journal of Sociology* 63 (1):31–38.

Schofer, Evan, and John W. Meyer. 2005. "The Worldwide Expansion of Higher Education in the Twentieth Century." *American Sociological Review* 70 (6):898–920.

Schuster, Liza, and John Solomos. 2002. "Rights and Wrongs Across European Borders: Migrants, Minorities and Citizenship." *Citizenship Studies* 6 (1):37–54.

Scott, John. 2005. "Who Will Speak, and Who Will Listen? Comments on Burawoy and Public Sociology." *The British Journal of Sociology* 56 (3):405–409.

Searle, John R. 1969. *Speech Acts: An Essay in the Philosophy of Language*. Cambridge: Cambridge University Press.

Seidman, Steven. 1991. "The End of Sociological Theory: The Postmodern Hope." *Sociological Theory* 9 (2): 131–146.

Sellars, Kirsten. 2002. *The Rise and Rise of Human Rights*. Stroud: Sutton Pub Limited.

Sen, Amartya. 1995. *Inequality Reexamined*. Boston, MA: Harvard University Press.

Sen, Amartya. 1999. *Development as Freedom*. Oxford and New York: Oxford University Press.

Seu, Irene Bruna. 2012. "'In Countries like That…' Moral Boundaries and Implicatory Denial in Response to Human Rights Appeals." *The International Journal of Human Rights* 16 (8):1170–1182.

Shafir, Gershon, and Alison Brysk. 2006. "The Globalization of Rights: From Citizenship to Human Rights." *Citizenship Studies* 10 (3):275–287.

Shapira, Anita. 1998. "The Holocaust: Private Memories, Public Memory." *Jewish Social Studies* 4 (2):40–58.

Shestack, Jerome J. 1998. "The Philosophic Foundations of Human Rights." *Human Rights Quarterly* 20 (2):201–234.

Shilling, Chris, and Philip A. Mellor. 2001. *The Sociological Ambition*. London: Sage.

Short, Damien. 2010. "Cultural Genocide and Indigenous Peoples: A Sociological Approach." *The International Journal of Human Rights* 14 (6):833–848.

Shue, Henry. 1980. *Basic Rights: Subsistence, Affluence, and US Foreign Policy.* Princeton, NJ: Princeton University Press.

Silbey, Susan S. 2005. "After Legal Consciousness." *Annual Review of Law and Social Science* 1:323–368.

Silk, Leonard, and Mark Silk. 1980. *The American Establishment.* New York: Basic Books.

Simmons, Beth A. 2009. *Mobilizing for Human Rights: International Law in Domestic Politics.* Cambridge and New York: Cambridge University Press.

Sismondo, Sergio. 2011. *An Introduction to Science and Technology Studies.* Chichester: John Wiley & Sons.

Sjoberg, Gideon. 2009. "Corporations and Human Rights." In *Interpreting Human Rights: Social Science Perspectives*, edited by S. Turner Bryan and Rhiannon Morgan, 157–176. London: Routledge.

Sjoberg, Gideon, Elizabeth A. Gill, and Norma Williams. 2001. "A Sociology of Human Rights." *Social Problems* 48 (1):11–47.

Skaar, Elin. 2011. *Judicial Independence and Human Rights in Latin America: Violations, Politics, and Prosecution.* New York: Palgrave Macmillan.

Skillington, Tracey. 2012. "Climate Change and the Human Rights Challenge: Extending Justice Beyond the Borders of the Nation State." *The International Journal of Human Rights* 16 (8):1196–1212.

Slaughter, Anne-Marie. 2004. *A New World Order.* Princeton, NJ: Princeton University Press.

Slaughter, Joseph. 2009. *Human Rights, Inc: The World Novel, Narrative Form, and International Law.* New York: Fordham University Press.

Sliwinski, Sharon. 2011. *Human Rights in Camera.* Chicago and London: University of Chicago Press.

Sluga, Glenda. 2013. *Internationalism in the Age of Nationalism.* Philadelphia, PA: University of Pennsylvania Press.

Smith, Anthony. 1991. *National Identity.* Reno, NV: University of Nevada Press.

Smith, Brian H. 1979. "Churches and Human Rights in Latin America: Recent Trends in the Subcontinent." *Journal of Interamerican Studies and World Affairs* 21 (1):89–127.

Smith, Dorothy E. 1999. *Writing the Social: Critique, Theory, and Investigations.* Toronto: University of Toronto Press.

Smith, James A. 1993. *Idea Brokers: Think Tanks and the Rise of the New Policy Elite.* New York: Simon and Schuster.

Snyder, Emily. 2014. "Indigenous Feminist Legal Theory." *Canadian Journal of Women and the Law* 26 (2):365–401.

Snyder, Jack, and Leslie Vinjamuri. 2006. "Trials and Errors: Principle and Pragmatism in Strategies of International Justice." *International Security* 28 (3):5–44.

Snyder, Sarah B. 2011. *Human Rights Activism and the End of the Cold War: A Transnational History of the Helsinki Network*. Cambridge and New York: Cambridge University Press.

Somers, Margaret R. 1993. "Citizenship and the Place of the Public Sphere: Law, Community, and Political Culture in the Transition to Democracy." *American Sociological Review* 58 (5):587–620.

Somers, Margaret R. 1994a. "Rights, Relationality, and Membership: Rethinking the Making and Meaning of Citizenship." *Law & Social Inquiry* 19 (1):63–114.

Somers, Margaret R. 1994b. "The Narrative Constitution of Identity: A Relational and Network Approach." *Theory and Society* 23 (5):605–649.

Somers, Margaret R. 1997. "Deconstructing and Reconstructing Class Formation Theory: Narrativity, Relational Analysis and Social Theory." In *Reworking Class*, edited by R. John Hall, 73–106. Ithaca and London: Cornell University Press.

Somers, Margaret R. 2008. *Genealogies of Citizenship*. Cambridge and New York: Cambridge University Press.

Somers, Margaret R., and Fred Block. 2005. "From Poverty to Perversity: Ideas, Markets, and Institutions over 200 Years of Welfare Debate." *American Sociological Review* 70 (2):260–287.

Somers, Margaret R., and Christopher N. J. Roberts. 2008. "Toward a New Sociology of Rights: A Genealogy of 'Buried Bodies' of Citizenship and Human Rights." *Annual Review of Law and Social Science* 4:385–425.

Soysal, Yasemin Nuhoğlu. 1994. *Limits of Citizenship: Migrants and Postnational Membership in Europe*. Chicago and London: University of Chicago Press.

Soysal, Yasemin Nuhoğlu. 2012. "Citizenship, Immigration, and the European Social Project: Rights and Obligations of Individuality." *The British Journal of Sociology* 63 (1):1–21.

Spiro, Peter J. 2008. *Beyond Citizenship: American Identity After Globalization*. Oxford and New York: Oxford University Press.

Stammers, Neil. 2009. *Human Rights and Social Movements*. London: Pluto Press.

Staples, Amy L. S. 2006. *The Birth of Development: How the World Bank, Food and Agriculture Organization, and World Health Organization Changed the World, 1945–1965*. Kent, OH: Kent State University Press.

Stein, Arlene. 2014. *Reluctant Witnesses: Survivors, Their Children, and the Rise of Holocaust Consciousness*. Oxford and New York: Oxford University Press.

Stohl, Michael, David Carleton, and Steven E. Johnson. 1984. "Human Rights and US Foreign Assistance from Nixon to Carter." *Journal of Peace Research* 21 (3):215–226.

Strang, David, and John W. Meyer. 1993. "Institutional Conditions for Diffusion." *Theory and Society* 22 (4):487–511.

Sum, Ngai-Ling, and Bob Jessop. 2013. *Towards a Cultural Political Economy: Putting Culture in Its Place in Political Economy*. Cheltenham: Edward Elgar Publishing.

Sunstein, Cass. 2009. *The Second Bill of Rights: FDR's Unfinished Revolution – And Why We Need It More Than Ever*. New York: Basic Books.

Swidler, Ann. 1986. "Culture in Action: Symbols and Strategies." *American Sociological Review* 51 (2):273–286.

Taylor, Charles. 2002. "Modern Social Imaginaries." *Public Culture* 14 (1):91–124.

Teeple, Gary. 2005. *The Riddle of Human Rights*. Toronto: University of Toronto Press.

Thornhill, Chris. 2011. *A Sociology of Constitutions: Constitutions and State Legitimacy in Historical-Sociological Perspective*. Cambridge and New York: Cambridge University Press.

Thornhill, Chris. 2013. "State Building, Constitutional Rights and the Social Construction of Norms: Outline for a Sociology of Constitutions." In *Making Human Rights Intelligible: Towards a Sociology of Human Rights*, edited by Mikael Rask Madsen and Gert Verschraegen, 25–59. Oxford and Portland Oregon: Hart Publishing.

Tilly, Charles. 2007. *Democracy*. Cambridge and New York: Cambridge University Press.

Tittle, Charles R. 2004. "The Arrogance of Public Sociology." *Social Forces* 82 (4):1639–1643.

Tolley Jr, Howard B. 1994. *The International Commission of Jurists: Global Advocates for Human Rights*. Philadelphia: University of Pennsylvania Press.

Toussaint, Laura. 2011. "Promoting Cultural Rights." In *Sociology and Human Rights: A Bill of Rights for the Twenty-First Century*, edited by Judith Blau and Mark Frezzo. Los Angeles and London: Sage.

Triadafilopoulos, Triadafilos. 2011. "Illiberal Means to Liberal Ends? Understanding Recent Immigrant Integration Policies in Europe." *Journal of Ethnic and Migration Studies* 37 (6):861–880.

Triandafyllidou, Anna, Tariq Modood, and Nasar Meer, eds. 2011. *Beyond Post-National Citizenship. Access, Consequence, Conditionality*. Edinburgh: Edinburgh University Press.

Tunnicliffe, Jennifer. 2013. "A Limited Vision: Canadian Participation in the Adoption of the International Covenants on Human Rights." In *Taking Liberties: A History of Human Rights in Canada*, edited by Stephen J. Heathorn and David Goutor, 166–187. Don Mills, ON: Oxford University Press.

Tunnicliffe, Jennifer. 2014. "Canada and the Human Rights Framework: Historiographical Trends." *History Compass* 12 (10):807–817.

Turner, Bryan S. 1990. "Outline of a Theory of Citizenship." *Sociology* 24 (2):189–217.

Turner, Bryan S. 1993. "Outline of a Theory of Human Rights." *Sociology* 27 (3):489–512.

Turner, Bryan S. 1997. "Citizenship Studies: A General Theory." *Citizenship Studies* 1 (1):5–18.

Turner, Bryan S. 2006. *Vulnerability and Human Rights*. Philadelphia: Penn State Press.

Turner, Bryan S. 2009. "10 A Sociology of Citizenship and Human Rights." *Interpreting Human Rights: Social Science Perspectives* 47:177.

Turner, Jonathan H. 2005. "Is Public Sociology such a Good Idea?" *The American Sociologist* 36 (3–4):27–45.

Turner, Victor. 1985. *On the Edge of the Bush: Anthropology as Experience*. Tuscon: University of Arizona Press.

Turner, Victor. 1986. *The Anthropology of Performance*. New York: PAJ Publications.

Unger, Roberto Mangabeira. 1983. *The Critical Legal Studies Movement: Another Time, a Greater Task*. Boston, MA: Harvard University Press.

Urry, John. 2012. *Sociology Beyond Societies: Mobilities for the Twenty-First Century*. London: Routledge.

Vaïsse, Justin. 2010. *Neoconservatism: The Biography of a Movement*. Cambridge, MA: Harvard University Press.

Valverde, Mariana. 2003a. "'Which Side Are You On?' Uses of the Everyday in Sociolegal Scholarship." *PoLAR: Political and Legal Anthropology Review* 26 (1):86–98.

Valverde, Mariana. 2003b. *Law's Dream of a Common Knowledge*. Princeton and Oxford: Princeton University Press.

Van Drunen, Saskia Paula Caecilia. 2010. *Struggling with the Past: The Human Rights Movement and the Politics of Memory in Post-Dictatorship Argentina, 1983–2006*. Amsterdam: Rozenberg.

Van Krieken, Robert. 2004. "Legal Reasoning as a Field of Knowledge Production: Luhmann, Bourdieu and Law's Autonomy." Law and Society Association Conference, Chicago.

Verschraegen, Gert. 2013. "Differentiation and Inclusion: A Neglected Sociological Approach to Fundamental Rights." In *Making Human Rights Intelligible: Towards a Sociology of Human Rights/Madsen, M.[edit.]; Ea*, edited by Gert Verschraegen and Mikael Rask Madsen, 61–80. Oxford and Portland Oregon.

Vincent, Raymond John. 1986. *Human Rights and International Relations*. Cambridge and New York: Cambridge University Press.

Waever, Ole. 1998. "The Sociology of a Not so International Discipline: American and European Developments in International Relations." *International Organization* 52 (4):687–727.

Waites, Matthew. 2010. "Human Rights, Sexual Orientation and the Generation of Childhoods: Analysing the Partial Decriminalization of 'Unnatural Offences' in India." *The International Journal of Human Rights* 14 (6):971–993.

Waters, Malcolm. 1996. "Human Rights and the Universalization of Interests: Towards a Social Constructionist Approach." *Sociology* 30 (3):593–600.

Weber, Max. 2009. *From Max Weber: Essays in Sociology*. London: Routledge.

Weinreb, Lloyld L. 2005. *Legal Reason: The Use of Analogy in Legal Argument*. Cambridge and Malden, MA: Cambridge University Press.

Weisberg, Kelly, ed. 1993. *Feminist Legal Theory: Foundations*. Philadelphia: Temple University Press.

Wellman, Carl. 2010. *The Moral Dimensions of Human Rights*. Oxford: Oxford University Press.

Wendt, Alexander. 1999. *Social Theory of International Politics*. Cambridge and New York: Cambridge University Press.

Wiener, Antje. 2003. "Constructivism: The Limits of Bridging Gaps." *Journal of International Relations and Development* 6 (3):252–275.

Wilson, Alex, and Ellen Pence. 2006. "In the Lives of Battered Women: An Indigenous Assessment." In *Institutional Ethnography as Practice*, edited by Dorothy E. Smith, 199–225. New York: Rowman & Littlefield.

Wilson, Richard A. 1997. "Introduction." In *Human Rights, Culture and Context: Anthropological Perspectives*. London: Pluto Press.

Wilson, Richard A. 2001. *The Politics of Truth and Reconciliation in South Africa: Legitimizing the Post-Apartheid State*. Cambridge and New York: Cambridge University Press.

Wilson, Richard A. 2009. "Representing Human Rights Violations: Social Contexts and Subjectivities." In *Human Rights: An Anthropological Reader*, edited by Mark Goodale, 134–160. Oxford and New York: Wiley Blackwell.

Woodiwiss, Anthony. 1992. *Law, Labour and Society in Japan*. London: Routledge.

Woodiwiss, Anthony. 1993. *Postmodernity USA: The Crisis of Social Modernism in Postwar America*. London and New York: SAGE Publications Limited.

Woodiwiss, Anthony. 1997. "Against 'Modernity': A Dissident Rant." *Economy and Society* 26 (1):1–21.

Woodiwiss, Anthony. 1998. *Globalisation, Human Rights and Labour Law in Pacific Asian*. Cambridge: Cambridge University Press.

Woodiwiss, Anthony. 2001. *The Visual in Social Theory*. London: The Athlone Press.

Woodiwiss, Anthony. 2003. *Making Human Rights Work Globally*. London: The Glass House Press.

Woodiwiss, Anthony. 2005a. *Human Rights*. London and New York: Routledge.

Woodiwiss, Anthony. 2005b. *Scoping the Social*. London and New York: McGraw-Hill Education.

Woodiwiss, Anthony. 2011. "Making the Sociology of Human Rights More Sociological." *Development and Society* 40 (1):117–138.

Woodiwiss, Anthony. 2012. "Asia, Enforceable Benevolence and the Future of Human Rights." *Sociology* 46 (5):966–981.

Wright, Charles W. 2004. "Particularity and Perspective Taking: On Feminism and Habermas' Discourse Theory of Morality." *Hypatia* 19 (4):47–74.

Wrong, Dennis H. 1961. "The Oversocialized Conception of Man in Modern Sociology." *American Sociological Review*, Journal Article:183–193.

Yashar, Deborah J. 2002. "Globalization and Collective Action." *Comparative Politics* 34 (3):355–375.

Young, Iris Marion. 1989. "Polity and Group Difference: A Critique of the Ideal of Universal Citizenship." *Ethics* 99 (2):250–274.

Žižek, Slavoj. 2005. "Against Human Rights." *New Left Review* 34 (July–August):115–131.

Zolo, Danilo. 2009. *Victors' Justice: From Nuremberg to Baghdad*. London: Verso Books.

Zulaika, Joseba, and William A. Douglass. 1996. *Terror and Taboo: The Follies, Fables, and Faces of Terrorism*. London and New York: Routledge.

Index[1]

[1] Note: Page numbers followed by 'n' refer to notes.

J. Julián López, *Human Rights as Political Imaginary*,
https://doi.org/10.1007/978-3-319-74274-8